Digital Constitutionalism in Europe

Reframing Rights and Powers in the Algorithmic Society

This book is about rights and powers in the digital age. It is an attempt to reframe the role of constitutional democracies in the algorithmic society. By focusing on the European constitutional framework as a lodestar, this book examines the rise and consolidation of digital constitutionalism as a reaction to digital capitalism. The primary goal is to examine how European digital constitutionalism can protect fundamental rights and democratic values against the charm of digital liberalism and the challenges raised by platform powers. Firstly, this book investigates the reasons leading to the development of digital constitutionalism in Europe. Secondly, it provides a normative framework analysing to what extent European constitutionalism provides an architecture to protect rights and limit the exercise of unaccountable powers in the algorithmic society. This title is also available as open access on Cambridge Core.

Giovanni De Gregorio is Postdoctoral Researcher at the Centre for Socio-Legal Studies, University of Oxford. His research deals with digital constitutionalism, platform governance and digital policy.

Cambridge Studies in European Law and Policy

The focus of this series is European law broadly understood. It aims to publish original monographs in all fields of European law, from work focusing on the institutions of the EU and the Council of Europe to books examining substantive fields of European law as well as examining the relationship between European law and domestic, regional and international legal orders. The series publishes works adopting a wide variety of methods: comparative, doctrinal, theoretical and inter-disciplinary approaches to European law are equally welcome, as are works looking at the historical and political facets of the development of European law and policy. The main criterion is excellence i.e. the publication of innovative work, which will help to shape the legal, political and scholarly debate on the future of European law.

Books in the Series

Digital Constitutionalism in Europe: Reframing Rights and Powers in the Algorithmic Society
Giovanni De Gregorio

Can the European Court of Human Rights Shape European Public Order?
Kanstantsin Dzehtsiarou

The Constitutional Boundaries of European Fiscal Federalism
Brady Gordon

Private Selves: Legal Personhood in European Privacy Protection
Susanna Lindroos-Hovinheimo

Fissures in EU Citizenship: The Deconstruction and Reconstruction of the Legal Evolution of EU Citizenship
Martin Steinfeld

The Boundaries of the EU Internal Market: Participation without Membership
Marja-Liisa Öberg

The Currency of Solidarity: Constitutional Transformation during the Euro Crisis
Vestert Borger

Empire of Law: Nazi Germany, Exile Scholars and the Battle for the Future of Europe
Kaius Tuori

In the Court We Trust: Cooperation, Coordination and Collaboration between the ECJ and Supreme Administrative Courts
Rob van Gestel and Jurgen de Poorter

Beyond Minimum Harmonisation: Gold-Plating and Green-Plating of European Environmental Law
Lorenzo Squintani

The Court of Justice of the European Union as an Institutional Actor: Judicial Lawmaking and Its Limits
Thomas Horsley

The Politics of Justice in European Private Law: Social Justice, Access Justice, Societal Justice
Hans-W. Micklitz

The Transformation of EU Treaty Making: The Rise of Parliaments, Referendums and Courts Since 1950
Dermot Hodson and Imelda Maher

Redefining European Economic Integration
Dariusz Adamski

Human Rights in the Council of Europe and the European Union: Achievements, Trends and Challenges
Steven Greer, Janneke Gerards and Rosie Slowe

Core Socio-Economic Rights and the European Court of Human Rights
Ingrid Leijten

Green Trade and Fair Trade in and with the EU: Process-based Measures within the EU Legal Order
Laurens Ankersmit

New Labour Laws in Old Member States: Trade Union Responses to European Enlargement
Rebecca Zahn

The Governance of EU Fundamental Rights
Mark Dawson

The International Responsibility of the European Union: From Competence to Normative Control
Andrés Delgado Casteleiro

Frontex and Non-Refoulement: The International Responsibility of the EU
Roberta Mungianu

Gendering European Working Time Regimes: The Working Time Directive and the Case of Poland
Ania Zbyszewska

EU Renewable Electricity Law and Policy: From National Targets to a Common Market
Tim Maxian Rusche

European Constitutionalism
Kaarlo Tuori

Brokering Europe: Euro-Lawyers and the Making of a Transnational Polity
Antoine Vauchez

Services Liberalization in the EU and the WTO: Concepts, Standards and Regulatory Approaches
Marcus Klamert

Referendums and the European Union: A Comparative Enquiry
Fernando Mendez, Mario Mendez and Vasiliki Triga

The Allocation of Regulatory Competence in the EU Emissions Trading Scheme
Jospehine van Zeben

The Eurozone Crisis: A Constitutional Analysis
Kaarlo Tuori and Klaus Tuori

International Trade Disputes and EU Liability
Anne Thies

The Limits of Legal Reasoning and the European Court of Justice
Gerard Conway

New Governance and the Transformation of European Law: Coordinating EU Social Law and Policy
Mark Dawson

The Lisbon Treaty: A Legal and Political Analysis
Jean-Claude Piris

The European Union's Fight Against Corruption: The Evolving Policy Towards Member States and Candidate Countries
Patrycja Szarek-Mason

The Ethos of Europe: Values, Law and Justice in the EU
Andrew Williams

State and Market in European Union Law: The Public and Private Spheres of the Internal Market before the EU Courts
Wolf Sauter and Harm Schepel

The European Civil Code: The Way Forward
Hugh Collins

Ethical Dimensions of the Foreign Policy of the European Union: A Legal Appraisal
Urfan Khaliq

Implementing EU Pollution Control: Law and Integration
Bettina Lange

European Broadcasting Law and Policy
Jackie Harrison and Lorna Woods

The Transformation of Citizenship in the European Union: Electoral Rights and the Restructuring of Political Space
Jo Shaw

The Constitution for Europe: A Legal Analysis
Jean-Claude Piris

The European Convention on Human Rights: Achievements, Problems and Prospects
Steven Greer

Social Rights and Market Freedom in the European Constitution: A Labour Law Perspective
Stefano Giubboni

EU Enlargement and the Constitutions of Central and Eastern Europe
Anneli Albi

Digital Constitutionalism in Europe

Reframing Rights and Powers in the Algorithmic Society

Giovanni De Gregorio

University of Oxford

CAMBRIDGE
UNIVERSITY PRESS

CAMBRIDGE
UNIVERSITY PRESS

University Printing House, Cambridge CB2 8BS, United Kingdom

One Liberty Plaza, 20th Floor, New York, NY 10006, USA

477 Williamstown Road, Port Melbourne, VIC 3207, Australia

314–321, 3rd Floor, Plot 3, Splendor Forum, Jasola District Centre, New Delhi – 110025, India

103 Penang Road, #05–06/07, Visioncrest Commercial, Singapore 238467

Cambridge University Press is part of the University of Cambridge.

It furthers the University's mission by disseminating knowledge in the pursuit of education, learning, and research at the highest international levels of excellence.

www.cambridge.org
Information on this title: www.cambridge.org/9781316512777
DOI: 10.1017/9781009071215

When citing this work, please include a reference to the DOI 10.1017/9781009071215

First published 2022

A catalogue record for this publication is available from the British Library.

ISBN 978-1-316-51277-7 Hardback

Contents

Foreword

It is a pleasure and a privilege to have the opportunity to introduce Giovanni De Gregorio's book, which, as far as I am aware, is the first monograph to provide a comprehensive analysis of the developing notion of 'digital constitutionalism'. In writing this book, Giovanni has made four major contributions, thus consolidating his leading position within debates among researchers concerning the relationship between public law and digital technologies.

First, Giovanni looks behind the 'label' of digital constitutionalism. Through a highly thoughtful, convincing and innovative analysis, the author seeks to 'unpack' digital constitutionalism, by situating this notion within its temporal and material dimension and also emancipating it from a 'monolithic' conceptualisation. As he rightly argues, digital constitutionalism should be seen not as a unique concept but as the expression of different constitutional approaches to digital technologies which are connected to political and institutional dynamics.

A second important merit of this book consists of deploying the concept of digital constitutionalism as a core instrument for dispelling the hypocritical narrative affirming that the freedom to conduct business, and even more importantly competition law, should occupy a dominant position in online platform regulation.

In looking at digital constitutionalism as the embodiment of the limits to the exercise of powers in a networked society, Giovanni explores the transformation of online platforms from (simply) economic actors into private powers capable of competing with public authorities. According to the author, this shift has systemic implications. The most important, in my view, is that the constitutional perspective is of an increasingly crucial significance. More specifically, as I have tried to explore in *Judicial Protection of Fundamental Rights on the Internet: A Road Towards Digital Constitutionalism?* (Hart 2021), constitutionalism has a congenital mission of limiting power. Until recently, the challenge was to limit public (generally governmental) power within the classic vertical dimension: (public) authority versus individual liberty.

As Giovanni persuasively argues, the geometry of power, and the resulting challenge for constitutional law, is becoming more complex and articulated: aside from the vertical dimension, there is a growing horizontal relationship which connects individuals with private digital powers competing with, and often prevailing over, public powers in the algorithmic society. As demonstrated by this book, the core issue at the new frontier of digital constitutionalism is precisely how to deal with the rise of private powers, bearing in mind that there cannot be any constitutional law if the aim is not to protect freedoms and limit power.

As a third point, this research reaches beyond a synchronic analysis of the current conceptual framework and adopts a highly innovative retrospective and prospective approach, which enhances the normative contribution of this research.

Retrospectively, the author demonstrates in an original way how the European approach to online expression and data has evolved since the turn of the century, through the gradual rise of a more constitutional and European institution-based approach. This approach, as Giovanni shows, has two prongs. Firstly, there is a judicial aspect. The Court of Justice of the European Union is finally able to draw on the Nice Charter as a bill of rights, establishing itself as a European constitutional court in the digital age. Secondly, the European approach has a legislative aspect relating to the codification of the ECJ's case law and the limitation of online platform powers within the framework of the Digital Single Market. In this context, at the end of 2020, the European Commission proposed a new digital package that fits within this framework.

As regards the prospective analysis, Giovanni focuses on the potential path of European digital constitutionalism by addressing three constitutional challenges: digital humanism versus digital capitalism; public authority versus private ordering; and constitutional imperialism versus constitutional protectionism. Facing these apparent dilemmas, the author raises a highly original question about whether the characteristics of European digital constitutionalism will be capable of leading to a European third way (a digital sustainable approach) among these global trends, and how this can be achieved eventually.

Fourthly, and finally, Giovanni has the invaluable merit of further emancipating the debate surrounding law and technology from the still dominant perspective of technocrats, privacy and intellectual property lawyers, by introducing a precious and increasingly necessary constitutional dimension.

Oreste Pollicino

Acknowledgements

This book is the result of a mix of places and people. It is an attempt not only to fill a gap in the debate around constitutionalism, public law and technology but also to give voice to those who have led me to address the challenges for constitutional democracies in the algorithmic society.

My research interest in this area has been primarily supported by my academic community in Milan, particularly by Oreste Pollicino who has kindly written the Foreword for this book as a symbol of his role in my academic path and my supervisor Giulio Enea Vigevani who has always contributed to enriching my research ideas. And I cannot escape from a special mention to Marco Bassini who has always been a great source of academic advice and guidance.

An invaluable part of these years has been travelling and exchanging views with different academic communities which have profoundly contributed to this research. My experience in Oxford has played a critical role in encouraging me to look beyond constitutionalism. In this sense, Linda Mulcahy and Nicole Stremlau have played a critical role in showing that there is life beyond the law. Also, Roxana Radu has tremendously contributed to my studies on Internet governance. I could express the same feeling for my visiting fellowship in Haifa where I had the pleasure to meet Niva Elkin-Koren and Maayan Perel. Both have enriched my research on content moderation and platform governance moving my perspective beyond public law, looking at the role of private ordering.

Participating in academic networks has also been critical for this research. I have always learned from talking about digital constitutionalism with Francisco De Abreu Duarte, Nicolas Suzor, Dennis Redeker, Edoardo Celeste, Amelie Heldt, Clara Iglesias Keller and Nicola Palladino. The community of the Internet Governance Forum and, particularly, the Dynamic Coalition on Platform Responsibilities have also played an important role. In this case, I cannot escape from mentioning Luca Belli and Nicolo Zingales who have contributed to my research on the powers of online platforms. Likewise, the IACL Research Group on 'Algorithmic State, Society and Market' has been an infinite source for studying algorithmic governance and, in this case, the merit is of Giovanni Sartor, Amnon Reichman, Andrea Simoncini, Hans-W. Micklitz and Erik Longo. Besides, my studies on policy have been particularly enriched by the collaboration with Elena Perotti and my participation in the Internet and Jurisdiction Policy Network, led by Bertrand de la Chapelle and Frane Maroevic who continuously push the debate further in terms of content regulation and platform governance.

I cannot delay further from mentioning at least two scholars who have been continuously supportive during these years, Sofia Ranchordas and Catalina Goanta. Both have encouraged me to move my research forwards and have always created an environment for me to grow and learn from senior scholars.

When it comes to this book, special thanks go to Pietro Dunn who has provided incredible feedback and the editors at Cambridge University Press, Tom Randall and Becky Jackman, for their invaluable support, to Helen Kitto who has taken care of the copy-editing work, Akash Datchinamurthy for the type-setting and Ruth Martin for the indexing.

I consider this book to be the result of conversations and exchanges of views. It is not just the result of my doctoral studies but also of relationships which, in some cases, have also led to new friendships. Reading and writing have been critical in these years, but the most relevant part has been played by people.

Giovanni De Gregorio

1 Digital Constitutionalism: An Introduction

1.1 Reframing Constitutionalism in the Digital Age

This is a book about rights and powers in the digital age. It is an attempt to reframe the role of constitutional democracies in the information or network society,[1] which, in the last twenty years, has transmuted into the algorithmic society as the current societal background featuring large, multinational social platforms 'sit between traditional nation states and ordinary individuals and the use of algorithms and artificial intelligence agents to govern populations'.[2] Within this framework, states are not the only source of concern any longer. Global online platforms, such as Facebook, Amazon or TikTok, increasingly play a critical role at the intersection between public authority and private ordering.[3] By focusing on the European constitutional framework as lodestar, this book looks at the rise and consolidation of European constitutionalism as a reaction to new digital powers. It also provides a normative strategy to face the opportunities and challenges of digital capitalism which, in the last twenty years, have not only led to a market revolution,[4] and to the rise of platform capitalism,[5] but have also impacted on the constitutional

[1] Manuel Castells, *The Rise of the Network Society: The Information Age: Economy, Society, and Culture* (Blackwell 2009); John Feather, *The Information Society: A Study of Continuity and Change* (American Library Association 2013).

[2] Jack M. Balkin, 'Free Speech in the Algorithmic Society: Big Data, Private Governance, and New School Speech Regulation' (2018) 51 U.C. Davis Law Review 1151.

[3] José van Dijck, Thomas Poell and Martijn de Waal, *The Platform Society: Public Values in a Connective World* (Oxford University Press 2018).

[4] Daniel Schiller, *Digital Capitalism: Networking the Global Market System* (MIT Press 1999).

[5] Nick Srnicek, *Platform Capitalism* (Polity Press 2016).

dimension of democracy as information capitalism,[6] or surveillance capitalism.[7]

This research unpacks the path of the Union moving from neoliberal positions towards democratic shores guided by the beacon of European constitutionalism. Since the end of the last century, the charm of accommodating the promises of digital technologies has led to neglecting and forgetting the role of constitutionalism, and then constitutional law, in protecting fundamental rights and limiting the rise and consolidation of unaccountable powers abusing constitutional values. Neoliberal reverences, also driven by technological optimism and the consolidation of liberal narratives around Internet governance,[8] have indeed encouraged constitutional democracies to subject public functions in the digital environment to the logic of the market by delegation or inertia. This process has contributed to the consolidation of new founding powers escaping public oversight and providing quasi-constitutional models which compete with public authorities. The case of global online platforms operating on a transnational base is a paradigmatic example of this trend. The challenges raised by the discretionary deplatforming of President Trump or the electoral concerns around the Cambridge Analytica scandal are just two major events that raised constitutional questions which are still unanswered in terms of legitimacy, power and democracy in the algorithmic society.

Rather than solving this issue by relying on the self-correction of the market, these questions constitute a call for action for scholars to reframe the role of constitutional law as an overarching framework of values and principles of the algorithmic society. If the digital environment has been an opportunity to offer cross-border services and exercise individual freedoms in a new space where information and data flow, on the other hand, it has also increased the threats to individual rights and freedoms which are no longer subject just to public interferences but also to private determinations. In other words, reframing constitutionalism in the algorithmic society requires understanding

[6] Julie E. Cohen, *Between Truth and Power: The Legal Constructions of Informational Capitalism* (Oxford University Press 2020).

[7] Shoshana Zuboff, *The Age of Surveillance Capitalism: The Fight for a Human Future at the New Frontier of Power* (Public Affairs 2018).

[8] Jean-Marie Chenou, 'From Cyber-Libertarianism to Neoliberalism: Internet Exceptionalism, Multi-stakeholderism, and the Institutionalisation of Internet Governance in the 1990s' (2014) 11(2) Globalizations 205.

the exercise of freedoms and new relationships of powers driven by the consolidation of digital technologies.

The question is not just about whether constitutional democracies could inject democratic values in the technological architecture. Technology is just a means for mediating the relationship of power between humans. Behind digital technologies, including artificial intelligence, there are actors defining the characteristics of these systems. These technologies are not autonomous or neutral but make decisions about human beings based on principles which are primarily shaped by other human beings. In order to face the challenges of 'algocracy',[9] it is critical to find a way to preserve the role of human expertise.[10] Therefore, the primary challenge for constitutional law in the algorithmic society is not to regulate technology but to address the threats coming from the rise of unaccountable transnational private powers, whose global effects increasingly produce local challenges for constitutional democracies.

In a sense, the mission of modern constitutionalism is to protect fundamental rights while limiting the emergence of powers outside any control.[11] Constitutions have been developed with a view to limiting governmental powers, thus shielding individuals from interference by public authorities. From a constitutional law perspective, the notion of power has traditionally been vested in public authorities. Constitutions already provide systems of checks and balances for limiting public powers. Still, they have not been conceived as a general barrier against the consolidation of paralegal systems or the exercise (rather abuse) of private freedom. On the contrary, constitutions aim to protect pluralism and freedoms of individuals against interferences by public actors while leaving public authorities the responsibility to intervene to ensure that fundamental rights are respected even at the horizontal level between private actors. This constitutional turn from the vertical to the horizontal dimension is generally the exception and occurs in the context of the

[9] John Danaher, 'The Threat of Algocracy: Reality, Resistance and Accommodation' (2016) 29 Philosophy & Technology 245.

[10] Frank Pasquale, *New Laws of Robotics: Defending Human Expertise in the Age of AI* (Belknap Press 2020).

[11] András Sajó and Renáta Uitz, *The Constitution of Freedom: An Introduction to Legal Constitutionalism* (Oxford University Press 2017); Jeremy Waldron, 'Constitutionalism: A Skeptical View' (2012) NYU, Public Law Research Paper No. 10–87 https://papers.ssrn.com/sol3/papers.cfm?abstract_id=1722771&rec=1&srcabs=1760963&alg=1&pos=1 accessed 21 November 2021. Constitutionalism has also a positive side encouraging public actors to promote the well-being and common good. See Adrian Vermeule, *Common Good Constitutionalism* (Wiley & Sons, forthcoming); Nicolas Barber, *The Principles of Constitutionalism* (Oxford University Press 2018).

horizontal application of fundamental rights or when constitutional values permeate legal norms by regulation.[12]

In the algorithmic society, the primary threats for constitutional democracies do not come any longer exclusively from public authorities, since they come primarily from private actors governing spaces which are formally private spaces, but exerting in practice, and without any safeguard, functions traditionally vested in public authorities without any safeguard. This challenge, however, does not imply the need to revolutionise the grounding roots of modern constitutionalism but that to reframe the role of constitutional law and interpret the challenges of the algorithmic society under the lens of digital constitutionalism. As Suzor observes, 'digital constitutionalism requires us to develop new ways of limiting abuses of power in a complex system that includes many different governments, businesses, and civil society organisations'.[13] Put in a different way, digital constitutionalism consists of articulating the limits to the exercise of power in a networked society.[14]

As the expression suggests, digital constitutionalism is made of two souls. While the first term ('digital') refers to technologies based on the Internet such as automated technologies to process data or moderate content, the second ('constitutionalism') refers to the political ideology born in the eighteenth century where, according to the Lockean idea, the power of governments should be legally limited, and its legitimacy depends upon complying with these limitations.[15] Despite this chronological gap, the adjective 'digital' entails placing constitutionalism in a temporal and material dimension. Digital constitutionalism indeed refers to a specific timeframe, precisely the aftermath of the Internet at the end of the last century. Moreover, from a material perspective, this adjective qualifies constitutionalism, moving the focus to how digital technologies and constitutionalism affect each other. Merging the expressions 'digital' and 'constitutionalism' does not lead to revolutionising the pillars of modern constitutionalism. Instead, it aims to understand how to interpret the (still hidden) role of constitutional law in the algorithmic society. Therefore, digital constitutionalism should be seen

[12] Eleni Frantziou, *The Horizontal Effect of Fundamental Rights in the European Union: A Constitutional Analysis* (Oxford University Press 2019).

[13] Nicolas Suzor, *Lawless: The Secret Rules That Govern Our Digital Lives* 173 (Cambridge University Press 2019).

[14] Claudia Padovani and Mauro Santaniello, 'Digital Constitutionalism: Fundamental Rights and Power Limitation in the Internet Eco-System' (2018) 80 International Communication Gazzette 295.

[15] Peter Grimm, *Constitutionalism: Past, Present and Future* (Oxford University Press 2016).

not as a monolith but as the expression of different constitutional approaches to digital technologies from an internal and external point of view.

From an internal angle, digital constitutionalism does not provide a unique way to solve the challenges of the algorithmic society. Despite the relevance of global constitutionalism,[16] still the way in which constitutional law reacts to the challenges of the algorithmic society is driven by regional and local constitutional traditions and cultures. This internal dimension is primarily because, even in a phase of internationalisation of constitutional law,[17] constitutions represent the identity and values of a certain community which, by definition, is connected to territorial boundaries. Although the protection of constitutional rights or the rule of law are missions shared by constitutional democracies, nonetheless, how these values are effectively protected depends on the political, institutional and social dynamics of different constitutional systems. Therefore, from an internal perspective, the constitutional answers to the challenges of the algorithmic society could not always overlap but lead to diverging paths. In this book, the European and US strategies to face the challenges of platform governance provide an example of the multiple faces of digital constitutionalism across the Atlantic.

The external point of view of digital constitutionalism shows how the constitutional reactions to the challenges of the algorithmic society are different when looking not only at the internal peculiarities of constitutional models around the world but also beyond the traditional boundaries of political and legal constitutionalism.[18] In particular, states' constitutions are not the only sources of norms and principles. Even outside the framework of digital technologies, constitutional law has struggled with maintaining its role in relation to the consolidation of normative principles resulting from international organisations, transnational corporations and standard-setting entities, defining the consolidation of societal constitutionalism,[19] or, more broadly, legal

[16] Antje Wiener and others, 'Global Constitutionalism: Human Rights, Democracy and the Rule of Law' (2012) 1 Global Constitutionalism 1.

[17] Sergio Bartole, *The Internationalisation of Constitutional Law* (Hart 2020).

[18] Nico Krisch, *Beyond Constitutionalism: The Pluralist Structure of Postnational Law* (Oxford University Press 2010).

[19] Angelo Jr. Golia and Gunther Teubner, 'Societal Constitutionalism: Background, Theory, Debates' Max Planck Institute for Comparative Public Law & International Law (MPIL) Research Paper No. 2021-08 https://papers.ssrn.com/sol3/papers.cfm?abstrac

and constitutional pluralism.[20] This form of pluralism leads to looking at legal constitutionalism under a broader umbrella where the link between law and territory is increasingly replaced by the relationship between norms and powers coming from different autonomous rationalities shaping each other in a process of mutual influence.

The rise of the algorithmic society highlights this path, underlining both the internal and external angle of digital constitutionalism. Constitutional democracies rely on policies to address common challenges but based on different constitutional values. For instance, the way in which freedom of expression promotes or limits platform power across the Atlantic shows a different constitutional sensitivity. This difference shows how, even if linked by common principles, constitutional democracies do not always share the same internal understanding of rights and powers, thus leading to diverging reactions. Likewise, the external point of view of digital constitutionalism can be examined by looking at how multiple entities influence Internet governance by imposing their internal values, while defining standards of protection competing externally with the principles and safeguards of constitutional democracies. The institutionalisation of social media councils such as the Facebook Oversight Board or the increasing power of online platforms to set the standards of protection on a global scale are nothing else than paths of constitutionalisation beyond the traditional boundaries of modern constitutionalism.

1.2 Paths of Constitutionalisation

Since the end of the twentieth century, daily life has increasingly gone digital towards an 'onlife' dimension.[21] Individuals increasingly experience their rights and freedom in a ubiquitous digital environment,[22] which differs from the end of the last century.[23] Within this framework, social relationships are mediated by a mix of entities expressing forms of public authority and private ordering. The pandemic season has been

t_id=3804094 accessed 20 November 2021; Gunther Teubner, *Constitutional Fragments: Societal Constitutionalism and Globalization* (Oxford University Press 2012).

[20] Paul S. Berman, *Global Legal Pluralism: A Jurisprudence of Law beyond Borders* (Cambridge University Press 2012). Neil Walker, 'The Idea of Constitutional Pluralism' (2002) 65(3) The Modern Law Review 317–59.

[21] Luciano Floridi (eds.), *The Onlife Manifesto: Being Human in a Hyperconnected Era* (Springer 2015).

[22] Laura De Nardis, *The Internet in Everything: Freedom and Security in a World with No Off Switch* (Yale University Press 2020).

[23] Sherry Turkle, *Life on the Screen, Identity in the Age of Internet* (Simon & Schuster 1997).

a litmus test in this sense. Amazon provided deliveries during the lockdown phase, while Google and Apple offered their technology for contact tracing apps. These actors have played a critical role in providing services which other businesses or even the state failed to deliver promptly. The COVID-19 crisis has led these actors to become increasingly involved in daily lives, underlining how they are part of the social infrastructure.[24] This situation has highlighted how transnational private actors are considered essential platforms or digital infrastructures.[25]

In this digital transition, law, technology and society, as examples of social systems, have not ceased to produce internal norms,[26] while continuously shaping each other in a process of mutual influence or rather digital constitutivity.[27] The law is indeed the result not only of its own logics but also of a compromise between technological architecture, social norms and market forces competing online.[28] At the same time, the law indirectly influences the other systems which, even if they produce their norms in an internal environment, are inevitably part of a greater picture. Usually, legal categories such as rules, authority or rights and freedoms contribute to shaping the boundaries of recognised powers. Although these definitions do not exist outside the legal framework but are created within the rationality of the law, these legal notions are exposed to systemic interferences from other (sub)systems. Likewise, the influence of legal systems shapes the boundaries and characteristics of technology and society.[29] In other words, the peculiarity of the law as a social system is to define spaces as delegated and autonomous manifestations of powers.

The rise of digital technologies has contributed to influencing the previous equilibrium among social systems, defining what Kettemann calls the normative order of the Internet.[30] And constitutional law was

[24] Jennifer Cobbe and Elettra Bietti, 'Rethinking Digital Platforms for the Post-COVID-19 Era' CIGI (12 May 2020) www.cigionline.org/articles/rethinking-digital-platforms-post-covid-19-era accessed 21 November 2021.

[25] Nikolas Guggenberger, 'Essential Platforms' (2021) 24 Stanford Technology Law Review 237.

[26] Niklas Luhman, *Social System* (Stanford University Press 2016).

[27] Gunther Teubner, *Law as an Autopoietic System* (Blackwell 1993).

[28] Lawrence Lessig, *Code: And Other Laws of Cyberspace. Version 2.0* (Basic Books 2006).

[29] David Delaney, 'Legal Geography I: Constitutivities, Complexities, and Contingencies' (2015) 39(1) Progress in Human Geographies 96.

[30] Matthias Kettemann, *The Normative Order of the Internet: A Theory of Rule and Regulation Online* (Oxford University Press 2020).

not spared in this process. The shift from atoms to bits at the end of the last century has affected constitutional values such as the protection of fundamental rights and democracy,[31] ultimately leading to a new digital constitutional phase at the door of the algorithmic society.[32] At the end of the last century, digital technologies have triggered the development of new channels, products and services, extending the opportunities to exercise economic freedoms and fundamental rights such as freedom of expression or the freedom to conduct business.[33] The Internet has fostered the possibilities to share opinions and engage with other ideas, thus fostering civil and political rights. This positive framework for democratic values was also one of the primary reasons justifying the technological optimism at the end of the last century, which considered the digital environment not as a threat but as an opportunity to empower freedoms while limiting interferences by public authorities.[34]

From a constitutional standpoint, this revolution has led to a positive alteration of the constitutional stability. At first glance, the benefits of this bottom-up constitutionalisation would have compensated for the drawbacks of self-regulation, especially when thinking about public surveillance and monitoring. Nonetheless, the digital age is far from being outside any form of control. Apart from the interferences of public actors,[35] the digital environment is subject to the governance (or authority) of private actors. Google, Facebook, Amazon or Apple are paradigmatic examples of digital forces competing with public authorities in the exercise of powers online.

Within this framework, constitutional democracies are increasingly marginalised in the algorithmic society. The power of lawmakers has

[31] Andrea Simoncini and Erik Longo, 'Fundamental Rights and the Rule of Law in the Algorithmic Society' in Hans-W. Micklitz and others (eds.), *Constitutional Challenges in the Algorithmic Society* 27 (Cambridge University Press 2021); Oreste Pollicino and Graziella Romeo (eds.), *The Internet and Constitutional Law: The Protection of Fundamental Rights and Constitutional Adjudication in Europe* (Routledge 2016).

[32] Paul Nemitz, 'Constitutional Democracy and Technology in the age of Artificial Intelligence' (2018) Royal Society Philosophical Transactions A 376.

[33] Yochai Benkler, *The Wealth of Networks: How Social Production Transforms Markets and Freedom* (Yale University Press 2006).

[34] David R. Johnson and David Post, 'Law and Borders: The Rise of Law in Cyberspace' (1996) 48(5) Stanford Law Review 1371.

[35] Justin Clark and others, 'The Shifting Landscape of Global Internet Censorship' (2017) Berkman Klein Center for Internet & Society Research Publication https://dash.harvard.edu/handle/1/33084425 accessed 21 November 2021.

been scaled back, and it is not a surprise that courts have taken the lead to overcome legislative inertia in the digital age.[36] The events around the Australian Competition and Consumer Commission News Media and Digital Platforms Mandatory Bargaining Code are a paradigmatic example of the power online platforms can hold in shaping public policies and decision-making.[37] As an answer to this political move, Facebook first decided to ban Australian publishers and users from sharing or viewing Australian as well as international news content. Second, just a couple of days later, the social media platform changed its view, once the Australian government decided to step back and negotiate with Facebook. Facebook's (temporary) choice to ban news in Australia is not just a business decision, reflecting the platform's economic freedoms. This case shows a 'power move' to push the Australian government, which had worked for months on the bill in question, to step back and negotiate with Facebook overnight. This interaction is not just an example of how Facebook can influence public policies, but it also shows how powers are relocated among different actors in the algorithmic society, within the push towards a new phase of digital constitutionalism.

This example demonstrates why the reactions of lawmakers and courts are not the result of a constitutional moment in Ackerman's terms.[38] Ackerman's theory looks at constitutional values not just as a mix of expressions and interpretations of the courts, but as the set of principles agreed upon by the people in an extraordinary moment of constitutional participation. Instead, the rise and consolidation of digital private powers represents an example of the constitutionalisation of global private spheres. In this process, constitutional values as translated by lawmakers and interpreted by courts are under a process of extraconstitutional amendment or, better, a reframing which is not expressed by codification but by the constitutional contamination of private determinations. This case is a clear example of how the internal rules produced by social systems compete with the autopoietic characteristics of (constitutional) law. By referring to Teubner, this framework

36 Oreste Pollicino, *Judicial Protection of Fundamental Rights on the Internet: A Road Towards Digital Constitutionalism?* (Hart 2021).

37 Giovanni De Gregorio, Oreste Pollicino and Elena Perotti, 'Flexing the Muscles of Information Power: On the Australian News Media Mandatory Bargaining Code' (2021) Verfassungsblog (26 February 2021) https://verfassungsblog.de/facebook-flexing/ accessed 20 November 2021.

38 Bruce Ackerman, *We The People: Transformations* (Belknap Press 1998).

could be described as 'the constitutionalisation of a multiplicity of autonomous subsystems of world society'.[39]

The constitutionalisation of global private spheres in the algorithmic society should not be seen only as an isolated phenomenon but as a piece of the puzzle in the process of globalisation which has increasingly promoted the meeting, and conflict, of different legal systems and rationalities,[40] while raising questions about the idea of networked statehood.[41]

In the last thirty years, globalisation has affected legal systems, thus causing a constitutional distress.[42] Traditional legal categories have been put under pressure. Different entities beyond state actors have extended their rules on a global scale.[43] Financial markets or environmental standards are paradigmatic examples of sectors where political choices are increasingly taken outside traditional democratic circuits, showing the law-making power of private actors.[44]

From a transnational constitutional perspective, constitutional democracies struggle with extending their reach to transnational phenomena occurring outside their territory.[45] Local dynamics and values still constitute the basic roots of each constitutional system. Still, supranational and international bundles, as in the case of the consolidation of multilevel constitutionalism in the European experience,[46] or the constitutionalisation of international law,[47] lead to the emancipation of

[39] Gunther Teubner, 'Societal Constitutionalism: Alternatives to State-Centered Constitutional Theory?' in Christian Joerges, Inger-Johanne Sand and Gunther Teubner (eds.), *Transnational Governance and Constitutionalism* 3 (Hart 2004).

[40] Lars Viellechner, 'Responsive Legal Pluralism: The Emergence of Transnational Conflicts Law' (2015) 6(2) Transnational Legal Theory 312; Detlef von Daniels, *The Concept of Law from a Transnational Perspective* (Ashgate 2010); Gralf-Peter Calliess and Peer Zumbansen *Rough Consensus and Running Code: A Theory of Transnational Private Law* (Hart 2010).

[41] Angelo Jr. Golia and Gunther Teubner, 'Networked Statehood: An Institutionalised Self-contradiction in the Process of Globalisation?' (2021) 12(1) Transnational Legal Theory 7.

[42] Mark Tushnet, 'The Inevitable Globalization of Constitutional Law' (2009) 49 Virginia Journal of International Law 985.

[43] Saskia Sassen, *Losing Control? Sovereignty in the Age of Globalization* (Columbia University Press 1996).

[44] Louis L. Jaffe, 'Law Making by Private Groups' (1937) 51(2) Harvard Law Review 201.

[45] Eric C. Ip, 'Globalization and the Future of the Law of the Sovereign State' (2010) 8(3) International Journal of Constitutional Law 636.

[46] Ingolf Pernice, 'Multilevel Constitutionalism and the Crisis of Democracy in Europe' (2015) 11(3) European Constitutional Law Review 541.

[47] Jan Klabbers, Anne Peters and Geir Ulfsein, *The Constitutionalisation of International Law* (Oxford University Press 2009).

constitutional values from its local roots towards a more global character where constitutional systems increasingly meet in a process of global hybridisation.

Within this framework, the rise of the Internet has not only challenged the traditional Westphalian principles of sovereignty and territory,[48] as in the case of monetary policy,[49] or underlined global and local tensions.[50] This situation was already clear in the aftermath of the *Licra* v. *Yahoo* case,[51] and the following debate on Internet jurisdiction.[52] The consolidation of the Internet has also led to wondering about the relationship between freedoms and power in the digital age.

1.3 Governing the Algorithmic Society

The role of constitutionalism has not been central in the debate about Internet governance and regulation. At the end of the last century, scholars, opposing liberal and anarchic approaches, struggled with explaining whether and to what extent the digital environment could be governed.[53] Likewise, Reidenberg focused on technology and communication networks as sources of information policy rules consisting of default rules that went beyond law and government regulation.[54] Murray went ever further underlining how the effectiveness of such regulation did not only depend on the modality of regulation (e.g. network architecture) but also the power that each point of the network can exercise over other dots.[55] It was already clear that the Internet

[48] Henry H. Perritt, Jr., 'The Internet as a Threat to Sovereignty? Thoughts on the Internet's Role in Strengthening National and Global Governance' (1998) 5 Indiana Journal of Global Legal Studies 423.

[49] Katharina Pistor, 'Statehood in the Digital Age' (2020) 27(3) Constellations 3.

[50] Oreste Pollicino and Marco Bassini, 'The Law of the Internet between Globalisation and Localization' in Miguel Maduro, Kaarlo Tuori and Suvi Sankari (eds.), *Transnational Law: Rethinking European Law and Legal Thinking* 346 (Cambridge University Press 2016).

[51] Tribunal de Grande Instance de Paris, Ligue contre le racisme et l'antisémitisme et Union des étudiants juifs de France c. Yahoo! Inc. et Société Yahoo! France (2000).

[52] Dan Jerker B. Svantesson, *Solving the Internet Jurisdiction Puzzle* (Oxford University Press 2017); Uta Kohl, *Jurisdiction and the Internet: Regulatory Competence over Online Activity* (Cambridge University Press 2007).

[53] Jack L. Goldsmith, 'Against Cyberanarchy' (1998) 65 University of Chicago Law Review 1199.

[54] Joel Reidenberg, 'Lex Informatica: The Formulation of Information Policy Rules through Technology' (1997–1998) 76 Texas Law Review 553.

[55] Andrew Murray, 'Internet Regulation' in David Levi-Faur (ed.), *Handbook on the Politics of Regulation* (Edward Elgar 2011).

would not entirely overcome state regulation. States had already proved their ability to regulate the digital environment, such as in the case of China.[56]

Nonetheless, public actors are no longer the only powerful regulators but they are just one piece of the fragmented framework of online governance. As Lynskey underlined, 'the Internet can be regulated and Internet governance is no longer the sole purview of the State'.[57] Even if states have not lost their power over the digital environment,[58] there are new actors expressing their powers.[59] Online platforms have become more influential operating in the shadow of governments.[60] They have developed their functions as proxies or delegated entities of public authorities to enforce public policies online and autonomously rely on the mix between market power and technological asymmetry. Put another way, the economic power of business actors is now blurred with authority, so the notion of 'power' is meant in a broader sense than the notion of market power used, for example, in competition law.[61]

The problem of private power is not only economic but also political. The accumulation of arbitrary authority in the market outside any form of political accountability can be considered a similar exercise of power characterising the exercise of public authority.[62] When freedoms turn into forms of powers, ensuring democratic oversight and safeguards can preclude market dynamics from driving constitutional values. The different degree of interrelation between market and democracy is firmly linked to the openness and sensitivity of constitutional systems. In

[56] Ronald Deibert and others, *Access Denied: The Practice and Policy of Global Internet Filtering* (MIT Press 2008).

[57] Orla Lynskey, 'Regulating Platform Power' (2017), LSE Legal Studies Working Paper 1 http://eprints.lse.ac.uk/73404/1/WPS2017-01_Lynskey.pdf accessed 21 November 2021.

[58] Blayne Haggart, Natasha Tusikov and Jan A. Scholte (eds.), *Power and Authority in Internet Governance Return of the State?* (Routledge 2021).

[59] Lucie Greene, *Silicon States: The Power and Politics of Big Tech and What It Means for Our Future* (Counterpoint 2018).

[60] Hannah Bloch-Wehba, 'Global Platform Governance: Private Power in the Shadow of the State' (2019) 72 SMU Law Review 27.

[61] Natali Helberger and others, 'Governing Online Platforms: From Contested to Cooperative Responsibility' (2018) 34(1) The Information Society 1; Luca Belli, Pedro A. Francisco and Nicolo Zingales, 'Law of the Land or Law of the Platform? Beware of the Privatisation of Regulation and Police' in Luca Belli and Nicolo Zingales (eds.), *How Platforms Are Regulated and How They Regulate Us* 41 (FGV Rio 2017).

[62] Morris R. Cohen, 'Property and Sovereignty' (1927) 13 Cornell Law Review 8.

other words, where market meets democracy, it is there that it is possible to observe how constitutionalism defines its boundaries.

In the algorithmic society, transnational private corporations, primarily online platforms, exercise powers by governing digital spaces. In a ubiquitous digital environment, content and data can be easily disseminated on a global scale to access services provided for free, from e-mail services to social media platforms implementing algorithmic technologies to moderate content. Public powers still play a critical role in governing digital spaces and interfering with rights and freedoms. Nonetheless, the influence of private actors in the digital environment is increasingly raising concerns in terms of how these entities perform functions of public interest or, in some cases, mirror the exercise of public powers.

The fields of online content and data can provide interesting clues to explain how powers are relocated in the algorithmic society. In terms of speech, the digital environment has become a primary channel for individuals to exercise their rights and freedoms, especially freedom of expression.[63] The Internet has fostered the dissemination of information increasing the opportunities of each individual to share ideas and opinion on a global scale without supporting the infrastructural costs and be subject to the filters of traditional media outlets. A technological optimism characterised the early days of the digital environment. At the end of the last century, the Internet promised an emancipation of the public sphere and democracy from public controls through decentralisation and anonymity. This positive trend was confirmed in a countless number of cases. It would be enough to mention how social media and search engines have provided irreplaceable tools for exercising the two sides of freedom of expression, precisely the right to inform and be informed. Online speech has shown its ability to influence elections, raise the exchange of new ideas on a global scale as well as support minorities and political movements as an instrument of emancipation, like the Arab Spring.[64]

Although, at first glance, this picture may suggest that the digital environment has enhanced freedom of expression while emancipating individual freedom from the interferences of public authorities, however, a closer look reveals that the flow of information online is not without control. In the last years, states have somewhat regulated

[63] Jack M. Balkin, 'Digital Speech and Democratic Culture: A Theory of Freedom of Expression for the Information Society' (2004) 79(1) New York University Law Review 1.

[64] Gadi Wolfsfeld and others, 'Social Media and the Arab Spring: Politics Comes First' (2013) 18(2) The International Journal of Press/Politics 115.

online speech to tackle extreme content or the spread of unauthorised copyright content. In some cases, public actors have also relied on shutting down the Internet extensively despite the economic consequences.[65] Nonetheless, the control of online speech is not merely related to online censorship by public authorities which are already subject to constitutional obligations. The exercise of power over information also concerns private actors.[66] By implementing artificial intelligence systems to moderate content, platforms like Facebook or YouTube can decide how to moderate content by displaying and organising online information based on opaque criteria driven by their Silicon values.[67] Pariser and Sunstein have already underlined the risk of polarisation due to the creation of 'filter bubbles' or 'information cocoons'.[68] Although the Internet has enhanced access to different types of information, this positive effect is lessened by a substantial restriction in the autonomy of users subject to governance of online platforms.

From a constitutional point of view, the primary concern comes from the negative or vertical nature characterising the protection of the right to freedom of expression. Unlike public actors, online platforms are not required to ensure the same constitutional safeguards when they make decisions over the organisation or removal of speech online. These actors can enforce and balance the vast amount of online information outside any public safeguard, primarily the rule of law, as also shown by the block of Donald Trump's accounts by Facebook and Twitter.

Likewise, the field of data can tell a similar story across public and private powers. At the end of the last century, the digital environment was considered a space to ensure the protection of privacy through anonymity and decentralisation which were considered as ways to emancipate freedoms from public interferences. It is not by chance that one of the most famous slogans was 'On the Internet, nobody knows you are a dog'.[69] As quoted by Turckle from one interview with users, '[y]ou can be

[65] Giovanni De Gregorio and Nicole Stremlau, 'Internet Shutdowns and the Limits of Law' (2020) 14 International Journal of Communication 4224.

[66] Kate Klonick, 'The New Governors: The People, Rules, and Processes Governing Online Speech' (2018) 131 Harvard Law Review 1598.

[67] Jillian C. York, *Silicon Values: The Future of Free Speech Under Surveillance Capitalism* (Verso Books 2021).

[68] Eli Pariser, *The Filter Bubble: What the Internet Is Hiding from You* (Viking 2011); Cass R. Sunstein, *Republic.com 2.0* (Princeton University Press 2007).

[69] This is an adage by Peter Steiner and published by The New Yorker in 1993. Glenn Fleishmandec, 'Cartoon Captures Spirit of the Internet' The New York Times

whoever you want to be. You can completely redefine yourself if you want. You don't have to worry about the slots other people put you in as much. They don't look at your body and make assumptions. They don't hear your accent and make assumptions. All they see are your words'.[70]

However, this framework of anonymity and decentralisation has not been an obstacle for public actors that have increasingly relied on the digital environment as an instrument of surveillance.[71] The case of Snowden has been just one example not only of the consolidation of a surveillance society,[72] but also of the invisible handshake characterising the cooperation between the public and private sectors in the field of data surveillance. [73]

The paradigmatic idea of a public panopticon can be considered one of the primary concerns in the algorithmic society.[74] However, similarly to the case of freedom of expression, public actors have not been the only source of concerns for privacy and personal data. At the end of the last century, the development of new processing technologies driven by neoliberal narratives has allowed the rise of new business models based on the processing of multiple kinds of information, including personal data, which are increasingly collected, organised and processed not only by public actors pursuing public tasks but also by businesses seeking profit. The processing of personal data has already highlighted serious constitutional challenges at the beginning of this century,[75] especially with the evolution of profiling technologies.[76] As observed by Nissenbaum, 'in a flourishing online ecology, where individuals, communities, institutions, and corporations generate content, experiences, interactions, and services, the supreme currency is information, including information about people'.[77]

In this framework, online platforms play a critical role due to the vast amount of data they process and organise. Even if not exclusively, their

(14 December 2000) www.nytimes.com/2000/12/14/technology/cartoon-captures-spirit-of-the-internet.html accessed 21 November 2021.

70 Turkle (n. 23), 184–5.

71 Neil M. Richards, 'The Dangers of Surveillance' (2013) 126 Harvard Law Review 1935.

72 David Lyon, *Surveillance after Snowden* (Polity 2015).

73 Micheal Birnhack and Niva Elkin-Koren, 'The Invisible Handshake: The Reemergence of the State in the Digital Environment' (2003) 8 Virginia Journal of Law and Technology 6.

74 Michel Foucault, *Discipline and Punish: The Birth of a Prison* (Penguin 1991).

75 A. Michael Froomkin, 'The Death of Privacy?' (2000) 52 Stanford Law Review 1461.

76 Steve Lohr, *Data-Ism: The Revolution Transforming Decision Making, Consumer Behavior, and Almost Everything Else* (Blackstone 2015).

77 Helen Nissenbaum, 'A Contextual Approach to Privacy Online' (2011) 140(4) Daedalus 32, 33.

business model is based or highly relies on the processing of data for profiling purposes to make profits from advertising revenues, targeted services or analysis of data. As in the field of content, the value of data in the algorithmic society can be understood by focusing on artificial intelligence systems providing opportunities for extracting value from the processing of vast amounts of (personal) data.[78] The development and implementation of algorithmic technologies have increased the concerns for the protection of privacy and personal data subject to ubiquitous forms of control answering to the logic of accumulation, prediction and behavioural influences.[79] The consequences of this discretion leads to consequences for individuals who are subject to discrimination outcomes,[80] as particularly shown by the case of search engines.[81] Besides, the Cambridge Analytica scandal showed how these constitutional challenges do not just affect individual rights but also collective interests and, more in general, democratic values.[82] This framework at the intersection between public and private powers highlights the logic of information capitalism and explains why users experience a 'modulated democracy'.[83]

Since data and information constitute the new non-rival and non-fungible resources of the algorithmic society,[84] their accumulation and processing by private actors has complemented the economic with the political power. Technological evolutions, combined with a liberal constitutional approach across the Atlantic at the end of the last century, has led online platforms to set their standards and procedures on a global scale and erode areas of powers traditionally vested in public authorities. Digital firms are no longer market participants, since they

78 Solon Barocas and others, 'Governing Algorithms: A Provocation Piece', SSRN (4 April 2013) https://ssrn.com/abstract=2245322 accessed 21 November 2021; Caryn Devins and others, 'The Law and Big Data' (2017) 27 Cornell Journal of Law & Public Policy 357.

79 Shoshana Zuboff, 'Big Other: Surveillance Capitalism and the Prospects of an Information Civilization' (2015) 30(1) Journal of Information Technology 75; Mireille Hildebrandt and Serge Gutwirth (eds.), *Profiling the European Citizen: Cross-Disciplinary Perspectives* (Springer 2008).

80 Cathy O'Neil, *Weapons of Math Destruction: How Big Data Increases Inequality and Threatens Democracy* (Crown Pub 2016).

81 Safiya U. Noble, *Algorithms of Oppression: How Search Engines Reinforce Racism* (New York University Press 2018).

82 Brittany Kaiser, *Targeted: The Cambridge Analytica Whistleblower's Inside Story of How Big Data, Trump, and Facebook Broke Democracy and How It Can Happen Again* (Harper Collins 2019).

83 Julie E. Cohen, 'What Privacy Is For' (2013) 126 Harvard Law Review 1904.

84 Michele Loi and Paul-Olivier Dehaye, 'If Data Is the New Oil, When Is the Extraction of Value from Data Unjust?' (2018) 7(2) Philosophy & Public Issues 137.

'aspire to displace more government roles over time, replacing the logic of territorial sovereignty with functional sovereignty'.[85] These actors have been already named 'gatekeepers' to underline their high degree of control in online spaces.[86] As Mark Zuckerberg stressed, '[i]n a lot of ways Facebook is more like a government than a traditional company'.[87]

By implementing Terms of Service and community guidelines, platforms unilaterally establish the grounding values of the community and what rights users have within their digital spaces. Formally, these documents are private agreements between users and platforms. However, substantially, these instruments reflect a process of constitutionalisation of online spaces,[88] made by instruments of private ordering shaping the scope of fundamental rights and freedoms of billions of people by adopting a rigid top-down approach.[89] Online platforms can autonomously decide not only how people interact but also how they can assert their rights (and what those rights are) by privately regulating their digital infrastructure.

Online platforms do not impose limitations just to set the standards of protection of their digital spaces. They also embody other functions and tasks normally vested in public authorities, like courts or other jurisdictional bodies. The Facebook's Oversight Board is a paradigmatic example not only of a system of private adjudication,[90] but also of the institutionalisation of digital private powers. These dynamics lead to the

85 Frank Pasquale, 'From Territorial to Functional Sovereignty: The Case of Amazon' Law and Political Economy (6 December 2017) https://lpeblog.org/2017/12/06/from-territorial-to-functional-sovereignty-the-case-of-amazon accessed 20 November 2021.

86 Emily B. Laidlaw, 'A Framework for Identifying Internet Information Gatekeepers' (2012) 24(3) International Review of Computer Law and Technology 263; Jonathan Zittrain, 'History of Online Gatekeeping' (2006) 19(2) Harvard Journal of Law & Technology 253; Scott Burris, Peter Drahos and Clifford Shearing, 'Nodal Governance' (2005) 30 Australian Journal of Law and Policy 30.

87 Franklin Foer, 'Facebook's War on Free Will' The Guardian (19 September 2017) www.theguardian.com/technology/2017/sep/19/facebooks-war-on-free-will accessed 19 November 2021.

88 Edoardo Celeste, 'Terms of Service and Bills of Rights: New Mechanisms of Constitutionalisation in the Social Media Environment?' (2018) International Review of Law, Computers and Technology www.tandfonline.com/doi/abs/10.1080/13600869.2018.1475898 accessed 20 November 2021; Luca Belli and Jamila Venturini, 'Private Ordering and the Rise of Terms of Service as Cyber-Regulation' (2016) 5(4) Internet Policy Review https://policyreview.info/node/441/pdf accessed 20 November 2021.

89 Tomer Shadmy, 'The New Social Contract: Facebook's Community and Our Rights' (2019) 37 Boston University International Law Journal 307.

90 Kate Klonick, 'The Facebook Oversight Board: Creating an Independent Institution to Adjudicate Online Free Expression' (2020) 129(8) The Yale Law Journal 2232;

privatisation of fundamental rights protection.[91] While public enforcement has been for a long time the default option, based on the role of public authorities as monopoly holders in the context of fundamental rights adjudication, private enforcement has recently emerged as a new trend, when it comes to protecting fundamental rights in the digital realm.[92] Such privatisation of the protection of rights and liberties is just one of the countless processes underlining how constitutional democracies delegate public enforcement to private entities,[93] which then consolidate their powers by developing autonomous functions.

This form of technological regulation is different from legal regulation. As Hildebrandt underlined, technological regulation is not the result of a democratic process, excludes disobedience and does not allow being contested due to lack of transparency and accountability of decision-making.[94] The spread of automated decision-making systems makes the public and private powers even more opaque, and, therefore, unaccountable. Increasingly, private actors exercise their influence over decisions on the development of these technologies promising to globally affect society, even in the public sector. These private determinations are usually based on their own economic, legal and ethical frameworks.[95] Operational parameters for processing information and data are programmed by developers and, then, implemented by private entities which are not obliged to pursue any public interest and respect fundamental rights in the lack of any regulation or contractual arrangement.

The entire framework is even more multifaceted when observing that public actors rely on the private sector as a proxy in the digital environment.[96] The Pentagon's request to Amazon, Google, Microsoft

Evelyn Douek, 'Facebook's "Oversight Board:" Move Fast with Stable Infrastructure and Humility' (2019) 21(1) North Carolina Journal of Law & Technology 1.

91 Marco Bassini, 'Fundamental Rights and Private Enforcement in the Digital Age' (2019) 25(2) European Law Journal 182; Rory Van Loo, 'The Corporation as Courthouse' (2016) 33 Yale Journal on Regulation 547.

92 Giovanni De Gregorio, 'From Constitutional Freedoms to Powers: Protecting Fundamental Rights Online in the Algorithmic Society' (2019) 11(2) European Journal of Legal Studies 65.

93 Jody Freeman and Martha Minow (eds.), *Government by Contract: Outsourcing and American Democracy* (Harvard University Press 2009).

94 Mireille Hildebrandt, *Smart Technologies and the End(s) of Law* (Edward Elgar 2016).

95 Brent Mittelstadt and others, 'The Ethics of Algorithms: Mapping the Debate' (2016) 3 Big Data & Society https://journals.sagepub.com/doi/pdf/10.1177/2053951716679679 accessed 23 November 2021.

96 Niva Elkin-Koren and Eldar Haber, 'Governance by Proxy: Cyber Challenges to Civil Liberties' (2016) 82 Brookling Law Review 105.

and Oracle for bids on cloud contracts is a clear example of the critical role of public-private partnership where public and private values inevitably merge in a hybrid contractual framework.[97] Likewise, public actors usually rely on the algorithmic enforcement of individual rights online, as in the case of India ordering the removal of content during the pandemic.[98] In other words, the increasing intersection between public and private values could expose public actors to the charm of technological solutionism driven by private business interests.[99]

The consolidation of private powers in the algorithmic society does not only challenge the protection of individual fundamental rights, such as freedom of expression, privacy and data protection but also democratic values from two perspectives.

Firstly, democracy and fundamental rights are intimately intertwined. Among different angles, it is worth observing that, when digital technologies raise threats for fundamental rights, especially civil and political liberties, they also raise concerns for democratic values. Without expressing opinions and ideas freely, it is not possible to define a society as democratic. Likewise, without rules governing the processing of personal data, individuals may not express their identity if they fear a regime of private surveillance and they could not rely on a set of accountability and transparency safeguards to avoid marginalisation of individuals in opaque spheres of data ignorance.

Secondly, the consolidation of private powers is a troubling process for democracy. Even if, at first glance, democratic states are open environments for pluralism flourishing through fundamental rights and freedoms, at the same time, their stability can be undermined when those freedoms transform into new founding powers overcoming basic principles such as the respect of the rule of law. In this situation, there is no effective form of participation or representation of citizens in determining the rules governing their community and oversight on the exercise of private powers. The creation of private legal frameworks

97 Jordan Novet, 'Pentagon Asks Amazon, Google, Microsoft and Oracle for Bids on New Cloud Contracts' CNBC (19 November 2021) www.cnbc.com/2021/11/19/pentagon-asks-amazon-google-microsoft-oracle-for-cloud-bids.html accessed 20 November 2021.

98 Kim Lyons, 'India reportedly orders social media platforms to remove references to "Indian variant" of COVID-19' The Verge (23 May 2021) www.theverge.com/2021/5/23/22449898/india-social-media-platforms-remove-indian-variant-covid-19-coronavirus accessed 20 November 2021.

99 Evgeny Morozov, *To Save Everything, Click Here: The Folly of Technological Solutionism* (Public Affairs 2013).

outside any representative mechanism undermines the possibility for citizens to participate in the democratic designing of the rules governing the digital environment. In other words, the algorithmic society challenges one of the pillars of democratic systems, namely making laws chosen by the people.

Within this framework, individuals find themselves in a situation which resembles that of a new digital *status subjectionis*. Online platforms offer their services to billions of individuals by defining the contractual rules of the game. When users enter into an agreement with platforms, they have limited power of negotiation. They accept to relinquish their rights and freedoms while legitimising platforms as authorities to manage those rights, in a manner similar to the stipulation of a private social contract. The primary concern is that, unlike democratic countries, online platforms exercise this power without following any democratic procedures but, conversely by exercising an absolute authority. Even if these actors take decisions that affect fundamental rights and democratic values, users have little possibility of making their voices heard. It is precisely here that private freedoms tend to transmute to (unaccountable) powers.

1.4 The Forgotten Talent of European Constitutionalism

The research angle offered by digital constitutionalism can be considered a way to test the talent of European constitutional law to react against these challenges. The Union is a paradigmatic example of the constitutional reaction to the challenges of the algorithmic society. From a liberal imprinting at the end of the last century, the policy of the Union in the field of digital technologies has shifted to a constitutional-based approach. As explained in Chapter 2, this change of heart has been primarily driven by transnational corporations performing quasi-public functions on a global scale, thus competing with public actors and imposing their standards of protection.

Although the implementation of digital technologies by public actors also raises serious constitutional concerns, the rise of European digital constitutionalism is primarily the result of the role of online platforms, which, although vested as private actors, increasingly perform quasi-public tasks. The freedom to conduct business enshrined in the Charter of Fundamental Rights (Charter) has now turned into a new dimension,[100] namely that of private power, which brings significant challenges to the role and tools of constitutional law. If Google and Facebook can rely on financial resources more than entire states or rely on algorithmic technologies to gather information and data from billions of users, they can exercise functions which can compete with, if not overcome in some cases, the power of public authorities. If these actors can establish standards of protection of users' rights on a global scale, the principle of the rule of law and democratic values would be increasingly shaped, and maybe replaced, by market logic.

It is not by chance that the constitutional reaction to platform powers occurred in Europe. This shift of paradigm, which has been triggered by the talent of European constitutional law to react against the emergence of powers in the algorithmic society, is the result of a peculiar sensitivity of European constitutionalism that does not tolerate abuse of rights and aims to protect human dignity. Neoliberal approaches or excessive democratic tolerance which contribute to transforming freedoms into powers cannot be exploited to destroy democracy itself.[101] Since the horrors of the Second World War, European states started to incorporate and codify human dignity within its founding values.[102] The post-War scenario was a decisive moment for the emergence of dignity as a European constitutional principle,[103] thus elevating it to 'cornerstone of the postwar constitutional state'.[104] Besides, dignity is not an isolated concept but a foundational principle connected with the values and aspirations shaping European constitutionalism. Also driven by the international framework, human dignity has started to emancipate the eastern side of the Atlantic from the western where the liberal imprinting of constitutional law still remains the primary foundation of fundamental rights and liberties.[105] The consolidation of human dignity at the international level is evident even when focusing on the

[100] Charter of Fundamental Rights of the European Union (2012) OJ C 326/391.

[101] Christine Duprè, *The Age of Dignity: Human Rights and Constitutionalism in Europe* (Hart 2015).

[102] Paolo Becchi, 'Human Dignity in Europe: Introduction' in Paolo Becchi and Klaus Mathis (eds.), *Handbook of Human Dignity in Europe* (Springer 2019).

[103] James Q. Whitman, 'On Nazi "Honour" and the New European "Dignity"' in Christian Joerges and Navraj Singh Ghaleigh (eds.), *The Darker Legacies of Law in Europe* 243 (Hart 2003).

[104] Lorraine Weinrib, 'Human Dignity as a Rights-Protecting Principle' (2004) 17 National Journal of Constitutional Law 330.

[105] Giovanni Bognetti, 'The Concept of Human Dignity in European and U.S. Constitutionalism' in Georg Nolte (ed.), *European and US Constitutionalism* 95 (Cambridge University Press 2005).

European Convention on Human Rights (Convention).[106] The Strasbourg Court considers human dignity as underpinning values protecting all the other rights of the Convention.[107]

The influence of the Council of Europe and Member States can also be understood when moving to the framework of the Union. In *Omega*, the European Court of Justice (ECJ) held that 'the Community legal order undeniably strives to ensure respect for human dignity as a general principle of law'.[108] Likewise, the ECJ recognised human dignity as part of the Member States' public security and order.[109] The recognition of human dignity as a general principle of law before the entry into force of the Charter is an evident example of the consolidation of the process of European constitutionalisation to which the ECJ opened the door since *Stauder*,[110] as also evolved in *Internationale Handelsgesellschaft* and *Nold*.[111] In other words, the ECJ has played a primary role in the constitutionalisation of the European dimension even before the Charter.[112]

In addition, human dignity has been established as the first and autonomous fundamental right in the Charter. Its primacy and autonomy would suggest its role as an overarching principle but also as a fundamental right which does not leave room for any interference. Human dignity is not just enshrined in the preamble of the Charter, but it is protected as an autonomous and inviolable fundamental right.[113] Even if the Charter provides the possibility to limit fundamental rights,[114] a systematic interpretation reveals that this does not apply to human rights with absolute protection as those protected by the ECHR.[115] Therefore, even in the lack of accession of the Union's system

106 Christopher McCrudden, 'Human Dignity and Judicial Interpretation of Human Rights' (2008) 19(4) European Journal of International Law 655.

107 *Pretty* v. *United Kingdom* (1997) 24 EHRR (1997) 423, 65.

108 Case C-36/02, *Omega Spielhallen und Automatenaufstellungs- GmbH* v. *Oberbürgermeisterin der Bundesstadt Bonn* (2004) ECR I-9609, 34.

109 Joined Case C-331/ 16 and C-366/16, *K.* v. *Staatssecretaris van Veiligheid en Justitie* and *H. F.* v. *Belgische Staat* (2018), 47.

110 See Case 29/69, *Erich Stauder* v. *City of Ulm – Sozialamt* (1969).

111 Case 11/70, *Internationale Handelsgesellschaft mbH* v. *Einfuhr- und Vorratsstelle für Getreide und Futtermittel* (1970); Case 4/73, *J. Nold, Kohlen- und Baustoffgroßhandlung* v. *Ruhrkohle Aktiengesellschaft* (1977).

112 Marta Cartabia, 'Europe and Rights: Taking Dialogue Seriously' (2009) 5 European Constitutional Law Review 5.

113 Charter (n. 100), Art. 1. See also Arts. 25, 31.

114 Ibid., Art. 52.

115 Ibid., Art. 52(3).

to the ECHR, it is still possible to define an intimate bundle which characterises human dignity as the overarching principle of European constitutionalism.

Together with democracy, the rule of law and the protection of human rights, the Lisbon Treaty has recognised the role of human dignity as a pillar of European constitutionalism. Even if the preamble of the Treaty of the European Union (TEU) just mentions human rights and the inalienable rights of human persons,[116] human dignity has been enshrined as one of the primary common values of the Union.[117] The position in EU primary law is not neutral but constitutes a legal obligation to respect this human right for public actors and an objective driving all of the activities of the Union. Besides, the recognition of the Charter as a source of EU primary law has led to the consolidation of the European constitutional framework with the result that human dignity has become a mandatory point of reference.

Within this framework, dignity is not only an objective or a fundamental right but a promise for democracy after a phase of dehumanisation. Human dignity as a constitutional foundation is the result of the process of the European experience whose values aim to foster a vision of democracy where human beings can take decisions on their life and shape collective decisions. Human dignity is not just avoiding torture or ensuring equality, but it is the constitutional foundation of European democratic values.

Therefore, human dignity also aims to achieve a utopian goal while driving European constitutionalism towards individuals as the core of fundamental rights protection and critical part of democracy. As observed, 'there is no foolproof constitutional design that can immunise liberal democracy from the pressures of backsliding. At best, constitutional design features serve as speed bumps to slow the agglomeration and abuse of political power; they cannot save us from our worst selves completely'.[118] This risk does not concern only political or external forces which aim to overthrow democratic safeguards but also the interferences of private powers whose activities are backed by a liberal constitutional approach. In the algorithmic society, the predominance of digital capitalism leads human dignity to express its role as the beacon and the overarching framework of the European

[116] Treaty on the European Union (2012) OJ 326/13, preamble 2, 4.

[117] Ibid., Art. 2.

[118] Tom Ginsburg, Aziz Z. Huq and Mila Versteeg, 'The Coming Demise of Liberal Constitutionalism?' (2018) 85(2) The University of Chicago Law Review 239, 253.

constitutional systems. Therefore, the rise of European digital constitutionalism should not be seen as a mere answer, but rather as a long-term strategy to protect constitutional values from the interferences of private powers in the digital age. Put another way, rather than just a firm reaction, it is also a proactive approach calling the Union and Member States to intervene to mitigate the threats to democratic values.

Nonetheless, the European constitutional reaction to the challenges raised by private actors is not the general rule. While the Union framework is at the forefront of a new constitutional approach to the challenges of the algorithmic society, the United States seem to be following an opposite path. In the last twenty years, the US policy has adopted an 'omissive' approach based on a First Amendment dogma. Still, the responsibilities of platform activities are based on a legal framework adopted at the end of the last century based on immunity and exemption of liability.[119] In the field of data, apart from some national attempts,[120] there is not a harmonised approach at the federal level to privacy and data protection. Moving from the Congress to the Supreme Court, even in this case, there has been a restrictive approach towards any public attempt to regulate the digital environment,[121] or horizontal extension of constitutional rights.[122]

These non-exhaustive considerations on the constitutional approaches of the other side of the Atlantic would confirm that digital constitutionalism is not a unique expression. It is intimately connected with the constitutional framework of each legal and political system as intertwined with the alternative process of constitutionalisation. The rise of digital constitutionalism across the Atlantic is the result of paths guided by different constitutional premises. In the last twenty years, the US framework has not reacted to the rise of private powers but has highly defended the concept of liberty as set in stone within the First Amendment. The liberal approach of the United States could also be considered another expression of digital constitutionalism showing the different talent of US constitutional law which looks at online platforms as an enabler of liberties and democracy rather than a threat to such values. Such a framework of liberty has been increasingly abandoned on the eastern side of the Atlantic where the different constitutional humus

[119] Communications Decency Act (1996), Section 230; Digital Millennium Copyright Act (1997), Section 512.

[120] See, e.g., California Consumer Privacy Act (2020).

[121] See, e.g., *Packingham* v. *North Carolina*, 582 U.S. ___ (2017).

[122] See, e.g., *Manhattan Community Access Corp.* v. *Halleck*, No. 17-1702, 587 U.S. ___ (2019).

based on human dignity has paved the way towards a new constitutional phase.

Looking at the eastern side of the Atlantic, the challenges raised by the power of private actors in the digital environment leads to questioning the traditional boundaries of European constitutional law to understand to what extent it is possible to remedy the current situation of threat for fundamental rights and democracy. The research angles of European digital constitutionalism can contribute to defining the instruments to deal with platform powers as well as the guiding principles and remedies to restore the constitutional equilibrium. The primary mission of European digital constitutionalism consists of limiting the abuse of powers by framing and extending constitutional values in the algorithmic society.

1.5 Investigating European Digital Constitutionalism

This book aims to capture the emergence of a new phase of European constitutionalism in the algorithmic society defined as digital constitutionalism. This new moment is examined in a twofold way. Firstly, this work investigates the reasons leading to this new constitutional phase in Europe. Secondly, it provides a normative framework analysing how and to what extent European constitutional law can remedy the imbalances of powers threatening fundamental rights and democracy in the digital age. By focusing on fundamental rights and powers, this descriptive and normative framework provides a picture representing the role of European constitutionalism in the algorithmic society. The implied goal of this research is to fill an important gap concerning the role of constitutional law in the digital age, underlining the dynamic dialectic between constitutionalism and digital technologies. The book aims to create a bridge between the studies in constitutional and public law with the debates on technology, media and policy.

Within this framework, the first question to answer is: what are the reasons for the rise of European digital constitutionalism? Digital constitutionalism has been portrayed as the rise of a new constitutional moment,[123] analysed by mapping bills of rights and legislative attempts concerning the relationship between Internet and constitutions,[124] and

[123] Edoardo Celeste, 'Digital Constitutionalism: A New Systematic Theorization' (2019) 33 (1) International Review of Law, Computers and Technology 76.

[124] Dennis Redeker and others, 'Towards Digital Constitutionalism? Mapping Attempts to Craft an Internet Bill of Rights' (2018) 80 International Communication Gazette 302;

examined in specific cases.[125] At the end of the last century, Fitzgerald stressed that the exercise of power is shared between public and private actors in the information society.[126] Indeed, the mediation between powers and freedom involves the relationship between both sides of the same coin. The characteristics of the digital environment promoted a system in search for a balance between public intervention and private self-regulation. The idea of Fitzgerald is that 'information constitutionalism' should delimit the boundaries of self-regulation through which private actors determine their standards manipulating software (*rectius* technological architecture). In this view, private law is called to step in and solve the challenges of the digital age through the guide of constitutional values.

Moreover, Berman acknowledged the role of private actors in defining and using the code of the cyberspace to regulate the digital environment.[127] Berman proposed an approach towards 'constitutive constitutionalism' consisting of the possibility to open constitutional adjudication to private actors as a means to overcome the vertical dimension of the state action in US constitutional law and allow judges and individuals to address these pressing issues. Lessig also has tried to underline the challenges of digital technologies for constitutional law by looking not only at the role of technological architecture but also at that of courts.[128] Boyle questioned liberal approaches to the cyberspace as potentially leading to the consolidation of private powers.[129] Likewise, Netanel questioned the self-governance model and the underlined the challenges of private ordering from the perspective of democracy.[130] Pernice provided an analysis of the relationship between global constitutionalism and

Mauro Santaniello and others, 'The Language of Digital Constitutionalism and the Role of National Parliaments' (2018) 80 International Communication Gazette 320.

125 Monique Mann, 'The Limits of (Digital) Constitutionalism: Exploring the Private Security (Im)balance in Australia' (2018) 80 International Communication Gazette 369.

126 Brian Fitzgerald, 'Software as Discourse – A Constitutionalism for Information Society' (1999) 24 Alternative Legal Journal 144.

127 Paul S. Berman, 'Cyberspace and the State Action Debate: The Cultural Value of Applying Constitutional Norms to "Private" Regulation' (2000) 71 University of Colorado Law Review 1263.

128 Lawrence Lessig, 'Reading the Constitution in Cyberspace' (1996) 45(3) Emory Law Journal 869.

129 James Boyle, 'Foucault in Cyberspace: Surveillance, Sovereignty, and Hardwired Censors' (1997) 66 University of Cincinnati Law Review 177.

130 Neil W. Netanel, 'Cyberspace Self-Governance: A Skeptical View from the Liberal Democratic Theory' (2000) 88 California Law Review 401.

Internet underlining the challenges relating to the democratic deficit and global regulation.[131] Besides, Guimarães addressed the role of Google as a global private power and its relationship with the Union.[132] Suzor underlined that the power relationships in the digital age should be governed by public principles and platform legitimacy should be assessed through the lens of the rule of law.[133] According to Suzor, the project of digital constitutionalism is 'to rethink how the exercise of power ought to be limited (made legitimate) in the digital age'.[134]

Building on this framework, for the first time, this research would implement a comprehensive digital constitutional analysis within a specific constitutional legal order, precisely the European context. The goal is to shed light on the role of European constitutional law as a shield against the exercise of powers in the algorithmic society. The aforementioned debate neglected the role of European constitutionalism as a shield against emerging digital powers. This lack of attention is also the heritage of a debate which primarily focused on the regulatory powers of states over the Internet. Rather than understanding the influence of constitutional systems and values in the digital environment, libertarian and paternalistic answers focused more on how to ensure an effective regulation looking at the technological dimension outside any specific constitutional framework of reference. Even if there are several works addressing the impact of digital technologies over human and fundamental rights,[135] still, there is not a systematic constitutional perspective on how to address the challenges of the algorithmic society.

Investigating the rise and consolidation of European digital constitutionalism cannot neglect the analysis of online platform powers. This is

131 Ingolf Pernice, 'Global Constitutionalism and the Internet. Taking People Seriously' HIIG Discussion Paper Series Discussion Paper (10 March 2015) https://papers.ssrn.com/sol3/papers.cfm?abstract_id=2576697 accessed 20 November 2021.

132 Guilherme C. Guimarães, *Global Technology and Legal Theory: Transnational Constitutionalism, Google and the European Union* (Routledge 2019).

133 Nicolas Suzor, 'Digital Constitutionalism: Using the Rule of Law to Evaluate the Legitimacy of Governance by Platforms' (2018) 4(3) Social Media + Society https://journals.sagepub.com/doi/pdf/10.1177/ 2056305118787812 accessed 20 November 2021.

134 Ibid., 4.

135 See, e.g., Mireille Hildebrandt and Kieron O'Hara (eds.), *Life and the Law in the Era of Data-Driven Agency* (Edward Elgar 2020); Ben Wagner and others (eds.), *Research Handbook on Human Rights and Digital Technology: Global Politics, Law and International Relations* (Edward Elgar 2019); Pollicino and Romeo (n. 31); Mathias Klang and Andrew Murray (eds.), *Human Rights in the Digital Age* (Cavendish 2005).

why the second research question is: what are the characteristics and the limits of platform powers in the digital environment? Answers to this question are still fragmented, and there is a lack of attention to the notion of 'platform power' from the standpoint of constitutional law. So far, scholars have focused on powers from different perspectives. This term has been interpreted as market power in the context of competition law,[136] imbalances of power in the field of consumer law,[137] and even 'data power' in the field of data protection.[138]

The way in which these three areas look at the notion of power is not homogenous. Power is defined from an economic perspective which fails to provide a constitutional analysis of the threats coming from the consolidation of freedoms increasingly turning into powers. Competition law, contract law and consumer law only provide one side of the debate, especially that of the internal market. Indeed, they fail to picture the evolution of the constitutional dimension of the Union,[139] and the consolidation of a polity.[140] In other words, the lens of the internal market fails to address the other side of the coin which is represented by digital constitutionalism. This shift of attention does not imply that the internal market perspective does not participate in the puzzle of platform powers. Nonetheless, competition law or consumer law cannot be left without the guidance of constitutional law any longer.

[136] See, e.g., Nicolas Petit, *Big Tech and the Digital Economy: The Moligopoly Scenario* (Oxford University Press 2020); Viktoria H. S. E. Robertson, 'Excessive Data Collection: Privacy Considerations and Abuse of Dominance in the Era of Big Data' (2020) 57(1) Common Market Law Review 161; Damien Geradin, 'What Should EU Competition Policy do to Address the Concerns Raised by the Digital Platforms' Market Power?' (2018) TILEC Discussion Paper No. 2018-041 https://papers.ssrn.com/sol3/papers.cfm?abstract_id=3011188 accessed 20 November 2021; Inge Graef, *EU Competition Law, Data Protection and Online Platforms: Data As Essential Facility* (Wolters Kluwer 2016); Angela Daly, *Private Power, Online Information Flows and EU Law: Mind the Gap* (Hart 2016); Daniel Zimmer, 'Digital Markets: New Rules for Competition Law' (2015) 6(9) Journal of European Competition Law & Practice 627.

[137] See, e.g., Christoph Busch and others, 'The Rise of the Platform Economy: A New Challenge for EU Consumer Law?' (2016) 5 Journal of European Consumer and Market Law 3.

[138] Carissa Veliz, *Privacy Is Power: Why and How You Should Take Back Control of Your Data* (Bantam Press 2020); Orla Linskey, 'Grappling with "Data Power": Normative Nudges from Data Protection and Privacy' (2019) 20(1) Theoretical Inquiries in Law 189.

[139] Kaarlo Tuori, *European Constitutionalism* (Cambridge University Press 2015); Joseph H. H. Weiler and Marlene Wind (eds.), *European Constitutionalism beyond the State* (Cambridge University Press 2003); Joseph Weiler, *The Constitution of Europe* (Cambridge University Press 1999).

[140] Massimo Fichera, *The Foundations of the EU As a Polity* (Edward Elgar 2018).

This research aims to fill this gap. Precisely, platform powers are analysed from two perspectives, namely the indirect delegation of powers by public authorities and the autonomous powers which platforms exercise as resulting from the exploitation of private law and digital technologies based on the liberal constitutional approach adopted by the Union at the end of last century.

This constitutional analysis of platform powers is conducted at least from a regional perspective since constitutional law reflects the values and principles of a certain society. The focus on the European framework is critical for this research not only to anchor the analysis to a specific constitutional area but also for answering the third research question: which remedies can European constitutional law provide to solve the imbalances of power in the algorithmic society and mitigate the risks for fundamental rights and democratic values? This question concerns how European constitutionalism protects fundamental rights and democratic values such as the rule of law and democratic participation. While from a constitutional law perspective power has traditionally been vested in public authorities, a new form of (digital) private power has now come into play determining standards of protection and procedures based on their social, legal and ethical framework.

This research argues that the protection of rights and freedoms in the algorithmic society cannot just be based on the expansionistic rhetoric of constitutional safeguards. The quantitative perspective has shown its failure in the last years when looking at the attempts to codify Internet constitutions. Many propositions have been made in this respect, particularly in Brazil and Italy.[141] The failure to establish a general right to Internet access at the constitutional level is a clear example of the instruments that constitutional law could provide to lawmakers and judges.[142] Besides, these calls for new forms of constitutional protection

[141] Marco Civil da Internet, Law no. 12.965 (2014); Dichiarazione dei diritti in Internet (2015).

[142] Oreste Pollicino, 'Right to Internet Access: Quid Iuris?' in Andreas von Arnauld, Kerstin von der Decken and Mart Susi (eds.), *The Cambridge Handbook on New Human Rights. Recognition, Novelty, Rhetoric* 263 (Cambridge University Press 2019); Stephen Tully, 'A Human Right to Access the Internet? Problems and Prospects' (2014) 14(2) Human Rights Law Review 175; Paul De Hert and Darek Kloza, 'Internet (Access) As a New Fundamental Right: Inflating the Current Rights Framework?' (2012) 3(2) European Journal of Law and Technology www.ejlt.org/index.php/ejlt/article/view/123/268 accessed 23 November 2021; Nicola Lucchi, 'Freedom of Expression and the Right to Internet Access' in Monroe E. Price, Stefaan G. Verhulst and Libby Morgan (eds.), *Routledge Handbook of Media Law* (Routledge 2013).

have not led to concrete solutions to face the constitutional challenges of the algorithmic society. Traditional bills of rights limit public powers, and do not provide instruments to remedy the transparency and accountability gap among private actors.

Therefore, this research does not propose to introduce new constitutional rights but to focus on the 'quality' of protection. It is not the first time that scholars have looked at the ability of private actors to interfere with individual fundamental rights. A traditional answer given to this challenge has been the horizontal effects doctrine,[143] or state action doctrine in the US framework.[144] The background idea is to extend the scope of application of the existing bills of rights and human rights covenants between private parties to avoid freedoms turning to a justification to express hidden forms of power which do not reflect constitutional values. In the case of online platforms, the horizontal effect doctrine could look like a potential leeway to require these actors to comply with constitutional safeguards.[145] Nevertheless, even if the horizontal application could be a first step to protect individual rights, it could not provide a systematic solution due to its case-by-case structure which is likely to undermine the principle of legal certainty if extensively and incoherently applied by judicial bodies, especially in civil law countries where there is not a system based on the common law principle of *stare decisis*.

Nonetheless, there is a way to fill the gap of the horizontal effect doctrine, precisely by looking at another constitutional trigger: the positive obligations of states to protect fundamental rights and democratic values. Scholars have tried to deal with this constitutional angle,[146] but the debate still lacks constitutional guidance to deal with

[143] Sonya Walkila, *Horizontal Effect of Fundamental Rights in EU Law* (European Law Publishing 2016); Dorota Leczykiewicz, 'Horizontal Application of the Charter of Fundamental Rights' (2013) 38(3) European Law Review 479; Eleni Frantziou, 'The Horizontal Effect of the Charter of Fundamental Rights of the EU: Rediscovering the Reasons for Horizontality' (2015) 21(5) European Law Journal 657.

[144] Mark Tushnet, 'The Issue of State Action/Horizontal Effect in Comparative Constitutional Law' (2003) 1(1) International Journal of Constitutional Law 79; Stephen Gardbaum, 'The Horizontal Effect of Constitutional Rights' (2003) 102 Michigan Law Review 388.

[145] Jonathan Peters, 'The "Sovereigns of Cyberspace" and State Action: The First Amendment's Application (or Lack Thereof) to Third-Party Platforms' (2018) 32 Berkeley Technology Law Journal 988. See also Berman (n. 127).

[146] Barrie Sander, 'Democratic Disruption in the Age of Social Media: Between Marketized and Structural Conceptions of Human Rights Law' (2021) 32(1) European Journal of

the challenges of the algorithmic society in the next decades. For instance, scholars have focused on the right not to be subject to an automated decision-making process,[147] established by the General Data Protection Regulation (GDPR),[148] particularly focusing on the meaning and effectiveness of this data subject right.[149] Nonetheless, the issue of the right to explanation is only one of the issues questioning how fundamental rights and democratic values are conceived and protected in the algorithmic society. This research aims to fill this gap by underlining how European constitutional law can lead to a more systematic strategy.

To complete the analysis of European digital constitutionalism, it is worth looking at the road ahead by focusing on a fourth research question: which paths does the consolidation of European digital constitutionalism open to the Union in the next years? The rise of the algorithmic society has already highlighted some constitutional challenges that the Union will be called to address in the near future. The rise of European digital constitutionalism is still at the beginning of a long path to address the challenges raised by digital capitalism.

Firstly, it is worth questioning how to strike a fair balance between innovation in the internal market and the protection of fundamental rights and democratic values. To answer this question, the research will focus on understanding if the path of European digital constitutionalism will turn back to a neoliberal free-market approach as that dominating at the beginning of this century, following the promises of digital capitalism, or if this phase will design a constitutional path and

International Law 159; Aleksandra Kuczerawy, 'The Power of Positive Thinking: Intermediary Liability and the Effective Enjoyment of the Right to Freedom of Expression' (2017) 3 Journal of Intellectual Property, Information Technology and Electronic Commerce Law 182.

[147] Andrew D. Selbst and Julia Powles, 'Meaningful Information and the Right to Explanation' (2017) 7 International Data Privacy Law 233; Margot E. Kaminski, 'The Right to Explanation, Explained' (2019) 34 Berkeley Technology Law Journal 189.

[148] Regulation (EU) 2016/679 of the European Parliament and of the Council of 27 April 2016 on the protection of natural persons with regard to the processing of personal data and on the free movement of such data, and repealing Directive 95/46/EC (General Data Protection Regulation) OJ L 119/1.

[149] Sandra Wachter and others, 'Why a Right to Explanation of Automated Decision-Making Does Not Exist in the General Data Protection Regulation' (2017) 7 International Data Privacy Law 76; Gianclaudio Malgieri and Giovanni Comandè, 'Why a Right to Legibility of Automated Decision-Making Exists in the General Data Protection Regulation' (2017) 7 International Data Privacy Law 234; Lilian Edwards and Michael Veale, 'Slave to the Algorithm? Why a "Right to an Explanation" Is Probably Not the Remedy You Are Looking For' (2017) 16 Duke Law & Technology Review 18.

a cautious strategy aimed to protect individual rights and freedoms towards digital humanism. The Union has already shown its intention to focus on ethics and a human-centric approach in the field of artificial intelligence.[150] This political crossroads deserves particular attention in this research since this choice will be critical not only for the growth of the internal market but also for the protection of constitutional values, especially human dignity, in the long run.[151]

A second point that is worth exploring focuses on the dilemma between public authority and private ordering. This point leads to wondering which of these approaches can better ensure the implementation of public policies online guaranteeing innovation while protecting fundamental rights and democratic values. Under the Digital Single Market strategy, the Union has already implemented hard and soft legal measures to deal with the challenges raised by online platforms.[152] Nevertheless, it would be naïve to believe that the Union has abandoned (digital) internal market goals. Digitisation is one of the primary pillars of the strategy to shape the European digital future,[153] and the role of online platforms will be relevant in this transition. Therefore, it is critical to understand whether the promises of digital capitalism will indirectly force the Union to rely on self-regulation or de facto dilute the scope of hard regulation in order not to hinder the development of these technologies. In other words, the primary point is to understand whether European digital constitutionalism could provide instruments and procedures to bind forces with increasingly political power coming from a combination of economic and technological power.

Thirdly, the transnational dimension of these challenges leads to focusing on the extraterritorial scope of European constitutional values as shown in the field of data.[154] The clash among constitutional values

[150] High-Level Expert Group on Artificial Intelligence, 'Ethics Guidelines for Trustworthy AI' (8 April 2019) https://ec.europa.eu/newsroom/dae/document.cfm?doc_id=60419 accessed 24 November 2021.

[151] White Paper, 'On Artificial Intelligence – A European Approach to Excellence and Trust' COM(2020) 65 final.

[152] Oreste Pollicino and Giovanni De Gregorio, 'A Constitutional-Driven Change of Heart: ISP Liability and Artificial Intelligence in the Digital Single Market' (2019) 18 The Global Community Yearbook of International Law and Jurisprudence 237.

[153] Communication from the Commission to the European Parliament, the Council, the European Economic and Social Committee and the Committee of the Regions, Shaping Europe's digital future, COM(2020) 67 final.

[154] Paul De Hert and Michal Czerniawski, 'Expanding the European Data Protection Scope Beyond Territory: Article 3 of the General Data Protection Regulation in its Wider Context' (2016) 6(3) International Data Privacy Law 230, 240; Christopher Kuner,

could be the result of constitutional imperialism where models of digital sovereignty compete to shape the principles of the algorithmic society. Nonetheless, the trend towards constitutional imperialism is not the only consequence of how digital constitutionalism provides answers to the challenges of the algorithmic society. Indeed, conflicts resulting from an expansion of constitutional values could also be the reason for the rise of constitutional protectionism justified by the interest in shielding regional or local values from external influences. Therefore, understanding extraterritorial constitutional conflicts is crucial to underline the potential path of European digital constitutionalism.

To answer these research questions, this book follows a precise methodology. Firstly, in terms of the territorial scope of the research, the focus is on the European framework, precisely investigating digital constitutionalism within the framework of the Union and the Council of Europe. This research also takes into account the role of Member States at the national level within the supranational analysis. Likewise, a comparative approach with the US framework is also embedded in this research without, however, losing its European focus. The reference to the US legal framework is critical to this research due to the influence and interrelation between the two constitutional systems in the algorithmic society.

Secondly, regarding the material scope, another methodological pillar consists of taking the challenges for freedom of expression, privacy and data protection in the algorithmic society as paradigmatic examples. This twofold analysis characterises the entire research examining private powers through two of the most critical fundamental rights in the digital age. As already stressed, this choice should not surprise since freedom of expression and data protection are two democratic cornerstones. Without expressing ideas and opinions openly or accessing instruments of transparency and accountability concerning the protection of personal data, democracy is just a label failing to represent a situation of veiled authoritarianism.

Thirdly, the research addresses the topic of digital constitutionalism from a descriptive to a normative perspective. The mix between these two standpoints provides the grounding framework on which, then, the normative argument is built. Describing the reasons leading to the rise of European digital constitutionalism becomes a preliminary basis to

'Extraterritoriality and Regulation of International Data Transfers in EU Data Protection Law' (2015) 5(4) International Data Privacy Law 235.

address the normative part of the research, precisely looking at the remedies European constitutional law provides to address the challenges of the algorithmic society.

1.6 Research Structure

This research is articulated into four parts. After this introductory chapter, Chapters 2 to 4 describe the path leading to the rise of digital constitutionalism in Europe, the ability of platforms to exercise delegated and autonomous powers as well as the intimate relationship between expressions and personal data in the digital environment. This descriptive frame provides the grounds on which the normative claims are supported in Chapters 5 and 6. In particular, this part focuses on how to address the challenges raised by the private powers to freedom of expression, privacy and data protection by analysing the constitutional challenges of content moderation and the processing of personal data based on automated decision-making technologies. Chapter 7 provides the possible paths of European digital constitutionalism, precisely underlining three critical challenges raising questions whose answers can be found through the digital constitutional lens provided by this research.

Chapter 2 focuses on the rise of digital constitutionalism in Europe. It analyses the evolution of the European approach to regulate the flow of expressions and data online since the end of the last century. This path is described in three constitutional phases: digital liberalism, judicial activism and digital constitutionalism. The first phase illustrates how, at the end of the last century, the liberal approach concerning online intermediaries and data protection was rooted in the fear to slow the development of new digital products and services which promise to promote the economic growth of the internal market. The end of this first phase was the result of the emergence of the Nice Charter as a bill of rights and new challenges raised by private actors in the digital environment. In this phase, the ECJ has played a pivotal role in moving the European standpoint from fundamental freedoms to fundamental rights. This second phase has only anticipated a new phase of European constitutionalism (i.e, digital constitutionalism) based on codifying the ECJ's case law and limiting online platform powers within the framework of the Digital Single Market.

Chapter 3 examines the characteristics of platform powers. The reasons for the rise of European digital constitutionalism cannot be understood without explaining how platforms perform functions mirroring public powers. This chapter divides platform powers into two categories: delegated powers and autonomous powers. Despite the distinction, these two forms of power are interrelated. The first category includes functions which platforms exercise according to the delegation of public authorities, particularly legislative and judicial delegation of powers. For instance, the recognition of the role of tackling illegal content or the enforcement of the right to be forgotten online are just two examples of how powers have shifted from the public to the private sector. This process does not show a new trend since public actors increasingly rely on the private sector to perform public services. However, in this case, the primary concern is related to the lack of safeguards in the delegation of these powers. This limitless delegation has contributed to promoting an extension of private functions into forms of autonomous powers. In these cases, platforms have demonstrated their power to define and enforce the rule of their communities while also exercising a balancing activity between the fundamental rights at stake. These autonomous powers contribute to defining a para-constitutional framework where users are subject to a new *status subjectionis* in relation to private powers which do not ensure the separation of functions or democratic processes, and thus resemble authoritarian regimes.

Before focusing on the challenges of content moderation and automated decision-making in the field of data, Chapter 4 deals with another crucial piece of the puzzle: the intimate relationship between content and data in the algorithmic society. This chapter underlines how these two fields are not isolated but overlap. There is an intimate connection between the legal and technological regime governing content and data. These fields have been conceived as parallel tracks at the end of the last century. Nonetheless, the rise of the algorithmic society has blurred this traditional gap, thus increasing the technological convergence between content and data, despite the legal divergence of these two fields. From a merely passive role, online platforms such as search engines and social networks have acquired an increasingly active role in managing online content. At the same time, their role in deciding how to process personal data has transformed these actors from data processors to controllers. This evolving framework from passive to active intermediaries has led to the technological and legal convergence of parallel tracks which have started to overlap. In other words, the rise of the algorithmic society has contributed to reducing the technological distance between content and data, while increasing the need to increase the legal convergence to protect democratic values against abuses of powers.

Chapter 5 introduces the normative part of this research, analysing the challenges of content moderation. Although freedom of expression is one of the cornerstones on which democracy is based, this statement firmly clashes with the troubling evolution of the algorithmic society where algorithmic technologies govern the flow of information online according to opaque technical standards established by social media platforms. Therefore, the chapter argues that the liberal paradigm of protection of the right to free speech is no longer enough to protect democratic values in the digital environment, since the flow of information is actively organised by business interests, driven by profit-maximisation rather than democracy, transparency or accountability. Although the role of free speech is still paramount, it is necessary to focus on the positive dimension of this fundamental right by introducing procedural safeguards in online content moderation to shield platform business interests from fragmentation and uncertainty while protecting democratic values and fostering a new form of media pluralism online based on transparency and accountability.

Chapter 6 deals with the field of data and, in particular, with the use of artificial intelligence systems to process personal data. The chapter underlines how the characteristics of algorithmic technologies highly challenge the primary pillars on which the protection of personal data is based. The chapter firstly describes the clash between data protection principles and artificial intelligence systems, and then it proposes a constitutional-oriented interpretation. The chapter unveils the constitutional underpinning values of the GDPR, in particular the principles of human dignity, proportionality and due process. Unlike the field of content, in this case, the primary issue does not relate to the introduction of procedural safeguards but to their interpretation, which should look at the protection of democratic values while supporting the growth of the internal market.

Once described the reasons for the rise of European digital constitutionalism and the constitutional remedies to address platform powers, Chapter 7 focuses on the potential path of European digital constitutionalism by analysing three constitutional challenges: digital humanism versus digital capitalism; public authority versus private ordering;

constitutional imperialism versus constitutional protectionism. This chapter does not focus on these poles as trade-offs but underlines how the characteristics of European digital constitutionalism would lead to a sustainable approach characterising the European third way among these global trends. This analysis provides the potential paths of European digital constitutionalism, thus defining the characteristics of this new constitutional phase in the algorithmic society.

2 The Rise of European Digital Constitutionalism

2.1 Moving towards European Digital Constitutionalism

The shift of the Union from a liberal perspective to a constitutional democratic approach is a story about constitutional law meeting digital technologies. The rise of European digital constitutionalism can be described as a long process if it is compared with the rampant evolution of the digital environment in the last twenty years. The turn has not been immediate but has gradually followed a path towards the integration of economic with constitutional values,[1] which define European constitutionalism,[2] while digital technologies provided opportunities to offer cross-border services and exercise individual freedoms.[3] In this transformation, a constitutional strategy complemented the internal market imprinting of the Union which is increasingly oriented to the protection of fundamental rights and democratic values.

The reason for this European constitutional shift comes from the US and European liberal approach to the digital environment at the end of the last century. Both sides of the Atlantic considered online intermediaries as neutral service providers rather than active providers. These providers do not usually produce or create content even if they host and organise information and data for profit. In other words, online intermediaries just provide digital spaces where users share their views or access services. Likewise, the advent of European data protection was

[1] Gráinne de Búrca and Joseph H. H. Weiler (eds.), *The Worlds of European Constitutionalism* (Cambridge University Press 2012).

[2] Kaarlo Tuori, *European Constitutionalism* (Cambridge University Press 2015).

[3] Yochai Benkler, *The Wealth of Networks: How Social Production Transforms Markets and Freedom* (Yale University Press 2006).

considered a necessary step to ensure the free circulation of data in the internal market rather than to provide a comprehensive set of safeguards to protect privacy and personal data in the digital age.

This constitutional angle has encouraged the private sector to exploit the opportunities deriving from the use of a low-cost global communication technology for developing business models relying on a liberal approach migrating across the Atlantic. The consolidation of platform power can be considered the result of this liberal standpoint, which, at the end of the last century, encouraged private actors to gain areas of powers by processing data and information in a liberal constitutional environment. Even if the platformisation of the digital environment cannot be considered a single process,[4] it is possible to underline how the mix of this liberal approach and the development of digital technologies, primarily algorithmic systems, has enriched the functions of online platforms. The profiling of users or the organisation of content has led these actors to exercise a more pervasive control over information and data. Algorithmic technologies play a critical role in creating targeted services attracting more customers while providing precise windows of visibility and engagement for businesses and organisations to advertise their products and services.[5] To achieve this business purpose, the collection and organisation of a vast amount of data and content become a constitutive activity. The processing of information and data has entrusted these actors with almost exclusive control over online content and data, transforming their role into something more than a mere intermediary.

The consolidation of online platforms has led to a paradigmatic shift of power in the algorithmic society.[6] The private development of digital and automated technologies has not only, on the one hand, challenged the protection of individual fundamental rights such as freedom of expression and data protection. Even more importantly, on the other hand, this new technological framework has also empowered transnational corporations operating in the digital environment to perform

[4] Geoffrey G. Parker, Marshall W. Van Alstyne and Sangett P. Choudary, *Platform Revolution – How Networked Markets are Transforming the Economy – And How to Make Them Work for You* (WW Norton & Company Inc 2017); Anne Helmond, 'The Platformization of the Web: Making Web Data Platform Ready' (2015) 1(2) Social Media + Society 1.

[5] Tarleton Gillespie, 'The Relevance of Algorithms' in Tarleton Gillespie, Pablo J. Boczkowski, and Kirsten A. Foot (eds.) *Media Technologies Essays on Communication, Materiality, and Society* 167 (Oxford University Press 2014).

[6] Jack M. Balkin, 'Free Speech in the Algorithmic Society: Big Data, Private Governance, and New School Speech Regulation' (2018) 51 University of California Davis 1151.

quasi-public functions in the transnational context. The setting and enforcement of private standards through algorithmic technologies or the processing of vast amounts of information raise questions about the role of (constitutional) law.[7] Digital capitalism not only affects the individual dimension but also the collective sphere as demonstrated by the Cambridge Analytica scandal.[8]

The challenges raised by digital capitalism to democratic values are one of the primary reasons leading the Union to emancipate itself from the US technological optimism which looks at the First Amendment as the dogma of digital liberalism. On the other side of the Atlantic, the characteristics of European constitutionalism have increasingly encouraged the Union to follow a new path to address the challenges of the algorithmic society. As already underlined in Chapter 1, this process can be considered the result of different constitutional premises across the Atlantic where the consolidation of digital private powers has not led to the same constitutional reaction and shift towards a democratic strategy.

Within this framework, this chapter analyses the path leading the Union to shift from a liberal approach to a democratic constitutional strategy to address the consolidation of platform powers. This chapter aims to explain the reasons for this paradigmatic shift looking at content and data as the two emblematic areas symbolising the rise of a new phase of European digital constitutionalism. This chapter focuses on three phases: digital liberalism, judicial activism and digital constitutionalism. The first part of this chapter frames the first steps taken by the Union in the phase of digital liberalism at the end of the last century. The second part analyses the role of judicial activism in moving the attention from fundamental freedoms to fundamental rights online after the adoption of the Lisbon Treaty. The third part examines the path of the Union towards a constitutional democratic strategy and the consolidation of European digital constitutionalism.

[7] Caryn Devins and others, 'The Law and Big Data' (2017) 27 Cornell Journal of Law and Public Policy 357.

[8] Brittany Kaiser, *Targeted: The Cambridge Analytica Whistleblower's Inside Story of How Big Data, Trump, and Facebook Broke Democracy and How It Can Happen Again* (Harper Collins 2019).

2.2 The Charm of Digital Liberalism

The road of the Union towards digital liberalism has its roots in the European economic imprinting. The signing of the Treaty of Rome in 1957 set the primary goal of the European Economic Community: the establishment of a common market and the approximation of economic policies among Member States.[9] At that time, digital technologies were far from demonstrating their potentialities. The founding fathers could not foresee how the digital revolution would provide new possibilities for economic growth while introducing a new layer of complexity for the regulation of the internal market.

Until the adoption of the Nice Charter in 2000 and the recognition of its binding effects in 2009,[10] the European approach was firmly based on economic pillars, namely the fundamental freedoms. Even if not exclusively, the free movement of persons, the freedom of establishment, the freedom to provide goods and services and the free movement of capital can (still) be considered the primary drivers of European integration and the growth of the internal market.[11] The goal of this system was 'to protect society and create an equitable Internet environment'.[12] Therefore, the consolidation and harmonisation of the internal market was one of the primary drivers of the European approach at the end of the last century.

This liberal framework was also transposed in the regulation of critical areas for the growth of the digital environment. In the field of data and content, the Data Protection Directive and the e-Commerce Directive are two paradigmatic examples showing such a liberal frame oriented to ensure the smooth development of the internal market.[13] Precisely, online intermediaries have been exempted from liability for transmitting or hosting unlawful third-party content while the

[9] Kamiel Mortelmans, 'The Common Market, the Internal Market and the Single Market, What's in a Market?' (1998) 35(1) Common Market Law Review 101.

[10] Charter of Fundamental Rights of the European Union (2012) OJ C 326/391.

[11] Consolidated version of the Treaty on the Functioning of the European Union (2012) OJ C 326/47, Title II and IV.

[12] Matthew Feeley, 'EU Internet Regulation Policy: The Rise of Self-Regulation' (1999) 22(1) Boston College International and Comparative Law Review 159, 167.

[13] Directive 95/46/EC of the European Parliament and of the Council of 24 October 1995 on the protection of individuals with regard to the processing of personal data and on the free movement of such data (1995) OJ L 281/31; Directive 2000/31/EC of the European Parliament and of the Council of 8 June 2000 on certain legal aspects of information society services, in particular electronic commerce, in the Internal Market (2000) OJ L 178/1.

processing of personal data was harmonised to promote the free circulation of personal data in the internal market. Therefore, digital technologies were considered an enabler of economic prosperity. In other words, also considering the lack of a European constitutional framework at that time, the economic imprinting of the internal market has characterised the first approach of the Union in the field of digital technologies, namely digital liberalism.

Such a liberal approach does not only reflect the economic imprinting of the Union but it can also be framed within the debate about Internet regulation at the end of the last century. An extensive technological optimism from the western side of the Atlantic welcomed the advent of the Internet. As explained in Chapter 3, at that time, the digital environment was considered an area where public actors could not extend their sovereign powers and interfere with rights and freedoms. Barlow underlined that the digital space is a new world separate from the atomic dimension, where 'legal concepts of property, expression, identity, movement, and context do not apply'.[14] As for all new undiscovered worlds, the cyberspace was considered as an opportunity: a dreamland where social behaviours were not exposed to tyrannical constraints. In other words, the digital environment was considered as a new world completely separate from the atomic reality, thus preventing governments and lawmakers from exercising their traditional powers.

Johnson and Post also supported the independent nature of the digital environment.[15] Both consider a 'decentralised and emergent law', resulting from customary or collective private action, the basis for creating a democratic set of rules applicable to the digital community.[16] Put differently, these liberal ideas are based on a bottom-up approach: rather than relying on traditional public lawmaking powers to set the norms regulating the digital environment, digital communities would be capable of participating and creating the rules governing their online spaces.

This technological trust can also be explained by looking at the characteristics of the digital environment challenging the powers of governments and lawmakers. It is not by chance that Froomkin defines

[14] Ibid.

[15] David R. Johnson and David Post, 'Law and Borders: The Rise of Law in Cyberspace' (1996) 48(5) Stanford Law Review 1367, 1371.

[16] David R. Johnson and David Post, 'And How Shall the Net be Governed?' in Brian Kahin and James Keller (eds.) *Coordinating the Internet* 62 (MIT Press 1997).

the Internet as the 'Modern Hydra'.[17] No matter what the effort is to cut the heads of the mythical beast, others will grow up. As the mythical beast, the Internet has discouraged regulation since top-down attempts at regulating it (i.e. cutting off one of the Hydra's heads) would fail since communities would easily react against such interferences (i.e. the growth of new heads).

This metaphor does not only highlight the liberal narrative and challenges that governments face when trying to strike a fair balance between innovation and protection of constitutional rights. Even more importantly, this expression also represents some of the reasons why democratic constitutional states have adopted a free-market approach when dealing with the digital environment, while other systems have followed different paths.[18] At the end of the last century, the adoption of a paternalistic approach could have hindered the development of new digital services and the positive effects on the exercise of fundamental rights and freedoms. A strict regulation of the online environment would have damaged the growth of the internal market, exactly when new technologies were poised to revolutionise the entire society.

Besides, the rise of digital capitalism, or surveillance capitalism, was highly convenient not only for ensuring paths of economic growth and fostering fundamental freedoms but also for the exercise of public powers,[19] and so much so that even public actors exploited these opportunities for performing public tasks. The resilience of the liberal approach is also the result of an invisible handshake based on which governments have refrained to regulate private companies operating in the online environment to benefit from unaccountable cooperation.[20] The lack of transparency and accountability made it easier for public actors to rely on data for security and surveillance purposes, thus formally escaping constitutional safeguards. The cooperation between the public and private sector is still a relevant

[17] A. Michael Froomkin, 'The Internet as a Source of Regulatory Arbitrage' in Brian Kahin and Charles Nesson (eds.), *Borders in Cyberspace* (MIT Press 1997).

[18] Barney Warf, 'Geographies of Global Internet Censorship' (2011) 76 GeoJournal 1; Anupam Chander and Uyen P. Le, 'Data Nationalism' (2015) 64(3) Emory Law Journal 677.

[19] Shoshana Zuboff, *The Age of Surveillance Capitalism: The Fight for a Human Future at the New Frontier of Power* (Polity Press 2019); David Lyon, *Surveillance After Snowden* (Polity Press 2015).

[20] Michael Birnhack and Niva Elkin-Koren, 'The Invisible Handshake: The Reemergence of the State in the Digital Environment' (2003) 8(2) Virginia Journal of Law & Technology 1.

matter as also underlined by the Israeli Supreme Court stressing the lack of due process and the impact on freedom of expression of removal orders to social media by public authorities.[21]

The consolidation of digital liberalism across the Atlantic was primarily the result of a positive angle looking at digital technologies as an opportunity to grow and prosper when they did not represent a potential threat to individual constitutional rights and freedoms. The approach of the Union was more concerned about the potential impacts of regulatory burdens on economic (fundamental) freedoms and innovation rather than on the protection of constitutional values which, instead, a public intervention in the digital environment would have undermined. At that time, there were no reasons to fear the rise of new private powers challenging the protection of fundamental rights online and competing with public powers.

Within this framework, a migration of constitutional ideas has occurred across the Atlantic. As underlined by Christou and Simpson, the US vision of the Internet as a self-regulatory environment driven by neoliberal globalisation theories has influenced the European legal framework, even if the Union has always shown its cooperative approach to the regulation of the Internet.[22] This transatlantic influence is not casual, but it is the result of the interaction between two constitutional models. Nonetheless, as underlined in Chapter 1, this relationship does not always entail the same proximity of constitutional premises. The following sections analyse the phase of digital liberalism examining the path of the Union at the beginning of this century in the field of content and data.

2.2.1 Immunising Online Intermediaries

The starting point to examine the European liberal approach in the field of content could not depart from looking at the e-Commerce Directive. The reading of the first Recitals can unveil that the primary aim of the Union was to provide a common framework for electronic commerce for 'the proper functioning of the internal market by

[21] See, e.g., *Adalah et al* v. *Israeli Ministry of Justice's Cyber Unit et al* (2021).

[22] George Christou and Seamus Simpson, 'The Internet and Public–Private Governance in the European Union' (2006) 26(1) Journal of Public Policy 43. See also Edward Halpin and Seamus Simpson, 'Between Self-Regulation and Intervention in the Networked Economy: The European Union and Internet Policy' (2002) 28(4) Journal of Information Science 285.

ensuring the free movement of information society services between the Member States'.[23] As also observed by the Economic and Social Committee before the adoption of the e-Commerce Directive, to bring the possible benefits fully to bear, it is necessary both to eliminate legal constraints on electronic commerce and to create conditions, whereby potential users of electronic commercial services (both consumers and businesses) can have confidence in e-commerce. An optimum balance must be found between these two requirements'.[24]

This European system did not introduce a new model but was inspired by the US approach to online intermediaries, precisely the Communication Decency Act[25] and the Digital Millennium Copyright Act.[26] By recognising that online intermediaries are not involved in the creation of content, although in different ways, both these measures exempt online intermediaries from liability for transmitting or hosting unlawful third-party content.[27] When the US Congress passed Section 230 of the Communication Decency Act, one of primary aims was to encourage free expression and the development of the digital environment. In order to achieve this objective, the choice was to exempt computer service providers from liability for third-party conduct. Otherwise, online intermediaries would have been subject to a broad and unpredictable range of cases concerning their liability for editing third-party content since their activities consisted of transmitting and hosting vast amounts of content.

Since, in the lack of any legal shield, this situation would have negatively affected the development of new digital services, as some cases had already shown at that time,[28] the US policy aimed to encourage online intermediaries to grow and develop their business under the protection of the safe harbour and the Good Samaritan rule.[29] It is not by chance that Section 230 has been described as 'the twenty-six words that created the Internet'.[30] This provision has opened the door to the evolution of the digital

[23] e-Commerce Directive (n. 13), Recitals 1–3.

[24] Opinion of the Economic and Social Committee on the 'Proposal for a European Parliament and Council Directive on certain legal aspects of electronic commerce in the internal market' (1999) C 169, 36–42.

[25] Communication Decency Act, 47 U.S.C., Section 230.

[26] Digital Millennium Copyright Act, 17 U.S.C., Section 512.

[27] Mariarosaria Taddeo and Luciano Floridi (eds.), *The Responsibilities of Online Service Providers* (Springer 2017); Graeme B. Dinwoodie (ed.), *Secondary Liability of Internet Service Providers* (Springer 2017).

[28] *Cubby, Inc.* v. *CompuServe Inc.* 776 F. Supp. 135 (S.D.N.Y. 1991); *Stratton Oakmont, Inc.* v. *Prodigy Services Co.* WL 323710 (N.Y. Sup. Ct. 1995).

[29] *Zeran* v. *Am. Online, Inc.* 129 F.3d 327, 330 (4th Cir. 1997).

[30] Jeff Kosseff, *The Twenty-Six Words That Created the Internet* (Cornell University Press 2019).

environment and still constitutes the basic pillar legitimising platform powers,[31] showing the primacy of the First Amendment in US constitutionalism.[32]

The US model has influenced the political choice on the eastern side of the Atlantic. The e-Commerce Directive exempts Internet service providers (or online intermediaries) from liability for the unlawful conduct of third parties.[33] Among online intermediaries,[34] hosting providers are not liable for the information or content stored by their users unless, upon becoming aware of the unlawful nature of the information or content stored, they do not promptly remove or disable access to the unlawful information or content (i.e. notice and takedown).[35]

The aim of the European liability exemption is twofold. Firstly, the e-Commerce Directive focuses on fostering the free movement of information society services as a 'reflection in Community law of a more general principle, namely freedom of expression',[36] as enshrined at that time only in the Convention.[37] Here, the right to freedom of expression was strictly connected to the development of new digital services. In other words, according to the Union's approach, these new technologies would constitute a driver for promoting this fundamental right in the internal market. Secondly, the exemption of liability aims to avoid holding liable entities that do not have effective control over the content transmitted or hosted since they perform activities merely neutral, automatic and passive.[38] In order to achieve this purpose, the

[31] Danielle K. Citron and Benjamin Wittes, 'The Internet Will Not Break: Denying Bad Samaritans § 230 Immunity' (2017) 86 Fordham Law Review 401; Jeff Kosseff, 'Defending Section 230: The Value of Intermediary Immunity' (2010) 15 Journal of Technology Law & Policy 123; Jack M. Balkin, 'The Future of Free Expression in a Digital Age' (2009) 36 Pepperdine Law Review 427.

[32] Alexander Meiklejohn, 'The First Amendment is an Absolute' (1961) 1961 The Supreme Court Review 245.

[33] Patrick Van Eecke, 'Online Service Providers and Liability: A Plea for a Balanced Approach' (2011) 48 Common Market Law Review 1455; Lilian Edwards, 'The Problem of Intermediary Service Provider Liability' in Lilian Edwards (ed.), *The New Legal Framework for E-Commerce in Europe* 93 (Hart 2005).

[34] This legal regime applies to three categories of online intermediaries: access providers, caching providers and hosting providers. e-Commerce Directive (n. 13), Arts. 12–14.

[35] Ibid., Art. 14. Nonetheless, Member States have implemented this rule in different ways like Italy. See Marco Bassini, 'Mambo Italiano: The Italian Perilous Way on ISP Liability' in Tuomas Ojanen and Byliana Petkova (eds.), *Fundamental Rights Protection Online: The Future Regulation of Intermediaries* 84 (Edward Elgar 2020).

[36] e-Commerce Directive (n. 13), Recital 9.

[37] European Convention on Human Rights (1950), Art. 10.

[38] e-Commerce Directive (n. 13), Recital 42.

e-Commerce Directive does not only exempt online intermediaries from liability but also sets forth a general rule banning general monitoring imposed by Member States.[39]

Therefore, online intermediaries cannot be required to monitor the information transmitted or stored by users within their services, as well as seek facts or circumstances that reveal illegal activities conducted by their users through the relevant service.[40] This rule aims to avoid disproportionate interferences with the economic freedoms of online intermediaries which would be required to set additional financial and human resources, de facto making their activities not profitable due to the vast amount of content they transmit or host. Likewise, the ban on general monitoring also protects users' rights and freedoms by precluding public authorities from imposing surveillance obligations onto online intermediaries. Nonetheless, these limits only apply to public actors while online intermediaries enjoy margins of freedom in implementing voluntary measures to manage their digital spaces.

This legal regime highlights the architecture of freedom on which online intermediaries have been able to develop their business, and powers. These actors have been generally considered neither accountable nor responsible (i.e. safe harbour) since platforms are not aware (or in control) of illegal content transmitted or hosted. This legal framework looks reasonable as long as online intermediaries only performed passive activities, such as providing access or space to host third-party content. However, e-commerce marketplaces, search engines and social networks organising and moderating content through artificial intelligence technologies have firmly challenged the legal exemption of liability which is formally based on the lack of awareness and control over third-party content. If, on the one hand, the choice to exempt online intermediaries from liability was aimed to foster the development of new digital services, thus contributing to the internal market, on the other hand, such a liberal approach has led to the rise and consolidation of new areas of private powers in the internal market.

Furthermore, as examined in Chapter 3, by imposing upon hosting providers the obligation to remove online content based on their

[39] Ibid., Art. 15.

[40] Nevertheless, when implementing the e-Commerce Directive in their respective national legislation, Member States are free to impose on ISPs a duty to report to the competent public authority possible illegal activity conducted through their services or the transmission or storage within their services of unlawful information. Ibid., Art. 15(2).

awareness or control, this system of liability has entrusted online platforms with the power to autonomously decide whether to remove or block online content. Since these actors are private, and there is no requirement that public authorities assess the lawfulness of online content before removal or blocking, online platforms would likely apply a risk-based approach to escape liability from their failure to comply with their duty to remove or block (i.e. collateral censorship).[41] This liability regime incentivises online platforms to focus on minimising this economic risk rather than adopting a fundamental rights-based approach.

This system leaves platforms free to organise content based on the logic of moderation which is driven by profit maximisation. It works as a legal shield for online platforms[42] and, even more importantly, has encouraged private actors to set their rules to organise and moderate content based on business interests and other discretionary (but opaque) conditions.[43] The organisation of content driven by unaccountable business purposes can be considered one of the primary reasons explaining how online platforms shape the protection of fundamental rights and freedoms in the digital environment. As the next subsection shows, even the European approach to personal data has played a critical role in the rise of private powers in the digital age.

2.2.2 Ensuring the Free Circulation of Personal Data

At first glance, the Union has not adopted a liberal approach to personal data. Unlike the case of content, rather than exempting online intermediaries from liability, the Union introduced obligations concerning the processing of personal data to face the challenges coming from the increase in data usage and processing relating to the provision of new services and the development of digital technologies.[44]

[41] Jack M. Balkin, 'Old-School/New-School Speech Regulation' (2014) 128 Harvard Law Review 2296; Felix T. Wu, 'Collateral Censorship and the Limits of Intermediary Immunity' (2011) 87(1) Notre Dame Law Review 293.

[42] Frank Pasquale, 'Platform Neutrality: Enhancing Freedom of Expression in Spheres of Private Power' (2016) 17 Theoretical Inquiries in Law 487; Rebecca Tushnet, 'Power Without Responsibility: Intermediaries and the First Amendment' (2008) 76 George Washington Law Review 986.

[43] Danielle K. Citron and Helen L. Norton, 'Intermediaries and Hate Speech: Fostering Digital Citizenship for our Information Age' (2011) 91 Boston University Law Review 1436.

[44] Data Protection Directive (n. 13), Recital 4.

As Chapter 6 will explain in more detail, the rise of European data protection law can be examined looking at the consolidation of the constitutional dimension of privacy and the protection of personal data in the framework of the Council of Europe and Member States' national legislation.[45] Convention No. 108 has been the first instrument to deal with the protection of individuals with regard to automatic processing of personal data in 1981.[46] Even before the advent of artificial intelligence technologies, the aim of this instrument, subsequently modernised in 2018,[47] was to ensure the protection of personal data taking account of the increasing flow of information across frontiers.

The Data Protection Directive could perfectly fit within this framework of safeguards and guarantees. In 1995, the adoption of the Data Protection Directive could be considered the result of a constitutional reaction against the challenges raised by the information society, as also underlined by the approach of the Council of Europe. However, a closer look can reveal how the Union policy was oriented to encourage the free movement of data as a way to promote the growth of the internal market. The Data Protection Directive highlighted the functional nature of the protection of personal data for the consolidation and proper functioning of the internal market and, consequently, as an instrument to guarantee the fundamental freedoms of the Union.[48] The liberal imprinting and functional approach of data protection can be understood by focusing on the first proposal of the Commission in 1990.[49] According to the Commission, 'a Community approach towards the protection of individuals in relation to the processing of personal data is also essential to the development of the data processing industry and of value-added data communication services'.[50] Although the processing of personal data shall serve mankind and aim to protect the

[45] See, e.g., the *Datenschutzgesetz* adopted on 7 October 1970 in Germany; *Datalagen* adopted on 11 May 1973 in Sweden; Loi n. 78-17 on 6 January 1978 in France; Data Protection Act 1984 on 12 July 1984 in UK.

[46] Convention for the Protection of Individuals with regard to Automatic Processing of Personal Data (1981).

[47] Modernised Convention for the Protection of Individuals with regard to the Processing of Personal Data (2018).

[48] Data Protection Directive (n. 13), Recital 3.

[49] Proposal for a Council Directive concerning the protection of individuals in relation to the processing of personal data (1990) COM(90) 314 final.

[50] Ibid., 4.

privacy of data subjects,[51] the economic-centric frame of the European approach with regard to the protection of personal data cannot be disregarded.

Likewise, the Data Protection Directive does not seem to adopt a liberal approach also when looking at the principle of consent which, apparently, limits the possibility for data controllers to freely process personal data while requiring data controllers to comply with specific legal bases. The principle of consent in European data protection law ensures that data subjects can freely decide whether and how their personal data can be processed.[52] However, this liberal premise fostering autonomy and self-determination also implies that data subjects are autonomous and informed. And this would be possible thanks to the role of data protection in mitigating information asymmetry through transparency obligations and procedural safeguards. Nonetheless, despite the logic of this system, the principle of consent has not played a critical role to limit the discretion of data controllers which can rely on an alternative legal basis to process personal data or exploit their economic position, thus making consent a mandatory step and not a free choice for data subjects. This situation shows the relevance of consent, while underlining its limit and crisis in the digital age.[53]

Therefore, the European liberal approach in the field of data is counterintuitive. Despite the adoption of safeguards to deal with the processing of personal data, the European strategy aimed to reach internal market purposes, thus becoming the primary trigger of European data protection law. However, this approach should not surprise because this path was mandatory at that time. In 1995, the lack of a European constitutional framework protecting privacy and data protection was a limit to the constitutional scope of the Data

[51] Ibid., Recital 2.

[52] Antoinette Rouvroy and Yves Poullet, 'The Right to Informational Self-Determination and the Value of Self-Development: Reassessing the Importance of Privacy for Democracy' in Serge Gutwirth and others (eds.) *Reinventing Data Protection?* 45 (Springer 2009).

[53] Gabriela Zanfir-Fortuna, 'Forgetting About Consent: Why The Focus Should Be on "Suitable Safeguards" in Data Protection Law' in Serge Gutwirth, Ronald Leenes and Paul De Hert (eds.) *Reloading Data Protection* 237 (Springer 2014); Bert-J. Koops, 'The Trouble with European Data Protection Law' (2014) 4(4) International Data Privacy Law 250; Bart. W. Schermer, Bart Custers and Simone van der Hof, 'The Crisis of Consent: How Stronger Legal Protection May Lead to Weaker Consent in Data Protection' (2014) 16 Ethics and Information Technology 171.

Protection Directive which was based on the internal market clause.[54]

Besides, like in the field of content, the Union could not foresee how the digital environment would have affected the right to privacy and data protection. In 1995, the actors operating in the digital environment were primarily online intermediaries offering the storage, access and transmission of data across networks. There were no social media platforms, e-commerce marketplaces or other digital services. Although it was reasonable not to foresee serious concerns at that time due to the passive nature of online intermediaries, this consideration does not explain why the first proposal to revise European data protection law has been proposed only in 2012,[55] and the GDPR entered into force in 2016, even having binding effects until 2018.[56]

In the years after the adoption of the Data Protection Directive, the Union did not make steps forward to modernise data protection rules to address the new challenges raised by transnational private actors such as users' profiling. The time of adoption together with the lack of any amendment in more than twenty years could explain why European data protection law has failed to face the challenges raised by new ways of processing personal data in the digital environment. In other words, the (digital) liberal approach of the Union in this field is also the result of an omissive approach rather than a political choice like in the field of content.

Beyond these diachronic reasons, the characteristics of European directives can also underline the inadequacy of the European data protection law to face transnational digital challenges. Unlike regulations which are directly applicable once they enter into force without the need for domestic implementation, the norms provided by European directives outline just the result that Member States should achieve and are not generally applicable without domestic implementation. Therefore, minimum harmonisation should have

[54] Laima Jančiūtė, 'EU Data Protection and "Treaty-base Games": When Fundamental Rights are Wearing Market-making Clothes' in Ronald Leenes and others (eds.), *Data Protection and Privacy. The Age of Intelligent Machine* (Hart 2017).

[55] Proposal for a Regulation of the European Parliament and of the Council on the protection of individuals with regard to the processing of personal data and on the free movement of such data (General Data Protection Regulation) (2012) COM(2012) 11 final.

[56] Regulation (EU) 2016/679 of the European Parliament and of the Council of 27 April 2016 on the protection of natural persons with regard to the processing of personal data and on the free movement of such data, and repealing Directive 95/46/EC (General Data Protection Regulation) (2016) OJ L 119/1.

provided a common legal framework for promoting the free circulation of personal data in the Union. The Data Protection Directive left Member States free to exercise their margins of discretion when implementing data protection rules within their domestic legal order. Therefore, despite the possibility to rely on a harmonised framework in the Union, the Data Protection Directive could not ensure that degree of uniformity able to address transnational challenges.

Even if these considerations could also be extended to the e-Commerce Directive, in that case, the margins of Member States were limited in relation to the liability of online intermediaries. Besides, the Union introduced other legal instruments to tackle illicit content.[57] Whereas, in the framework of data, several Member States had already adopted their national laws on data protection before the adoption of the Data Protection Directive. These laws were already rooted in the legal tradition of each Member State as demonstrated by the case of France and Germany.[58] Therefore, the heterogeneous legal system of data protection in Europe coming from the mix of different domestic traditions and margins of discretion left by the Data Protection Directive to Member States can be considered one of the primary obstacles for data protection law to face the challenges raised by online platforms.

Within this framework, the fragmentation of domestic regimes and the lack of any revision at supranational level have left enough space for private actors to turn their freedoms into powers based on the processing of vast amounts of (personal) data on a global scale. In other words, in the field of data, the rise and consolidation of private powers in the algorithmic society have been encouraged by liberal goals and design as well as regulatory omissions. This expression of digital liberalism has played a critical role in the consolidation of digital private powers while also encouraging the rise of a new European constitutional strategy.

[57] See, e.g., Directive 2001/29/EC of the European Parliament and of the Council on the harmonisation of certain aspects of copyright and related rights in the information society (2001) OJ L 167/10; Council Framework Decision 2008/913/JHA on combating certain forms and expressions of racism and xenophobia by means of criminal law (2008) OJ L 328/55.

[58] Loi N° 78-17 Du 6 Janvier 1978 Relative à l'informatique, Aux Fichiers et Aux Libertés; Gesetz zum Schutz vor Mißbrauch personenbezogener Daten bei der Datenverarbeitung (Bundesdatenschutzgesetz - BDSG) of 27 January 1977.

2.3 Judicial Activism As a Bridge

The rampant evolution of the digital environment at the beginning of this century has started to challenge the liberal imprinting of the Union. At the very least, two macro-events have questioned the phase of digital liberalism and opened the door to a new step in the European constitutional path characterised by the creative role of the ECJ in framing fundamental rights in the digital environment.[59] The first event triggering this phase of judicial activism concerns the rise and consolidation of new private actors in the digital environment. The second is related to recognition of the Charter as a bill of rights of the Union after the adoption of the Lisbon Treaty.[60]

Firstly, since the end of the last century, the Internet has changed its face. From a channel to transmit and host information published on webpages made just of text and small pictures, it has started to become an environment where to offer products and information and data, primarily through online platforms.[61] In other words, from a mere channel of communication and hosting, the Internet became a social layer where freedoms and powers interact. Within this framework, new business models have started to emerge by benefiting from the characteristics of this global channel of communication.

Unlike traditional access or hosting providers, the primary activities of online platforms do not consist of providing free online spaces where users can share information and opinions. On the contrary, these actors gain profit from the processing and analysis of information and data which attract different forms of revenue such as advertising or allow them to increasingly attract new customers to their products and services.[62] In the case of social media, these actors need to firmly govern their digital spaces by implementing automated decision-making technologies to moderate online content

[59] Oreste Pollicino, *Judicial Protection of Fundamental Rights on the Internet: A Road Towards Digital Constitutionalism?* (Hart 2021).

[60] Sionhaid Douglas-Scott, 'The European Union and Human Rights after the Treaty of Lisbon' (2011) 11(4) Human Rights Law Review 645: Grainne De Burca, 'The Road Not Taken: The EU as a Global Human Rights Actor' (2011) 105(4) American Journal of International Law 649.

[61] Nick Srnicek, *Platform Capitalism* (Polity Press 2016).

[62] Martin Moore and Damian Tambini (eds.), *Digital Dominance: The Power of Google, Amazon, Facebook, and Apple* (Oxford University Press 2018).

and process data.[63] These systems help online platforms attracting revenues from the profiling of users by ensuring a healthy and efficient online community, thus contributing to corporate image and showing a commitment to ethical values. The increasing involvement of online platforms in the organisation of content and the profiling of users' preferences through the use of artificial intelligence technologies has transformed their role as hosting providers.

Secondly, the other primary driver of judicial activism, and of European digital constitutionalism, consisted of the adoption of the Lisbon Treaty which recognised the Charter as EU primary law. This step has contributed to codifying the constitutional dimension of the European (digital) environment.[64] Until that moment, the protection of freedom of expression, privacy and data protection in the European context was based not only on the domestic level but also on the Convention.[65] The Strasbourg Court has played a crucial role not only in protecting the aforementioned fundamental rights but also in underlining the constitutional challenges coming from digital technologies.[66] Nevertheless, although the Union made reference to the framework of the Convention as explicitly mentioned in the Recitals of the e-Commerce Directive and the Data Protection Directive, the lack of accession of the Union to the Convention has limited the dialogue between the two systems,[67] thus leaving Member States to deal with the Convention within their own domestic systems. However, the relationship between the Union and the Council of Europe is closer when looking at the judicial interaction between the ECJ and the ECtHR.[68]

[63] Tarleton Gillespie, *Custodians of The Internet. Platforms, Content Moderation, and the Hidden Decisions That Shape Social Media* (Yale University Press 2018).

[64] Consolidated version of Treaty on the European Union (2012) OJ C 326/13, Art 6(1).

[65] Convention (n. 37), Arts. 8, 10.

[66] Oreste Pollicino, 'Judicial Protection of Fundamental Rights in the Transition from the World of Atoms to the Word of Bits: The Case of Freedom of Speech' (2019) 25 European Law Journal 155.

[67] Bruno De Witte and Sejla Imanovic, 'Opinion 2/13 on Accession to the ECHR: Defending the EU Legal Order against a Foreign Human Rights Court' (2015) 5 European Law Review 683; Paul Craig, 'EU Accession to the ECHR: Competence, Procedure and Substance' (2013) 35 Fordham International Law Journal 111; Sionhaid Douglas-Scott, 'The Relationship between the EU and the ECHR Five Years on from the Treaty of Lisbon' in Sybe De Vries, Ulf Bernitz and Stephen Weatherill (eds.), *The EU Charter of Fundamental Rights as a Binding Instrument: Five Years Old and Growing* 41 (Hart 2015).

[68] Marta Cartabia, 'Europe and Rights: Taking Dialogue Seriously' (2009) 5(1) European Constitutional Law Review 5; Sionhaid Douglas-Scott, 'A Tale of Two Courts: Luxembourg, Strasbourg and the Growing European Human Rights Acquis' (2006) 43 Common Market Law Review 629.

The Lisbon Treaty has constituted a crucial step allowing the right to freedom of expression,[69] private and family life,[70] and the protection of personal data,[71] as already enshrined in the Charter, to become binding vis-à-vis Member States and European institutions,[72] which can interfere with these rights only according to the conditions established by the Charter.[73] Besides, similarly to the Convention,[74] the Charter adds another important piece of the European constitutional puzzle by prohibiting the abuse of rights, which consists of the 'destruction of any of the rights and freedoms recognised in this Charter or at their limitation to a greater extent than is provided for herein'.[75] In this sense, the evolution of European constitutional law is peculiar since the constitutional protection of fundamental rights and freedoms comes from the evolution of the European economic identity.

Within this new constitutional framework, the ECJ has started to act as quasi-constitutional court.[76] The Charter has become the parameter to assess the validity and interpret European legal instruments suffering the legislative inertia of the European lawmaker in relation to the challenges of the digital age. This proactive approach has led to shifting from a formal dimension to a substantial application of fundamental rights, or constitutional law in action. Nevertheless, this activity is not new to the ECJ that, even before the Maastricht Treaty entered into force, had underlined the role of fundamental rights as a limit to fundamental freedoms and common market principles.[77] Precisely, the recognition of fundamental rights as general principles of EU law has opened the doors towards a balancing exercise between fundamentals freedoms and rights, or between the economic and constitutional

[69] Charter (n. 10), Art. 11(1).

[70] Ibid., Art. 7.

[71] Ibid., Art. 8(1).

[72] Ibid., Art. 51.

[73] Koen Lenaerts, 'Exploring the Limits of the EU Charter of Fundamental Rights' (2013) 8 (3) European Constitutional Law Review 375.

[74] Convention (n. 37), Art. 17.

[75] Charter (n. 10), Art. 54.

[76] Grainne De Burca, 'After the EU Charter of Fundamental Rights: The Court of Justice as a Human Rights Adjudicator?' (2013) 20(2) Maastricht Journal of European and Comparative Law 168.

[77] See Case C-112/00, *Eugen Schmidberger, Internationale Transporte und Planzüge* v. *Republik Österreich* (2003) ECR I-905; Case C-36/02, *Omega Spielhallen- und Automatenaufstellungs-GmbH* v. *Oberbürgermeisterin der Bundesstadt Bonn* (2004) ECR I-9609; Case C-341/05, *Laval un Partneri Ltd* v. *Svenska Byggnadsarbetareförbundet* (2007) ECR I-11767; Case C-438/05, *Viking Line ABP* v. *The International transport Workers' Federation, the Finnish Seaman's Union* (2007) ECR I-10779.

dimension of the Union.[78] And this approach is still in the style of the ECJ as shown by the judicial approaches to the challenges raised by digital technologies.

Therefore, the Charter has arisen as a judicial tool to address digital challenges due to the lack of any intervention from the political power. As demonstrated by the next subsections, the ECJ has adopted a teleological approach to ensure the effective protection of constitutional rights and freedoms in relation to the threats of digital technologies implemented by public actors and private businesses such as online platforms. Given the lack of any legislative review of either the e-Commerce Directive or the Data Protection Directive, judicial activism has played a primary role to highlight the challenges for fundamental rights in the algorithmic society. This judicial approach has promoted the transition from a mere economic perspective towards a reframing of constitutional rights and democratic values defining a new phase characterising European digital constitutionalism.

2.3.1 The Constitutional Dimension of Online Intermediaries

The role of fundamental rights and democratic values is hidden between the lines of the system of content. Apart from the reference to Article 10 of the Convention, there are no other points in the e-Commerce Directive expressing the relationship between online intermediaries and fundamental rights. This gap was evident in the case law of the ECJ before the adoption of the Lisbon Treaty.

In *Google France*,[79] the ECJ underlined that, where an Internet-referencing service provider has not played an active role of such a kind as to give it knowledge of, or control over, the data stored, it cannot be held liable for the data that it has stored at the request of an advertiser, unless, having obtained knowledge of the unlawful nature of that data or of that advertiser's activities, it failed to act expeditiously to remove or to disable access to the data concerned. The original liberal frame characterising this decision can be understood by looking at the opinion of the Advocate General in this case. According to the Advocate General Poiares Maduro, search engine results are a 'product of

[78] See Case 29/69, *Erich Stauder* v. *City of Ulm – Sozialamt* (1969); Case 11/70, *Internationale Handelsgesellschaft mbH* v. *Einfuhr- und Vorratsstelle für Getreide und Futtermittel* (1970); Case 4/73, *J. Nold, Kohlen- und Baustoffgroßhandlung* v. *Ruhrkohle Aktiengesellschaft* (1977).

[79] Cases C-236/08, C-237/08 and C-238/08, *Google France* v. *Louis Vuitton Malletier SA*, *Google France SARL* v. *Viaticum SA and Luteciel SARL*, and *Google France SARL* v. *Centre national de recherche en relations humaines (CNRRH) SARL and others* (2010) ECR I-2417.

automatic algorithms that apply objective criteria in order to generate sites likely to be of interest to the Internet user' and, therefore, even if Google has a pecuniary interest in providing users with the possibility to access the more relevant sites, 'however, it does not have an interest in bringing any specific site to the internet user's attention'.[80] Likewise, although the ECJ recognised that Google established 'the order of display according to, inter alia, the remuneration paid by the advertisers',[81] this situation does not deprive the search engine from the exemption of liability established by the e-Commerce Directive.[82] Although neither the Advocate General nor the ECJ did recognise the active role of this provider, the role of automated processing systems had already shown their relevance in shaping the field of online content.

The ECJ made a step forward in *L'Oréal*.[83] In this case, the offering of assistance, including the optimisation, presentation or promotion of the offers for sale, was not considered a neutral activity performed by the provider.[84] It is worth observing how, firstly, the court did not recall the opinion of Poiares Maduro in *Google France*, thus limiting the scope of the economic interests of online platforms in providing their services. Secondly, its decision acknowledged how automated technologies have led some providers to perform an active role rather than the mere passive provisions of digital products and services.

Still, both decisions are the results of a judicial frame based on the economic imprinting of the Union. The predominance of the economic narrative in the judicial reasoning of the ECJ was also the result of the lack of European constitutional parameters to assess the impact on fundamental rights and freedoms. It is not by chance that, after the adoption of the Lisbon Treaty, the ECJ changed its judicial approach moving from a merely economic perspective to a fundamental rights-based approach.

The adoption of a constitutional interpretative angle came up when addressing two cases involving online intermediaries and, primarily, the extent of the ban on general monitoring. In *Scarlet* and *Netlog*,[85] the

80 Opinion of Advocate General Poiares Maduro in the case *Google France* C-236/08, 144.

81 Cases C-236/08, C-237/08 and C-238/08 (n. 79), 115.

82 Ibid., 116.

83 Case 324/09, *L'Oréal SA and Others* v. *eBay International AG and Others* (2011) ECR I-06011.

84 Ibid., 116.

85 Case C-70/10, *Scarlet Extended SA* v. *Société belge des auteurs, compositeurs et éditeurs SCRL (SABAM)* (2011) ECR I-11959; Case C-360/10, *Belgische Vereniging van Auteurs, Componisten en Uitgevers CVBA (SABAM)* v. *Netlog NV* (2012). See Stefan Kulk and Frederik

question of the domestic court aimed to understand whether Member States could allow national courts to order online platforms to set filtering systems of all electronic communications for preventing the dissemination of illicit online content. The e-Commerce Directive prohibits Member States from imposing either a general obligation on providers to monitor the information that they transmit or store or a general obligation to actively seek facts or circumstances indicating illegal activity.

Therefore, the primary question of the national court concerned the proportionality of such an injunction, thus leading the ECJ to interpret the protection of fundamental rights in the Charter. The ECJ dealt with the complex topic of finding a balance between the need to tackle illegal content and users' fundamental rights, precisely the right to privacy and freedom of expression as well as the interests of the platforms not to be overwhelmed by monitoring systems. According to the ECJ, an injunction to install a general filtering system would have not respected the freedom to conduct business of online intermediaries.[86] Moreover, the contested measures could affect users' fundamental rights, namely their right to the protection of their personal data and their freedom to receive or impart information.[87] As a result, the Court held that Belgian content filtering requirements 'for all electronic communications ...; which applies indiscriminately to all its customers; as a preventive measure; exclusively at its expense; and for an unlimited period' violated the ban on general monitoring obligation.

From that moment, the ECJ has relied on the Charter to assess the framework of the e-Commerce Directive. For instance, in *Telekabel* and *McFadden*,[88] the ECJ addressed two similar cases involving injunction orders on online intermediaries which left the provider free to choose the measures to tackle copyright infringements while maintaining the exemption of liability by requiring a duty of care in respect of European fundamental rights. The ECJ upheld the interpretation of the referring national court on the same (constitutional) basis argued in *Scarlet* and

Zuiderveen Borgesius, 'Filtering for Copyright Enforcement in Europe after the Sabam Cases' (2012) 34(11) European Intellectual Property Review 791.

86 Case C-70/10 (n. 85), 50.

87 Charter (n. 10), Arts. 8, 11.

88 Case C-314/12, *UPC Telekabel Wien GmbH* v. *Constantin Film Verleih GmbH and Wega Filmproduktionsgesellschaft mbH* (2014); Case C-484/14, *Tobias McFadden* v. *Sony Music Entertainment Germany GmbH* (2016). See Martin Husovec, 'Holey Cap! CJEU Drills (yet) Another Hole in the e-Commerce Directive's Safe Harbours' (2017) 12(2) Journal of Intellectual Property Law and Practice 115.

Netlog, by concluding that the fundamental rights recognised by European law have to be interpreted as not precluding a court injunction such as that of the case in question. This constitutional interpretation has led the ECJ to extend constitutional safeguards to the digital environment underlining how the economic frame could not be considered enough to address new digital challenges. Even more recently, as examined in Chapter 5, the ECJ has interpreted the framework of the e-Commerce Directive in *Eva Glawischnig-Piesczek*, defining additional safeguards in the removal of identical and equivalent content.[89]

Besides, the ECJ has not been the only European court to stress the relevance of fundamental rights in the field of content. The Strasbourg Court also underlined how the activities of online intermediaries involve fundamental rights. The Court has repeatedly addressed national measures involving the responsibility of online intermediaries for hosting unlawful content such as defamatory comments.[90] Precisely, the Court has highlighted the potential chilling effect on freedom of expression online resulting from holding platforms liable in relation to third-party conduct.[91]

Despite these judicial efforts, the challenges raised by online platforms are far from being solved. European courts have extensively addressed the problem of enforcement in the digital age.[92] Still, the challenge of content moderation raises constitutional concerns. The increasing active role of online platforms in content moderation questions not only the liability regime of the e-Commerce Directive but also constitutional values such as the protection of fundamental rights and the rule of law. Nonetheless, the ECJ's approach has played a crucial part in defining the role of constitutional values in the field of content, driving the evolution of European digital constitutionalism. As underlined in the next sections, the Union has adopted a constitutional strategy in the field of content by orienting its approach towards the introduction of transparency and accountability safeguards in content moderation.

[89] Case C-18/18 *Eva Glawischnig-Piesczek* v. *Facebook Ireland Limited* (2019).

[90] See *Delfi AS* v. *Estonia*, Judgment (2015); *Magyar Tartalomszolgáltatók Egyesülete and Index.Hu Zrt* v. *Hungary*, Judgment (2016); *Rolf Anders Daniel Pihl* v. *Sweden*, Judgment (2017).

[91] Robert Spano, 'Intermediary Liability for Online User Comments under the European Convention on Human Rights' (2017) 17(4) Human Rights Law Review 665.

[92] Martin Husovec, *Injunctions against Intermediaries in the European Union. Accountable but Not Liable?* (Cambridge University Press 2017).

2.3.2 The Judicial Path towards Digital Privacy

The role of the ECJ in these cases provides some clues about the role of judicial activism in adjusting constitutional values to a different technological environment and answering the legislative inertia of the European lawmaker. In the field of data, the ECJ has not only focused on underlining the relevance of fundamental rights but also consolidating and emancipating the right to data protection in the European framework.[93] Both the recognition of the Charter as a primary source of EU law and the increasing relevance of data in the digital age have encouraged the ECJ to overcome the economic-functional dimension of the Data Protection Directive to a constitutional approach.

As a first step, in *Lindqvist*,[94] the ECJ highlighted the potential clash between internal market goals and fundamental rights. The objectives of harmonising national rules including the free flow of data across Member States can clash with the safeguarding of constitutional values.[95] Precisely, the court underlined how the case in question required to strike a fair balance between conflicting rights, especially the right to freedom of expression and privacy.[96] However, in this case, the judicial focus was still on the right to privacy. Some years later, in *Promusicae*,[97] the ECJ enlarged its view to the right to data protection. In a case involving the scope of a judicial order to disclose the identities and physical addresses of certain persons whom it provided with Internet access services, the ECJ recognised the role of data protection 'namely the right that guarantees protection of personal data and hence of private life',[98] despite its functional link with the protection of privacy.[99]

[93] Orla Lynskey, *The Foundations of EU Data Protection Law* (Oxford University Press 2015); Paul De Hert and Serge Gutwirth, 'Data Protection in the Case Law of Strasbourg and Luxembourg: Constitutionalisation in Action' in Serge Gutwirth and others (eds.), *Reinventing Data Protection* 3 (Springer 2009).

[94] Case C-101/01, *Lindqvist* (2003) ECR I-2971.

[95] Ibid., 79–81.

[96] Ibid., 86.

[97] Case C-275/06, *Productores de Música de España (Promusicae)* v. *Telefónica de España SAU* (2008) ECR I-271, 63.

[98] Ibid., 63.

[99] Juliane Kokott and Christoph Sobotta, 'The Distinction between Privacy and Data Protection in the Jurisprudence of the CJEU and the ECtHR' (2013) 3 International Data Privacy Law 222.

This scenario changed with the entry into force of the Lisbon Treaty. Thereafter, the ECJ has started to apply the Charter to assess the threats to privacy and data protection. Unlike the field of content, the Charter has introduced a new fundamental right consisting of the right to protection of personal data.[100] Therefore, the ECJ has not just framed the scope of application of the right to privacy online, but it has played a crucial role in consolidating the constitutional dimension of data protection within the European context.

The mix of this constitutional addition together with the challenges of the information society has led the ECJ to invalidate the Data Retention Directive,[101] due to its disproportionate effects over fundamental rights. In *Digital Rights Ireland*,[102] by assessing, as a constitutional court, the interferences and potential justifications with the rights of privacy and data protection established by the Charter, the ECJ proved to be aware of the risks for the protection of the fundamental rights of European citizens. The retention of all traffic data 'applies to all means of electronic communication. ... It therefore entails an interference with the fundamental rights of practically the entire European population'.[103] Moreover, with regard to automated technologies, the ECJ observed that '[t]he need for such safeguards is all the greater where ... personal data are subjected to automatic processing and where there is a significant risk of unlawful access to those data'.[104] The influence of this approach can also be examined in further decisions of the ECJ on data retention and, precisely in *Tele 2* and *La Quadrature du Net*.[105]

The same constitutional approach can be appreciated in *Schrems*,[106] where the ECJ invalidated the safe harbour decision, which was the

[100] Charter (n. 10), Art. 8.

[101] Directive 2006/24/EC of the European Parliament and of the Council of 15 March 2006 on the retention of data generated or processed in connection with the provision of publicly available electronic communications services or of public communications networks and amending Directive 2002/58/EC (2006) OJ L 105/54.

[102] Cases C-293/12 and C-594/12, *Digital Rights Ireland Ltd* v. *Minister for Communications, Marine and Natural Resources and Others and Kärntner Landesregierung and Others* (2014). See Federico Fabbrini, 'The European Court of Justice Ruling in the Data Retention Case and its Lessons for Privacy and Surveillance in the U.S.' (2015) 28 Harvard Human Rights Journal 65.

[103] Cases C-293/12 and C-594/12 (n. 102), 56.

[104] Ibid., 55.

[105] Case 203/15, *Tele2 Sverige AB contro Post- och telestyrelsen e Secretary of State for the Home Department* v. *Tom Watson e a.* (2016); C-511/18, *La Quadrature du Net and Others* v. *Premier ministre and Others* (2020).

[106] Case C-362/14, *Maximillian Schrems* v. *Data Protection Commissioner* (2015). See Oreste Pollicino and Marco Bassini, 'Bridge Is Down, Data Truck Can't Get Through ...

legal basis allowing the transfer of data from the EU to the United States.[107] Also in this case, the ECJ provided an extensive interpretation of the fundamental right to data protection when reviewing the regime of data transfers established by the Data Protection Directive,[108] in order to ensure 'an adequate level of protection' in the light of 'the protection of the private lives and basic freedoms and rights of individuals'.[109] It is interesting to observe how the ECJ has manipulated the notion of 'adequacy', which, as a result of this new constitutional frame, has moved to a standard of 'equivalence' between the protection afforded to personal data across the Atlantic.[110] Therefore, according to the ECJ, the adequate level of protection required of third states for the transfer of personal data from the EU should ensure a degree of protection 'essentially equivalent' to the EU 'by virtue of Directive 95/46 read in the light of the Charter'.[111] The ECJ adopted the same extensive approach also in the second decision involving the transfer of personal data to the United States. As examined in Chapter 7, the need to ensure an essentially equivalent level of protection has led the ECJ to invalidate even the adequacy decision called Privacy Shield.[112]

These cases underline the role of the Charter in empowering the ECJ and extending (or adapting) the scope of the Data Protection Directive vis-à-vis the new digital threats coming from the massive processing of personal data both inside and outside the European boundaries. Nevertheless, the case showing the paradigmatic shift from an economic to a constitutional perspective in the field of data is *Google Spain*, for at least two reasons.[113] Firstly, as in *Digital Rights Ireland* and *Schrems*, the ECJ has provided an extensive constitutional interpretation

A Critical View of the Schrems Judgment in the Context of European Constitutionalism' (2017) 16 Global Community Yearbook of International Law and Jurisprudence 245.

107 Commission Decision of 26 July 2000 pursuant to Directive 95/46/EC of the European Parliament and of the Council on the adequacy of the protection provided by the safe harbour privacy principles and related frequently asked questions issued by the US Department of Commerce (2000) OJ L 215/7.

108 Data Protection Directive (n. 13), Art. 25.

109 Case C-362/14 (n. 106), 71.

110 Ibid., 73.

111 Ibid.

112 Case C-311/18 *Data Protection Commissioner* v. *Facebook Ireland Limited and Maximillian Schrems* (2020).

113 Case C-131/12, *Google Spain SL and Google Inc.* v. *Agencia Española de Protección de Datos (AEPD) and Mario Costeja González* (2014). See Orla Lynskey, 'Control Over Personal Data in a Digital Age: Google Spain V AEPD and Mario Costeja Gonzalez' (2015) 78 Modern Law Review 522.

of the right to privacy and data protection to ensure their effective protection. Secondly, unlike the other two cases, the *Google Spain* ruling demonstrates a first judicial attempt to cope with the power of online platforms and answer to the legislative inertia of the Union, thus laying the foundation of digital constitutionalism.

The way in which the ECJ recognised that a search engine like Google falls under the category of 'data controller' shows the predominant role of privacy and data protection as fundamental rights. When interpreting the scope of application of the Data Protection Directive, the ECJ observed that not only a literal but also teleological interpretation, which looks at the need to ensure the effective and complete protection of data subjects, would lead to considering search engines as data controllers over the personal data published on the web pages of third parties.[114] In other words, considering Google as a mere data processor would have not ensured effective protection to the rights of the data subjects.

Secondly, the same consideration also applies to the definition of establishment. The ECJ ruled that processing of personal data should be considered as being conducted in the context of the activities of an establishment of the controller in the territory of a Member State, within the meaning of that provision, when the operator of a search engine sets up, in a Member State, a branch or subsidiary that is intended to promote and sell advertising space offered by that engine and that orientates its activities towards the inhabitants of that Member State.[115] As the ECJ observed, '[I]t cannot be accepted that the processing of personal data ... should escape the obligations and guarantees laid down by Directive 95/46, which would compromise ... the effective and complete protection of the fundamental rights and freedoms of natural persons which the directive seeks to'.[116] In this case, the ECJ broadly interpreted the meaning of 'in the context of establishment' to avoid that fundamental rights are subject to a disproportionate effect due to a formal interpretation.

Thirdly, the ECJ entrusted search engines to delist online content connected with personal data of data subjects even without requiring the removal of the content at stake.[117] As a result, it is possible to argue that this interpretation just unveiled an existing legal basis in the Data Protection Directive to enforce this right against private actors.

[114] Ibid., 34.
[115] Ibid., 58.
[116] Ibid., 60.
[117] Ibid., 97.

However, by framing this decision within the new constitutional framework, the ECJ has recognised a right to be forgotten online through the interpretation of the Data Protection Directive. Such a constitutional-oriented interpretation can be considered the expression of a horizontal enforcement of the fundamental rights enshrined in the Charter. In this way, as also addressed in Chapter 3, the ECJ has delegated to search engines the task of balancing fundamental rights when assessing users' requests to delist, thus promoting the consolidation of private ordering.[118]

These landmark decisions show the role of judicial activism in underlining the role of constitutional law in the digital environment. Nonetheless, as underlined in the case of content, judicial activism has not been enough to solve the issue raised in the field of data. The aforementioned cases just touched the constitutional challenges raised by the processing of personal data through automated decision-making technologies. Therefore, although the ECJ has contributed to the consolidation of the constitutional dimension of privacy and data protection in the Union, the next section demonstrates how the GDPR, as one of the expressions of European digital constitutionalism, has led to the codification of these judicial steps and provided a new harmonised framework of European data protection law.

2.4 The Reaction of European Digital Constitutionalism

The changing landscape of the digital environment has led the ECJ to take the initiative, thus overcoming the inertia of political power. The ECJ's judicial activism has paved the way for a shift from the first approach based on digital liberalism to a new phase of digital constitutionalism characterised by the reframing of fundamental rights and the injection of democratic values in the digital environment.

This change of paradigm does not only concern the power exercised by public actors. As underlined in Chapter 1, public actors are still a primary source of concern but are no longer the only source of interference with individual fundamental rights and freedoms. Threats to constitutional values also come from transnational private actors, precisely online platforms such as social media and search engines whose freedoms are increasingly turning into forms of

[118] Jean-Marie Chenou and Roxana Radu, 'The "Right to Be Forgotten": Negotiating Public and Private Ordering in the European Union' (2017) 58 Business & Society 74.

unaccountable power. While constitutional safeguards bind the public sector, these do not generally extend to private actors. Given the lack of regulation or horizontal translation of constitutional values, constitutional law does not limit the freedom which private entities enjoy in performing their activities.

The constitutional gap between the exercise of power by public and private actors has led the Union to abandon the phase of digital liberalism and face new private forms of authority based on the exploitation of algorithmic technologies for processing content and data on a global scale.[119] As also supported by judicial activism, this reaction is not only linked to the protection of individual fundamental rights, such as freedom of expression and data protection, and, at the end, dignity.[120] Even more importantly, the consolidation of private powers raises concerns for the democratic system and, primarily, the principle of rule of law due to the increasing competition between public and private values.[121]

Within this framework, two primary drivers have characterised the rise of the democratic phase of European digital constitutionalism. Firstly, the Union codified some of the ECJ's judicial lessons. Secondly, the Union introduced new limits to private powers by adopting legal instruments by increasing the degree of transparency and accountability in content moderation and data processing. Both of these characteristics can be found in the Digital Single Market strategy.[122] According to the Commission, online platforms should 'protect core values' and increase 'transparency and fairness for maintaining user trust and safeguarding innovation'.[123] This is because the role of online platforms in the digital environment implies 'wider responsibility'.[124]

119 Luciano Floridi, *The Fourth Revolution: How the Infosphere Is Reshaping Human Reality* (Oxford University Press 2014).

120 Gunther Teubner, 'The Anonymous Matrix: Human Rights Violations by "Private" Transnational Actors' (2006) 69(3) Modern Law Review 327.

121 Paul Nemitz, 'Constitutional Democracy and Technology in the age of Artificial Intelligence' (2018) 376 Philosophical Transaction of the Royal Society A.

122 Communication from the Commission to the European Parliament, the Council, the European Economic and Social Committee and the Committee of the Regions, A Digital Single Market Strategy for Europe COM(2015) 192 final.

123 Communication from the Commission to the European Parliament, the Council, the European Economic and Social Committee and the Committee of the Regions, Online Platforms and the Digital Single Market Opportunities and Challenges for Europe COM (2016) 288 final.

124 Ibid.

Likewise, the Council of Europe has contributed to the reaction of the Union against the power of online platforms. Particularly, it underlined the relevance of the positive obligation of Member States to ensure the respect of human rights and the role and responsibility of online intermediaries in managing content and processing data. As observed, 'the power of such intermediaries as protagonists of online expression makes it imperative to clarify their role and impact on human rights, as well as their corresponding duties and responsibilities'.[125] Even the European Parliament proposed to clarify the boundaries of online intermediaries' liability and to provide more guidance defining their responsibilities.[126]

This political approach resulted in a new wave of soft-law and hard-law instruments whose objective is, inter alia, to mitigate online platform powers in the field of content and data. Like other fields such as net neutrality or the right to Internet access, the introduction of new safeguards constitutes the expressions of key values of the contemporary society.[127] Precisely, the Directive on copyright in the DSM (Copyright Directive),[128] the amendments to the audiovisual media services Directive (AVMS Directive),[129] the regulation to address online terrorist content (TERREG),[130] or the adoption of the GDPR are just some of the examples demonstrating how the Digital Single Market strategy has constituted a change of paradigm to face the consolidation of powers in the algorithmic society. The proposal for the Digital Services Act can be seen as a milestone of this

[125] Recommendation of the Committee of Ministers to member States on the roles and responsibilities of internet intermediaries CM/Rec(2018)2, 7.

[126] European Parliament resolution of 15 June 2017 on online platforms and the digital single market, 2016/2276(INI).

[127] Christoph B. Graber, 'Bottom-Up Constitutionalism: The Case of Net Neutrality' (2017) 7 Transnational Legal Theory 524.

[128] Directive (EU) 2019/790 of the European Parliament and of the Council of 17 April 2019 on copyright and related rights in the Digital Single Market and amending Directives 96/9/EC and 2001/29/EC (2019) OJ L 130/92.

[129] Directive (EU) 2018/1808 of the European Parliament and of the Council of 14 November 2018 amending Directive 2010/13/EU on the coordination of certain provisions laid down by law, regulation or administrative action in Member States concerning the provision of audiovisual media services (Audiovisual Media Services Directive) in view of changing market realities (2018) OJ L 303/69.

[130] Regulation (EU) 2021/784 of the European Parliament and of the Council of 29 April 2021 on addressing the dissemination of terrorist content online (2021) OJ L 172/79.

path,[131] as discussed in Chapter 5. The next subsections examine how the Union has built a constitutional strategy to protect rights and limit powers by introducing obligations and safeguards in the field of content and data.

2.4.1 Democratising Content Moderation

Within the framework of the Digital Single Market strategy, the Commission oriented the efforts towards fostering transparency and accountability in the field of content. To reduce the discretion of online platforms to organise and remove content, the Commission adopted a siloed approach defining new procedural safeguards in different sectors like copyright or audiovisual content.

For the first time after twenty years, the adoption of the Copyright Directive has changed the system of liability established by the e-Commerce Directive but applying only to some online platforms (i.e. online content-sharing service providers) and limited to the field of copyright.[132] Despite this scope, this step can be considered a watershed in the European policy, acknowledging that the activities of some online platforms cannot be considered passive any longer. The digital environment has gained in complexity. The services offered by platforms, particularly social media, allow access to a large amount of copyright-protected content uploaded by their users.[133]

Since rightholders bear financial losses due to the quantity of copyright-protected works uploaded on online platforms without prior authorisation, the Copyright Directive establishes, inter alia, a licensing

[131] Proposal for a Regulation of the European Parliament and of the Council on a Single Market for Digital Services (Digital Services Act) and amending Directive 2000/31/EC, COM(2020) 825 final.

[132] Martin Husovec, 'How Europe Wants to Redefine Global Online Copyright Enforcement' in Tatiana E. Synodinou (ed.), *Pluralism or Universalism in International Copyright Law* 513 (Wolter Kluwer 2019); Thomas Spoerri, 'On Upload-Filters and other Competitive Advantages for Big Tech Companies under Article 17 of the Directive on Copyright in the Digital Single Market' (2019) 10(2) Journal of Intellectual Property, Information Technology and E-Commerce Law 173; Giancarlo Frosio and Sunimal Mendis, 'Monitoring and Filtering: European Reform or Global Trend?' in Giancarlo Frosio (ed.), *The Oxford Handbook of Online Intermediary Liability* 544 (Oxford University Press 2020).

[133] Giancarlo Frosio, 'The Death of "No Monitoring Obligations": A Story of Untameable Monsters' (2017) 8(3) Journal of Intellectual Property, Information Technology 212.

system between online platforms and rightholders.[134] Precisely, the Copyright Directive establishes that online content-sharing service providers perform an act of communication to the public when hosting third-party content and, as a result, they are required to obtain licences from rightholders. If no authorisation is granted, online content-sharing service providers can be held liable for unauthorised acts of communication to the public, including making available to the public copyright-protected works unless they comply with the new conditions defining the exemption of liability focused on the notion of best efforts.[135]

The liability of online content-sharing service providers should be assessed based on 'the type, the audience and the size of the service and the type of works or other subject-matter uploaded by the users of the service; and the availability of suitable and effective means and their cost for service providers'.[136] Moreover, this regime partially applies to online content-sharing service providers whose services have been available to the public in the Union for less than three years and that have an annual turnover below €10 million.[137] Furthermore, the Copyright Directive extends the ban on general monitoring not only to Member States but also the cooperation between rightholders and online platforms.[138]

In this case, it is possible to observe the heritage of the ECJ rulings in terms of proportionality safeguards as influenced by the decisions in *Scarlet* and *Netlog*. The Copyright Directive does not introduce a general system applying to all information society services like the e-Commerce Directive, but aims to strike a fair balance between the interests of rightholders, the protection of users' rights and the freedom to conduct business, especially concerning small platforms.

This new system of liability is not the sole novelty. The Union has not only codified the findings of the ECJ but, even more importantly, has limited platform powers by introducing procedural safeguards in content moderation. Firstly, the Copyright Directive requires online content-sharing service providers to provide rightholders at their request with adequate information on the functioning of their practices with regard to the cooperation referred to and where licensing agreements are concluded between service providers and rightholders, information

[134] Copyright Directive (n. 128), Art. 2(6).
[135] Ibid., Art. 17.
[136] Ibid., Art. 17(5).
[137] Ibid., Art. 17(6).
[138] Ibid., Art. 17(8).

on the use of content covered by the agreements.[139] Moreover, these providers should put in place an effective and expeditious complaint and redress mechanism that is available to users of their services in the event of disputes over the disabling of access to, or the removal of, works or other subject matter uploaded by them.[140] Where rightholders request to have access to their specific works or other subject matter disabled or those works or other subject matter removed, they shall duly justify the reasons for their requests.[141] In general, complaints have to be processed without undue delay, and decisions to disable access to or remove uploaded content is subject to human review. Member States are also required to ensure that out-of-court redress mechanisms are available for the settlement of disputes.[142] Such mechanisms shall enable disputes to be settled impartially and shall not deprive the user of the legal protection afforded by national law, without prejudice to the rights of users to have recourse to efficient judicial remedies.

The Copyright Directive underlines how, on the one hand, the Union has codified the lessons of the ECJ in terms of proportionality and, on the other hand, has limited the exemption of liability of some online platforms for copyright-protected content. Likewise, the amendment to the AVMS Directive aims to increase the responsibilities of video-sharing platforms.[143] Unlike the Copyright Directive, the AVMS Directive specifies that video-sharing platforms' liability is subject to the provisions of the e-Commerce Directive.[144] As a result, the AVMS Directive has not introduced a specific liability of online platforms hosting audiovisual media services. Besides, Member States cannot oblige providers to monitor content or impose other active engagements.

Nonetheless, the AVMS Directive introduces further safeguards. Member States should ensure that video-sharing platform providers introduce 'appropriate measures' to achieve the objectives to protect minors from harmful content and the general public from audiovisual content which incite to hate against a group referred to Article 21 of the Charter or constitute specific criminal offences under EU law.[145]

139 Ibid.
140 Ibid., Art. 17(9).
141 Ibid.
142 Ibid.
143 AVMS Directive (n. 129), Art. 1(1)(b).
144 Ibid., Art. 28a(1).
145 Ibid., Art. 28a(1)(c), namely public provocation to commit a terrorist offence within the meaning of Art. 5 of Directive 2017/541/EU, offences concerning child pornography within the meaning of Art. 5(4) of Directive 2011/93/EU and offences concerning

Such appropriate measures should also regard audiovisual commercial communications that are not marketed, sold or arranged by those video-sharing platform providers. In this case, the AVMS Directive clarifies that it is necessary to take into consideration 'the limited control exercised by those video-sharing platforms over those audiovisual commercial communications'.[146] Another provision regards the duty of video-sharing platform providers to clearly inform users of the programmes and user-generated videos that contain audiovisual commercial communications, where the user who has uploaded the user-generated video in question declares that such video includes commercial communications or the provider has knowledge of that fact.

As already mentioned, the measure introduced by the Member States shall comply with the liability regime established by the e-Commerce Directive. The meaning of 'appropriate measure' is specified by the AVMS Directive.[147] Precisely, the nature of the content, the possible harm which it may cause, the characteristics of the category of person to be protected, the rights and the legitimate interests of subjects involved, including also those of video-sharing platforms and users, and the public interest should be considered. Such appropriate measures should also be practicable and proportionate, taking into consideration the size of the video-sharing platform service and the nature of the service provided.

The AVMS Directive provides a list of appropriate measures such as the establishment of mechanisms for users of video-sharing platforms to report or flag to the video-sharing platform provider or age verification systems for users of video-sharing platforms with respect to content which may impair the physical, mental or moral development of minors. The role of Member States is to establish mechanisms to assess the degree of appropriateness of these measures through their national regulatory authorities, together with mechanisms to ensure the possibility to complain and redress related to the application of appropriate measures. In this case, the AVMS Directive has not changed the liability of video-sharing providers. Nevertheless, the aforementioned considerations show how online platforms are not

racism and xenophobia within the meaning of Art. 1 of Framework Decision 2008/913/JHA.

146 Ibid., Art. 28a(2). The same provision extends the obligations established by Art. 9 regarding audiovisual commercial communications that are marketed, sold or arranged by those video-sharing platform providers. In this case, the difference consists in the role of the video-sharing platforms that, in this case, act as a content provider exercising a control over the product and services offered.

147 Ibid., Art. 28a(3).

considered so much as passive providers but as market players whose activities should be subject to regulation.

Similar observations apply to the TERREG which aims to establish a clear and harmonised legal framework to address the misuse of hosting services for the dissemination of terrorist content.[148] Firstly, the TERREG defines terrorist content.[149] As a result, since the definition is provided by law, online platforms' discretion would be bound by this legal definition when moderating terrorist content. Secondly, hosting service providers are required to act in a diligent, proportionate and non-discriminatory manner and considering 'in all circumstances' fundamental rights of the users, especially freedom of expression.[150]

Despite the relevance of these obligations, the implementation of these measures, described as 'duties of care',[151] should not lead online platforms to generally monitor the information they transmit or store, nor to a general duty to actively seek facts or circumstances indicating illegal activity. In any case, unlike the Copyright Directive, the TERREG does not prejudice the application of the safe harbour regime established by the e-Commerce Directive. Hosting providers are only required to inform the competent authorities and remove expeditiously the content of which they became aware. Besides, they are obliged to remove content within one hour of the receipt of a removal order from the competent authority.[152]

Although the TERREG has raised several concerns since the launch of the first proposal,[153] even in this case, the Union has injected procedural

[148] Joris van Hoboken, 'The Proposed EU Terrorism Content Regulation: Analysis and Recommendations with Respect to Freedom of Expression Implications' Transatlantic Working Group on Content Moderation Online and Freedom of Expression (2019) www.ivir.nl/publicaties/download/TERREG_FoE-ANALYSIS.pdf accessed 21 November 2021; Joan Barata, 'New EU Proposal on the Prevention of Terrorist Content Online', CIS Stanford Law (2018) https://cyberlaw.stanford.edu/files/publication/files/2018.10.11.Comment.Terrorism.pdf accessed 21 November 2021.

[149] TERREG (n. 148), Art. 2(1)(7).

[150] Ibid., Art. 5.

[151] Ibid., Art. 1(1)(a).

[152] Ibid., Art. 3.

[153] Jillian C. York and Christoph Schmon, 'The EU Online Terrorism Regulation: A Bad Deal' EFF (7 April 2021) www.eff.org/it/deeplinks/2021/04/eu-online-terrorism-regulation-bad-deal accessed 21 November 2021. See, also, FRA, 'Proposal for a Regulation on preventing the dissemination of terrorist content online and its fundamental rights implications. Opinion of the European Union Agency for Fundamental Right' (12 February 2019) https://fra.europa.eu/sites/default/files/fra_uploads/fra-2019-opinion-online-terrorism-regulation-02-2019_en.pdf accessed 21 November 2021.

safeguards. Hosting service providers are required, for example, to set out clearly in their terms and conditions their policy to prevent the dissemination of terrorist content.[154] Furthermore, competent authorities shall make publicly available annual transparency reports on the removal of terrorist content.[155] Transparency obligations are not the only safeguards. Where hosting service providers use automated tools in respect of content that they store, online platforms are obliged to set and implement 'effective and appropriate safeguard' ensuring that content moderation is accurate and well-founded (e.g. human oversight).[156] Furthermore, the TERREG recognises the right to an effective remedy requiring online platforms to put in place procedures allowing content providers to access remedy against decisions on content which has been removed or access to which has been disabled following a removal order.[157] As in the case of transparency obligations, this process aims to regulate content moderation. Firstly, online platforms are obliged to promptly examine every complaint they receive and, secondly, reinstate the content without undue delay where the removal or disabling of access was unjustified.[158] This process is not entirely discretionary. Within two weeks from the receipt of the complaint, online platforms do not only inform the notice provider but also provide an explanation when they decide not to reinstate the content.

These measures deserve to be framed within the attempts of the Commission to nudge online platforms to introduce transparency and accountability mechanisms.[159] The Recommendation on measures to effectively tackle illegal content online proposes a general framework of safeguards in content moderation.[160] This instrument encourages platforms to publish, in a clear, easily understandable and sufficiently detailed manner, the criteria according to which they manage the

[154] Ibid., Art. 7.
[155] Ibid., Art. 8.
[156] Ibid., Art. 5(2).
[157] Ibid., Art. 10.
[158] Ibid., Art. 10(2).
[159] Code of conduct on countering illegal hate speech online (2016) http://ec.europa.eu/newsroom/just/item-detail.cfm?item_id=54300 accessed 21 November 2021; Code of practice on disinformation (2018) https://ec.europa.eu/digital-single-market/en/news/code-practice-disinformation accessed 21 November 2021; Communication from the Commission to the European Parliament, the Council, the European Economic and Social Committee and the Committee of the Regions, Tackling Illegal Content Online Towards an enhanced responsibility of online platforms COM(2017) 555 final.
[160] Recommendation of 1 March 2018 on measures to effectively tackle illegal content online, C(18) 1177 final.

removal of or blocking of access to online content.[161] In the case of the removal of or blocking of access to the signalled online content, platforms should, without undue delay, inform users about the decision, stating their reasoning as well as the possibility to contest the decision.[162] Against a removal decision, the content provider should have the possibility to contest the decision by submitting a 'counter-notice' within a 'reasonable period of time'. The Recommendation in question can be considered the manifesto of the new approach to online content moderation in the Digital Single Market Strategy. This new set of rights aims to reduce the asymmetry between individuals and private actors implementing automated technologies.

Although the European constitutional framework has made some important steps forward in the field of content, however, the legal fragmentation of guarantees and remedies at supranational level could undermine the attempt of the Union to provide a common framework to address the cross-border challenges raised by online platforms. Instead, the Union does not seem to adopt a common strategy in this field but regulates platform by siloes. This situation also raises challenges at the national level as underlined by the implementation of the new licensing system introduced by the Copyright Directive.[163]

Despite the steps forward made in the last years at European level, this supranational approach has not pre-empted Member States in following their path in the field of content, precisely when looking at the laws introduced by Germany in the field of hate speech,[164] and France concerning disinformation.[165] The mix of supranational and national initiatives leads to a decrease in the effective degree of protection of fundamental freedoms and rights in the internal market, thus challenging the role of digital constitutionalism in protecting individual fundamental rights and limiting the powers of online platforms.

161 Ibid., 16.

162 Ibid., 9.

163 João P. Quintais and others, 'Safeguarding User Freedoms in Implementing Article 17 of the Copyright in the Digital Single Market Directive: Recommendations from European Academics' (2019) 10(3) Journal of Intellectual Property, Information Technology and E-Commerce Law 277.

164 Netzdurchsetzunggesetz, Law of 30 June 2017 (NetzDG).

165 Loi organique n° 2018-1201 du 22 décembre 2018 relative à la lutte contre la manipulation de l'information; Loi n° 2018-1202 du 22 décembre 2018 relative à la lutte contre la manipulation de l'information.

Therefore, as examined in Chapter 5, the advent of the Digital Services Act provides a common and horizontal framework supporting the increase of transparency and accountability of content moderation.

2.4.2 Centring a Personal Data Risk-Based Approach

The protection of personal data has reached a new step of consolidation not only after the adoption of the Lisbon Treaty thanks to the role of the ECJ but also with the adoption of the GDPR. The change in the strategy of the Union can be examined when comparing the first Recitals of the GDPR with the Data Protection Directive to understand the central role of data subjects' fundamental rights within the framework of European data protection law.[166] This focus on fundamental rights does not entail neglecting other constitutional rights and freedoms at stake or even the interests of the Union in ensuring the smooth development of the internal market by promoting innovation within the context of the data industry.[167] However, this change of paradigm in the approach of the Union underlines a commitment to protect fundamental rights and democratic values in the algorithmic society.

The entire structure of the GDPR is based on general principles which orbit around the accountability of the data controller, who should ensure and prove compliance to the system of data protection law.[168] Even when the data controller is not established in the Union,[169] the GDPR increases the responsibility of the data controller which, instead of focusing on merely complying with data protection law, is required to design and monitor data processing by assessing the risk for data subjects.[170] In other words, even in this field, the approach of the Union aims to move from formal compliance as a legal shield to substantive

[166] GDPR (n. 56), Recitals 1–2.

[167] Ibid., Recital 4.

[168] Ibid., Art. 5.

[169] Ibid., Art. 3(2).

[170] Raphael Gellert, 'Understanding the Notion of Risk in the General Data Protection Regulation' (2018) 34 Computer Law & Security Review 279; Claudia Quelle, 'Enhancing Compliance under the General Data Protection Regulation: The Risky Upshot of the Accountability- and Risk-based Approach' (2018) 9(3) European Journal of Risk Regulation 502; Milda Maceinate, 'The "Riskification" of European Data Protection Law through a Two-fold Shift' (2017) 8(3) European Journal of Risk Regulation 506.

responsibilities (or accountability) of the data controller guided by the principles of the GDPR as horizontal translation of the fundamental rights of privacy and data protection. The influence of the ECJ's lessons can be read by examining how the GDPR aims to overcome formal approaches (e.g. establishment) and adopt a risk-based approach to preclude data controllers from escaping the responsibility to protect data subjects' rights and freedoms.

Within this framework, the GDPR adopts a dynamic definition of the data controller's responsibility that considers the nature, the scope of application, the context and the purposes of the processing, as well as the risks to the individual rights and freedoms. On this basis, the data controller is required to implement appropriate technical and organisational measures to guarantee, and be able to demonstrate, that the processing is conducted in accordance with the GDPR's principles.[171] The principle of accountability can be considered a paradigmatic example of how the Union aims to inject proportionality in the field of data.

The principles of privacy by design and by default contributes to achieving this purpose by imposing an ex-ante assessment of compliance with the GDPR and, as a result, with the protection of the fundamental right to data protection.[172] Put another way, the GDPR focuses on promoting a proactive, rather than a reactive approach based on the assessment of the risks and context of specific processing of personal data. An example of this shift is the obligation for the data controller to carry out the Data Protection Impact Assessment, which explicitly also aims to address the risks deriving from automated processing 'on which decisions are based that produce legal effects concerning the natural person or similarly significantly affect the natural person'.[173] This obligation requires the data controllers to conduct a risk assessment which is not only based on business interests but also on data subjects' (fundamental) rights.

Furthermore, the GDPR has not only increased the degree of accountability of the data controller but also has also aimed to empower individuals by introducing new rights for data subjects. The case of the right to erasure can be considered a paradigmatic example of the codification

171 Ibid., Art. 24.
172 Ibid., Art. 25.
173 Ibid., Art. 35(3)(a).

process in the aftermath of the ECJ's case law, precisely *Google Spain*.[174] The right not to be subject to automated decisions and the right to data portability are only two examples of the new rights upon which users can rely.[175] In other words, the provisions of new data subjects' rights demonstrate how the Union intends to ensure that individuals are not marginalised vis-à-vis the data controller, especially when the latter processes vast amounts of data and information through the use of artificial intelligence technologies.

Among these safeguards, it is not by chance that the GDPR establishes the right not to be subject to automated decision-making processes as an example of the Union reaction against the challenges raised by artificial intelligence technologies. Without being exhaustive, the GDPR provides a general rule, according to which, subject to some exceptions,[176] the data subject has the right not to be subject to a decision 'based solely on automated processing, including profiling, which produces legal effects concerning him or her or similarly significantly affects him or her'.

As analysed in Chapter 6, despite this vague scope of this right which tries to provide a flexible approach to different automated decision-making systems, the GDPR aims to protect data subjects against this form of automated processing. By complementing this liberty with a positive dimension based on procedural safeguard consisting of the obligation for data controllers to implement 'at least' the possibility for the data subject to obtain human intervention, express his or her point of view and contest decisions, the GDPR aims to ensure not only the right to privacy and data protection but also individual autonomy and dignity.[177] The provision of the 'human intervention' as a minimum standard in automated processing would foster the role of data subjects in the algorithmic society. In other words, this right aims to increase the degree of transparency and accountability for individuals which can rely on their right to receive information about automated decisions involving their rights and freedoms.

However, that enhancing procedural safeguards could affect the freedom to conduct business or the performance of a public task due to additional human and financial resources required to adapt automated technologies to the data protection legal framework. More broadly, this situation could also contribute to the consolidation of existing platform

[174] Jef Ausloos, *The Right to Erasure in EU Data Protection Law* (Oxford University Press 2020).
[175] GDPR (n. 56), Arts. 20, 22.
[176] Ibid., Art. 22(2).
[177] Ibid., Art. 22(3).

powers creating a legal barrier for other businesses to use these technologies.[178] Secondly, the presence of a human being does not eliminate any risk of error or discrimination, especially considering that, in some cases, algorithmic biases are the results of data collected by humans or reflecting human prejudices.[179] Thirdly, the opacity of some algorithmic processes could not allow the data controller to provide the same degree of explanation in any case. This point is primarily connected to the debate around the right to explanation in European data protection law.[180]

Nevertheless, this provision, together with the principle of accountability, constitutes a crucial step in the governance of automated decision-making processes.[181] Since automated systems are developed according to the choice of programmers who, by setting the rules of technologies, transform legal language in technical norms, they contribute to defining transnational standards of protection outside the traditional channels of control. This situation raises threats not only for the principles of European data protection law, but even more importantly, the principle of the rule of law since, even in this case, legal norms are potentially replaced by technological standard and private determinations outside any democratic check or procedure.

The GDPR has not provided a clear answer to these challenges and, more in general, to the fallacies of European data protection law.[182] The potential scope of the principle of accountability leaves data controllers to enjoy margins of discretions in deciding the safeguards that are

178 Michal S Gal and Oshrit Aviv, 'The Competitive Effects of the GDPR' (2020) 16(3) Journal of Competition Law and Economics 349.

179 Andreas Tsamados and others. 'The Ethics of Algorithms: Key Problems and Solutions' (2021) AI & Society https://link.springer.com/article/10.1007/s00146-021-01154-8#cite as accessed 21 November 2021.

180 Andrew D. Selbst and Julia Powles, 'Meaningful Information and the Right to Explanation' (2017) 7 International Data Privacy Law 233; Margot E. Kaminski, 'The Right to Explanation, Explained' (2019) 34 Berkeley Technology Law Journal 189; Sandra Wachter and others, 'Why a Right to Explanation of Automated Decision-Making Does Not Exist in the General Data Protection Regulation' (2017) 7 International Data Privacy Law 76; Gianclaudio Malgieri and Giovanni Comandè, 'Why a Right to Legibility of Automated Decision-Making Exists in the General Data Protection Regulation' (2017) 7 International Data Privacy Law 234; Lilian Edwards and Michael Veale, 'Slave to the Algorithm? Why a "Right to an Explanation" Is Probably Not the Remedy You Are Looking For' (2017) 16 Duke Law & Technology Review 18.

181 Margot Kaminski, 'Binary Governance: Lessons from the GDPR's Approach to Algorithmic Accountability' (2019) 92 Southern California Law Review 1529.

182 Bert-Jaap Koops, 'The Trouble with European Data Protection Law' (2014) 4(4) International Data Privacy Law 250.

enough to protect the fundamental rights of data subjects in a specific context. As underlined in Chapter 3, the risk-based approach introduced by the GDPR could be considered a delegation to data controller of the power to balance conflicting interests, thus making the controller the 'arbiter' of data protection. Although the GDPR cannot be considered a panacea, it constitutes an important step forward in the field of data. Like in the case of content, the Union approach has focused on increasing the responsibility of the private sector while limiting the discretion in the use of algorithmic technologies by unaccountable powers.

2.5 Freedoms and Powers in the Algorithmic Society

The advent of the Internet has left its stamp on the evolution of European (digital) constitutionalism. The first phase of technological optimism coming from the western side of the Atlantic has spread on the other side of the ocean where the Union considered the digital environment as an enabler of economic growth for the internal market. The evolution of the digital environment has revealed how the transplant of the US neoliberal approach to digital technologies had not taken into account the different humus of European constitutional values. This transatlantic distance underlines why the first phase of digital liberalism was destined to fall before the rise of new private actors interfering with individual fundamental rights and challenging democratic values on a global scale.

It is difficult to imagine what would have been the approach of the Union if it had not followed the US path towards digital liberalism at the end of last century. Nonetheless, the new European approach to the challenges of the algorithmic society is a paradigmatic example of the talent of European constitutionalism to protect fundamental rights and democratic values from the rise of unaccountable powers. From a first phase characterised by digital liberalism where freedoms were incentivised as the engine of the internal market, the Union's approach moved to a constitutional-based approach. The ECJ has played a crucial role in this transition by building a constitutional bridge allowing the Union to move from digital liberalism to a democratic constitutional strategy. The Commission then codified and consolidated this shift as demonstrated by the approach taken with the Digital Single Market Strategy.

The rise of European digital constitutionalism can be considered a reaction against the challenges of the algorithmic society, and in particular the rise of platform powers. The liberal approach adopted by constitutional democracies recognising broad areas of freedom both in the field of content and data has led to the development of business models providing opportunities for fundamental rights and freedoms online. At the same time, the price to pay for leaving broad margin of freedoms to the private sector has contributed to turning freedoms into powers. In other words, the digital liberal approach of the Union has promoted the rise and consolidation of private ordering competing with public powers.

As analysed in Chapter 3, technological evolutions, combined with a liberal constitutional approach, have led online platforms to exercise delegated and autonomous powers to set their rules and procedures on a global scale. Therefore, users are subject to a 'private' form of authority exercised by online platforms through a mix of private law and automated technologies (i.e. the law of the platforms). The path of European digital constitutionalism is still at the beginning. As underlined in the next chapter, the powers exercised by online platforms, as transnational private actors, have raised constitutional challenges which still need to be addressed.

3 The Law of the Platforms

3.1 From Public to Private As from Atoms to Bits

In the 1990s, Negroponte defined the increasing level of digitisation as the movement from atoms to bits.[1] In general, a bit is only the sum of 0 and 1 but, as in the case of atoms, the interrelations between bits can build increasingly complex structures,[2] leading to the shift from materiality to immateriality.[3] The move from the industrial to the information society is primarily due to the move from rivalrousness to non-rivalrousness of traditional products and services.[4] Put another way, the bits exchanged through the Internet have driven the shift from analogue to digital technologies by creating revolutionary models to market traditional products or services and leading to wonder about the application of traditional rules to the digital environment.[5] The result is that the economy is no longer based on the creation of value through production but on values created through the flowing of information on a transnational architecture governed at the intersection between public authority and private ordering.

At the end of the last century, constitutional democracies across the Atlantic adopted a liberal approach to this technological shift which

1 Nicholas Negroponte, *Being Digital* (Alfred A. Knopf 1995).

2 Bill Gates, *The Road Ahead* (Viking Press 1995).

3 John P. Barlow, 'The Economy of Ideas: Selling Wine Without Bottles on the Global Net' in Peter Ludlow (ed.), *High Noon on the Electronic Frontier: Conceptual Issues in Cyberspace* (MIT Press 1999).

4 Yochai Benkler, *The Wealth of Networks: How Social Production Transforms Markets and Freedom* (Yale University Press 2006); Andrew Murray, *Information Technology Law: The Law and Society* (Oxford University Press 2013).

5 Frank H. Easterbrook, 'Cyberspace and the Law of the Horse' (1996) University of Chicago Legal Forum 207.

promised new paths of economic growth.[6] The rapid expansion of digital technologies combined with liberal goals have been two of the primary drivers for the accumulation of power by transnational private entities providing increasingly essential services. Instead of the democratic decentralised society pictured by technology optimists at the end of the last century, an oligopoly of private entities controls the exchange of online information and provide services which are increasingly critical for society at large as public utilities.[7] As already mentioned in Chapter 1, the global pandemic has revealed to what extent the services offered by these actors constitute critical bricks of daily life. As such, the platform-based regulation of the Internet has prevailed over the community-based model.[8]

Online platforms play a crucial role not only in providing products and services which are increasingly relevant but also in ensuring the enforcement of public policies online. The activity of content moderation and the enforcement of the right to be forgotten online are only two examples illustrating how public actors rely on online platforms to perform regulatory tasks in the field of content and data.[9] Online platforms enjoy a broad margin of discretion in deciding how to implement these functions. For instance, the decision to remove and consequently delete a video from YouTube is a clear interference with the user's right to freedom of expression but could also preserve other fundamental rights such as their right to privacy. However, this 'delegation' of responsibilities is not the only concern at stake. By virtue of the governance of their digital spaces, online platforms also perform autonomous quasi-public functions without the need to rely on the oversight of a public authority, such as for the definition and enforcement of their Terms of Services (ToS) by relying on the governance of the technological

[6] Rosa Hartmut, *Social Acceleration: A New Theory of Modernity* (Columbia University Press 2013); John G. Palfrey, 'Four Phases of Internet Regulation' (2010) 77(3) Social Research 981.

[7] K. Sabeel Rahman, 'The New Utilities: Private Power, Social Infrastructure, and the Revival of the Public Utility Concept' (2018) 39 Cardozo L. Rev. 1621; Alex Moazed and Nicholas L. Johnson, *Modern Monopolies: What It Takes to Dominate the 21st Century Economy* (St Martin's Press 2016); Robin Mansell and Michele Javary, 'Emerging Internet Oligopolies: A Political Economy Analysis' in Arthur S. Miller and Warren J. Samuels (eds.), *An Institutionalist Approach to Public Utilities Regulation* (Michigan State University Press 2002).

[8] Orly Lobel, 'The Law of the Platforms' (2016) 101 Minnesota Law Review 87.

[9] Niva Elkin-Koren and Eldar Haber, 'Governance by Proxy: Cyber Challenges to Civil Liberties' (2017) 82(1) Brooklyn Law Review 105.

architecture of their digital spaces.[10] In both cases, online platforms freely govern the relationship with their communities. They enforce and balance individual fundamental rights by implementing automated decision-making processes outside any constitutional safeguard.

This situation could not be seen as problematic from a constitutional standpoint. Rather, it could be considered as the expression of private freedoms. Given the lack of any regulation, platforms as private actors are not required to care about fundamental rights or other constitutional values. Despite multiple incentives such as corporate social responsibility, platforms are primarily driven by the maximisation of profits. This expression of freedom would not raise a constitutional concern as long as there are public safeguards to, eventually, limit the power which private actors exercise on fundamental rights and democratic values. This is not the case when looking at platforms shaping individual fundamental rights according to their legal, economic and ethical framework. When economic freedoms turn into forms of private powers, the lack of regulation translating constitutional principles into binding norms could lead to troubling challenges for democratic values such as transparency and the rule of law. The setting, enforcement and balancing of fundamental rights and freedoms in the algorithmic society is increasingly privatised and compete with constitutional standards of protection on a global scale. The consolidation of autonomous areas of powers extending their private rationality driven by private incentives is one of the primary calls for action for European digital constitutionalism to preserve democratic values from the influence of market dynamics.

Within this framework, this chapter highlights the reasons for the turning of online platforms' freedoms into more extensive forms of private power. Understanding the characteristics of platform power is critical to understand the remedies mitigating this constitutional challenge. Therefore, this chapter analyses the two interrelated forms through which platforms exercise powers in the digital environment: delegated and autonomous powers. The first part of the chapter

[10] Lawrence Lessig, *Code: And Other Laws of Cyberspace. Version 2.0* (Basic Books 2006); Tarleton Gillespie, 'The Relevance of Algorithms' in Tarleton Gillespie, Pablo J. Boczkowski and Kirsten A. Foot (eds.), *Media Technologies: Essays on Communication, Materiality, and Society* (MIT Press 2014); Helen Nissenbaum, 'From Preemption to Circumvention: If Technology Regulates, Why Do We Need Regulation (and Vice Versa)?' (2011) 26 Berkley Technology Law Journal 1367.

analyses the reasons for the governance shift from public to private actors in the digital environment. The second part examines delegated powers in the field of content and data while the third part focuses on the exercise of autonomous private powers competing with public authority.

3.2 The Governance Shift

In the last twenty years, global trends have underlined different patterns of convergence,[11] usually named 'globalisation' where the state-centric model has started to lose its power.[12] The decay of national sovereignty and territorial borders is represented by 'a world in which jurisdictional borders collapse, and in which goods, services, people and information "flow across seamless national borders"'.[13] This transformation has led to limits of states' control,[14] struggling with the rise of 'global law' to define a meta-legal system where different organisations and entities produce and shape norms with extraterritorial implications beyond the state.[15]

Constitutions traditionally embody the values and principles to which a specific community decides to adhere and respect. They represent an expression of the social contract between public power and citizens. Constitutions have seen the light in different contexts through different forms of constituent powers.[16] Nevertheless, it is possible to underline the intimate relationship between constitutions and certain areas of space (i.e. territory) over which the sovereign power is exercised and limited. The relationship between (constitutional) law and space is intricate. The law stands on a certain territorial space and relies on political processes legitimising its creation. Formally, outside the domestic legal framework, there are not any other legitimised binding forces over a certain territory unless authorised by the legal framework itself. Substantially, the law is only one of the systems influencing

[11] Neil Walker, *Intimations of Global Law* (Cambridge University Press 2015).

[12] Eric C. Ip, 'Globalization and the Future of the Law of the Sovereign State' (2010) 8(3) International Journal of Constitutional Law 636.

[13] Ran Hirschl and Ayelet Shachar, 'Spatial Statism' (2019) 17(2) International Journal of Constitutional Law 387.

[14] Saskia Sassen, *Losing Control?: Sovereignty in the Age of Globalization* (Columbia University Press 1996).

[15] Giuliana Ziccardi-Capaldo, *The Pillars of Global Law* (Ashgate 2008).

[16] Mattias Kumm, 'Constituent Power, Cosmopolitan Constitutionalism, and Post-Positivist Law' (2016) 14(3) International Journal of Constitutional Law 2016.

space. By moving from a unitary view of the law to pluralism, it is possible to observe how other systems develop their norms and principles. Therefore, the relationship between law and territory characterising state sovereignty tends to lose its exclusiveness, thus leaving space to the consolidation of another dyadic relationship: norms and spaces.

As already underlined in Chapter 1, this twofold-poietic relationship is based on the idea that the law is not a monolith but interacts with other social systems. Although these systems tend to be normatively closed since they autonomously develop their rules internally, however, they are cognitively open and influenced by other systems externally.[17] This form of autopoiesis leads to look at the law not just as the outcome of only legitimated political structure in a certain territory but as one of the fragments composing the constitutional puzzle on a global scale.[18]

An interesting example of this phenomenon can be found in the digital environment or the so-called cyberspace. At the end of the last century, Johnson and Post wrote that '[c]yberspace radically undermines the relationship between legally significant (online) phenomena and physical location'.[19] This is why the cyberspace was considered a self-regulatory environment where bottom-up regulation replaces top-down rules by public authorities lacking any power, effects, legitimacy and notice. Besides, unlike top-down norms affected by a high degree of rigidity and uniformity, bottom-up rules ensure more flexibility. Therefore, self-regulation was considered the way to provide a better regulatory framework than centralised rulemaking.[20]

These positions, representing the gap between law and space, are one of the reasons for the the positions firmly denying the idea of cyberspace as a new 'world' outside the influence of sovereign

[17] Gunther Teubner, *Law as an Autopoietic System* (Blackwell 1993).

[18] Gunther Teubner, *Constitutional Fragments: Societal Constitutionalism and Globalization* (Oxford University Press 2012).

[19] David R. Johnson and David Post, 'Law and Borders: The Rise of Law in Cyberspace' (1996) 48(5) Stanford Law Review 1367.

[20] I. Trotter Hardy, 'The Proper Legal Regime for "Cyberspace"' (1994) 55 University of Pittsburgh Law Review 993.

states.[21] Territorial boundaries are known for their ability to define limited areas where states can exercise their sovereignty. In the case of constitutions, these legal sources provide the rules and the principles of a certain group of people in a certain sovereign space. Inside a specific territory, people are expected to comply with the applicable law in that area. The digital environment is not outside this constitutional framework. Rather than a 'lawless place', states have shown their ability to impose their sovereignty, especially by regulating network architecture.[22] According to Reidenberg, the architecture of the cyberspace prescribes its rules constituting the basis of the digital regulation, while also providing instruments of regulation. [23] In the case of China, the adoption of the 'Great Firewall' is one of the most evident examples of how states can express their sovereign powers over the Internet by regulating the network's architectural dimension.[24] Precisely, one of the ways to express powers in the digital environment lies in the regulation of the online architecture.[25]

Nonetheless, although public authorities can exercise their sovereign powers over the digital environment within their territories, at the same time, other actors contribute to producing their norms in turn. It is not by chance that scholars identified a 'trend toward self-regulation'.[26] More specifically, this autopoietic trend in the cyberspace also results from the code's architecture that contributes to defining the constitutional norms of the digital environment. As underlined by

21 Joseph H. Sommer, 'Against Cyberlaw' (2000) 15 Berkeley Technology Law Journal 1145; Jack L. Goldsmith, 'Against Cyberanarchy' (1999) 40 University of Chicago Law Occasional Paper 1; Andrew Shapiro, 'The Disappearance of Cyberspace and the Rise of Code' (1998) 8 Seton Hall Constitutional Law Journal 703; Tim Wu, 'Cyberspace Sovereignty? The Internet and the International Systems' (1997) 10(3) Harvard Law Journal 647.

22 Lawrence Lessig and Paul Resnick, 'Zoning Speech on the Internet: A Legal and Technical Model' (1998) 98 Michigan Law Review 395; Jack L. Goldsmith, 'The Internet and the Abiding Significance of Territorial Sovereignty' (1998) 5 Indiana Journal of Global Legal Studies 474; Joel R. Reidenberg, 'Governing Networks and Rule-Making Cyberspace' (1996) 45 Emory Law Journal 911.

23 Joel R. Reidenberg, 'Lex Informatica: The Formulation of Information Policy Rules through Technology' (1997–8) 76 Texas Law Review 553.

24 Jonathan Zittrain and Benjamin Edelman, 'Empirical Analysis of Internet Filtering in China' (2003) Harvard Law School Public Law Research Paper No. 62.

25 Lessig (n. 10); Francesca Musiani, 'Network Architecture as Internet Governance' (2013) 2(4) Internet Policy Review https://policyreview.info/node/208/pdf accessed 21 November 2021.

26 Jack L. Goldsmith, 'The Internet, Conflicts of Regulation and International Harmonization' in Christoph Engel (ed.), *Governance of Global Networks in the Light of Differing Local Values* 197 (Nomos 2000).

Sassen, '[p]rivate digital networks are also making possible forms of power other than the distributed power made possible by public digital networks'.[27] Likewise, Perrit underlines the dispersion of governance in the cyberspace among a variety of public and private institutions.[28]

Therefore, understanding the overlapping points among social systems becomes crucial to understand the relationship of power in the digital environment. Unlike the static vision of the 'pathetic dot',[29] public and private actors are 'active dots' since they contribute to defining their rules and express regulatory powers over social systems.[30] The relationship of power in the cyberspace is more complicated than it appears at first glance. There are different micro-communities which are isolated and independently interact without knowing each other.[31] However, there are some points in the network where communities overlap. In those places, it is possible to observe the exercise of powers over the information flow. Examples of these points are Internet service providers, search engines such as Google, social network platforms such as Facebook or Twitter, governments, and other private organisations. All these actors participate in shaping the environment where communities meet creating rooms for sharing values and ideas. As underlined by Greenleaf, regulating the architecture of the cyberspace is not a neutral activity but reflects the values of its governors.[32]

Notwithstanding all the actors contribute to shaping the overall picture, nodes have not the same influence on the network. Some dots in the network play the role of gatekeepers,[33] affecting the structure of the cyberspace more than others. According to Network Gatekeeper

[27] Saskia Sassen, 'On the Internet and Sovereignty' (1998) 5 Indiana Journal of Global Legal Studies 545, 551.

[28] Henry H. Perritt, 'Cyberspace Self-Government: Town Hall Democracy or Rediscovered Royalism?' (1997) 12 Berkeley Technology Law Journal 413.

[29] Lawrence Lessig, 'The New Chicago School' (1998) 27(2) The Journal of Legal Studies 661.

[30] Andrew Murray, *The Regulation of Cyberspace* (Routledge 2007).

[31] Cass R. Sunstein, *Republic.com 2.0* (Princeton University Press 2007).

[32] Graham Greenleaf, 'An Endnote on Regulating Cyberspace: Architecture vs Law?' (1998) 2(2) University of New South Wales Law Journal 593.

[33] Karine Barzilai-Nahon, 'Toward a Theory of Network Gatekeeping: A Framework for Exploring Information Control' (2008) 59(9) Journal of the American Society for Information Science and Technology 1493.

Theory's scholars, '[a]ll nodes are not created equal. Nodes vary in their accessibility, their efficacy, the other nodes they can influence and how that influence is exerted. ... The capacity of a node to influence or regulate depends in large part upon its resources broadly defined to include a wide range of forms of capital in the Bourdieuian sense'.[34] The node's structure plays a fundamental role in the functioning of societies. Briefly, this model does not consider the individual as isolated in a specific environment, but every subject is part of a node which has the power to govern the network. Nodes do not have the same dimension or the same degree of development but, as centres of power, they share some common features: a strategy to govern (mentalities), modalities to govern (technologies), a definition of funds (resources) and a structure (institutions).[35]

States can be an example of powerful nodes. Governments define the strategy and modalities to govern, choose the resources needed to make them effective while also relying on an institutional structure to execute decisions. This model can also be applied to other entities. Some actors can exercise a stronger influence over the structure of the cyberspace than other dots. In other words, by virtue of their 'gravity', some actors, or nodes, in the network can attract other active dots shaping online communities and, as a result, the entire network.[36] These actors are usually called macro-nodes or gatekeepers.[37] In other words, these actors mediate in a horizontal manner among spaces, for example, the state, the market and society.[38] For instance, governments are powerful actors influencing and attracting other nodes. However, the influence of nodes is not always equal. In states with a high degree of public intervention in the Internet sector like China or the Arabic states, these nodes can exercise more influence than constitutional democracies where public restrictions need to be justified and based on the rule of law. Online platforms are another example of powerful nodes which can impose their rules over the digital environment by defining and enforcing their standards on a global scale. The different weight of

[34] Scott Burris, Peter Drahos and Clifford Shearing, 'Nodal Governance' (2005) 30 Australian Journal of Legal Philosophy 30.

[35] Less Johnston and Clifford Shearing, *Governing Security. Explorations in Policing and Justice* (Routledge 2003).

[36] Andrew Murray, 'Nodes and Gravity in Virtual Space' (2011) 5(2) Legisprudence 195.

[37] Emily B. Laidlaw, 'A Framework for Identifying Internet Information Gatekeepers' (2012) 24(3) International Review of Law, Computers & Technology 263.

[38] Julia Black, 'Constitutionalising Self-Regulation' (1996) 59(1) The Modern Law Review 24.

nodes confirms that communities are dynamic concepts whose evolution is the consequence of the relations between systems expressing different degree of powers.

Despite the ability of these systems to create their spaces, their rules are not generated outside any logic but are influenced by other forces including (constitutional) legal norms. It is precisely when constitutionalism overcomes state boundaries and penetrates the transnational context, including the private sector, that it loses a state-centric perspective and leads to processes of 'constitutionalisation without the state',[39] or beyond the state.[40] According to Teubner, this process cannot be understood just from the perspective of traditional public institutions but it can be considered as the expression of different autonomous subsystems of the global society.[41] In the case of the digital environment, social, technical and legal processes intertwine, with the result that the governance of these spaces results from the clash of different rationalities where the architecture constitutes the paradigm of power.

The scope of the norms produced by public and private actors is not equal across the globe but is affected by the legal environment in which these norms are created. It is not by chance that these kinds of norms tend to flourish in liberal democracies since these systems are characterised by general tolerance for pluralism and the principle of equality. On the contrary, these self-autonomous systems are weaker in authoritarian regimes where tolerance is replaced by instruments of control and surveillance.

The constitutional asymmetry among the approaches of states to the digital environment is not the only relevant point. New actors operating in the digital environment such as online platforms enjoy new areas of power deriving not just from a mix of business opportunities and technologies,[42] but also from the openness of democracies oriented to digital liberalism which has left these actors accumulating powers. While authoritarian models of governance aim to control and monitor online activities, on the opposite side, democratic models tend to digital

[39] Gunther Teubner, 'Societal Constitutionalism: Alternatives to State-Centred Constitutional Theory?' in Christian Joerges, Inger-Johanne Sand and Gunther Teubner (eds.), *Transnational Governance and Constitutionalism* 3, 8 (Hart 2004).

[40] Nico Krisch, *Beyond Constitutionalism: The Pluralist Structure of Postnational Law* (Oxford University Press 2010).

[41] Ibid.

[42] Nicolas Suzor, *Lawless: The Secret Rules That Govern Our Digital Lives* (Cambridge University Press 2019).

liberalism by nature in order to respect private freedoms and promote economic and social growth.

Nonetheless, as analysed in Chapter 2, this approach devoted to digital liberalism has reduced the influences of states on the private actors which have been able to develop their system of governance by relying on constitutional freedoms. A new phase of liberalism based on a fundamental transformation towards privatisation and deregulation has triggered the development of a new space of power operating in the digital environment.[43] In other words, legal tolerance characterising constitutional democracies has played a crucial role in defining the boundaries of platform geography as a space where online platforms self-generate their rules on a global scale. This process could be described not only just by 'the annihilation of law by space',[44] but also as 'the annihilation of law by law'. Merging the socio-legal and constitutional perspective, this phenomenon can be considered as expressing the rise of civil constitutions on a global scale.[45]

In order to better understand how the shift of powers from public to private actors primarily concerns constitutional democracies, the next subsections focus on two constitutional asymmetries. The first concerns the relationship between democratic and authoritarian models of digital governance while the second focuses on the asymmetry between democratic and platform governance.

3.2.1 The First Constitutional Asymmetry

The constitutional asymmetry between liberal and illiberal models of governance provides a first angle to understand the challenges raised by private powers for constitutional democracies. Particularly in countries where forms of surveillance and control over information are diffused, like China and the Arab states,[46] the Internet has been subject to public controls leading to the monitoring of data,[47] or to Internet shutdowns.[48] States around the world have not taken the

[43] Joshua Barkan, 'Law and the Geographic Analysis of Economic Globalization' (2011) 35 (5) Progress in Human Geography 589.

[44] Bruce D'Arcus, 'Extraordinary Rendition, Law and the Spatial Architecture of Rights' (2014) 13 ACME: An International E-Journal for Critical Geographies 79.

[45] Teubner (n. 39), 3.

[46] Barney Warf, 'Geographies of Global Internet Censorship' (2011) 76 GeoJournal 1.

[47] Anupam Chander and Uyen P. Le, 'Data Nationalism' (2015) 64(3) Emory Law Journal 677.

[48] Giovanni De Gregorio and Nicole Stremlau, 'Internet Shutdowns and the Limits of Law' (2020) 14 International Journal of Communication 4224.

same road towards a free-market approach to the Internet which Johnson and Post identified as the solution for the governance of the cyberspace.[49] While a liberal approach became the standard across the Atlantic at the end of the last century, illiberal regimes have shown how public actors can regulate the digital environment, thus confirming the paternalistic positions of scholars who have criticised the libertarian approach,[50] and considered network architecture as the primary source of regulatory powers.[51]

Unlike democratic systems considering the Internet as an instrument to foster fundamental freedoms and rights, primarily freedom of expression, authoritative or illiberal regimes have shown less concern in censoring the digital environment.[52] In this case, Internet censorship is merely a political decision to pursue political purposes prevailing over any other conflicting rights and interest with the regime. The central authority aims to protect its power by dissolving any personal freedoms and other constitutional values and principles such as the rule of law.[53] These models do not deny constitutional principles and limits but manipulate them as an instrument to pursue political purposes transforming political constitutions into a façade.[54] Within this framework, the lack of pluralism and solid democratic institutions does not promote any form of freedom whose boundaries can extend so broadly to undermine the central authority. In the lack of any safeguard and tolerance for pluralism, censoring the digital environment is not a matter of freedom and right any longer, but is equated to other discretionary measures implemented for political purposes. Therefore, it should not come as a surprise if the first aim of authoritarian and illiberal regimes is to suppress or control the degree of pluralism to avoid any interference with the central authority.

49 Johnson and Post (n. 19).

50 Jack Goldsmith and Tim Wu, *Who Controls the Internet? Illusions of a Borderless World* (Oxford University Press 2006).

51 Lessig (n. 10); Reidenberg (n. 23).

52 Justin Clark and others, 'The Shifting Landscape of Global Internet Censorship' (2017) Berkman Klein Center for Internet & Society Research Publication http://nrs.harvard.edu/urn-3:HUL.InstRepos:33084425 accessed 20 November 2021; Ronald Deibert and others, *Access Denied: The Practice and Policy of Global Internet Filtering* (MIT Press 2008).

53 Tom Ginsburg and Alberto Simpser (eds.), *Constitutions in Authoritarian Regimes* (Cambridge University Press 2014).

54 Giovanni Sartori, 'Constitutionalism: A Preliminary Discussion' (1962) 56(4) The American Political Science Review 853.

The Internet is a paradigmatic enabler of pluralism which these systems aim to suppress or limit. Digital technologies provide instruments to express fundamental rights and freedoms and particularly civil and political rights which could potentially undermine the central authority. The example of Internet shutdowns before elections or during protests or less intrusive forms of digital censorship like the suppression of false content have demonstrated how governments implement these practices without providing explanations or relying on a general legal basis.[55]

In the opposite scenario, liberal and democratic models are open environments for pluralism. The expression 'liberal democracy' evokes values and principles such as liberty, equality, liberalism and participation rights. On the contrary, as already underlined, authoritarianism is based on narratives based on public interests, paternalism and pragmatic decision-making. On the opposite, the respect of fundamental rights and freedoms is at the basis of democratic systems. Without protecting equality, freedom of expression or assembly, it would not be possible to enjoy a democratic society. This shows why fundamental rights and democracy are substantially intertwined. Because of this substantive relationship, fundamental rights cannot easily be exploited to pursue unaccountable political ends.[56]

This first constitutional asymmetry has led to the polarisation of the models to govern the digital environment. While authoritarian and illiberal systems have focused on developing their digital political economy by controlling the market and platforms as in the case of China,[57] democratic systems have followed a liberal approach to strike a fair balance between different rights and interests at stake, primarily the freedom to conduct business of online platforms or freedom of expression. The digital environment is a crucial vehicle to foster fundamental rights and freedoms, especially through the services offered by private actors such as social media and search engines. Intervening in this market requires constitutional democracies to assess not only the drawbacks for innovation but also the potential disproportionate interference with economic freedoms and fundamental rights.

55 Ben Wagner, 'Understanding Internet Shutdowns: A Case Study from Pakistan' (2018) 12 International Journal of Communication 3917.

56 Susan Marks, *The Riddle of All Constitutions: International Law, Democracy, and the Critique of Ideology* (Oxford University Press 2004).

57 Yun Wen, *The Huawei Model: The Rise of China's Technology Giant* (University of Illinois Press 2020).

The openness to legal pluralism is one of the reasons for the asymmetry among models of internet governance. This gap also provides clues to understand that the rise of digital private powers primarily affects constitutional democracies. Democratic systems tend to ensure a political and institutional environment where private actors can potentially consolidate their powers. On the opposite, in authoritarian countries, there is not enough space for the private sector not only to exercise freedoms but also to turn this area into forms of powers.

The liberal framework driving constitutional democracies across the Atlantic has led to the consolidation of private powersin governing the flow of information online and developing instruments of surveillance based on the processing of a vast amount of personal data. The spread of disinformation and the misuse of data are only two examples of the challenges raised by the role of private actors in the digital environment.[58] As underlined in the next subsection, these challenges are primarily the result of a constitutional asymmetry between public and private powers. While constitutional democracies are not free to restrict rights and freedoms by imposing their authority without balancing conflicting interests, private actors perform their business without being bound by constitutional limits given the lack of regulation.

3.2.2 The Second Constitutional Asymmetry

Governing the Internet is far from simple for constitutional democracies. Democratic systems cannot freely pursue their goals, but they are (positively) stuck in respect of the principle of the rule of law as well as the protection of fundamental rights and freedoms. The respect of these constitutional values is crucial to safeguard democratic values. For instance, from a European constitutional standpoint, disproportionate measures to regulate the Internet are not tolerated. In the case of online platforms, Member States are required to respect the freedom to conduct business as recognised by the Charter,[59] and the Treaties protecting fundamental freedoms, especially the freedom to provide services.[60]

[58] Giovanni Pitruzzella and Oreste Pollicino, *Hate Speech and Disinformation: A European Constitutional Perspective* (Bocconi University Press 2020).

[59] Charter of Fundamental Rights of the European Union (2012) OJ C 326/391, Art. 16.

[60] Consolidated version of the Treaty on the Functioning of the European Union (2012) OJ C 326/47, Arts. 56–62.

Each attempt to regulate online platforms should comply with the test established by the Charter setting a test based on the principle of legality, legitimacy and proportionality.[61] Therefore, in order to impose limitations on platform freedoms, it is necessary to comply with this test, which does not only consider the limitation of platform freedoms but also the impact of regulation on individual rights such as freedom of expression, privacy and data protection.

The ban on abuse of rights complements this system. According to the Charter, 'nothing in this Charter shall be interpreted as implying any right to engage in any activity or to perform any act aimed at the destruction of any of the rights and freedoms recognised in this Charter or at their limitation to a greater extent than is provided for herein'.[62] Therefore, the Union cannot recognise absolute protection just to economic freedoms or fundamental rights. Instead, it is necessary to ensure that the enjoyment of fundamental rights does not lead to the destruction of other constitutional values. As a result, Member States need to strike a fair balance between platform freedoms and individual rights, thus respecting the core protection of these constitutional values.

Looking at the other side of the Atlantic, online platforms enjoy even broader protection since the constitutional ground to perform their business does not merely lies in economic freedoms but also in the right to free speech as recognised by the First Amendment. Precisely, the US Supreme Court applies a strict scrutiny test according to which any such law should be narrowly tailored to serve a compelling state interest, as the case *Reno* v. *ACLU* already underlined at the end of the last century.[63] Despite the differences between the two models, in both cases, online platforms enjoy a 'constitutional safe area' whose boundaries can be restricted only by a disproportionate prominence over other fundamental rights or legitimate interests. Despite the passing of years and opposing positions, this liberal approach has been reiterated more recently in *Packingham* v. *North Carolina*.[64] In the words of

61 Charter (n. 59), Art. 52.

62 Ibid., Art. 54.

63 Reno v. American Civil Liberties Union, 521 U.S. 844 (1997). Oreste Pollicino and Marco Bassini, 'Free Speech, Defamation and the Limits to Freedom of Expression in the EU: A Comparative Analysis' in Andrej Savin and Jan Trzaskowski (eds.), *Research Handbook on EU Internet Law* 508 (Edward Elgar 2014).

64 *Packingham* v. *North Carolina* (2017) 582 US ___.

Justice Kennedy: 'It is cyberspace – the "vast democratic forums of the Internet" in general, and social media in particular'.[65] Therefore, social media enjoy a safe constitutional area of protection under the First Amendment, which, in the last twenty years, has constituted a fundamental ban on any regulatory attempt to regulate online speech.[66]

Therefore, when addressing the challenges raised by the algorithmic society, constitutional democracies cannot just rely on general justifications or political statements arguing the need to protect public security or other public interests. In order to restrict fundamental rights and freedoms, constitutional democracies are required to comply with constitutional procedures and safeguards. Furthermore, the respect of other constitutional rights plays a crucial role in limiting the possibility to recognise absolute protection to some values rather than others and promote the development of pluralism.

Historically, the first bills of rights were designed to restrict the power of public actors rather than interfere with the private sphere. As a result, constitutional provisions have been conceived, on the one hand, as a limit to the power of the state and, on the other hand, as a source of positive obligation for public actors to protect constitutional rights and liberties. Within this framework, the primary threats to individual rights and freedoms do not derive from the exercise of unaccountable freedoms by private actors but from public powers.

The increasing areas of power enjoyed by transnational corporations such as online platforms challenge this constitutional paradigm. The rapid expansion of new digital technologies combined with the choice of constitutional democracies to adopt a liberal approach regarding the digital environment are two of the reasons which have promoted the rise of online platforms as private powers.

Neoliberal ideas rejecting market intervention have paved the way towards a self-regulatory environment based on individual autonomy and freedom from public interferences. The application of neoliberal approaches to the digital environment have led to neglecting the critical role of public actors to ensure democratic principles against the

[65] Ibid.

[66] See, for example, Reno (n. 63); *Ashcroft* v. *Free Speech Coalition* (2002) 535 US 234; *Aschroft* v. *American Civil Liberties Union* (2002) 535 US 564.

consolidation of actors imposing their powers in the digital age.[67] Particularly, the consolidation of online platforms come from the exploitation of the same neoliberal narrative that constitutional democracies aim to ensure to promote pluralism and freedom.

While illiberal regimes have shown their ability to address this situation maintaining their power by implementing instruments of control and surveillance, the laissez-faire approach of democratic systems has led to the emergence of private powers underlining, de facto, a second constitutional asymmetry in the digital environment. In this case, given the lack of any regulation, online platforms can regulate their digital spaces without the obligation to protect constitutional values. Like illiberal regimes, platforms escape from constitutional obligations to pursue their business purposes.

Despite these challenges, instead of regulating online platforms to preclude private actors from expanding their powers, in the last decades, constitutional democracies have indirectly delegated public functions to online platforms. These observations just introduce some of the reasons leading private actors to expand their regulatory influence in the digital age and develop autonomous forms of power. In order to understand this situation from a constitutional perspective, the next sections address the power of online platforms to exercise delegated and autonomous functions.

3.3 Delegated Exercise of Quasi-Public Powers Online

The consolidation of platform powers has not been by chance, following the evolution of the digital environment. Law and policies have contributed to supporting the consolidation of platform capitalism. Online platforms have not just exploited the opportunities of digital technologies. The rise of digital private powers can primarily be considered the result of an indirect delegation of public functions. The shift from public to private in the digital environment is not an isolated case, but it is the result of a general tendency towards the transfer of functions or public tasks from lawmakers to specialised actors both in the public and the private sector.[68]

[67] Neil W. Netanel, 'Cyberspace Self-Governance: A Skeptical View from the Liberal Democratic Theory' (2000) 88 California Law Review 401.

[68] Jody Freeman and Martha Minow (eds.), *Government by Contract Outsourcing and American Democracy* (Harvard University Press 2009).

The result of this complexity is part of a larger system of delegation which does not involve anymore the relationship between the lawmaker and the Government (legislative-executive) but also two new branches, respectively public bodies such as agencies (fourth branch) and private entities dealing with delegated public tasks (fifth branch). The delegation of public functions is not just a unitary phenomenon. It can include agreements between public and private actors based on public-private partnership schemes allowing private entities to provide goods or services.[69] The cases of smart cities or governmental services are clear examples of the shift of responsibilities from the public sector to private entities through instruments of public procurement.[70] In other cases, the delegation of public functions consists of the creation of new (private or public) entities to perform public tasks such as the provisions of products and services or the support to rule-making activities. In this case, the establishment of new government corporation or agency is one of the most evident examples.[71]

More than fifteen years ago, this shift of power from public to private actors in the digital environment captured the attention of scholars who started to think how public law can be extended to a multi-stakeholder and decentralised system like the Internet. Boyle already wondered whether the Internet would have led to a transformation challenging basic assumptions not only concerning economics but also constitutional and administrative law.[72] As reported by Kaplan in the aftermath of the ICANN's foundation, Zittrain referred to a 'constitutional convention in a sense'.[73] At that time, it was clear that ICANN was in a position of governing the Internet architecture in 'a position to exercise a substantial degree of power over the supposedly ungovernable world of the Internet'.[74] The case of ICANN has been the first example of the delegation to agency or other entities of regulatory powers over the digital environment. Froomkin underlined how, in the case of ICANN, the

69 Albert Sánchez Graells, *Public Procurement and the EU Competition Rules* (Hart 2015).

70 Sofia Ranchordas and Catalina Goanta, 'The New City Regulators: Platform and Public Values in Smart and Sharing Cities' (2020) 36 Computer Law and Security Review 105375.

71 Marta Simoncini, *Administrative Regulation Beyond the Non-Delegation Doctrine: A Study on EU Agencies* (Hart 2018).

72 James Boyle, 'A Nondelegation Doctrine for the Digital Age?' (2000) 50 Duke Law Journal 5.

73 Carl S. Kaplan, 'A Kind of Constitutional Convention for the Internet' The New York Times (23 October 1998) www.nytimes/com/library/tech/98/10/cyber/cyberlaw/23law .html accessed 21 November 2021.

74 Boyle (n. 72).

Government was violating the Administrative Procedures Act (APA) and going beyond the non-delegation doctrine coming from the interpretation of Article 1 of US Constitution and the separation of powers principle.[75] Likewise, Weinberg underlined how ICANN played the role of a public authority since 'a private entity wielding what amounts to public power may be subjected to constitutional restraints designed to ensure that its power is exercised consistently with democratic values'.[76]

These challenges had already unveiled some of the primary concerns that are relevant for examining platform powers. At the beginning of this century, scholars have defined the cooperation between public actors and online intermediaries as the 'invisible handshake',[77] based on the idea that public actors rely on private actors online to pursue their aims online outside constitutional safeguards. For instance, the use of online intermediaries for law enforcement purposes could support public tasks by mitigating enforcement complexity in the digital environment. In this case, online intermediaries would provide the infrastructural capabilities to pursue public policies online since they govern the digital spaces where information flows online, no matter if it crosses national borders. In other words, online intermediaries, as other private entities, were considered an instrument for public actors to ensure the enforcement of public policies rather than a threat leading to the rise of new powers online. The size of the infrastructure they provide is of particular interest for public authorities that are interested in accessing information to pursue public tasks.

When focusing on the digital environment, rather than a trend towards agencification, public actors have recognised the role of online intermediaries in enforcing public policies online. At the beginning of this century, Reidenberg underlined the dependency of the public sector on online intermediaries. He defined three modalities to ensure the enforcement of legal rules online: network intermediaries, network engineering and technological instruments.[78] Regarding the first approach, Reidenberg explained how public actors can rely on online platforms to ensure the enforcement of public policies online. States do

[75] A. Michael Froomkin, 'Wrong Turn in Cyberspace: Using ICANN to Route Around the APA and the Constitution' (2000) 50 Duke Law Journal 17.

[76] Jonathan Weinberg, 'ICANN and the Problem of Legitimacy' (2000) 50 Duke Law Journal 187, 217.

[77] Micheal D. Birnhack and Niva Elkin-Koren, 'The Invisible Handshake: The Reemergence of the State in the Digital Environment' (2003) 8 Virginia Journal of Law & Technology 1.

[78] Joel R. Reidenberg, 'States and Internet enforcement' (2004) 1 University of Ottawa Law & Techonology Journal 213.

not own the resources to pursue any wrongdoer acting in the digital environment. Already at the beginning of this century, the spread of peer-to-peer and torrent mechanisms unveiled the complexities of investigating, prosecuting and sanctioning millions of infringers every day. In such situations, online providers can function as 'gateway points' to identify and block illicit behaviours acting directly on the network structure. In this way, governments would regain control over the Internet using platforms as proxies to reaffirm their national sovereignty online.[79] In the last years, different regulatory models have arisen, thus moving from traditional approaches like 'command and control' to other models,[80] such as co-regulation, self-regulation and codes of conduct.[81] The choice for models outside the control of public actors comes from expertise increasingly found outside the government.[82]

The shift of power from the public to the private sector can be interpreted not only as the consequence of economic and technical forces but also as the result of the changing influence of constitutional democracies in the field of Internet governance.[83] The delegation of public functions to online platforms is linked to the opportunity to rely on entities governing transnational areas such as the digital environment. Governments have increasingly started to rely on online platforms, for instance, to offer public services or improve their quality through digital and automated solutions like in the case of the urban environment.[84] However, this cooperation leads, firstly, to tech companies to hold a vast amount of information coming from the public sector, including personal data. Secondly, since public actors are increasingly technologically dependent on private actors, platforms can impose their conditions when agreeing on partnerships or other contractual arrangements with public actors. For instance, the use of artificial intelligence developed by private companies and then

79 Elkin-Koren and Haber (n. 9).

80 Ian Brown and Christopher Marsden, *Regulating Code: Good Governance and Better Regulation in the Information Age* (MIT Press 2013).

81 Monroe E. Price and Stefaan G. Verhulst, *Self-Regulation and the Internet* (Kluwer 2004).

82 Dennis D. Hirsch, 'The Law and Policy of Online Privacy: Regulation, Self-Regulation, or Co-Regulation?' (2011) 34 Seattle University Law Review 439.

83 Uta Kohl (ed.), *The Net and the Nation State Multidisciplinary Perspectives on Internet Governance* (Cambridge University Press 2017).

84 Robert Brauneis and Ellen P. Goodman, 'Algorithmic Transparency for the Smart City' (2018) 20 Yale Journal of Law and Technology 103; Lilian Edwards, 'Privacy, Security and Data Protection in Smart Cities: A Critical EU Law Perspective' (2016) 1 European Data Protection Law 26.

implemented by public authorities in welfare programs or criminal justice is another example where the (private) code and the accompanying infrastructure mediate individual rights and public functions.[85] Besides, governments have also forfeited power to private actors providing national services based on digital infrastructure governed by the private sector.[86] In other words, rather than preserving public functions or creating a new administrative body to deal with these areas of power, public actors have considered it more convenient to rely on entities which know how to do their job. Online platforms can indeed influence public policy due to the dependency of the public sector, especially for surveillance purposes, and the interests of citizens to access digital services which otherwise would not be offered by the public sector. The case of online contact tracing of COVID-19 has showed this intimate relationship between public and private actors in the algorithmic society.[87]

Even if online platforms can play a critical role in ensuring the enforcement of policies in the digital environment, delegating public functions to the private sector entails the transfer of power to set the rule of the game through a mix of law and technology. Online platforms can indeed set the technical rules and the degree of transparency of their technologies, thus precluding public actors from exercising any form of oversight. Whether direct or indirect, the delegation of public functions to private actors touches upon some of the most intimate features of constitutional law: the constitutional divide between public and private actors, the separation of power, the principle of rule of law and, even more importantly, the democratic system. Although the gap between public and private actors could be formal at first glance, this distinction involves the core of constitutional law and, especially, how constitutional provisions apply vertically only to public bodies, while private actors are not required to comply with these boundaries given the lack of any regulatory intervention.

[85] Aziz Z. Huq, 'Racial Equity in Algorithmic Criminal Justice' (2019) 68 Duke Law Journal 1043.

[86] Aaron Gregg and Jay Greene, 'Pentagon Awards Controversial $10 Billion Cloud Computing Deal to Microsoft, Spurning Amazon' Washington Post (26 October 2019) www.washingtonpost.com/business/2019/10/25/pentagon-awards-controversial-billion-cloud-computing-deal-microsoft-spurning-amazon/ accessed 22 November 2021.

[87] Teresa Scassa, 'Pandemic Innovation: The Private Sector and the Development of Contact-Tracing and Exposure Notification Apps' (2021) 6(2) Business and Human Rights Journal 352.

This constitutive difference can explain why the transfer of public functions to the private sector is subject to constitutional limits. These boundaries aim to control to what extent lawmakers can transfer or delegate authority to other (public or private) entities and the constitutional safeguards that should apply to avoid a dangerous marginalisation of democratic values in favour of non-accountable logics. These challenges have already emerged in other sectors where financial institutions, telecom companies and other infrastructure own the resources and the means to impose private standards on public values.[88] This concern was already expressed by Brandeis who defined this situation as the 'curse of bigness' to underline the role of corporations and monopolies in the progressive era.[89] However, unlike traditional forms of delegating public functions, online platforms can exercise powers deriving from an indirect form of delegation which is not backed by public safeguards and oversight.

Delegating online platforms to perform public tasks online is not problematic per se. It is the lack of procedural and substantive safeguards that raises constitutional challenges since it leaves the private sector free to consolidate its power. Precisely the idea of a government 'of the people, by the people, for the people' is put under pressure when public functions are left to the discretion of non-accountable private actors establishing standards driven by business interests. Looking at US constitutional law, the ban for the Congress to delegate power 'is a principle universally recognized as vital to the integrity and maintenance of the system of government ordained by the Constitution'.[90] Moving to the European framework, the ECJ has clarified the boundaries of delegation from the Union's institutions to agency and private actors by, de facto, creating a judicial non-delegation doctrine.[91] As observed by the Strasbourg Court, 'the State cannot absolve itself from responsibility by delegating its obligation to private bodies or individuals'.[92] Because 'the fact that a state chooses a form of delegation in which some of its powers are exercised by another body cannot be

88 Tim Wu, *The Curse of Bigness: How Corporate Giants Came to Rule the World* (Atlantic Books 2020).

89 Louis D. Brandeis, 'The Curse of Bigness' in Osmond K. Fraenkel (ed.), *The Curse of Bigness: Miscellaneous Papers of Louis D. Brandeis* (Viking Press 1934).

90 *Field* v. *Clark* 143 US 649 (1892), 692.

91 Robert Schutze, '"Delegated" Legislation in the (New) European Union: A Constitutional Analysis' (2011) 74(5) Modern Law Review 661.

92 *Costello-Roberts* v. *United Kingdom* (1993) 19 EHRR 112 27–8.

decisive for the question of State responsibility . . . ; [t]he responsibility of the respondent State thus continues even after such a transfer'.[93]

This view has not only been questioned by the increasing reliance of public powers on other public bodies such as agencies and independent administrative authorities to face the technocratic reality of the administrative state.[94] It has also been challenged by a general trust in the role of the private sector or rather the belief that digital liberalism would have been the most suitable approach for the digital environment at the end of the last century. Therefore, when delegating public functions to private actors, public safeguards limit the consolidation of unaccountable powers. In other words, the aim of these safeguards is to avoid a dangerous uncertainty resulting from the mix of, quoting Boyle when referring to ICANN, 'public and private, technical harmonization and political policy choice, contractual agency relationship and delegated rulemaker, state actor and private corporation'.[95]

The rise of digital liberalism at the end of the last century has led to a shift of power and responsibility from public actors to the private sector based on technological optimism which, however, given the lack of any safeguard, is misplaced for at least two reasons. Firstly, private actors are not bound by limits to respect constitutional values and principles such as fundamental rights. Therefore, the absence of any regulatory safeguard or incentive leads private actors free to choose how to shape constitutional values based on their business interests. Secondly, even supporting self-regulation leaves the private sector free to impose standards which do not only influence public values but also private entities suffering the exercise of horizontal forms of authority coming from a mix of regulatory, economic and technological factors.

The next subsections underline how public actors have indirectly delegated public functions to online platforms. In the field of content, the analysis focuses on how the liability regime of online intermediaries has played a part in encouraging platforms to moderate content and setting the standard of protection of freedom of expression in the digital environment. The second subsection focuses on the role of European data protection law in entrusting online platforms with discretion on the processing of personal data.

93 *Wos* v. *Poland* (2007) 45 EHRR 28, 72.

94 Gary Lawson, 'The Rise and Rise of the Administrative State' (1994) 107 Harvard Law Review 1231.

95 Boyle (n. 72), 8.

3.3.1 Delegating Powers on Content

The US and European regimes of online intermediaries could be considered examples of delegating public functions in the field of content. The Communications Decency Act,[96] together with the Digital Millennium Copyright Act[97] and the e-Commerce Directive,[98] have not only introduced a special regime of immunity or exemption of liability for online intermediaries, acknowledging, *in abstracto*, their non-involvement as content providers.[99] These instruments have also recognised the power of intermediaries to make decisions on content, thus determining the lawlessness of online speech.

Despite this allocation of power, these systems do not provide any procedural safeguard while nor do they require any administrative or judicial filter determining ex ante whether content is illicit in a specific case. The e-Commerce Directive refers to the protection of freedom of expression only when underlining its functional role to the free movement of information society services,[100] and clarifying that the removal or disabling of access to online content must be undertaken in the observance of the principle of freedom of expression and procedures established for this purpose at national level. It is not by chance if another Recital clarifies that Member States can require service providers to apply 'duties of care' to detect and prevent certain types of illegal activities. These provisions are not binding since they simply play the role of interpretative guidelines for Member States implementing the e-Commerce Directive.[101] Moreover, even if the Recitals of the e-Commerce Directive refer to the need that online intermediaries respect the right to free speech when they moderate content, it is not clear whether this interpretative statement refers to the protection ensured, at that time, by Article 10 of the Convention or, also, to a functional dimension of freedom of expression resulting from the need to ensure the freedom to movement of information society services. This acknowledgement contributes to entrusting online

[96] Communications Decency Act (1996), Section 230(c)(1).

[97] Digital Millennium Copyright Act (1997), Section 512.

[98] Directive 2000/31/EC of the European Parliament and of the Council of 8 June 2000 on certain legal aspects of information society services, in particular electronic commerce, in the Internal Market (2000) OJ L 178/1.

[99] Mariarosaria Taddeo and Luciano Floridi (eds.), *The Responsibilities of Online Service Providers* (Springer 2017).

[100] Ibid., Recital 9.

[101] Guarantees of some Member States.

platforms with the power to enforce and adjudicate disputes in the field of online content based on a standard of protection which is not only unclear but also based on business interests. Therefore, this system of liability has contributed to entrusting online intermediaries with the power to decide how to organise information as well as whether to remove or block content, thus creating the basis for business models based on third-party content sharing with limited risks of secondary liability. Therefore, due to the lack of transparency and accountability safeguards, online platforms are not required to consider the impact of their activities on fundamental rights and democratic values.

Moreover, the notice and takedown approach leads online platforms to perform this function based on the risk to be held liable, thus raising questions around collateral censorship.[102] Since online platforms are run privately, these actors would try to avoid the risks of being sanctioned for non-compliance with this duty by removing or blocking especially content whose illicit nature is not fully evident. The case of disinformation can provide an interesting example. Since it is not always possible to understand whether a false content is unlawful and eventually on which legal basis, this legal uncertainty encourages online platforms to monitor and remove even lawful speech to avoid any risk of liability.[103] This obligation encourages online intermediaries to censor even content whose illicit nature is not clear as a means to avoid economic sanctions.[104] The Strasbourg Court has also underlined this risk which can produce chilling effects for freedom of expression.[105] In other words, online intermediaries, as business actors,

[102] Jack M. Balkin, 'Free Speech and Hostile Environments' (1999) Columbia Law Review 2295.

[103] Oreste Pollicino, Giovanni De Gregorio and Laura Somaini, 'The European Regulatory Conundrum to Face the Rise and Amplification of False Content Online' (2020) 19(1) Global Yearbook of International Law and Jurisprudence 319.

[104] Felix T. Wu, 'Collateral Censorship and the Limits of Intermediary Immunity' (2013) 87 Notre Dame Law Review 293; Seth F. Kreimer, 'Censorship by Proxy: The First Amendment, Internet Intermediaries, and the Problem of the Weakest Link' (2006) 155 University of Pennsylvania Law Review 11; Jack M. Balkin, 'Free Speech and Hostile Environments' (1999) 99 Columbia Law Review 2295.

[105] *Delfi AS* v. *Estonia* (2015); *Magyar Tartalomszolgáltatók Egyesülete and Index.Hu Zrt* v. *Hungary* (2016). According to para 86: 'Such liability may have foreseeable negative consequences on the comment environment of an Internet portal, for example by impelling it to close the commenting space altogether. For the Court, these consequences may have, directly or indirectly, a chilling effect on the freedom of expression on the Internet. This effect could be particularly detrimental to a non-commercial website such as the first applicant'.

would likely focus on minimising this economic risk rather than adopting a fundamental-rights-based approach, thus pushing private interests to prevail over constitutional values

If the moderation of content is not an issue when online intermediaries just perform passive hosting functions, the same trust on private enforcement might be questioned by observing how platforms profit from moderating the content of billions of users on a daily basis. In this case, the role of online platforms is not merely passive in terms of their interest to organise and remove content which is driven by business purposes. It is here that the trust in the market turns into a fear that these actors can influence not only individual rights but also democratic values. Therefore, such delegated activity implies, inter alia, that platforms can take decisions affecting fundamental rights and democratic values.[106]

Even if, as analysed in Chapter 2, the Union has started to limit platform discretion in content moderation, there are still constitutional drawbacks. Firstly, taking decisions on the lawfulness of content is a function traditionally belonging to public authorities. Instead, platforms are called to assess the lawfulness of the content in question to remove it promptly. Given the lack of any regulation of this process, online platforms are free to assess whether expressions are unlawful and make a decision regarding the removal or blocking of online content based on the contractual agreement with users. As a result, this anti-system has led platforms to acquire an increasing influence on the enforcing and balancing of users' fundamental rights. For example, the choice to remove or block defamatory content or hate speech videos interferes with the right to freedom of expression of the users. Likewise, the decision about the need to protect other conflicting rights such as the protection of minors or human dignity is left to the decision of private actors without any public guarantee.

This change of responsibility would also lead to calling for introducing effective and appropriate safeguards to ensure the prevention of unintended removal of lawful content and respect the fundamental rights and democratic values.[107] However, this is not the current situation. As already stressed, the e-Commerce Directive does not provide

[106] Orla Lynskey, 'Regulation by Platforms: The Impact on Fundamental Rights' in Luca Belli and Nicolo Zingales (eds.), *Platform Regulations How Platforms Are Regulated and How They Regulate Us* (FGV Direito Rio 2017); James Grimmelmann, 'Speech Engines' (2014) 98 Minnesota Law Review 868.

[107] e-Commerce Directive (n. 98), Recital 42.

any safeguards limiting platforms' discretion. Obligations are indeed directed to Member States while online platforms, as hosting providers, are just required to remove content once they become aware of their illicit presence online.

Within this framework, as examined in Chapter 5, the primary issue is the lack of any accountability, transparent procedure or redress mechanisms limiting platform power in the field of content. For example, platforms are neither obliged to explain the reasoning of the removal or blocking of online content, nor to provide remedies against their decisions even if they process a vast amount of content. While waiting for the effects of the Digital Services Act,[108] users cannot rely on a horizontal legal remedy against autonomous decisions of online platforms affecting their rights and freedoms. This situation raises concerns even for democratic systems. Delegating online platforms to make decisions on content empowers these private actors to influence public discourse. The case of the deplatforming of the former US president Trump is a paradigmatic example of the power an online platform can exercise on online speech. This issue is also connected to the autonomous powers these private entities can exercise by setting the standard of protection of fundamental rights online, including the right to freedom of expression, which is one of the cornerstones of democracy.

Nonetheless, the expansion of digital private powers does not concern just the field of content. As the next subsection will examine, even in the field of data, the Union has contributed to extending the power of the platform to make decisions based on a risk-based approach.

3.3.2 Delegating Powers on Data

The field of data has also experienced a process of delegation of public functions to the private sector. Unlike the case of content, however, the primary concerns are not related to the lack of safeguards but to the risk-based approach which the Data Protection Directive introduced in 1995.[109] The WP29 stressed the role of a risk-based approach in data

[108] Proposal for a Regulation of the European Parliament and of the Council on a Single Market for Digital Services (Digital Services Act) and amending Directive 2000/31/EC, COM(2020) 825 final.

[109] Directive 95/46/EC of the European Parliament and of the Council of 24 October 1995 on the protection of individuals with regard to the processing of personal data and on the free movement of such data (1995) OJ L 281/31.

protection underlining how risk management is not a new concept in data protection law.[110]

Even the Council of Ministers of the Organisation for Economic Co-operation and Development (OECD) implemented a risk-based approach when revising the Guidelines Governing the Protection of Privacy and Transborder Flows of Personal Data, first adopted in 1980,[111] for instance, concerning the implementation of security measures.[112] According to the Data Protection Directive, security measures must 'ensure a level of security appropriate to the risks represented by the processing and the nature of the data to be protected'.[113] Even more importantly, the assessment of risk was also considered one legal basis for the processing of personal data when the processing was 'necessary for the purposes of the legitimate interest pursued by the controller or by the third party or parties to whom data are disclosed, except where such interests are overridden by the interests for fundamental rights and freedoms of the data subjects'.[114] In both cases, this assessment rested in the hands of the data controller which 'determines the purposes and means of the processing of personal data'. This definition can explain how the governance of personal data is not just determined by public authorities but is also firmly dependent on the choices of the data controller. Unlike these cases, the relevance of risk also extends to Member States through data protection authorities to assess specific risks coming from the processing of personal data.[115]

The GDPR has consolidated this approach by introducing a comprehensive risk-based approach built upon the principle of accountability of the data controller.[116] As underlined in Chapter 2, the principle of accountability requires the controller to prove

[110] Working Party 29, 'Statement on the Role of a Risk-Based Approach in Data Protection Legal Frameworks' (2014) https://ec.europa.eu/justice/article-29/documentation/opinion-recommendation/files/2014/wp218_en.pdf accessed 21 November 2021.

[111] OECD, Guidelines Governing the Protection of Privacy and Transborder Flows of Personal Data (2013).

[112] Christopher Kuner and others, 'Risk Management in Data Protection' (2015) 5(2) International Data Privacy Law 95.

[113] Data Protection Directive (n. 109), Art. 17.

[114] Ibid., Art. 7(f).

[115] Ibid., Art. 20.

[116] Regulation (EU) 2016/679 of the European Parliament and of the Council of 27 April 2016 on the protection of natural persons with regard to the processing of personal data and on the free movement of such data, and repealing Directive 95/46/EC (General Data Protection Regulation) (2016) OJ L 119/1, Art. 5.

compliance with the general principles of the GDPR by establishing safeguards and limitations based on the specific context of the processing, especially on the risks for data subjects. The GDPR modulates the obligation of the data controller according to the specific context in which the processing takes place.[117] As observed by Macenaite, 'risk becomes a new boundary in the data protection field when deciding whether easily to allow personal data processing or to impose additional legal and procedural safeguards in order to shield the relevant data subjects from possible harm'.[118] It would be enough to focus on the norms concerning the Data Protection Impact Assessment,[119] or the appointment of the Data Protection Officer,[120] to understand how the GDPR has not introduced mere obligations to comply but a flexible risk-based approach which leads to different margins of responsibility depending on the context at stake.[121] In other words, the GDPR has led to the merge of a rights-based approach with a risk-based approach based on a case-by-case assessment about the responsibility of data controllers.

However, the risk-based approach leads data controllers to playing a critical role in defining not whether but how to comply with the GDPR. This system entrusts data controllers to decide the appropriate safeguards and procedures which, in a specific context, would be enough to be aligned with the general principles of the GDPR. This approach is also the result of a dynamic definition of the data controller's responsibilities based on the nature, the scope of application, the context and the purpose of the processing, as well as the risks to the individuals' rights and freedoms. On this basis, the data controller is required to implement appropriate technical and organisational measures to guarantee, and be able to demonstrate, that the processing is conducted in accordance with the GDPR.[122] The principles of privacy by

[117] Raphaël Gellert, *The Risk-Based Approach to Data Protection* (Oxford University Press 2020).

[118] Milda Macenaite, 'The "Riskification" of European Data Protection Law through a Two-fold Shift' (2017) 8(3) European Journal of Risk Regulation 506.

[119] GDPR (n. 116), Art. 35.

[120] Ibid., Art. 37.

[121] Raphaël Gellert, 'Understanding the Notion of Risk in the General Data Protection Regulation' (2018) 34 Computer Law & Security Review 279; Claudia Quelle, 'Enhancing Compliance under the General Data Protection Regulation: The Risky Upshot of the Accountability- and Risk-based Approach' (2018) 9(3) European Journal of Risk Regulation 502.

[122] GDPR (n. 116), Art. 24.

design and by default contributes to achieving this purpose by imposing an ex-ante assessment of compliance with the GDPR and, as a result, with the protection of the fundamental right to data protection.[123] Put another way, the GDPR focuses on promoting a proactive, rather than a reactive approach based on the assessment of the risks and context of specific processing of personal data. A paradigmatic example of this shift is the obligation for the data controller to carry out the Data Protection Impact Assessment, which, however, is a mandatory step only in the cases defined by the GDPR and based on the data controller sensitivity.[124] This obligation requires data controllers to conduct a risk assessment which is not only based on business interests but also on data subjects' (fundamental) rights. In other words, the risk-based approach introduced by the GDPR could be considered a delegation to the data controller of the power to balance conflicting interests, thus making the controller the 'arbiter' of data protection.

However, the GDPR does not exhaust the concern about delegation in the field of data. Even before the adoption of the GDPR, the ECJ had contributed to extending platform powers in delisting online content. Even without analysing the well-known facts of the landmark decision in *Google Spain*,[125] the ECJ has brought out a new right to be forgotten as a part of the right to privacy and data protection in the digital age.[126] In order to achieve this aim, the ECJ, as a public actor, interpreted the framework of fundamental rights together with the dispositions of the Data Protection Directive and de facto entrusted private actors, more precisely search engines, to delist online content without removing information on the motion of the individual concerned.

However, unlike the case of content, both the ECJ and the EDPB, and before the WP29, have identified some criteria according to which platforms shall assess the request of the data subject.[127] Moreover, the recent European codification of the right to erasure has contributed to

[123] Ibid., Art. 25.

[124] Ibid., Art. 35(3)(a).

[125] Case C-131/12 *Google Spain SL and Google Inc.* v. *Agencia Española de Protección de Datos (AEPD) and Mario Costeja González* (2014).

[126] Oreste Pollicino and Marco Bassini, 'Reconciling Right to Be Forgotten and Freedom of Information in the Digital Age. Past and Future of Personal Data Protection in the EU' (2014) 2 Diritto pubblico comparato ed europeo 641.

[127] European Data Protection Board, Guidelines 5/2019 on the criteria of the Right to be Forgotten in the search engines cases under the GDPR, 2 December 2019; Working Party Article 29, 'Working Party on the Implementation of the Court of Justice of the European Union Judgment on "Google Spain and Inc v. Agencia Española de Protección de Datos (AEPD) and Mario Costeja González" C-131/12', http://ec.europa

clarifying the criteria to apply the right to delist. Precisely, the data subject has the right to obtain from the controller, without undue delay, the erasure of personal data concerning him or her according to specific grounds,[128] and excluding such rights in other cases,[129] for example when the processing is necessary for exercising the right to freedom of expression and information.

Although the data subject can rely on a legal remedy by lodging a complaint to the public authority to have their rights protected, the autonomy of platforms continues to remain a relevant concern. When addressing users' requests for delisting, the balancing of fundamental rights is left to the assessment of online platforms. As explained in Chapter 4, this issue overlaps with the concerns about the notice and takedown mechanism in the field of content since search engines enjoy a broad margin of discretion when balancing fundamental rights and enforcing their decisions. In the case of the right to be forgotten online, search engines decide whether the exception relating to the freedom to impart information applies in a specific case. They delist search results by relying only on their internal assessments and they are not obliged to provide any reason for their decision or redress mechanism. Therefore, the online enforcement of the right to be forgotten is another example of (delegated) powers that platforms exercise when balancing and enforcing fundamental rights online.

Even if, in the field of data, the primary concerns do not result from the lack of procedural safeguards, the adoption of the risk-based approach still demonstrates the risk of entrusting private actors with functions which increasingly mirror the powers exercised by public authorities. Even if, as underlined in Chapter VI, the risk-based approach plays a critical role for European digital constitutionalism, it should not be neglected how the structure of European data protection law has entrusted the private sector with important decision-making functions on fundamental and democratic values. It is not by chance that, as in the field of content, the delegation of power to online

.eu/justice/article-29/documentation/opinion-recommendation/files/2014/wp225_en .pdf accessed 21 November 2021.

128 GDPR (n. 116), art. 17(1).

129 Ibid., art. 17(3).

platforms has also contributed to consolidating autonomous powers outside the oversight of public authorities.

3.4 Autonomous Exercise of Quasi-Public Powers Online

The indirect delegation of public functions has not only expanded platform powers. It has also contributed to extending the autonomy of online platforms, leading these actors to consolidate areas of power beyond delegation. Indeed, the liberal constitutional approach across the Atlantic has encouraged online platforms to exploit technology not only to become proxies of public actors but also rely on their freedoms to set their standards and procedures.

Although online platforms are still considered service providers, the consequences of their gatekeeping role cannot be neglected. The possibility to autonomously set the rules according to which information flows and is processed on a global scale leads to an increase in the discretion of these private actors. As Pasquale observed, 'in functional arenas from room-letting to transportation to commerce, persons will be increasingly subject to corporate, rather than democratic, control'.[130] Daskal underlined the ability of private actors in setting the rules governing the Internet.[131] Intermediaries have increasingly arisen as surveillance infrastructures,[132] as well as governors of digital expressions.[133]

These functional expressions of power increasingly compete with states' authority based on the exercise of sovereign powers on a certain territory.[134] This consideration highlights why some scholars have referred to this phenomenon as the rise of the law of the

[130] Frank Pasquale, 'From Territorial to Functional Sovereignty: The Case of Amazon. Law and Political Economy' LPE (12 June 2017) https://lpeblog.org/2017/12/06/from-territorial-to-functional-sovereignty-the-case-of-amazon/ accessed 22 November 2021.

[131] Jennifer C. Daskal, 'Borders and Bits' (2018) 71 Vanderbilt Law Review 179.

[132] Alan Z. Rozenshtein, 'Surveillance Intermediaries' (2018) 70 Stanford Law Review 99.

[133] Kate Klonick, 'The New Governors: The People, Rules, and Processes Governing Online Speech' (2018) 131 Harvard Law Review 1598; Jack M. Balkin, 'Free Speech in the Algorithmic Society: Big Data, Private Governance, and New School Speech Regulation' (2018) 51 U.C. Davis Law Review 1151

[134] Kristen E. Eichensehr, 'Digital Switzerlands' (2018) 167 University Pennsylvania Law Review 665.

platforms.[135] Put another way, online platforms have developed their private geography on a global scale. The possibility to autonomously set the rules according to which data flows and is processed leads to an increase in the discretion of private actors.[136] In the *laissez-faire* scenario, data and information have started being collected globally by private actors for business purposes. Whereas the Internet has allowed private actors to gather information and develop their businesses, today algorithmic technologies enable such actors to process vast amounts of data (or Big Data) to extract value. Their processing has led to an increase in the economic and political power of some private actors in the digital age where the monopoly over knowledge does not belong exclusively to public authorities anymore but also to private actors. From a transnational constitutional perspective, this phenomenon can be described as the rise of a civil constitution outside institutionalised politics. According to Teubner, the constitution of a global society cannot result from a unitary and institutionalised effort but emerges from the constitutionalisation of autonomous subsystems of that global society.[137]

Therefore, these challenges do not just concern the limit faced by public actors in regulating the Internet, but, more importantly, how constitutional democracies can avoid the consolidation of private powers the nature of which is more global than local.[138] As already underlined, constitutional democracies aim to protect freedoms and pluralism. The primary challenge is when such tolerance contributes to the rise of private powers centralising and excluding any form of pluralism. In other words, in a circular way, the rise of private power would threaten the goal of constitutional democracies to protect a pluralistic environment. This is why the next subsection focuses on examining the exercise of autonomous powers by online platforms. The first part examines how the situation can be considered as a new status of *subjectionis* or digital social contract. The second describes how platforms enjoy areas of

[135] Luca Belli, Pedro A. Francisco and N. Zingales, 'Law of the Land or Law of the Platform? Beware of the Privatisation of Regulation and Policy' in Belli and Zingales (n. 106), 41.

[136] Yochai Benkler, 'Degrees of Freedom Dimension and Power' (2016) 145 Daedalus 18.

[137] Gunther Teubner, *Constitutional Fragments: Societal Constitutionalism and Globalization* (Oxford University Press 2012).

[138] Gunther Teubner, 'The Anonymous Matrix: Human Rights Violations by "Private" Transnational Actors' (2006) 69 Modern Law Review 327.

freedoms that de facto represent the exercise of quasi-public powers online.

3.4.1 A New Status *Subjectionis* or Digital Social Contract

In 2017, Zuckerberg stated that 'Great communities have great leaders' and 'we need to give more leaders the power to build communities'.[139] These expressions might not raise concerns at first glance. Nevertheless, they indirectly picture the inspirational values of Facebook. The success of online communities does not come from users' participation and involvement but from the power of its leader. The will of the leader, receiving its investiture from the company, shapes communities. This narrative is far from looking democratic. However, these pharaonic statements should not surprise since online platforms, as business actors, are not keen on democratic forms of participation based on transparency and accountability. They care more to ensure a sound and stable governance driven by profit maximisation.

Therefore, the starting point to understand the exercise of autonomous powers by online platforms is to focus on the vertical regulation of users reflecting the relationship between authority and subjects. At first glance, a contractual agreement governs the relationship between users and online platforms. Users decide spontaneously to adhere to the rules established in ToS and community guidelines. Nonetheless, ToS are not just contracts but instruments of governance. It is not by chance that these agreements have been analysed as the constitutional foundation of online platforms' activities.[140] As Radin explained, generally businesses try to exploit new forms of contracts to overrule legislation protecting parties' rights.[141] Contract law allows private actors to exercise a regulatory authority over a private relationship 'without using the appearance of authoritarian forms'.[142] According to Slawson, contracts, and especially standard forms, hide an antidemocratic tendency '[s]ince

[139] Mark Zuckerberg, 'Bringing the World Closer Together' Facebook (22 June 2017) https://www.facebook.com/notes/mark-zuckerberg/bringing-the-world-closer-together/10154944663901634/ accessed 22 November 2021.

[140] Edoardo Celeste, 'Terms of Service and Bills of Rights: New Mechanisms of Constitutionalisation in the Social Media Environment?' (2018) 33(2) International Review of Law, Computers & Technology 122.

[141] Margaret J. Radin, *Boilerplate the Fine Print, Vanishing Rights, and the Rule of Law* (Princeton University Press 2013).

[142] Fredrick Kessler, 'Contract of Adhesion – Some Thoughts about Freedom of Contract' (1943) 43 Columbia Law Review 629, 640.

so much law is made by standard form it is important that it be made democratically'.[143] Users enter into digital spaces where private companies are 'both service providers and regulatory bodies that govern their own and their users' conduct'.[144] It is not by chance that Zuboff describes the aim of ToS as a 'form of unilateral declaration that most closely resembles the social relations of a pre-modern absolutist authority'.[145] Likewise, MacKinnon describes this situation as a Hobbesian approach to governance, where users give up their fundamental rights to access and enjoy digital services.[146] In other words, moving from private to constitutional law, platforms vertically govern their communities and the horizontal relationship between users through a mix of instruments of technology and contract law.[147]

Besides, the role of online platforms as social infrastructures annihilates any contractual power of the user making the relationship between users and platforms vertical rather than horizontal. The digital dominance of online platforms plays a critical role in daily lives.[148] They contribute to offering people services, for example, to find resources online (i.e. search engines), buy products and services (i.e. e-commerce marketplaces), communicate and share information and data with other people (i.e. social media). And this role has been confirmed even during the pandemic. Without considering their market power, it would be enough to look at the number of users of Facebook or Google to understand that their community is bigger than entire regions of the world,[149] so that the definition of a 'company-town' would seem reductive.[150]

The inhabitants of these digital spaces consider online platforms as primary channels for news or even managing intimate and professional relationships as well as advertising their businesses. According to

143 David Slawson, 'Standard Forms of Contract and Democratic Control of Lawmaking Power' (1967) 84 Harvard Law Review 529, 530.

144 Omri Ben-Shahar and Carl E. Schneider, *More Than You Wanted to Know: The Failure of Mandated Disclosure* 27 (Princeton University Press 2016).

145 Shoshana Zuboff, 'Big Other: Surveillance Capitalism and the Prospects of an Information Civilization' (2015) 30(1) Journal of Information Technology 75.

146 Rebecca MacKinnon, *Consent of the Networked: The Worldwide Struggle for Internet Freedom* (Basic Books 2013).

147 Tal Z. Zarsky, 'Social Justice, Social Norms and the Governance of Social Media' (2014) 35 Pace Law Review 154.

148 Martin Moore and Damian Tambini (eds.), *Digital Dominance. The Power of Google, Amazon, Facebook, and Apple* (Oxford University Press 2018).

149 Anupam Chander, 'Facebookistan' (2012) 90 North Carolina Law Review 1807.

150 Zarsky (n. 147).

Pasquale, the real product here is users' information and data.[151] The company can exercise a form of private monitoring over content and data shared, not so differently from governmental surveillance. Indeed, Kim and Telman underline how 'private data mining is just as objectionable and harmful to individual rights as is governmental data mining',[152] and 'because corporate actors are now empowered to use their technological advantages to manipulate and dictate the terms on which they interact with the public, they govern us in ways that can mimic and even supersede governance through democratic processes'.[153] Therefore, platform power is not just a matter of quantity but also of quality. In other words, online platforms have acquired their areas of power not only as resulting from the amount of data or their scale but also from their gatekeeping role based on the organisation of online spaces for billions of users.[154]

These digital spaces governed by online platforms are not based on horizontal systems where communities decide and shape their rules but on vertical contractual relationships resembling a new *pactum subjectionis* or digital social contract. Users bargain their constitutional rights to adhere to conditions determined through a top-down approach driven by business interests. As the ruler of digital space, the governance of online platforms defines a private geography of power based on norms and spaces whose boundaries escape the traditional notion of territorial sovereignty.

The mix of automated technologies of moderation with internal and community guidelines reproduces a system of constitutional rules and principles governing communities. As Evans explains, the rules and penalties imposed by the platform mirror (and, in some cases, substitute) those adopted by public authorities.[155] In this para-constitutional framework, the vertical and horizontal relationship of users and, therefore, the exercise of their rights and freedoms are privately determined without the substantive and

[151] Frank A. Pasquale, 'Privacy, Autonomy, and Internet Platforms' in Marc Rotenberg, Julia Horwitz and Jeramie Scott (eds.), *Privacy in the Modern Age, the Search for Solutions* (The New Press 2015).

[152] Nancy S. Kim and D. A. Telman, 'Internet Giants as Quasi-Governmental Actors and the Limits of Contractual Consent' (2015) 80 Missouri Law Review 723, 730.

[153] Ibid.

[154] Orla Lynskey, 'Regulating Platform Power' (2017) LSE Legal Studies Working Paper 1 http://eprints.lse.ac.uk/73404/1/WPS2017-01_Lynskey.pdf accessed 22 November 2021.

[155] David S. Evans, 'Governing Bad Behavior by Users of Multi-Sided Platforms' (2012) 27 Berkeley Technology Law Journal 1201.

procedural safeguards democratic constitutional norms traditionally offer. Within this authoritarian framework, as observed by Shadmy, 'corporate services ... transforms rights in the public imaginary into privileges that the company grants and can revoke, according to its own will and interest'.[156]

Besides, the power to shape and determine rights and freedoms in the digital environment is not the only concern. The vertical relationship between community and platform reflects the characteristics of an absolute regime rather than that of a private constitutional order. Online platforms set the rules governing their communities without involving users, who have no instrument of participation to determine the rules of the game. Even if online platforms offer their spaces as instruments to foster democracy, there is no space for democratic participation.[157] Although online platforms base their narrative on their role in establishing a global community, it is worth wondering how it is possible to reach an agreement upon common rules between communities which, in some cases, are made up to two billion people. Someone could argue that users can participate in the platforms' environment by selecting to hide news or opt-in to specific data regimes. However, it should not be forgotten that online platforms set these options, thus leaving users the mere feeling of freedom in their digital spaces.

In this regard, Jenkins distinguishes between participation and interactivity.[158] According to Jenkins, 'Interactivity refers to the ways that new technologies have been designed to be more responsive to consumer feedback' while 'Participation, on the other hand, is shaped by the cultural and social protocols'. Translating this distinction in the field of online platforms, it is possible to observe how there is no participation since online platforms autonomously define the protocols while inviting users to engage and interact. Platforms foster interactivity as an alternative to participation which create a reasonable feeling of trust and involvement in online platforms' determinations. The rights and freedoms in the digital environment are not just the result of democratic participation ('bottom-up') but also of the privileges granted

[156] Tomer Shadmy, 'The New Social Contract: Facebook's Community and Our Rights' (2019) 37 Boston University International Law Journal 307, 329.

[157] Laura Stein, 'Policy and Participation on Social Media: The Cases of YouTube, Facebook, and Wikipedia' (2013) 6(3) Communication, Culture & Critique 353.

[158] Henry Jenkins, *Convergence Culture: Where Old and New Media Collide* (New York University Press 2006).

by online platforms ('top-down'). In this case, constitutional values and principles compete with discretionary private determinations which are not required to respect constitutional safeguards and act like an absolute power.

The lack of any participatory instrument or transparency makes individuals subject to the autonomous powers exercised by online platforms, leading to a process of 'democratic degradation'.[159] Therefore, it is not just a matter of formal adherence to boilerplate clauses but the lack of participation in activities which affect the rights and freedoms of billions of people in the world. This situation also extends to the lack of transparency and redress mechanisms. Although data protection law provides more safeguards on this point, it is possible to generally observe how online platforms escape from accountability for their conducts. Within this framework, it would be possible to argue that the power exercised by online platforms mirrors, to some extent, the same discretion which an absolute power can exercise over its subjects.

3.4.2 The Exercise of Autonomous Powers

The vertical relationship between platform powers and users is not the only piece of this authoritarian puzzle. It is also critical to understand how online platforms express autonomous forms of power. By ToS and community guidelines, platforms unilaterally establish what users can do in their digital spaces. Platforms rely on private freedoms to regulate relationships with their online communities, precisely determining how content and data are governed online. In the field of content, this is particularly evident as underlined in Chapter 2. In the lack of any regulation of the process through which expression is moderated, platforms are free to set the rules according to which speech flows online. While, in the field of data, on the one hand, the GDPR introduces safeguards and obligations, on the other hand, it leaves data controllers broad margins of discretion in assessing the risks for data subject's fundamental rights and their ability to prove compliance with data protection principles according to the principle of accountability.

Regulating speech and data is usually the result of legislative fights and constitutional compromises. On the opposite, online platforms autonomously set standards and procedures through instruments of contract law even if they operate transnationally and are driven by

[159] Radin (n. 141), 16.

their business purposes. At first glance, the significance of this situation under a public (or rather constitutional) law perspective may not be evident, both because boilerplate contracts are very common even in the offline world and ToS do not seem to differ from the traditional contractual model.[160] Boilerplate contracts provide clauses based on standard contractual terms that are usually included in other agreements.[161] However, as Jaffe underlined in the first half of the last century, contract law could be considered as a delegation of lawmaking powers to private parties,[162] and this extends to the private governance of the digital environment.[163] Put another way, these agreements compete with the traditional way norms and powers are conceived as expression of public authorities.

By defining the rules to enforce private standards as well as the procedural and technical tools underpinning their ToS, platforms govern their digital spaces.[164] In this case, it would be possible to observe how ToS constitute the expression of a quasi-legislative power. The lack of transparency and accountability of the online platforms' decision-making processes does not allow assessing whether platforms comply with legal standards, internal guidelines or other business purposes.[165] These instruments do not ensure the same degree of protection as public safeguards.[166] Although this autonomy is limited in some areas such as data protection, the global application of their services and the lack of any legal rule regulating online content moderation leave a broad margin of political discretion in their hands when drafting their ToS. In other words, similarly to the law, these private determinations can be considered as the legal basis according to which platforms

[160] Peter Zumbansen, 'The Law of Society: Governance Through Contract' (2007) 14(1) Indiana Journal of Global Legal Studies 19.

[161] Woodrow Hartzog, 'Website Design as Contract' (2011) 60(6) American University Law Review 1635.

[162] Louis Jaffe, 'Law Making by Private Groups' (1937) 51 Harvard Law Review 201.

[163] Lee A. Bygrave, *Internet Governance by Contract* (Oxford University Press 2015).

[164] Luca Belli and Jamila Venturini, 'Private Ordering and the Rise of Terms of Service as Cyber-Regulation' (2016) 5(4) Internet Policy Review https://policyreview.info/node/441/pdf accessed 22 November 2021.

[165] Paul S. Berman, 'Cyberspace and the State Action Debate: The Cultural Value of Applying Constitutional Norms to "Private" Regulation' (2000) 71 University of Colorado Law Review 1263.

[166] Ellen Wauters, Eva Lievens and Peggy Valcke, 'Towards a Better Protection of Social Media Users: A Legal Perspective on the Terms of Use of Social Networking Sites' (2014) 22 International Journal of Law & Information Technology 254.

exercise their powers or an expression of how platforms can promote an autopoietic set of rules which compete with the law.

Besides, the exercise of quasi-legislative functions is not the only expression of platform powers. Online platforms can enforce contractual clauses provided for in the ToS directly without relying on public mechanisms such as a judicial order or the intervention of law enforcement authorities. For instance, the removal of online content or the erasure of data can be performed directly and discretionarily by online platforms without the involvement of any public body ordering the infringing party to fulfil the related contractual obligations. This technological asymmetry constitutes the grounding difference from traditional boilerplate contracts. Their enforcement is strictly dependent on the role of the public authority in ensuring the respect of the rights and obligations which the parties have agreed upon. Here, the code assumes the function of the law,[167] and the network architecture shows its role as modality of regulation.[168] Platforms can directly enforce their rights through a quasi-executive function. This private enforcement is the result of an asymmetrical technological position with respect to users. Platforms are the rulers of their digital space since they can manage the activities which occur within their boundaries. This power, which is not delegated by public authorities but results from the network architecture itself, is of special concern from a constitutional perspective since it represents not only a form of disintermediation of the role of public actors but also the constitutionalisation of self-regulation.[169]

Together with these normative and executive functions, online platforms can also exercise a quasi-judicial power. Platforms have showed that they perform functions which are similar to judicial powers and especially mirror the role of constitutional courts, namely the balancing of fundamental rights. When receiving a notice from users asking for content removal or delisting, platforms assess which fundamental rights or interests should prevail in the case at issue to render a decision. Taking as an example the alleged defamatory content signalled by a user, the platform could freely decide that the right to inform prevails over human dignity. The same consideration applies when focusing on how the right to privacy should be balanced with

[167] Lessig (n. 10).
[168] Reidenberg (n. 23).
[169] Black (n. 38).

freedom of expression. This situation is evident not only when platforms moderate content but also when processing personal data exploiting the loopholes of data protection law. These decisions are based on their business purposes without being obliged to respect or take into account fundamental rights. The result of this situation leads to a chilling effect for fundamental rights and, even more importantly, to the establishment of paralegal frameworks in the algorithmic society.

Furthermore, adding another layer of complexity – and concern – is the possibility that these activities can be executed by using automated decision-making technologies. On the one hand, algorithms can be considered as technical instruments facilitating platform's functionalities, such as the organisation of online content and the processing of data. However, on the other hand, such technologies can constitute technical self-executing rules, obviating even the need for a human executive or judicial function.

The use of automated decision-making technologies is not neutral from a constitutional law perspective. Humans and machines shape the choices of online platforms.[170] The lack of transparency and accountability in these systems challenges fundamental rights and democratic values.[171] The new relationship between human and machine in the algorithmic society leads to the increase of platform powers. Within this framework, there is no room for users to complain against abuse of powers. The governance of decision-making is not shared but centralised and covered by unaccountable purposes. As underlined by Hartzog, Melber and Salinger, 'our rights are established through non-negotiable, one-sided and deliberately opaque "terms of service" contracts. These documents are not designed to protect us. They are drafted by corporations, for corporations. There are few protections for the users – the lifeblood powering social media'.[172]

[170] Ira Rubinstein and Nathan Good, 'Privacy by Design: A Counterfactual Analysis of Google and Facebook Privacy Incidents' (2013) 28 Berkeley Technology Law Journal 1333; Robert Brendan Taylor, 'Consumer-Driven Changes to Online Form Contracts' (2011–12) 67 NYU Annual Survey of American Law 371.

[171] Frank Pasquale, *The Black Box Society: The Secret Algorithms that Control Money and Information* (Harvard University Press 2015); Matteo Turilli and Luciano Floridi, 'The Ethics of Information Transparency' (2009) 11(2) Ethics and Information Technology 105; Tal Zarsky, 'Transparent Predictions' (2013) 4 University of Illinois Law Review 1507.

[172] Woodrow Hartzog, Ari Melber and Evan Salinger, 'Fighting Facebook: A Campaign for a People's Terms of Service' Center for Internet and Society (22 May 2013) http://cybe

From a constitutional perspective, users, as members of online communities, are subject to the exercise of a contractual authority exercised by platforms through instruments of private law mixed with technology (i.e. the law of the platforms). The three traditional public powers are centralised when focusing on platforms quasi-public functions: the definition of the rules to assess online content, the enforcement and the balancing of rights are all practised by the platform without any separation of powers. Constitutionalism has primarily been based on the idea of the separation of powers, as theorised by Charles De Secondat,[173] and the protection of rights and freedoms.[174] In contrast, the governance of online platforms reflects a private order whose characteristics are not inspired by democratic constitutionalism but are more similar to the exercise of absolute power. Precisely, this is not the rise of a 'private constitutional order' since neither the separation of powers nor the protection of rights are granted in this system.[175] This framework has led some authors to refer to this phenomenon as a return to feudalism,[176] or to the *ancien régime*.[177]

3.5 Converging Powers in the Algorithmic Society

The rise of online platforms as digital private powers is not an unexpected consequence if framed within the global trends challenging constitutional democracies. Globalisation as also driven by neoliberal narratives has contributed to the rise of transnational actors producing and shaping norms beyond national boundaries. This situation contributes to weakening the relationship between 'law and territory' and enhancing that between 'norms and space'. The evolution of different systems leads to the emergence of different institutions which operate according to their internal rationality. As a result, the unitary of the state and the role of law is slowly replaced by the fragmentation of new institutions expressing their principles and values on a global scale.

rlaw.stanford.edu/blog/2013/05/fighting-facebook-campaign-people%E2%809699s-terms-service accessed 22 November 2021.

173 Charles De Secondat, *L'esprit des loi* (1748).

174 Charles Howard McIlwain, *Constitutionalism: Ancient and Modern* (Amagi 2007).

175 The French Declaration of the Rights of Man and Citizens art. 16 states: 'Any society in which the guarantee of rights is not assured, nor the separation of powers determined, has no Constitution'. Declaration of the Right of Man and the Citizen, 26 August 1789.

176 James Grimmelmann, 'Virtual World Feudalism' (2009) 118 Yale Law Journal Pocket Part 126.

177 Belli and Venturini (n. 164).

The digital environment constitutes a sort of battlefield between these systems. Different rationalities influence each other since they are cognitively open, although they develop their rules according to their internal norms and procedures which are based on autonomous principles. On the one hand, public authorities can express binding rules censoring content or restricting access to the Internet, also enjoying the exclusive monopoly on the use of force. On the other hand, online platforms develop standards and procedures answering their business logic, thus inevitably providing a model competing with public powers. Both systems develop their rules according to their internal procedures and logic in a continuous interaction defining different relationship of power.

Against these challenges, while authoritarian systems have replied to these threats by extending their powers to the digital environment to protect the central authority, constitutional democracies, which instead are open environments for freedoms, have adopted a liberal approach entrusting online platforms with public tasks in the digital environment. Such a transfer of responsibilities has also been driven by the ability of platforms to enforce public policies online as gatekeepers. Although the delegation to private actors of public tasks should not be considered a negative phenomenon per se, the lack of safeguards leaves these actors free to exercise private powers. Unlike public actors, online platforms are not required to pursue public interests such as the protection of fundamental rights and democratic values.

Therefore, without providing instruments to foster transparency and accountability, even the indirect delegation of public functions contributes to the consolidation of economic and political power as well as to the exercise of autonomous functions by private actors. Moreover, delegated powers are not the only source of concern. Platforms can exercise private powers over their online spaces through instruments based on contract law and technology. In the field of content and data, platform governance mirrors the exercise of quasi-public functions by defining the values and the principles on which their communities are based. This discretion in setting the standard of their communities or the possibility to balance and enforce fundamental rights through automated systems are examples of a private order mirroring an absolute regime resulting from a mix of constitutional freedoms and technology.

The fields of content and data have provided a critical angle to examine the exercise of platform powers. This is not a coincidence, but it is the result of the intimate relationship between these two fields in the algorithmic society. Therefore, the next chapter focuses on how the evolution of the digital environment has led to the convergence of content and data, showing how, even if they are based on different constitutional premises, freedom of expression, privacy and data protection share the same constitutional direction.

4 From Parallel Tracks to Overlapping Layers

4.1 The Intimate Connection between Content and Data

The consolidation of platform powers raises concerns for constitutional democracies. Delegated and autonomous powers question the role of constitutionalism in protecting fundamental rights while limiting the exercise of powers. Nonetheless, the role of European digital constitutionalism cannot be entirely understood without examining another layer of complexity, precisely the intimate relationship between content and data in the algorithmic society. The challenges for fundamental rights like freedom of expression, privacy and data protection do not just come from platform powers but also from the blurring boundaries between the technological framework and legal regimes governing content and data.

At the end of the last century, the Union approached the liability of online intermediaries in relation to content and data in separate ways. While the e-Commerce Directive was introduced to govern the field of online content by defining the legal responsibility of online intermediaries concerning third-party illicit content,[1] the Data Protection Directive focused on regulating the processing of personal information.[2] Both systems provide definitions, pursue specific objectives and are encapsulated by different legal instruments. The legal divergence between the two regimes has also been expressly clarified by the

[1] Directive 2000/31/EC of the European Parliament and of the Council of 8 June 2000 on certain legal aspects of information society services, in particular electronic commerce, in the Internal Market (2000) OJ L 178/1.

[2] Directive 95/46/EC of the European Parliament and of the Council of 24 October 1995 on the protection of individuals with regard to the processing of personal data and on the free movement of such data (1995) OJ L 281/31.

e-Commerce Directive whose scope of application does not include 'questions relating to information society services covered by Directives 95/46/EC and 97/66/EC'.[3] In other words, the Data Protection Directive and the e-Commerce Directive started running on parallel tracks from a legal point of view.

This political choice made perfect sense in the aftermath of the Internet. At that moment, online intermediaries were predominantly performing passive activities offering access or hosting services mainly to businesses rather than to billions of consumers. It is not a coincidence that the relationship between content and data was of limited concern for the European Commission when drafting the respective legal regimes. Online intermediaries offer services without interfering with the information they transmit and host while acting as processors in relation to the data uploaded by third parties. Therefore, the technological divergence between the field of content and that of data was one of the primary reasons for the legal divergence in the regulation of these fields.

In the meantime, the fields of content and data have experienced a process of technological convergence. Online intermediaries have become more active by offering services to share information which is indexed and organised through the processing of data.[4] Over the years, several actors have developed new services based on the processing of content and data. Together with the traditional providers of Internet access providers and hosting providers, new players have started to offer their digital services such as search engines (e.g. Google and Yahoo), platforms that allow communication, exchange and access to information (e.g. Facebook and Twitter), cloud computing services (e.g. Dropbox and

[3] e-Commerce Directive (n. 1), Article 1(5)(b). Recital 14 defines this rigid separation by stating that: 'The protection of individuals with regard to the processing of personal data is solely governed by Directive 95/46/EC . . . and Directive 97/66/EC . . . These Directives already establish a Community legal framework in the field of personal data and therefore it is not necessary to cover this issue in this Directive in order to ensure the smooth functioning of the internal market, in particular the free movement of personal data between Member States'. However, the same Recital does not exclude that 'the implementation and application of this Directive should be made in full compliance with the principles relating to the protection of personal data, in particular as regards unsolicited commercial communication and the liability of intermediaries; this Directive cannot prevent the anonymous use of open networks such as the Internet'.

[4] Giovanni Sartor, 'Providers Liability. From the eCommerce Directive to the Future' (2017) in-depth analysis for the IMCO Committee www.europarl.europa.eu/RegData/etudes/IDAN/2017/614179/IPOL_IDA(2017)614179_EN.pdf accessed 21 November 2021.

Google Drive), e-commerce marketplaces (e.g. e-Bay and Amazon) and online payment systems (e.g. Paypal).

This framework has inevitably affected the legal regimes of content and data. Despite the original parallel track, content and data have started to overlap even from a legal standpoint as an answer to the challenges driven by technological convergence. Within the framework of the Digital Single Market strategy, the Union has introduced new legal instruments indirectly leading to a legal convergence between content and data. In other words, the shift from parallel tracks to overlapping layers (or the move from technological and legal divergence to convergence) is a crucial piece of the puzzle to understand the framework in which platforms exercise their powers and shape democratic values. The blurred lines in the field of content and data are not neutral from a constitutional perspective. The technological convergence has challenged the parallel tracks in the fields of content and data, thus raising several challenges for the protection of legal certainty as well as fundamental rights.

Within this framework, the shift from parallel tracks to overlapping layers contributes to examining platform powers and understanding the role of European digital constitutionalism. This chapter aims to analyse the evolving technological and legal intersection between content and data in the algorithmic society. The first part examines the points of convergence and divergence between the legal regimes introduced by the e-Commerce Directive and the Data Protection Directive. In the second part, two examples underline how the relationship between the two systems has evolved, looking in particular at how technological convergence has led to overlapping layers between the two legal fields which were conceived on parallel tracks. The third part examines three paths of legal convergence in the phase of European digital constitutionalism.

4.2 An Evolving Relationship on Different Constitutional Grounds

At the end of the last century, the Union could not have foreseen how content and data would have started to become increasingly interrelated. When the liability regimes for content and data saw the light, there were no social media platforms, e-commerce marketplaces and other digital services. The role of intermediaries was merely that of passively offering storage, access and transmission of data across the network.

Within this framework, content and data were running on parallel tracks as also showed by the minimum interaction between the Data Protection Directive and the e-Commerce Directive. This gap was also the result of different constitutional paths for freedom of expression, privacy and data protection in Europe. When dealing with freedom of expression in Europe, it is possible to look at such fundamental right from at least three different perspectives. Freedom of expression is enshrined in the Charter and in the Convention as well as in each Member State's Constitution.[5] The predominance of freedom of expression in Europe finds its roots in the French Declaration of the Rights of Man and of the Citizen which protected 'the free communication of thoughts and of opinions'.[6] Since the nineteenth century, freedom of expression has been developed as an answer to the political power exercised by public authorities and then became the basis for protecting other rights such as the right to education and research.

Instead, the European path towards the constitutional recognition of privacy and data protection as fundamental rights started from the evolution of the concept of privacy in the US framework.[7] From a merely negative perspective, the right to be left alone, or the right to privacy, characterised by predominant liberal imprinting, has firstly emerged in Europe within the framework of the Convention. As will be examined in Chapter 6, this liberty has then evolved towards a positive dimension consisting in the right to the protection of personal data as an answer to the progress of the welfare state, the development of new automated processing techniques like databases[8] and then digital technologies.

Therefore, data protection in the European framework constitutes a relatively new individual right developed as a response to the rise of the information society driven by new automated technologies and, primarily, the Internet. In other words, if the right to privacy was enough to meet the interests of individuals' protection, in the information society, the widespread processing of personal data, also through automated means, has made it no longer sufficient to just safeguard

[5] Eric Barendt, *Freedom of Speech* (Oxford University Press 2017).

[6] French Declaration of the Rights of Man and of the Citizen (1789), Art. 11.

[7] Samuel D. Warren and Louis D. Brandeis, 'The Right to Privacy' (1890) 4 Harvard Law Review 193.

[8] Alan F. Westin, *Privacy and Freedom* (Atheneum 1967).

privacy but has also led to complementing this negative protection with a positive dimension consisting of the right to data protection.

Nonetheless, even indirectly, the fields of content and data have shared some points of contact since the adoption of the Data Protection Directive and the e-Commerce Directive. Both instruments were adopted to face the challenges of new information technologies to the internal market.[9] As underlined in Chapter 2, the Union was more concerned with focusing on ensuring the smooth development of the internal market by pursuing a digital liberal approach. To ensure this goal, the Union underlined the need to protect fundamental values. On the one hand, the Data Protection Directive identifies the right to privacy and data protection as the beacon to follow to 'contribute to economic and social progress, trade expansion and the well-being of individuals',[10] whereas the e-Commerce Directive protects freedom of expression since 'the free movement of information society services can in many cases be a specific reflection in Community law of a more general principle, namely freedom of expression'.[11] As a result, the two legal regimes have been conceived with a clear political perspective: ensuring the smooth development of the internal market by providing new rules and adapting fundamental freedoms to the new technological scenario.

These constitutional observations do not exhaust the relationship between the two systems. The parallel track between content and data is also based on other grounding differences between the two regimes. The e-Commerce Directive focuses on exempting online intermediaries from liability and tackling illegal content rather than establishing procedures in this case, while the Data Protection Directive follows the opposite path. European data protection law does not focus on

[9] Data Protection Directive (n. 2), Recital 4. Moreover, Recital 14 states that 'given the importance of the developments under way, in the framework of the information society, of the techniques used to capture, transmit, manipulate, record, store or communicate sound and image data relating to natural persons, this Directive should be applicable to processing involving such data'. e-Commerce Directive (n. 1), Recital 1. 'The European Union is seeking to forge ever closer links between the States and peoples of Europe, to ensure economic and social progress; in accordance with Article 14(2) of the Treaty, the internal market comprises an area without internal frontiers in which the free movements of goods, services and the freedom of establishment are ensured; the development of information society services within the area without internal frontiers is vital to eliminating the barriers which divide the European peoples'.

[10] Data Protection Directive (n. 2), Recital 2.

[11] e-Commerce Directive (n. 1), Recital 9.

exempting secondary liability or prohibiting the processing of personal data but rather on tackling unlawful processing. The two regimes have been built on parallel tracks characterised by different focal points. On the one hand, the content regime under the e-Commerce Directive is based on secondary liability for third-party illegal content or behaviours. On the other hand, the Data Protection Directive has introduced a system of liability of the controller independent from third-party conducts.

However, even these considerations are just a part of the jigsaw. When focusing on the liability regime system of content and data, some scholars observed that the two regimes should not be considered as mutually exclusionary but should be understood beyond a literal interpretation.[12] Precisely, before the adoption of the e-Commerce Directive, the Commission recognised the horizontal nature of the liability of online intermediaries involving 'copyright, consumer protection, trademarks, misleading advertising, protection of personal data, product liability, obscene content, hate speech, etc.'.[13] Even after the adoption of the e-Commerce Directive, the Commission stressed the general scope of the liability of online intermediaries in relation to third-party content.[14] Besides, the e-Commerce Directive provides another clue when it specifies that different civil and criminal regime of liability at domestic level could negatively affect the internal market.[15] This interpretative provision could be understood as a goal towards harmonisation of the liability systems covering any type of online content to reduce legal fragmentation which would undermine the development of the internal market.

Within this framework based on a parallel track, content and data started to overlap at least in three cases.[16] First, when users commit an

[12] Mario Viola de Azevedo Cunha and others, 'Peer-to-Peer Privacy Violations and ISP liability: Data Protection in the User-Generated Web' (2012) 2(2) International Data Privacy Law 50.

[13] Resolution on the communication from the Commission to the Council, the European Parliament, the Economic and Social Committee and the Committee of the Regions on a European Initiative in Electronic Commerce (COM(97)0157 C4-0297/97), 203.

[14] Report from the Commission to the European Parliament, the Council and the European Economic and Social Committee, First Report on the application of Directive 2000/31/EC of the European Parliament and of the Council of 8 June 2000 on certain legal aspects of information society services, in particular electronic commerce, in the Internal Market (Directive on electronic commerce), COM(2003) 702 final.

[15] e-Commerce Directive (n. 1), Recital 40.

[16] Bart van der Sloot, 'Welcome to the Jungle: The Liability of Internet Intermediaries for Privacy Violations in Europe' (2015) 3 Journal of Intellectual Property, Information Technology and Electronic Commerce Law 211.

infringement through online intermediaries' networks (e.g. defamation), the e-Commerce Directive applies, thus shielding the liability of online platforms. Therefore, online platforms are not liable provided that they remove the infringing content if they become aware of the users' illicit conduct. Second, when users infringe privacy and data protection rules through online intermediaries' networks, the Data Protection Directive applies in relation to users. In this case, platforms are liable just for primary infringements of data protection rules and not for users' illicit conducts. Third, where users infringe a right falling outside the scope of data protection rules (e.g. hate speech) and platforms are required to provide details about the infringing users or to implement filtering systems, both the e-Commerce Directive and the Data Protection Directive apply.

In the last case, it is possible to find a first (but indirect) point of contact between the two regimes. More specifically, in *Promusicae*,[17] a collecting society representing producers and publishers of musical and audiovisual recordings asked Telefonica, as access provider, to reveal personal data about its users due to alleged access to the IP-protected work of the collecting society's clients without authors' prior authorisation. The question referred to the ECJ was directed at understanding if an access provider could be obliged to provide such information to the collecting society according to the legal framework provided for by the Enforcement Directive,[18] the Infosoc Directive,[19] and the e-Privacy Directive.[20] The ECJ found that Member States are not required to lay down an obligation requiring intermediaries to share personal data to ensure effective protection of copyright in the context of civil proceedings. It is for Member States to strike a fair balance between the rights at issue and take care to apply general principles of proportionality. However, even in this case, although the system of content and data (in this case, the e-Privacy Directive) participated in the same reasoning of the ECJ, the mutual influence between the two regimes was still not clear at that time.

[17] Case C-275/06 *Productores de Música de España (Promusicae)* v. *Telefónica de España SAU* (2008).

[18] Directive 2004/48/EC of the European Parliament and of the Council of 29 April 2004 on the enforcement of intellectual property rights (2004) OJ L 195/16.

[19] Directive 2001/29/EC of the European Parliament and of the Council of 22 May 2001 on the harmonisation of certain aspects of copyright and related rights in the information society (2001) OJ L 167/1.

[20] Directive 2002/58/EC of the European Parliament and of the Council of 12 July 2002 concerning the processing of personal data and the protection of privacy in the electronic communications sector (2002) OJ L 201/37.

Likewise, in *LSG*,[21] the ECJ recognised that the rules of the Enforcement Directive, the Infosoc Directive and the e-Privacy Directive do not prevent Member States from establishing a reporting obligation for online intermediaries concerning third parties' traffic data in order to allow civil proceedings to commence for violations of copyright. Even in this case, the ECJ specified that such a system is compatible with Union law provided that Member States ensure a fair balance between the different fundamental rights at stake. The same orientation was confirmed in *Bonnier Audio*,[22] where the ECJ stated that EU law does not prevent the application of national legislations which, in order to identify an Internet subscriber or user, allow in civil proceedings to order an online intermediary to give a copyright holder or its representative information on the subscriber to whom the Internet service provider provided an IP address which was allegedly used for an infringement.

The overlap between content and data started to be clear to the ECJ even in *Google France*.[23] According to the ECJ, Google 'processes the data entered by advertisers and the resulting display of the ads is made under conditions which Google controls'.[24] The court then observed that this activity does not deprive Google of the exemptions from liability provided for in the e-Commerce Directive. Likewise, in the *L'Oreal* case,[25] the court did not follow the aforementioned path, recognising, instead, that eBay processes the data entered by its customer-sellers. Besides, the ECJ observed that the provision of assistance like the optimisation of the presentation of the offers for sale in question or promoting those offers leads the provider to playing an active role since it controls the data relating to the offers. Therefore, '[i]t cannot then rely, in the case of those data, on the exemption from liability referred to in Article 14(1) of Directive 2000/31'.[26] In these cases, the ECJ identified a connection between the data processed by the platform and its active role in relation to the exemption of liability.

[21] Case C-557/07 *LSG-Gesellschaft zur Wahrnehmung von Leistungsschutzrechten GmbH* v. *Tele2 Telecommunication GmbH* (2009).

[22] Case C-461/10 *Bonnier Audio AB, Earbooks AB, Norstedts Förlagsgrupp AB, Piratförlaget AB, Storyside AB* v. *Perfect Communication Sweden AB* (2012).

[23] Joined cases C-236/08 to C-238/08 *Google France SARL and Google Inc.* v. *Louis Vuitton Malletier SA* (C-236/08), *Google France SARL* v. *Viaticum SA and Luteciel SARL* (C-237/08) and *Google France SARL* v. *Centre national de recherche en relations humaines (CNRRH) SARL and Others* (C-238/08) (2010).

[24] Ibid., 115.

[25] Case C-324/09 *L'Oréal SA and Others* v. *eBay International AG and Others* (2011).

[26] Ibid., 116.

Although these cases could provide a first overview of a primordial legal overlap between the regimes of data and content, both systems remained formally far from each other. In other words, this phase was still characterised by technological and legal divergence in the field of content and data. These considerations do not provide any significant ground for understanding how and why the two regimes have started to overlap. The parallel tracks in the legal regime of content and data are not just the result of the adoption of two different legal instruments but also of a different technological environment at the end of the last century. The next section examines how the rise of online platforms has triggered the technological convergence of content and data and underline the legal convergence of the two fields.

4.3 The Blurring Lines between Content and Data

Online platforms are complex creatures playing multiple roles in the algorithmic society. On the one hand, they operate as data controllers when deciding the means and the purposes of processing personal data, but they can also be considered processors for the data they host. On the other hand, platforms actively organise users' content according to the data they collect from users while also hosting content and relying on an exemption of liability for third-party illicit conducts.

Social media are the most evident example of the intersection between content and data. The moderation of content and the processing of data is not performed by chance. Expressions are moderated with the precise scope of ensuring a peaceful environment where users can share their ideas and opinions. These expressions are also data whose processing allows platforms to offer micro-targeting advertising services.[27] Likewise, search engines organise their content according to billions of search results for providing the best targeted services to attract advertising revenues. These examples do not exhaust the way in which content and data are increasingly converging from a technological perspective, but they can lead to defining the intimate relationship between the two fields.

[27] Tarleton Gillespie, *Custodians of the Internet. Platforms, Content Moderation, and the Hidden Decisions That Shape Social Media* (Yale University Press 2018).

The blurring lines between content and data in the digital environment challenge these two systems based on parallel legal regimes. In the framework of content, online intermediaries are defined as entities offering access, caching or hosting services whose activity is exempted from secondary liability due to their passive nature.[28] These providers are shielded from liability due to the technical operations they perform. They can be liable when they start to play a more active role showing awareness of the content they host. In other words, the more providers perform their activities in an active way (e.g. creating content), the more they could be subject to liability. Access providers are not responsible provided that they do not initiate the transmission, select the receiver of the transmission, select or modify the information contained in the transmission.[29] Without focusing on caching providers,[30] hosting providers are not liable for the information stored in their digital spaces provided that two alternative conditions are satisfied. Firstly, online intermediaries are not liable when they do not have actual knowledge of illegal activity or information and, as regards claims for damages, are not aware of facts or circumstances from which the illegal activity or information is apparent. Secondly, the exemption of liability also covers the case when online intermediaries, upon obtaining such knowledge or awareness, act expeditiously to remove or disable access to the information.[31]

While there are no issues in considering Vodafone or Verizon as access providers and Facebook or Twitter as hosting providers, the situation is more complicated when focusing on search engines like Google (i.e. information location tool services). The definition of 'information society service' would cover their activities.[32] Nonetheless, it is not entirely clear if search engines fall under any of the three types of

[28] e-Commerce Directive (n. 1), Recital 42. 'The exemptions from liability established in this Directive cover only cases where the activity of the information society service provider is limited to the technical process of operating and giving access to a communication network over which information made available by third parties is transmitted or temporarily stored, for the sole purpose of making the transmission more efficient; this activity is of a mere technical, automatic and passive nature, which implies that the information society service provider has neither knowledge of nor control over the information which is transmitted or stored'.

[29] Ibid., Art. 12(1)(a–c).

[30] Ibid., Art. 13(1)(a–e).

[31] Ibid., Art. 14(1)(a–b).

[32] Ibid. According to Recital 18: '[I]nformation society services are not solely restricted to services giving rise to online contracting but also, in so far as they represent an economic activity, extend to services which are not remunerated by those who receive

service providers mentioned above. It is not by chance that the e-Commerce Directive clarifies that '[i]n examining the need for an adaptation of this Directive, the report shall in particular analyse the need for proposals concerning the liability of providers of hyperlinks and location tool services', thus leaving Member States this choice.[33]

Moving to the field of data, the Data Protection Directive adopts a different approach. It does not exempt online intermediaries from liability according to their passive roles but provides a comprehensive definition of data controllership.[34] 'Data controller' is indeed defined as 'the natural or legal person, public authority, agency or any other body which alone or jointly with others determines the purposes and means of the processing of personal data'.[35] Within this framework, the data controller can be defined as the governor of personal data since it can exercise a form of decision-making.[36] This power consists of the possibility to select the 'purposes and means', thus subjecting the data subject's personal data to the goals of the data controller.[37]

Unlike the field of content, this definition reflects an active engagement rather than a passive and technical role. Online intermediaries falling within this definition govern the processing of personal data. In other words, these definitions reflect the lack of a common starting point between the two regimes. On the one hand, as far as the legal regime of content is concerned, online intermediaries are depicted as

them, such as those offering on-line information or commercial communications, or those providing tools allowing for search, access and retrieval of data'.

33 Ibid., Art. 21. The reasons for such a choice came from the passive activity of search engines which do not take editorial decisions over content. They are not either the source of information they index or able to remove this information online. For instance, Some Member States (e.g. Portugal and Spain) have considered search engine services as hosting providers. See Joris van Hoboken, 'Legal Space for Innovative Ordering: On the Need to Update Selection Intermediary Liability in the EU' (2009) 13 International Journal of Communication Law & Policy 1.

34 The ECJ has shown how much this definition could be interpreted broadly. See Case C-210/16 *Unabhängiges Landeszentrum für Datenschutz Schleswig-Holstein v. Wirtschaftsakademie Schleswig-Holstein GmbH* (2018).

35 Data Protection Directive (n. 2), Art. 2(d).

36 Brendan Van Alsenoy, 'Allocating Responsibility Among Controllers, Processors, And "Everything In Between": The Definition of Actors and Roles in Directive 95/46' (2012) 28 Computer Law & Security Review 30.

37 It is worth mentioning that this situation becomes more intricate when data controllership is exercised by more than one entity. In this case, two or more actors govern the processing of personal data and, therefore, determining which entity is in control or responsible could be not an easy question to answer.

passive entities responsible only when they perform activities as content providers. Whereas data controllers are the key players of the data protection system since they actively define the modalities according to which data is processed.

The data controller is not the only relevant figure in the field of data. The Data Protection Directive also provides the definition of 'processor', who is the 'natural or legal person, public authority, agency or any other body which processes personal data on behalf of the controller'.[38] It is evident how the role of data processors is subject to the data controllers' guidelines and, therefore, its role can be defined as passive rather than active. In other words, the data controller is the brain of data governance, the processor is the brawn. The definition of data processor fits with purely passive providers, that neither determine the means nor the purpose of the data processing. According to the WP29, '[a]n ISP providing hosting services is in principle a processor for the personal data published online by its customers, who use this ISP for their website hosting and maintenance. If, however, the ISP further processes for its own purposes the data contained on the websites then it is the data controller with regard to that specific processing'.[39] Put another way, when online intermediaries only process data of third-party services such as hosting a specific website, they operate as mere passive providers and data processors. Whereas, when the data is processed for the purposes and according to the modalities defined by online intermediaries, this actor plays the role of an active provider and of a data controller.

As Erdos underlined, it is possible to identify '(i) those that are not only intermediary "hosts" but also only data protection "processors" (labelled "processor hosts"), (ii) those which are intermediary "hosts" but also data protection "controllers" (labelled "controller hosts") and (iii) those which are data protection 'controllers' and not intermediary "hosts" (labelled "independent intermediaries")'.[40] While the exemption of liability for online intermediaries was introduced to protect entities by virtue of their passive role, nowadays, the use of automated

[38] Data Protection Directive (n. 2), Art. 2(e).

[39] Working Party Article 29, 'Opinion 1/2010 on the concepts of "controller" and "processor"' (2010) https://ec.europa.eu/justice/article-29/documentation/opinion-recommendation/files/2010/wp169_en.pdf accessed 21 November 2021.

[40] David Erdos, 'Intermediary Publishers and European Data Protection: Delimiting the Ambit of Responsibility for Third-Party Rights through a Synthetic Interpretation of the EU Acquis' (2018) 26 International Journal of Law and Information Technology 189, 192.

systems of filtering and processing preferences have led these entities to perform activities whose passive nature is hard to support. As a result, nowadays, some online intermediaries perform no longer a merely passive role, but they are increasingly involved in active tasks. Therefore, the old-school rules in the framework of online intermediaries could not fit within the algorithmic society where online platforms actively run their business at the intersection between content and data.

While mere hosting services would fall under the first category (passive provider/data processor), online platforms, such as social networks and search engines, are likely to fall under the second relationship (active providers/data controllers). Passive hosting providers such as web service applications do not choose how to process large amounts of data, but they limit themselves to offering hosting services playing the role of data processor. This shift should not surprise since, as examined in Chapter 3, online platforms process content and data for profit relying on automated decision-making technologies. This active role at the intersection between content and data transforms the role of online intermediaries from passive providers and data processors to active providers and data controllers.

These considerations are the grounding reasons to understand how online platforms play the double role of hosting providers and data controllers in the algorithmic society. This situation is the primary example of the technological convergence between the two fields which has been characterised by legal divergence since the end of the last century. The following subsections examine the evolution of this relationship by focusing on two landmark cases showing how technological convergence has challenged the legal regime of content and data, thus paving the way towards legal convergence overcoming parallel tracks.

4.3.1 Active Providers and Data Controllers

Looking at the Italian framework, the *Google* v. *Vivi Down* saga provides clues to understand the evolution of the relationship between content and data.[41] The case arose from a video showing an autistic boy being bullied by his classmates uploaded to the Google video platform.[42] This

[41] It is worth mentioning that this case is not the only example of how Member States have interpreted the intersection between the fields of content and data in the last years. Nevertheless, the Italian saga allows us to deal with the core of this chapter. See Erdos (n. 40).

[42] See Oreste Pollicino and Ernesto Apa, *Modeling the Liability of Internet Service Providers: Google vs. Vivi Down. A Constitutional Perspective* (Egea 2013); Giovanni Sartor and Mario

situation involved both content, that is, in this case, the video itself as uploaded to Google Video, and data, most notably the health data of the victim which was ultimately processed through the hosting of the footage. It should thus not come as a surprise that the charges brought against the executives of Google concerned, on the one hand, the failure to prevent the crime of defamation against the minor, pursuant to Articles 40 and 595 of the Italian criminal code, and, on the other hand, the unlawful processing of personal data pursuant to Article 167 of Legislative Decree 196/2003.

The Court of Milan acquitted the defendants from the crime of defamation, excluding that Google, as a hosting provider, had an obligation to prevent crimes committed by its users.[43] Legislative Decree 70/2003, implementing the e-Commerce Directive in the Italian legal order, excludes the obligation to monitor content disseminated by users. Instead, the Milan Court of first instance condemned three executives from Google for the crime of unlawful processing of personal data, sentencing them to a six-month suspended conviction. According to the court, Google should have warned the uploaders about the obligations to respect when uploading online content as well as the consequences of potential violations.

The Milan Court of Appeals overturned the 2010 first instance ruling and found the Google executives not guilty of unlawful data processing.[44] Therefore, Google was not responsible for either defamation nor unlawful processing of personal data. The appeal decision was based on the general principle that Google was not aware of the content since it had no general duty to monitor user-uploaded content on its systems. Besides, the search engine could not be considered a data controller. Service providers were completely alien to the information stored when the e-Commerce Directive was introduced. However, according to the court, today such a statement is arguably not consistent any more with the state of the art. In today's world, the services that online intermediaries offer are not limited to the technical process that simply sets up and provides access to the network. They make possible for users to share their own content and other people's content on the

Viola de Azevedo Cunha, 'The Italian Google-Case: Privacy, Freedom of Speech and Responsibility of Providers for User-Generated Contents' (2010) 18(4) International Journal of Law & Information Technologies 15; Raul Mendez, 'Google Case in Italy' (2011) 1(2) International Data Privacy Law 137.

43 Court of Milan, decision no. 1972/2010.

44 Court of Appeals of Milan, decision no. 8611/2013.

network and they cannot escape from complying with data protection laws.

By recalling the decision of the court of first instance, the court observed that active hosting providers could be subject to more onerous duties than passive hosting providers. This extension of duties would descend from the organisation and selection of information. Data processing would then make online intermediaries aware of the indistinct flow of data. Nevertheless, the court clarified that this situation does not lead to a sort of chain reaction resulting in an extension of online intermediaries' liability for whatever third-party offences relating to the communication and upload of particular categories of data. In this case, the court argued that Google could not be considered a data controller.

The mix of these observations reflects how the layers of content and data tend to overlap. In this case, the core issue regards data protection since it concerns the assessment of the crime of unlawful data processing, so that the Data Protection Directive applies. As a result, Google could not rely on the exemption of liability since these rules are enshrined in a separate legal instrument whose scope of application does not extend to matters involving data protection. Nevertheless, the Milan Court of Appeals mixed the two systems in its reasoning with the result that the boundaries between the two regimes started to become increasingly blurred.

The Italian Supreme Court, upholding the decision of the Milan Court of Appeals, clarified the boundaries of the previous decision in relation to the qualification of hosting providers as data controller.[45] The Supreme Court dismissed the appeal of the public prosecutor confirming that hosting providers are not required to generally monitor data entered by third parties in its digital rooms. According to the court, although the illegal processing of personal data had occurred, as the video actually contained health data of the minor, this criminal conduct was only attributable to the uploader. The hosting provider was not aware of the illicit content and, as soon as the authority notified the provider, the content was promptly removed from the online platform.

In this case, the Supreme Court expressly addressed the topic of the coordination between the regime of the liability of online intermediaries and data protection, as implemented in the Italian legal order respectively by Legislative Decree 70/2003 and 196/2003. The court

[45] Italian Supreme Court, decision no. 5107/2014.

observed that the exclusion of data protection from the scope of application of Legislative Decree 70/2003 clarifies that the protection of personal data is governed by rules outside the scope of platform liability for hosting third-party content. Therefore, the two regimes should be interpreted together, meaning that the regime of online intermediaries clarifying and confirming the scope of the data protection regime. The role of the data controller implies the existence of decision-making powers with regard to the purposes, the methods of personal data processing and the tools used. Put another way, the data controller is the only subject who can fulfil these tasks. In the view of the Supreme Court, this role is compatible with the system of the e-Commerce Directive. Precisely, the court observed that as long as the illicit data is unknown to the service provider, this entity cannot be considered as the data controller, because it lacks any decision-making power on the data itself. When, instead, the provider is aware of the illicit data and does not take action for its immediate removal or to make it inaccessible in any case, it fully assumes the status of data controller.

The decision of the Supreme Court was based on a mix between the legal regimes of content and data. Even more importantly, this observation underlines a critical evolution of the role of online intermediaries whose neutral functions turned into a more active involvement characterised by the determination of the scope and purposes of personal data processing.

4.3.2 From the Takedown of Content to the Delist of Data

Another opportunity to examine the evolving relationship between content and data in the algorithmic society comes from the ECJ. Judicial activism has not only played a critical role in building a bridge between digital liberalism and the new phase of European digital constitutionalism but has also contributed to indirectly underlining how the regimes of content and data are destined to overlap in the framework of the algorithmic society. The *Google Spain* case is a landmark decision for several reasons but, for the purposes of this chapter, it is a clear example of convergence between the regimes of content and data.[46]

Without going back on the facts of the case and on the primary legal issues already underlined in the previous chapter and analysed by extensive literature,[47] it is interesting to highlight how, although the

[46] Case C-131/12 *Google Spain SL and Google Inc.* v. *Agencia Española de Protección de Datos (AEPD) and Mario Costeja González* (2014).

[47] See Aleksandra Kuczerawy and Jef Ausloos, 'From Notice-and-Takedown to Notice-and-Delist: Implementing Google Spain' (2016) 14 Columbia Technology

Google Spain case focused on data protection law, it shares similarities with the field of content. Like in the framework of the e-Commerce Directive, the case concerns the removal (*rectius* delisting) of online content including personal data. Under Spanish law, this action would have triggered the responsibility of the search engine, as a hosting provider, to remove the content at stake. In the *Google Spain* case, however, the matter was addressed from the data perspective.

This case still shows some first steps towards legal convergence. The opinion of the Advocate General Jääskinen provides interesting clues, precisely, when he rejected the idea of search engines as data controllers.[48] This conclusion came from the interpretation of the notion of data controller based on the idea of 'responsibility' over the personal data processed 'in the sense that the controller is aware of the existence of a certain defined category of information amounting to personal data and the controller processes this data with some intention which relates to their processing as personal data'.[49] This last view circularly comes back to the argument of the Italian Supreme Court when underlining the link between the notion of data controller and its responsibility in terms of awareness. This argument highlights the potential merge of the fields of content and data. In other words, the responsibility of data controllers results from their awareness when they process personal data, such as is the case of online intermediaries in the field of content. According to the Advocate General, the search engine provider just supplies an information location tool which does not make it aware of the existence of personal data in any other sense than as a statistical fact web pages are likely to include personal data. More particularly, he observed that '[i]n the course of processing of the source web pages for the purposes of crawling, analysing and indexing, personal data does not manifest itself as such in any particular way'.[50]

Law Journal 219; Frank Pasquale, 'Reforming the Law of Reputation' (2015) 47 Loyola University of Chicago Law Journal 515; Oreste Pollicino and Marco Bassini, 'Reconciling Right to Be Forgotten and Freedom of Information in the Digital Age. Past and Future of Personal Data Protection in the EU' (2014) 2 Diritto pubblico comparato ed europeo 641.

48 Opinion of the Advocate General Jääskinen in the case *Google Spain* C-131/12, 25 June 2013.

49 Ibid., 82.

50 Ibid., 84.

The Advocate General did not exclude that upon certain conditions even a search engine does exercise control on personal data and may therefore be subject to the obligations set forth under the Data Protection Directive in its capacity as data controller. The owner of a search engine has control over the index and can filter or block certain content.[51] A search engine can be required to apply exclusion codes on source pages to prevent the retrieval of specific content. Even with respect to the cache copy of the content of websites, in the case of a request for its updating by the owner, the search engine has actual control over personal data.[52]

The assumption behind this finding is based on considering the liability of search engines dependent on their active role based on awareness. In light of that, the opinion reached the conclusion that Google could not be considered a data controller.[53] The conclusion of the Advocate General shows how the two legal regimes inevitably overlap. The assessment about whether a search engine can be considered a data controller has been based on legal arguments resembling the framework of the e-Commerce Directive. In other words, the impossibility to control personal data in the case of delisting was connected to a passive role incompatible with data controllership.

Focusing on the ECJ's decision, even though the court agreed that the indexing of information retrieved from the website of third parties amounts to a processing of personal data, this point has remained the only common finding between the opinion of the Advocate General and the decision of the court. As far as the divergence between the two approaches is concerned, it is when answering the question as to the nature of the search engine as data controller that the court takes an opposite path. The ECJ's decision firmly recognised that search engines are data controllers, especially because these actors play a decisive role 'in the overall dissemination of those data in that it renders the latter accessible to any internet user making a search on the basis of the data subject's name, including to internet users who otherwise would not have found the web page on which those data are published'.[54] Therefore, the ECJ abandoned the idea of awareness and responsibilities advanced by the Advocate General and focused on the current effects of

[51] Ibid., 92.
[52] Ibid., 93.
[53] Ibid., 100.
[54] C-131/12 (n. 46), 36, 37–40.

the search engines' activities. Put another way, the court dismantled any potential convergence going back to parallel tracks.

A critical point lies within the ECJ's observation that excluding search engines from the notion of data controller would be contrary to the objective of the provision, which is to ensure effective and complete protection of data subjects. In order to ensure an effective protection of data subjects, it is necessary to adopt a broader definition of data controller. This consideration is also explained by the interest of the ECJ in ensuring effective protection of the right to privacy as underlined in Chapter 2. The finding of the court in *Google Spain* does not seem to be supported by the actual manner in which search engines act when indexing third-party webpages, but rather by the crucial implications that said activity produces with regard to the protection of personal data. The argument advanced by the Advocate General, according to whom an online intermediary qualifies as data controller only upon certain conditions, is thus rejected. The search engine provider amounts to a data controller regardless of the fact that the owner of a website has chosen to implement exclusion protocols or taken other arrangements for excluding the content of the same from being retrieved. The fact that the owner of a website does not indicate that, in the view of the court, does not release the search engine from its responsibility for the processing of personal data carried out as such.

It cannot be excluded that defining search engines as data controllers would be incompatible with data protection law since these actors would not be able to comply with all the obligations applicable to data controllers.[55] It is worth underlining that, when recognising Google as a data controller, the ECJ has underlined that such role should be carried out 'within the framework of its responsibilities, powers and capabilities', thus providing a safety valve against the disproportionate extension of data protection law obligations to search engines.[56]

Although this part of the decision would show the lack of intention to reduce the gap between the legal regimes of content and data, an example of the blurring line between the two fields comes from the paragraphs of the decisions where the ECJ supported the right to delist by interpreting the provisions of the Data Protection Directive.[57] The ruling of the ECJ raises several questions on the legal regime of search

55 Miquel Peguera, 'The Shaky Ground of the Right to Be Delisted' (2016) 18 Vanderbilt Journal of Entertainment & Technology Law 507.

56 C-131/12 (n. 46), 38.

57 Data Protection Directive (n. 2), Arts. 12(b), 14(a).

engines in the field of data and content. The primary question is whether search engines' results have not been considered as third-party content since they are generated from content providers such as users and hosted by search engines as service providers. It is true that the ECJ was called to answer the questions raised by the national judge through the preliminary reference mechanism focused on data protection laws. Nonetheless, since the right to delist has been clustered within the framework of personal data, the application of the e-Commerce Directive is not under discussion. The *Google Spain* decision did not refer to the legal framework of the e-Commerce Directive. The ECJ just focused on whether Google should be considered subject to European data protection law and its obligations without thinking about the consequences for the moderation of third-party content subject to delisting. Without knowing it, the ECJ built an important bridge between the fields of content and data.

The exclusive focus on data protection law does not mean that the decision had not produced effects on the regime of liability in the field of content. In this case, the ECJ led to the creation of a new complaint-based system mirroring the notice-and-takedown system established by the e-Commerce Directive.[58] From a broader perspective, the decision affects the framework of liability of search engines. Despite the high level of protection of fundamental rights, the ECJ has also delegated to search engines the task of balancing fundamental rights when assessing users' requests to delist online content. The right to delisting provides a broader remedy than the obligation to remove required of online platforms in case of awareness of illicit content. Search engines are required to assess users' requests which should not be based on alleged illicit content but on their personal data. Therefore, platforms can exercise their discretion in deciding whether to proceed with the delisting, so that, in this case, search engines perform a 'data moderation' rather than a 'content moderation'.

The two takedown procedures are not identical but similar. The notice-and-takedown mechanism was introduced in the field of content not only as the result of the liability exemption to online intermediaries but also to incentivise these actors to keep their spaces clean from illegal

[58] Stavroula Karapapa and Maurizio Borghi, 'Search Engine Liability for Autocomplete Suggestions: Personality, Privacy and the Power of the Algorithm' (2015) 23 International Journal of Law & Information Technology 261.

content online.[59] The 'notice-and-takedown' and the 'notice-and-delist' mechanisms are different, especially since they come from two different legal frameworks. Notice-and-takedown aims to tackle illegal third-party content while, in the field of data, notice-and-delist deals with legal content linked by the search engines' activities. The former mainly concerns the liability for third-party behaviours while the latter focuses on platforms' primary misconducts.

Nonetheless, both procedures affect content. Even if, at first glance, the right to delist would address the removal of links to publication including personal data, such an activity is highly dependent on the content in question due to the balancing between data protection and freedom of expression. It is not by chance that Keller underlined that the case of the right to be forgotten online looks like 'a textbook intermediary liability law'.[60] Even more importantly, failing to comply with these systems upon receiving users' notice would lead search engines to be liable. The fact that engines are data controllers would mean that they can exercise a sort of control over information and, particularly, on personal data. This situation seems to be in contrast with the ban on general monitoring obligations established by the e-Commerce Directive. In other words, although the *Google Spain* case does not deal with the framework of content, this decision moves the notice-and-takedown approach from the field of content to data without assessing the technological and legal boundaries between the two regimes.

4.4 From Legal Divergence to Convergence

The regimes of content and data have already shown a certain degree of technological convergence in the digital environment. While the relationship data processor/passive provider (e.g. web hosting) does not raise particular issues, the second model (data controller/active provider) questions the legal separation of the two regimes.

Despite the increasing connection between content and data, at first glance, this intersection has not led the Union to adopt a new approach to platform liability in the framework of the algorithmic society. In the field of content, the Union has introduced new rules addressing the

59 OECD, 'The Role of Internet Intermediaries in Advancing Public Policy Objectives' (2011) www.oecd.org/internet/ieconomy/48685066.pdf accessed 21 November 2021.

60 Daphne Keller, 'The Right Tools: Europe's Intermediary Liability Laws and the Eu 2016 General Data Protection Regulation' (2018) 33 Berkley Technology Law Journal 297, 354.

intersection between content and data.[61] A parallel track approach is still primary when looking at the Directive on Copyright in the Digital Single Market (Copyright Directive),[62] and the amendments in the framework of the Audiovisual Media Service Directive (AVMS Directive).[63] Similarly, the GDPR, as well as the Proposal for a Regulation on Privacy and Electronic Communications,[64] govern privacy and data protection law.

The rise of digital constitutionalism in Europe does not imply that the Union's approach can be considered coherent with the intertwined challenges in the fields of expressions and data. Within this framework, in *La Quadrature du Net*,[65] the ECJ addressed a case concerning the intersection between the legal regimes of content and data. The case concerned the lawfulness of Member States' legislation, laying down an obligation for providers of electronic communications services to forward users' traffic data and location data to a public authority or to retain such data in a general or indiscriminate way. The ECJ confirmed that EU law precludes this form of surveillance, precisely, the general and indiscriminate transmission or retention of traffic data and location data for the purpose of combatting crime in general or of safeguarding national security.[66] For the

[61] Several European legal instruments provide a specific legal framework in respect of specific types of illegal contents online. In particular, Directive 2011/93/EU requires Member States to take measures to remove web pages containing or disseminating child pornography and allows them to block access to such web pages, subject to certain safeguards. Directive (EU) 2017/541 regards online content removal in respect of online content constituting public provocation to commit a terrorist offence. It should not be forgetting also Directive 2004/48/EC of the European Parliament and of the Council on the enforcement of intellectual property rights, it is possible for competent judicial authorities to issue injunctions against intermediaries whose services are being used by a third party to infringe an intellectual property right.

[62] Directive (EU) 2019/790 of the European Parliament and of the Council of 17 April 2019 on copyright and related rights in the Digital Single Market and amending Directives 96/9/EC and 2001/29/EC (2019) OJ L 130/92.

[63] Directive (EU) 2018/1808 of the European Parliament and of the Council of 14 November 2018 amending Directive 2010/13/EU on the coordination of certain provisions laid down by law, regulation or administrative action in Member States concerning the provision of audiovisual media services (Audiovisual Media Services Directive) in view of changing market realities (2018) OJ L 303/69.

[64] Proposal for a Regulation of the European Parliament and of the Council concerning the respect for private life and the protection of personal data in electronic communications and repealing Directive 2002/58/EC (Regulation on Privacy and Electronic Communications), COM(2017) 10 final.

[65] Joined Cases C-511/18, C-512/18 and C-520/18 *La Quadrature du Net and Others* v. *Premier ministre and Others* (2020).

[66] See also Case C-207/16 *Ministerio Fiscal* (2018); Joined Cases C-203/15 and C-698/15 *Tele2 Sverige AB* v. *Post- och telestyrelsen* and *Secretary of State for the Home Department* v. *Tom Watson and Others* (2016); Joined Cases C-293/12 and C-594/12 *Digital Rights Ireland Ltd*

purposes of understanding the relationship between content and data, it is worth stressing that the ECJ observed that the protection of the confidentiality of communications and of natural persons with regard to the processing of personal data in the context of information society services is governed only by European data protection law.[67] The court has not only underlined that this field falls within the field of data but also that 'the protection that Directive 2000/31 is intended to ensure cannot, in any event, undermine the requirements under Directive 2002/58 and Regulation 2016/679'.[68]

Notwithstanding the parallel tracks approach seems predominant from this formal perspective, the substantive margins of convergence between the field of content and data underline a trend towards legal convergence as driven by European digital constitutionalism. The convergence between these two systems can be analysed from at least three perspectives described in the next subparagraphs. Firstly, paths of convergence between content and data in the digital environment are the result of the relationship between freedom of expression and data protection at the constitutional level. If, on the one hand, these two fundamental rights have led to parallel legal regimes, on the other hand, they pursue the same constitutional mission to protect democratic values. Secondly, the regime of content is increasingly approaching the system of data based on procedural safeguards. The Union has shifted its attention to regulating the procedures based on which content is processed without dealing with their legal qualification. The third path of convergence looks at the overlapping layers between the regimes of liability in the field of content and data.

4.4.1 Constitutional Conflict and Converging Values

It is no mystery that the information society has increasingly raised the attention on the protection of freedom of expression, privacy and personal data. In the case of the Union, the threats of digital technologies implemented by transnational private actors are one of the primary reasons triggering the rise of a new phase of digital constitutionalism. Nevertheless, what is worth observing in this case does not only concern the risks for these fundamental rights but also the increasing paths

v. *Minister for Communications, Marine and Natural Resources and Others and Kärntner Landesregierung and Others* (2014).

67 Joined Cases C-511/18, C-512/18 and C-520/18 (n. 65), 199.

68 Ibid., 200.

of converging values between freedom of expression, privacy and data protection.

Even before the advent of online platforms, freedom of expression has met, firstly, privacy as the right to be left alone, and, then, data protection due to the rise of new processing technologies. For instance, the interest to access relevant information for the public interest typically clashes with the right to privacy. The notion of 'intellectual privacy' can show the intersection between private sphere and freedom of expression.[69] As underlined by Richards, intellectual privacy is 'a zone of protection that guards our ability to make up our minds freely'.[70] Surveillance affects not only privacy and data protection but also freedom of expression. Users cannot only be concerned about the control of their private spheres, but also limit the sharing of their opinions and ideas. This could also happen when digital technologies enabling the profiling of users' behaviours are used to manipulate opinions. The conflictual connection between expressions and privacy has become closer through the passing of time. Their interrelation has not basically changed with the rise of the information society. There has been an amplification of cases where these fundamental rights clash with each other.

In the European framework, the scope of the Data Protection Directive confirms this tension between data and content since it did not only introduce a broad notion of personal data but also covered models of processing and disseminating information protected by the right to freedom of expression enshrined in the Charter and the Convention. Therefore, it is possible to agree that 'from its inception, the entirety of European data protection has been correctly understood to be in inherent tension with such rights'.[71] Even beyond the extensive definitions in the field of data, the Data Protection Directive also provided a specific exemption from data protection obligations 'solely for journalistic purposes or the purpose of artistic or literary expression ... only if they are

[69] Julie Cohen, 'Intellectual Privacy and Censorship of the Internet' (1998) 8(3) Seton Hall Constitutional Law Journal 693.

[70] Neil Richards, *Intellectual Privacy: Rethinking Civil Liberties in the Digital Age* 95 (Oxford University Press 2015).

[71] David Erdos, 'From the Scylla of Restriction to the Charybdis of Licence? Exploring the Scope of the "Special Purposes" Freedom of Expression Shield in European Data Protection' (2015) 52 Common Market Law Review 119, 121.

necessary to reconcile the right to privacy with the rules governing freedom of expression'.[72]

It is also possible to observe that, as also indirectly suggested in *Lindqvist*,[73] the Data Protection Directive already embedded a certain balance by allowing data protection to influence the standard of the right to freedom of expression.[74] This system of exemption subjected the right to freedom of expression to the logics of the data protection system whose scope is likely to cover different forms of expressions.

There is not a general hierarchy between these two fundamental rights at the European constitutional level. Even in *Google Spain*, it is true that the ECJ recognised the prevalence of the fundamental rights of data subjects over the interest of Internet users to access information. At the same time, the ECJ observed that the balance may depend on 'specific cases, on the nature of the information in question and its sensitivity for the data subject's private life and on the interest of the public in having that information, an interest which may vary, in particular, according to the role played by the data subject in public life'.[75]

This clash is the result of two different constitutional goals aimed to protect conflicting rights like secrecy and public disclosure. In other words, the meeting of freedom of expression, privacy and data protection is the result of a conflict rather than a convergence between constitutional interests. From this perspective, the relationship between these rights can be defined as adversarial (freedom of expression versus privacy/data protection). The solution to this natural conflict has traditionally consisted of the balancing between fundamental rights made *ex ante* by lawmakers and *ex post* by courts.[76] At first glance, the conflict between these two rights could be considered a form of convergence since both rights contribute to influencing the scope of

[72] Data Protection Directive (n. 2), Art. 9. See *Google Spain* (n. 46); Case C-73/07 *Tietosuojavaltuutettu* v. *Satakunnan Markkinapörssi Oy and Satamedia Oy* (2008) ECR I-9831.

[73] Case C-101/01 *Lindqvist* (2003) ECR I-12971, 82.

[74] Magdalena Jozwiak, 'Balancing the Rights to Data Protection and Freedom of Expression and Information by the Court of Justice of the European Union. The Vulnerability of Rights in an Online Context' (2016) 23(3) Maastricht Journal of European and Comparative Law 404.

[75] *Google Spain* (n. 46), 81.

[76] Eric Barendt, 'Balancing Freedom of Expression and Privacy' (2009) 1(1) Journal of Media Law 49.

protection of each other through balancing activities. Nevertheless, their clash can also be considered as an example of divergence since both systems aim to protect different rights from their constitutional perspective.

Although these considerations are still applicable in the algorithmic society, the relationship between freedom of expression, privacy and data protection is not only adversarial but also cooperative (freedom of expression and privacy/data protection). This cooperation lies in the joint mission underpinning these fundamental rights consisting of protecting democratic values. Freedom of expression, privacy and data protection are pillars of democratic societies. Without the possibility of expressing opinion and ideas freely, it is not possible to qualify a society as democratic. Likewise, without relying on the protection of the private sphere and procedures on the processing of personal data, it would not be possible to safeguard privacy and tackle an imbalance of powers between data controllers and subjects coming from the consolidation of an opaque sphere of data ignorance.

The common mission of these two fundamental rights emerged when examining the rise of a democratic phase of digital constitutionalism. Despite their natural conflictual relationship, both fundamental rights have shown their ability to provide the Union with constitutional instruments to answers platform powers. The measures adopted at the European level to regulate the process of content moderation and processing of automated decision-making processes are two clear examples of the mission of freedom of expression, privacy and data protection to protect democratic values in the algorithmic society. Their conflictual relationship can also be seen as a cooperative relationship linked by a common democratic goal.

4.4.2 From Content to Process

Another path of legal convergence comes from the transformation of content regulation that is now closer to the structure of data protection law grounded on procedural safeguards. The field of content is not structured on procedures but on qualifying and tackling illegal content. Put another way, the focus is on the *an* but not on the *quomodo*. The e-Commerce Directive does not introduce safeguards in the processing of content when online intermediaries process them as in the case of content moderation. It just defines the roles and responsibilities of online intermediaries when dealing with illegal content. Hosting providers are just obliged to remove illegal content based on their awareness without any specific procedures. The e-Commerce Directive leaves Member States free to set further safeguards in this process without however requiring them to ensure a minimum and harmonised standard of protection.[77] The only limit is the ban for Member States to introduce general monitoring obligations applying to online intermediaries.[78]

On the other side, European data protection law provides rules governing the procedures for collecting, organising and making available personal data. It determines according to which conditions data should be considered personal, the role and responsibilities of controllers and processors as well as the procedures to follow in the processing of personal data. Failure to comply with this system triggers the liability of data controllers and processors. In other words, the data protection law framework does not care whether data are illicit per se, but whether their processing is unlawful. On the opposite, in the field of content, the focus is on substantive rather than procedural obligations.

The steps in the field of the Digital Single Market strategy have affected this original legal divergence. The fields of content and data look more similar in terms of structure and obligations. As examined in Chapter 2, the Copyright Directive and the AVMS Directive highlight this path of convergence. The Copyright Directive introduces several procedural safeguards in online platforms' content moderation of copyright content.[79] For instance, online platforms are required to put in place an effective and expeditious complaint and redress mechanism which users can access in the event of disputes over the disabling of access to, or the removal of, works or other subject-matter uploaded by them.[80] This obligation leads online platforms to proceduralising their activities like in the field of data. Likewise, the AVMS Directive provides a list of appropriate measures such as the establishment of mechanisms for users of video-sharing platforms to report or flag, or age verification systems for users with respect to content which may impair the physical, mental or moral development of minors. It is worth mentioning that the Union has not abandoned its focus on defining illicit content rather setting managing procedures. The TERREG still tends to define

[77] e-Commerce Directive (n. 1), Recital 46.
[78] Ibid., Art. 15.
[79] Copyright Directive (n. 62), Art. 17.
[80] Ibid., Art. 17(9).

illicit content.[81] The scope of terrorist content is limited by legal definitions and includes cases of incitement and solicitation.[82] At the same time, the TERREG introduces accountability and transparency safeguards in the moderation of terrorist content by hosting providers.[83] Therefore, despite the hybrid solution, this case is another example of how the process of moderation is increasingly going towards procedural obligations characterising the field of data.

The first examples of the shift from content to procedure are primarily the result of the new phase of digital constitutionalism. As discussed in Chapter 5, the Digital Services Act will be another critical step of this convergence, thus making the field of content closer to that of data. [84] It will increasingly move the perspective from content to process by providing horizontal procedural safeguards. The primary threats to freedom of expression in the digital age are connected to the lack of transparency and accountability in the moderation of content. To solve this imbalance of power, the structural shift from content to process has triggered a new path of legal convergence in the algorithmic society.

4.4.3 Content and Data Liability

The GDPR triggered the third path of legal convergence between content and data, precisely concerning the application of the system of the e-Commerce Directive in the field of data protection. The GDPR underlines that its scope should not affect the application of the rules provided for by the e-Commerce Directive, including the provisions on the liability of online intermediaries. However, while waiting for the adoption of the Digital Services Act, which has introduced the same provision in relation to the application of its rules without prejudice to European data protection law,[85] the provision limiting the scope of the e-Commerce Directive is still in force.

81 Regulation (EU) 2021/784 of the European Parliament and of the Council of 29 April 2021 on addressing the dissemination of terrorist content online OJ L 172/79.
82 Ibid., Art. 2.
83 Ibid., Arts. 9–11.
84 Proposal for a Regulation of the European Parliament and of the Council on a Single Market for Digital Services (Digital Services Act) and amending Directive 2000/31/EC COM(2020) 825 final.
85 Digital Services Act (n. 84), Art. 1(5)(i).

A literal and narrow reading of the e-Commerce Directive would suggest that the liability exemption only applies to content without concerning the liability of online intermediaries for third-party data protection infringements or the liability of data controllers since these matters would be governed by the Data Protection Directive. As a result, even if online platforms can benefit from the exemption of liability established by the e-Commerce Directive, they remain liable for primary infringements in the field of data. As stated in the e-Commerce Directive, '[t]he implementation and application of this Directive should be made in full compliance with the principles relating to the protection of personal data, in particular as regards ... the liability of intermediaries'.[86] Likewise, the e-Commerce Directive states that 'the protection of individuals with regard to the processing of personal data is solely governed by [data protection laws], which are fully applicable to information society services; these Directives already establish a Community legal framework in the field of personal data and therefore it is not necessary to cover this issue in this Directive'.[87]

Consequently, there are two potential interpretations. Firstly, nothing has changed since the GDPR could not affect the scope limitation established by the e-Commerce Directive. Secondly, it is possible to picture a potential convergence between the two legislative instruments since the GDPR states that its application should not prejudice the application of the e-Commerce Directive, especially concerning the liability of online intermediaries. However, it does not draw a clear line regarding the extension of online intermediaries exemption of liability in the field of data protection.

In the past, scholars addressed this question supporting the abolition of the 'data protection exceptionalism' according to which online intermediaries could not rely on the exemption of liability for third-party data.[88] The solution would consist of deferring to 'data-protection law for the specification of what processing of personal data is illegal, while giving providers immunity for all illegal processing taking place on their platform (including processing that is illegal because of violations of data protection law)'.[89] This perspective is also confirmed by the potential application of the safe harbour regime only to third-party

[86] e-Commerce Directive (n. 1), Recital 14.

[87] Ibid.

[88] Giovanni Sartor, '"Providers" Liabilities in the New EU Data Protection Regulation: A Threat to Internet Freedoms?' (2013) 3(1) International Data Privacy Law 3.

[89] Ibid., 5.

content. The extension of this regime should not be considered as an exemption of liability from unlawful processing of personal data performed directly by online intermediaries. Whereas, in relation to online content violating data protection rules, in this case, online intermediaries could rely on the liability regime established by the e-Commerce Directive.

The potential applicability of the e-Commerce Directive in the field of data would not put aside the other provisions of data protection law. On the opposite, it would just lead to derogating provisions of liability for the distribution and storage of third-party content infringing data protection law which would remain the normative point of reference to assess the lawfulness of users' content. Nevertheless, it is worth underlining that an exemption of liability in this case would raise challenges when online intermediaries are also data controllers, so that they would have an active role in processing third-party content infringing data protection law.

Other limitations to the application of the e-Commerce Directive can also be found in the GDPR itself such as the exclusion of the application of data protection rules for 'purely personal or household activity'.[90] However, in this last case, it is necessary to mention that Recital 18 excludes these activities from the scope of the GDPR except for the case in which data controllers or processors provide the means for processing personal data for such personal or household activities.[91] As a result, according to this interpretative provision, even in this case, online intermediaries could be subject to the application of the GDPR while they could rely on their exemption of liability in the field of data if users process data within the scope of the aforementioned exception.

Besides, the GDPR does not refer to the e-Commerce Directive when addressing the liability of data controllers and processors. Regarding the liability of the data controller, the GDPR provides that a controller or processor shall be exempt from liability if they prove that they are not in any way responsible for the event giving rise to the damage. At this point, it would be possible to argue that online intermediaries as passive providers when exercising their functions as data controllers or processors should not be considered liable for third-party conducts.[92] It is necessary to observe that, unlike the Data Protection Directive, the

[90] GDPR, Art. 2(2)(c).
[91] Ibid., Recital 18.
[92] Ibid., Art. 82(3).

GDPR does not provide examples of how a controller might prove the lack of any liability: *force majeure* or error on the part of the data subject.[93] Although the provision could be interpreted in the same meaning that it refers only to events beyond the control of the controller or the processor, however, it is not clear whether even this provision could be used as a defence against third-party illicit behaviours.

These interpretations underline the overlap between the two fields. The extension of the regime of the e-Commerce Directive to third-party content infringing data protection law could also come from a constitutional interpretation based on the balancing between platforms' freedom to conduct business and users' fundamental rights. It is possible to observe that the extension of the scope of the e-Commerce Directive would increase uniformity in online content moderation.[94] If online intermediaries were able to rely on the safe harbour against illicit data processing perpetrated by third-parties, their content moderation processes could benefit from a general extension also to that online content in terms of the freedom to conduct business of online intermediaries. This is also why Keller underlined that the extension of the e-Commerce rule to the field of data would be a matter of fairness.[95]

Since the e-Commerce Directive allows Member States to impose injunctions and filtering systems to online intermediaries to address specific cases, a downside of the potential positive effects of such a system could be the risk of intermediaries encourage intermediaries to proactively monitoring data, most notably personal data, disseminated through their platform as a means to tackle third-party violations. Since, in the algorithmic society, online intermediaries play a more active role in processing data and performing content moderation, this safe harbour extension could encourage platforms to increase their monitoring activities with potential chilling effects for freedom of expression and with troubling effects also on other users'

[93] According to Recital 55, '[A]ny damage which a person may suffer as a result of unlawful processing must be compensated for by the controller, who may be exempted from liability if he proves that he is not responsible for the damage, in particular in cases where he establishes fault on the part of the data subject or in case of force majeure; whereas sanctions must be imposed on any person, whether governed by private or public law, who fails to comply with the national measures taken under this Directive'.

[94] Brendan Van Alsenoy, 'Liability under EU Data Protection Law from Directive 95/46 to the General Data Protection Regulation' (2016) 9(2) Journal of Intellectual Property, Information Technology and Electronic Commerce Law 271.

[95] Keller (n. 60).

fundamental rights like privacy.[96] Besides, the lack of harmonisation between different systems of notice-and-takedown conflicts with the GDPR's harmonisation goal.

It should also not be neglected that allowing online platforms to benefit from the exemption of liability even for third-party content infringing personal data could reduce the procedural safeguards limiting platforms powers. The e-Commerce Directive framework does not provide safeguards in this process. Therefore, users could not complain against platforms' refusal to remove certain data due to the fact that platforms are free to decide the fate of the information they host, especially when that information is likely not to be illicit, such as in the case of delisting requests. Instead, the GDPR recognises data subjects' rights. Even if, as already stressed, these obligations could be an incentive for online intermediaries to extensively monitor their spaces to escape responsibility, however, it is also a way to require them to take users' requests seriously. This framework will raise less concerns once the Digital Services Act is adopted introducing procedural safeguards even in the field of content.

As a result, it is worth wondering how *Google Vivi Down* and *Google Spain* would have been adjudicated if the GDPR was in force at that time. In the lack of judicial interpretation about the two regimes of liability, it is not possible to foresee how the Italian courts and ECJ would have interpreted the two cases. According to this system, as underlined in *La Quadrature du Net*, the ECJ can decide which regime applies by putting aside one of them. Besides, the adoption of the Digital Services Act would not contribute to clarifying this relationship since it just provides that the scope of application should be without prejudice to the application of the GDPR.[97] The only clarification introduced by the Digital Services Act, which adopts the same approach of the GDPR in terms of limiting its scope in relation to European data protection law, concerns the information relating to advertisement, which should be without prejudice to the provision of the GDPR relating to 'the right to object, automated individual decision-making, including profiling and specifically the need to obtain consent of the data subject prior to the processing of personal data for targeted advertising'.[98] One of the primary

[96] See Case C-70/10 *Scarlet Extended SA* v. *Société belge des auteurs, compositeurs et éditeurs SCRL (SABAM)* (2011); Case C-360/10 *Belgische Vereniging van Auteurs, Componisten en Uitgevers CVBA (SABAM)* v. *Netlog NV* (2012).

[97] COM(2020) 825 final (n. 84), Art. 1(5)(i).

[98] Ibid., Recital 52.

consequences of this approach is to blur the boundaries between the two regimes, precisely between the notion of 'data controller' and 'active provider' affecting the application of the rules in the field of content and data.

4.5 The Challenges Ahead in the Field of Content and Data

The relationship between content and data has increasingly become intimate with the rise and consolidation of the algorithmic society. Online platforms have led to revolutionary changes in the processing of information and data. Different types of data are published and mixed with other information through systems that organise, promote and aggregate content. From a first phase of technological and legal divergence at the beginning of this century, the legal regimes of online intermediaries and data have slowly started a dialogue triggered by a trend of technological convergence.

From the first contact in *Promusicae*, such a relationship has become more blurred with the advent of online platforms whose business was based on data-driven models. Both layers have started to technologically overlap when focusing on online intermediaries such as search engines and social media which do not merely perform the activity of data processors or passive providers any longer. In *Google Vivi Down* and *Google Spain*, the interpretation of the Italian courts and the ECJ highlighted the complexities in applying a rigid separation between the two systems. The mix of active provider and data controller implies that the rigid distinction in the application of the two regimes (and their parallel track) is questioned by the passive role of online intermediaries. Put another way, if it is not a surprise that the e-Commerce Directive excluded privacy and data protection matters from its scope of application, nowadays, the same political choice would look different when applied to online platforms.

The Union has maintained a system based on a parallel track even in the framework of the Digital Single Market Strategy. There are paths of legal convergence increasingly highlighting the relationship between content and data. Despite the historical differences between the two fields in question, freedom of expression and data protection have shown their ability to overcome the aforementioned legal divergence by sharing the common goal to protect democratic values. This trend is evident in the phase of digital constitutionalism where, as examined in Chapter 2, the need to protect both fundamental rights has led to a positive regulatory reaction. Likewise, the introduction of procedural safeguards in the field of content is another critical sign of convergence towards the creation of a more transparent and accountable digital environment. The introduction of the Digital Services Act could contribute to providing horizontal procedural safeguards reflecting the system of data protection. Besides, the system of liability in the field of content and data is another example of potential legal convergence even if, in this case, it is still not clear whether the GDPR opens the doors towards overlaps between the two regimes in terms of responsibilities and liability for third-party content and data.

Therefore, although the two systems have been conceived as being on parallel tracks, the path of European digital constitutionalism has led to legal convergence as an answer to technological convergence. It would not be hazardous to argue that the evolution of artificial intelligence technologies will increasingly lead the two systems to collide where data controllers and hosting providers decide how to exploit the value coming from the interrelation of content and data. The cases of content moderation and automated decision-making processes provide some clues of this evolution. Therefore, they deserve to be further analysed within the framework of European digital constitutionalism designing a path to protect fundamental rights and democratic values in the algorithmic society.

5 Digital Constitutionalism and Freedom of Expression

5.1 Expressions in the Algorithmic Society

Freedom of expression is one of the cornerstones of democratic society.[1] This non-exhaustive statement is of particular relevance in the digital age.[2] In the last twenty years, the Internet has become one of the primary means to exercise rights and freedoms. The possibility to access online services and content ubiquitously has played a critical role in promoting opinions and ideas on a global scale.[3] Users can connect with different communities to build social and professional relationships at a global level simply by using a personal device. The global pandemic has revealed the importance of online services to overcome the limits of social distancing.

Nevertheless, this flourishing democratic framework driven by digital communication technologies firmly clashes with the troubling evolution of the algorithmic society where online platforms govern the flow of information online.[4] By making decisions on expressions, they contribute to shaping the boundaries of freedom of expression in the digital age. More than two billion users are today governed by

[1] Cass Sunstein, *Democracy and the Problem of Free Speech* (The Free Press 1995).

[2] Jack M. Balkin, 'Digital Speech and Democratic Culture: A Theory of Freedom of Expression for the Information Society' (2004) 79(1) New York University Law Review 1.

[3] Henry Jenkins, *Convergence Culture: Where Old and New Media Collide* (New York University Press 2006).

[4] Niva Elkin-Koren and Maayan Perel, 'Guarding the Guardians: Content Moderation by Online Intermediaries and the Rule of Law' in Giancarlo Frosio (ed.), *Oxford Handbook of Online Intermediary Liability* (Oxford University Press 2020); Kate Klonick, 'The New Governors: The People, Rules, and Processes Governing Online Speech' (2018) 131 Harvard Law Review 1598; Kyle Langvardt, 'Regulating Online Content Moderation' (2018) 106 The Georgetown Law Journal 1353.

Facebook's community guidelines,[5] and YouTube decides how to host and distribute billions of hours of video each week.[6]

This quantitative consideration just provides a partial picture of power. An oligopoly of private entities organises transnationally online information for profit by using algorithmic technologies.[7] The organisation of social media news feeds or the results provided by a search engine are only some examples of the role of automated decision-making systems in online content moderation, thus pushing to rethink the public sphere.[8] The decisions of Facebook and Twitter to block the account of the former president Donald Trump in the aftermath of the violent conflict at Capitol Hill or the Facebook ban of Australian publishers as an answer to the adoption of the News Media and Digital Platforms Mandatory Bargaining Code are just two examples of their power over online information. Since algorithmic technologies are programmed according to the economic and ethical values of online platforms without any involvement of the users, the extent to which freedom of expression is protected is subject to private determinations driven by opaque business purposes.[9] Even if political and social movements have spread in the digital environment,[10] the governance of online content is increasingly privatised,[11] and, therefore, oriented to private purposes which would not lead to putting much hope in the safeguards of democratic values online.[12]

If content moderation plays a crucial role in shaping the boundaries of freedom of expression in the algorithmic society, it is worth wondering how to avoid freedom of expression being subject to opaque private

[5] Ben Popper, 'A Quarter of the World's Population now Uses Facebook Every Month' The Verge (3 May 2017) www.theverge.com/2017/5/3/15535216/facebook-q1-first-quarter-2017-earnings accessed 21 November 2021.

[6] Jack Nicas, 'YouTube Tops 1 Billion Hours of Video a Day, on Pace to Eclipse TV' Wall Street Journal (27 February 2017) www.wsj.com/articles/youtube-tops-1-billion-hours-of-video-a-day-on-pace-to-eclipse-tv-1488220851 accessed 21 November 2021.

[7] Jack M. Balkin, 'Free Speech in the Algorithmic Society: Big Data, Private Governance, and New School Speech Regulation' (2018) 51 University of California Davis 1151.

[8] Andras Koltay, *New Media and Freedom of Expression. Rethinking the Constitutional Foundations of the Public Sphere* (Hart 2019).

[9] Josè Van Dijk and Thomas Poell, 'Understanding Social Media Logic' (2013) 1(1) Media and Communication 2; Tarleton Gillespie, 'The Politics of Platforms' (2010) 12(3) News Media & Society 347.

[10] Manuel Castells, *Networks of Outrage and Hope: Social Movements in the Internet Age* (Polity Press 2012).

[11] Andrew Tutt, 'The New Speech' (2014) 41 Hastings Constitutional Law Quarterly 235.

[12] Evgeny Morozov, *The Net Delusion: The Dark Side of Internet Freedom* (Public Affairs 2011).

interests rather than public values. Indeed, the primary point is to understand which remedies can mitigate the risk of exposing users just to content reflecting business logics rather than pluralism. The informational (and power) asymmetry between users and platforms leads to questioning whether the traditional liberal and negative dimension of the right to freedom of expression can ensure democratic values in the algorithmic era.

Within this clash between democratic public values and non-democratic business interests, this chapter focuses on the challenges of freedom of expression in the algorithmic society and on how European digital constitutionalism can provide remedies to deal with this troubling scenario for democracy and the rule of law. This challenge is particularly relevant for democratic societies. As underlined in Chapter 3, democratic states are open environments for pluralism and values such as liberty, equality, transparency and accountability. On the contrary, the activity of online platforms is based on business interests, opaque procedures and unaccountable decision-making. Democracy relies on individual self-determination and autonomy which are the primary drivers for developing opinions and participation in decision-making processes. The lack of pluralism as driven by online platforms could undermine the ability of users to make decisions based on a multiplicity of voices concurring to develop ideas. Therefore, freedom of expression is not only a individual fundamental right subject to the interference of powers but also a constitutional instrument to foster autonomy in a democratic society, reflecting the framework of dignity characterising European constitutionalism.

As examined in Chapter 3, the law of the platform competes with the authority exercised by public actors. While online platforms have a responsibility rather than a duty to guarantee the respect of fundamental rights and freedoms, democratic states are required to safeguard these interests to protect the entire democratic system. Such duty also encompasses a positive obligation to protect individuals against acts committed by private persons or entities.[13] Without protecting equality, freedom of expression or assembly, it would not be possible to enjoy a democratic society.

[13] UN Human Rights Committee (HRC), 'General comment no. 31 [80], The nature of the general legal obligation imposed on States Parties to the Covenant', 26 May 2004 www.refworld.org/docid/478b26ae2.html accessed 21 November 2021.

This chapter underlines that the vertical and negative nature of freedom of expression is no longer enough to protect democratic values in the digital environment, since the flow of information is actively organised by business interests, driven by profit-maximisation rather than democracy, transparency or accountability. This chapter demonstrates how the development of the algorithmic society has challenged the liberal paradigm of free speech requiring a complementary shift from a negative and active to a positive and passive dimension. Therefore, this chapter examines how European digital constitutionalism leads to reframing media pluralism to protect freedom of expression in the algorithmic society.

The first part of this chapter analyses the shift from a liberal economic narrative based on the metaphor of the free marketplace of ideas to the rise of platform power to moderate online content. Precisely, it focuses on the logic of content moderation, the rise of the algorithmic public sphere and the challenges to the protection of the right to freedom of expression raised by the private enforcement of fundamental rights. The second part focuses on the current status quo, underlining the first step of European digital constitutionalism towards limiting platform power and focusing on the horizontal effect doctrine as a potential way to fill the regulatory gap in the field of content moderation. The third part examines the approach of European digital constitutionalism to address the challenges of content moderation, focusing on rethinking online media pluralism through transparency and procedural safeguards.

5.2 From the Free Marketplace of Ideas . . .

The right to freedom of expression in modern and contemporary history has liberal roots. Like other civil and political liberties risen at the end of the nineteenth century,[14] the right to free speech is based on the idea that liberties and freedoms can be ensured by limiting interferences coming from public actors.[15] The possibility to express opinions and ideas freely is the grounding condition to develop personal identity and ensures the right to self-determination in a democratic society.

It is not by chance that one of the most suggestive legal metaphors in this field is that of the 'free marketplace of ideas',[16] as coined for the

[14] The Declaration of the Rights of Man and of the Citizen (1789).

[15] Eric Barendt, *Freedom of Speech* (Oxford University Press 2017).

[16] See, e.g., Daniel E. Ho and Frederik Schauer, 'Testing the Marketplace of Ideas' (2015) 90 New York University Law Review 1161; Eugene Volokh, 'In Defense of the Market Place

first time by Justice Douglas in *United States* v. *Rumely*.[17] This liberalist belief can be contextualised in the classical theory of market balance applied to the field of ideas.[18] Since individuals act rationally, they can choose the best products and services in a free market. As in a competitive market where the best products or services prevail, the same mechanism would apply to the best information resulting from market balance.

However, the liberal grounds of freedom of expression are more in depth and older. In the seventeenth century, Milton, opposing the English Parliament's Press Ordinance, which had introduced a system of censorship to punish the promoters of ideas considered illegal, argued that freedom of expression should not be limited to allow the truth to prevail thanks to the free exchange of opinion.[19] Milton compares the truth to a streaming fountain whose water constitutes the flow of information saving men from prejudice. According to this perspective, it is necessary to avoid any interference with the flow of information to lead men to the highest level of knowledge. Two centuries later, Mill shared a liberal approach to freedom of expression.[20] Even falsehood could contribute to reaching the truth.[21] Otherwise, censoring falsehood would make meaningless

of Ideas / Search for Truth as a Theory of Free Speech Protection' (2011) 97(3) Virginia Law Review 591; Joseph Blocher, 'Institutions in the Marketplace of Ideas' (2008) 57(4) Duke Law Journal 820; Paul H. Brietzke, 'How and Why the Marketplace of Ideas Fails' (1997) 31(3) Valparaiso University Law Review 951; Alvin I. Goldman and James C. Cox, *Speech, Truth, and the Free Market for Ideas* (Cambridge University Press 1996).

17 *United States* v. *Rumely* 345 U.S. 41 (1953). 'Of necessity I come then to the constitutional questions. Respondent represents a segment of the American press. Some may like what his group publishes; others may disapprove. These tracts may be the essence of wisdom to some; to others their point of view and philosophy may be anathema. To some ears their words may be harsh and repulsive; to others they may carry the hope of the future. We have here a publisher who through books and pamphlets seeks to reach the minds and hearts of the American people. He is different in some respects from other publishers. But the differences are minor. Like the publishers of newspapers, magazines, or books, this publisher bids for the minds of men in the market place of ideas'.

18 Ronald Coase, 'Markets for Goods and Market for Ideas' (1974) 64(2) American Economic Review 1974.

19 John Milton, *Aeropagitica* (1644). According to Milton: 'So Truth be in the field, we do injuriously, by licensing and prohibiting, to misdoubt her strength. Let her and Falsehood grapple; who ever knew Truth put to the worse, in a free and open encounter?'

20 John S. Mill, *On Liberty* (1859).

21 Ibid. '[If] any opinion is compelled to silence, that opinion may, for aught we can certainly know, be true. To deny this is to assume our own infallibility'.

the comparison between ideas and opinions with the risk of dogmatising the current truth.[22] Both Milton and Mill agreed that the right to freedom of expression is effective when it is free from censorship and from the interferences of power.

The scope of these liberal ideas opposing public actors' interferences also emerged in the US legal framework. Justice Holmes' dissenting opinion in *Abrams* v. *United States* can still be considered the constitutional essence of freedom of expression in the United States as enshrined in the First Amendment.[23] The case concerned the distribution of leaflets calling for ammunition factories to strike to express a clear message of resistance against the US military intervention in Russia. According to Justice Holmes, although men try to support their positions by criticising opposing ideas, they must not be persuaded that their opinions are certain. Only the free exchange of ideas can confirm the accuracy of each position.[24] Freedom of speech is functional to ensure that individuals are autonomous and, therefore, responsible moral agents participating in a political society.[25] According to Meiklejohn, the constitutional protection of free speech aims to foster citizens' awareness about public matters.[26]

This liberal approach has also been expressed, more recently, in the framework of the digital environment, at least in two landmark decisions of the US Supreme Court. In 1997, in *Reno* v. *ACLU*,[27] the Supreme Court ruled that the provisions of the Communication Decency Act concerning the criminalisation of obscene or indecent materials to

22 Ibid. '[E]ven if the received opinion be not only true, but the whole truth; unless it is suffered to be, and actually is, vigorously and earnestly contested, it will, by most of those who receive it, be held in the manner of a prejudice, with little comprehension or feeling of its rational grounds'.

23 *Abrams* v. *United States* (1919) 250 U.S. 616: 'Persecution for the expression of opinions seems to me perfectly logical. If you have no doubt of your premises or your power and want a certain result with all your heart you naturally express your wishes in law and sweep away all opposition ... But when men have realized that time has upset many fighting faiths, they may come to believe even more than they believe the very foundations of their own conduct that the ultimate good desired is better reached by free trade in ideas. ... The best test of truth is the power of the thought to get itself accepted in the competition of the market, and that truth is the only ground upon which their wishes safely can be carried out'.

24 Sheldon Novick, *Honorable Justice* (Laurel 1990).

25 Ronald Dworkin, *Freedom's Law: The Moral Reading of the American Constitution* (Oxford University Press 1999).

26 Alexander Meiklejohn, *Free Speech and Its Relation to Self-Government* (Lawbook Exchange 2011).

27 *Reno* v. *American Civil Liberties Union* 521 U.S. 844 (1997).

any person under eighteen was unconstitutional.[28] As observed by the Supreme Court, unlike traditional media outlets, 'the risk of encountering indecent material by accident is remote because a series of affirmative steps is required to access specific material'.[31] According to Justice Stevens, the Internet plays the role of a 'new marketplace of ideas' observing that 'the interest in encouraging freedom of expression in a democratic society outweighs any theoretical but unproven benefit of censorship'.[29] Besides, he observed that the growth of the Internet as been phenomenal and, therefore, 'we presume that governmental regulation of the content of speech is more likely to interfere with the free exchange of ideas than to encourage it. The interest in encouraging freedom of expression in a democratic society outweighs any theoretical but unproven benefit of censorship'.[30] This decision can be considered the first step towards a transformation of the public forum doctrine.[31]

Despite the passing of years and opposing positions, this liberal approach has been reiterated more recently in *Packingham* v. *North Carolina*.[32] The case involved a statute banning registered sex offenders from accessing social networking services to avoid any contact with minors. The US Supreme Court placed the Internet and social media on the same layer of public places where the First Amendment enjoys a broad scope of protection. In the words of Justice Kennedy: 'It is cyberspace – the "vast democratic forums of the Internet" in general, and social media in particular'.[33] The metaphor of the (digital) free marketplace of ideas is still firm in the jurisprudence of the US Supreme Court. Social media are indeed considered as an enabler of democracy rather than as a threat for public discourse. This would also contribute to explaining why social media enjoy a safe constitutional area of protection under the First Amendment, which, in the last twenty years, has constituted a fundamental ban on any attempt to regulate speech online,[34] thus showing the role of the First Amendment in US

[28] Communication Decency Act (1996).

[29] 521 U.S. 844 (n. 27).

[30] Ibid., 885.

[31] Dawn C. Nunziato, 'The Death of The Public Forum in Cyberspace' (2005) 20 Berkeley Technology Law Journal 1115.

[32] *Packingham* v. *North Carolina* (2017) 582 U.S. ___.

[33] Ibid.

[34] See, e.g., *Ashcroft* v. *Free Speech Coalition* (2002) 535 U.S. 234; *Ashcroft* v. *American Civil Liberties Union* (2002) 535 U.S. 564.

constitutionalism,[35] as 'the paramount right within the American constellation of constitutional rights'.[36]

Nevertheless, it would be enough just to cross the Atlantic to understand how this general trust for a vertical paradigm of free speech is not shared worldwide by other democracies, especially when the right to freedom of expression is framed in the digital environment. While, in the United States, the Internet and social media still benefit from the frame coming from the traditional liberal metaphor of the free marketplace of ideas as a safeguard for democracy,[37] in Europe, freedom of expression online does not enjoy the same degree of protection.[38] In the European framework, the right to freedom of expression is subject to a multilevel balancing,[39] precisely with other rights enshrined in the Charter,[40] the Convention[41] and national constitutions. Unlike the US Supreme Court, the Strasbourg Court has shown a more restrictive approach to the protection of the right to freedom of expression in the digital environment, perceived more like a risk rather than as an opportunity for the flourishing of democratic values.[42]

Such a cautious approach in Europe does not only aim to balance different constitutional interests but also to avoid that granting absolute protection to one right could lead to the destruction of other

[35] See, e.g., Lee C. Bollinger and Geoffrey R. Stone (eds.), *The Free Speech Century* (Oxford University Press 2019); Floyd Abrams, *The Soul of the First Amendment* (Yale University Press 2017); Frederik Schaurer, 'The Exceptional First Amendment' in Michael Ignatieff (ed.), *American Exceptionalism and Human Rights* 29 (Princeton University Press 2005); Alexander Meiklejohn, 'The First Amendment Is an Absolute' (1961) The Supreme Court Review 245.

[36] Michel Rosenfeld and Andras Sajo, 'Spreading Liberal Constitutionalism: An Inquiry into the Fate of Free Speech Rights in New Democracies' in Sujit Choudhry (ed.), *The Migration of Constitutional Ideas* 152 (Cambridge University Press 2007).

[37] Claudia E. Haupt, 'Regulating Speech Online: Free Speech Values in Constitutional Frames' Northeastern University School of Law Research Paper No. 402-2021 (22 July 2021) https://papers.ssrn.com/sol3/papers.cfm?abstract_id=3794884 accessed 19 November 2021.

[38] Oreste Pollicino and Marco Bassini, 'Free Speech, Defamation and the Limits to Freedom of Expression in the EU: A Comparative Analysis' in Andrej Savin and Jan Trzaskowski (eds.), *Research Handbook on EU Internet Law* 508 (Edward Elgar 2014); Vincenzo Zeno-Zencovich, *Freedom of Expression: A Critical and Comparative Analysis* (Routledge 2008).

[39] Ingolf Pernice, 'The Treaty of Lisbon: Multilevel Constitutionalism in Action' (2009) 15 (3) Columbia Journal of European Law 349.

[40] Charter of Fundamental Rights of the European Union (2012) OJ C326/12, Arts. 11, 52.

[41] European Convention on Human Rights (1950), Art. 10.

[42] Oreste Pollicino, 'Judicial Protection of Fundamental Rights in the Transition from the World of Atoms to the World of Bits: The Case of Freedom of Speech' (2019) 25(2) European Law Journal 155.

fundamental interests undermining de facto their constitutional relevance.[43] This is an expression of the different understanding of the role of dignity on the western side of the Atlantic as mentioned in Chapter 1. In Europe, freedom of expression is not just a liberal value whose protection needs to be safeguarded at any cost to protect democracy. Allowing such an approach would also entail that speech could be used as a constitutional excuse to hinder democracy itself. From a European constitutional perspective, freedom of expression is instead a fundamental right whose protection needs to take into account the other constitutional interests at stake. Unlike the frame of liberty in the US constitutional framework, freedom of expression in Europe does not enjoy absolute protection but is subject to the logic of balancing intimately connected to human dignity.[44] Bognetti underlined the European reluctancy to read freedom of speech in ways that would sacrifice other constitutional values. He observed: 'At times the necessity of preserving the values of liberal democracy has been felt so intensely as to lead to the prohibition of political parties and to deny legitimacy to speech that has been seen to undermine these values'.[45]

This non-exhaustive framework provides clues to understand why the Union has not adopted an omissive approach to the challenges to freedom of expression raised by the algorithmic society, thus paving the way towards a new approach, precisely focusing on regulating the process of content moderation. Despite the difference in the protection of the right to freedom of expression in the EU and the United States, this fundamental right is still the prerequisite for a democratic society. However, in the digital environment, the protection of this fundamental right is no longer a matter of quantity but a matter of quality because of the crucial role of online platforms in determining the standard of protection of freedom of expression and other fundamental rights on a global scale. The case of disinformation is a paradigmatic example of the challenges to the right to freedom of expression in the algorithmic society.[46] In other words, the primary challenge for democracies is no longer that of

[43] Charter (n. 40), Art. 54; Convention (n. 41), Art. 17.

[44] Mattias Kumm and Alec D. Walen, 'Human Dignity and Proportionality: Deontic Pluralism in Balancing' Grant Huscroft and others (eds.), *Proportionality and the Rule of Law: Rights, Justification, Reasoning* (Cambridge University Press 2014).

[45] Giovanni Bognetti, 'The Concept of Human Dignity in U.S. and European Constitutionalism' in Georg Nolte (ed.), *European and US Constitutionalism* 77 (Cambridge University Press 2005).

[46] Giovanni Pitruzella and Oreste Pollicino, *Disinformation and Hate Speech: An European Constitutional Perspective* (Bocconi University Press 2020).

protecting freedom of expression extensively by granting access to new digital channels and avoiding interferences from public actors, but, rather, that of ensuring exposure and pluralism in a democratic digital environment.

5.3 ... To the Algorithmic Marketplace of Ideas

At the World Summit on the Information Society in 2004, Lessig underlined the significant potentialities afforded by the digital environment: '[f]or the first time in a millennium, we have a technology to equalize the opportunity that people have to access and participate in the construction of knowledge and culture, regardless of their geographic placing'.[47] Likewise, Shapiro stated: 'Hierarchies are coming undone. Gatekeepers are being bypassed. Power is devolving down to "end users" ... No one is in control except you'.[48] These were positive news for the free marketplace of ideas. Information sources have spread online. The new online communication channels have enabled users to potentially reach a global audience without relying any longer on the traditional channels of communications in the hand of publishers like newspapers and televisions.[49] Put another way, the Internet as a new channel of communication promised to overcome the problem of concentration of power in traditional media warned of by Habermas.[50]

Although it is true that the possibility for users to express opinions and ideas without traditional filters cannot be contested, nonetheless, the lack of control over information online has been revealed to be just a libertarian dream. It is true that users can still run their blogs and websites to share their ideas or opinions, sell products or keep social relationships. However, it would be naïve to believe that this is how most information flows online. As underlined in Chapter 3, to exercise online rights and freedoms, it is almost necessary to rely on online platforms, primarily social media. These entities aim to maximise

[47] Lawrence Lessig, 'An Information Society: Free or Feudal' (2004) World Summit on the Information Society (WSIS) www.itu.int/wsis/docs/pc2/visionaries/lessig.pdf accessed 22 November 2021.

[48] Andrew L. Shapiro, *The Control Revolution: How the Internet is Putting Individuals in Charge and Changing the World we Know* 11, 30 (Public Affairs 1999).

[49] Jack M. Balkin, 'Old-School/New-School Speech Regulation' (2014) 127 Harvard Law Review 2296.

[50] Marianne Franklin, *Digital Dilemmas: Power, Resistance, and the Internet* (Oxford University Press 2013).

their profit, and expressions – to say nothing of data – are the perfect means to achieve this purpose. By processing content, platforms can extract information, collect data and even map emotions to provide the most granular advertising services on the market and finding new ways to attract customers.[51] It would be enough to observe the business models of Facebook and Google based on more than 80 per cent on advertising revenues coming from advertising services.[52] Just these two platforms absorb 75 per cent of the $73 billion digital advertising market in the United States.[53] In other words, users are subject to the private governance of the space where information flows based on business logic of online platforms.

The moderation of expressions for profit reflects the logic of digital capitalism, or better information capitalism, which leads platforms to express surveillance and governance as expressions of powers.[54] At first glance, there would be not so many differences with traditional media outlets governing and filtering information. Nonetheless, in the digital environment, the source of platform power comes primarily from algorithmic technologies processing a vast amount of data and information that platforms can accumulate, revealing users' intimate information which is enormously valuable for commercial interests, governments' public tasks and political campaigns. If these considerations are mixed with the immunity of online intermediaries from liability for hosting third-party content, it should not come as a surprise how profitable it is for platforms to run their business with a very low degree of risk. In other words, by relying on their immunity, platforms have developed business models profiting from online speech without accountability.

However, although the private governance of content frames online speech in a mercantilist environment where the space for democratic values is only a matter of business incentives, the role of algorithms in organising content as well has positive effects to help users interact and

[51] Vindu Goel, 'Facebook Tinkers with Users' Emotions in News Feed Experiment, Stirring Outcry' The New York Times (29 June 2014) www.nytimes.com/2014/06/30/technology/facebook-tinkers-with-users-emotions-in-news-feed-experiment-stirring-outcry.html accessed 21 November 2021.

[52] Mathew Ingram, 'How Google and Facebook Have Taken Over the Digital Ad Industry' Fortune (4 January 2017) https://fortune.com/2017/01/04/google-facebook-ad-industry/ accessed 21 November 2021.

[53] Shannon Bond, 'Google and Facebook Build Digital Duopoly' Financial Times (14 March 2017) ft.com/content/30c81d12-08c8-11e7-97d1- 5e720a26771b accessed 21 November 2021.

[54] Julie Cohen, *Between Truth and Power: The Legal Constructions of Informational Capitalism* (Oxford University Press 2019).

access the vast amount of information in a framework of scarcity of time and attention.[55] Information has spread online with the result that what is now scarce is not the source of information but the attention of the listeners.[56] This change has led to the emergence of the 'attention economy' pushing towards new strategies to attracts consumers.[57] If social media programme their algorithms to achieve business purposes through content moderation, it should not come as a surprise that content moderation does not reflect necessarily democratic values like diversity or truthfulness. The primary goal is just increasing the probability of an interaction between users and the time and quantity of content they share on social media spaces. Even more importantly, as examined in Chapter 3, such discretion in the moderation of expressions contributes to shaping online speech and the principle of the rule of law. The price to pay for such an intermediation consists of accepting the private values translated by algorithmic determinations.

These considerations show why considering public actors as the only source of interference for freedom of expression online could today seem anachronistic. A further challenge raised by the algorithmic society concerns how to address the discretion of private actors freely influencing the limits of freedom of expression on a global scale without any public guarantee. The metaphor of the marketplace of ideas is critical now more than ever to represent the current situation, but with a small makeup. The difference consists of the change of the expression 'free' with 'algorithmic', that moves the perspective from democratic and collective values to business and individualist purposes. Ideas do not reach a market balance through the invisible hand, but are driven by oligopolist logics where decisions are centralised. In the algorithmic marketplace of ideas, speech is still central but not quite as much from the perspective of users' freedoms as from that of platforms' profits. Within this framework, the following subsections focus on the characteristics of the algorithmic public sphere, the logic of moderation and the private enforcement of freedom of expression online.

55 Natali Helberger, 'On the Democratic Role of News Recommenders' (2019) 7(8) Digital Journalism 993.

56 Herbert A. Simon, 'Designing Organizations for an Information-Rich World' in Martin Greenberger (ed.), *Computers, Communications, and the Public Interest* 37 (Johns Hopkins Press 1971).

57 Tim Wu, *The Attention Merchants: The Epic Scramble to Get Inside our Heads* (Knopf 2016).

5.3.1 The Public Sphere in the Age of Algorithms

'Imagine a future in which your interface agent can read every newswire and newspaper and catch every TV and radio broadcast on the planet, and then construct a personalised summary. This kind of newspaper is printed in an edition of one'. These were the words of Negroponte in 1995 in the aftermath of the Internet.[58] The situation of centralisation and personalisation of expression which users are experiencing was already in these sentences.

In the algorithmic society, online platforms mediate the ability of users to share their opinions and ideas online. The use of Google or Facebook is almost a mandatory step for entering the public debate and building social interactions online.[59] Already in 1962, Habermas observed that 'the process in which societal power is transformed into political power is as much in need of criticism and control as the legitimate exercise of political domination over society'.[60] The lack of control in the shift from social to political is what already happened in the field of traditional media outlets. Once again, Habermas already underlined the debasement of the public sphere consisting of the high societal barriers to access channels of communication (e.g. print media) and the intertwined relationship with politics.[61] In this bottleneck, a bunch of national mass media institutions governed public discourse.

These considerations would not sound brand new in the digital environment. Like any other libertarian dream, the idea of an alternative space overcoming traditional forms of control failed. Together with states, other entities contribute to producing norms regulating spaces. As Fraser explained, it is not possible to think a public sphere free from manipulation in a capitalist economy where different forces tend to influence the formation of the public opinion and societal beliefs.[62] Benkler already underlined how the digital environment projects users in a 'networked public sphere'.[63] The difference is the mediating subject which has changed from a bunch of traditional media outlets to

[58] Nicholas Negroponte, *Being Digital* 153 (Alfred A. Knopf 1995).

[59] Taina Bucher, 'Want to Be on the Top? Algorithmic Power and the Threat of Invisibility on Facebook' (2012) 14(7) New Media & Society 1164.

[60] Jürgen Habermas, *The Structural Transformation of the Public Sphere: An Inquiry into a Category of Bourgeois Society* 210 (MIT Press 1991).

[61] Jürgen Habermas, *Between Facts and Norms* (MIT Press 1998).

[62] Nancy Fraser, 'Rethinking the Public Sphere: A Contribution to the Critique of Actually Existing Democracy' (1990) 25/26 Social Text 56.

[63] Yochai Benkler, *The Wealth of Networks: How Social Production Transforms Markets and Freedom* (Yale University Press 2006).

an oligopoly of online providers. While, at first glance, the digital environment could be a solution to overcome centralised powers in the media sector, realising Habermas' dream of a bourgeois public sphere, a closer look shows how similar dynamics of centralisation and control over information have been reproduced in the digital environment creating a quasi-public sphere.[64] Platforms' ability to massively organise or amplify certain voices (and decide how to do that) leads to thinking about the future of the public sphere online.

This framework of power does not mean that the digital environment has not provided opportunities to express ideas and opinions. Although the rise of information pluralism should generally be welcomed for the development and maintenance of a democratic environment, the characteristics of the information flow online and its moderation raise serious concerns in terms of 'quantity' and 'quality' of the information sources.

From a quantitative perspective, in the last twenty years, a high degree of concentration of the online platforms' market has characterised the digital environment. As foreseen by Zittrain,[65] the characteristics of the information society have led to the creation of monopolies,[66] linked to the platformisation of the Internet,[67] which Srnicek would call the era of 'platform capitalism'.[68] This market concentration empowers a limited number of platforms to set the conditions on which vast amounts of content and data flow online. The effect of this process is to create barriers for entering the market of information and increase the dependency of traditional media outlets from the new opportunities of visibility offered by social media. Although, at first glance, the digital environment has empowered users to access new channels to share ideas and access sources of information, however, the aforementioned digital convergence dangerously affects media pluralism from a quantitative perspective.

[64] Jillian C. York, 'Policing Content in the Quasi-Public Sphere' Open Net Initiative' Bulletin (September 2010) https://opennet.net/policing-content-quasi-public-sphere accessed 21 November 2021.

[65] Jonathan Zittrain, *The Future of the Internet and How to Stop It* (Yale University Press 2008).

[66] Robin Mansell and Michele Javary, 'Emerging Internet Oligopolies: A Political Economy Analysis' in Arthur S. Miller and Warren J. Samuels (eds.), *An Institutionalist Approach to Public Utilities Regulation* (Michigan State University Press 2002).

[67] Anne Helmond, 'The Platformization of the Web: Making Web Data Platform Ready' (2015) 1(2) Social Media + Society 1.

[68] Nick Srnicek, *Platform Capitalism* (Polity Press 2016).

From a qualitative standpoint, pluralism is based on different manifestations of thinking and promotes heterogeneous ideas. In the digital environment, the use of artificial intelligence for online content moderation mitigates this positive effect. The European High-Level Expert Group on Media diversity underlined this point explaining the negative impact on democracy by noting that, while 'increasing filtering mechanisms make it more likely for people to only get news on subjects they are interested in, and with the perspective, they identify with', '[this reality] will also tend to create more insulated communities as isolated subsets within the overall public sphere'.[69] Democracy indeed needs a public sphere where the meeting of ideas and opinions can be a 'societal glue'.[70] Otherwise, individuals are likely to be attracted by extreme and dogmatic poles, forgetting the alternative ideas which are the basis for consensus in a democratic society. The Habermasian idea of the public sphere is hard to realise in the digital environment where ideas are formulated, negotiated and distributed by machines. In other words, the public sphere in the age of algorithms is not under the control and guidance of public opinion but instead is governed by opaque business purposes.

In a footnote within a larger article of 2006, Habermas underlined the critical role of digital technologies for democracy, looking particularly at authoritarian regimes. However, '[i]n the context of liberal regimes, the rise of millions of fragmented chat rooms across the world tend instead to lead to the fragmentation of large but politically focused mass audiences into a huge number of isolated issue publics'.[71] Despite the criticisms and disappointment sparked by this non-exhaustive comment,[72] these sentences underline the double face of the online public sphere: a great opportunity for democracy as a liberation

[69] High-Level Group on Media Freedom and Pluralism, 'A free and pluralistic media to sustain European democracy' (2013), 27 https://ec.europa.eu/digital-single-market/sites/digital-agenda/files/HLG%20Final%20Report.pdf accessed 22 November 2021.

[70] Cass R. Sunstein, *Republic.com* 9 (Princeton University Press 2002).

[71] Jurgen Habermas, 'Political Communication in Media Society: Does Democracy Still Enjoy an Epistemic Dimension? The Impact of Normative Theory on Empirical Research' (2006) 16(4) Communication Theory 411, 423.

[72] Howard Rheingold, 'Habermas Blows Off Question about the Internet and the Public Sphere', SmartMobs (5 November 2007) www.smartmobs.com/2007/11/05/habermas-blows-off-question-about-the-internet-and-the-public-sphere/ accessed 19 November 2021; Stuart Geiger, 'Does Habermas Understand the Internet? The Algorithmic Construction of the Blogo/Public Sphere' (2009) 10(1) Gnovis: A Journal of Communication, Culture, and Technology www.gnovisjournal.org/2009/12/22/does-habermas-understand-internet-algorithmic-construction-blogopublic-sphere/ accessed 19 November 2021.

technology, but also as a risk for the fragmentation of the public sphere driven by business purposes. According to Habermas, a solid democracy is highly dependent on the public opinion. The shift from 'public' to 'artificial' opinion due to the lack of ability of individuals to act as rational agents is one of the reasons why democracy could be threatened in the algorithmic society.

Such a liberal root of the public sphere, naturally and deeply connected with that of freedom of expression, is not just put under pressure, but it is is basically frustrated. It is worth wondering how individuals can be rational users in the algorithmic public sphere if they are subject to a top-down power exercised by online platforms driving the public sphere through artificial intelligence systems whose decision-making processes cannot be always explained. In other words, the same failure of freedom of expression as a negative right to protect democratic values also extends to the liberal vision of the digital public sphere.

A digital liberal approach to the public sphere based on the autonomy and rationality of users seems not to be enough to ensure democratic values any longer. The shift from the 'free' to the 'algorithmic' marketplace of ideas has shown the fallacies of the traditional instruments of pluralism when implemented in the digital environment. Accessing more information does not necessarily imply accessing better information. The organisation of content aims to engage users based on their data and preferences, leading to the polarisation of the debate due to the creation of 'filter bubbles' or 'information cocoons',[73] which Sunstein defines as 'communication universes in which we hear only what we choose and only what comforts us and pleases us'.[74] The personalisation of online content leads to the creation of echo chambers,[75] where each user is isolated and marginalised from opposing positions as resulting

[73] Eli Pariser, *The Filter Bubble: What the Internet Is Hiding from You* (Viking 2011); Cass R. Sunstein, *Republic.com 2.0* (Princeton University Press 2007).

[74] Cass R. Sunstein, *Infotopia: How Many Minds Produce Knowledge* 9 (Oxford University Press 2006).

[75] Empirical evidence of filter bubbles is scarce. See, e.g., see Judith Moeller and Natali Helberger, 'Beyond the Filter Bubble: Concepts, Myths, Evidence and Issues for Future Debates. A Report Drafted for the Dutch Media Regulator' (2018) https://dare.uva.nl/search?identifier=478edb9e-8296-4a84-9631-c7360d593610 accessed 19 November 2021; Richard Fletcher and Rasmus K. Nielsen, 'Are News Audiences Increasingly Fragmented? A Cross-National Comparative Analysis of Cross-Platform News Audience Fragmentation and Duplication' (2017) 67(4) Journal of Communication 476; Ivan Dylko and others, 'The Dark Side of Technology: An Experimental Investigation of the Influence of Customizability Technology on Online Political Selective Exposure' (2017) 73 Computers in Human Behavior 181.

from a mere algorithmic calculation. There are already studies showing the role of algorithmic bias in reflecting and amplifying existing human beliefs.[76] In other words, users are encouraged to interact only with information inside the area of their preferences.

This effect primarily results from the logic of moderation. Personalisation, more than removal or organisation, allows indeed platforms to maximise online attention, thus meeting the interests of companies interested in advertising their products and services online. Social media exploit the characteristics of human communication based on the tendency to avoid dissensus.[77] Since advertising revenues are highly dependent on attracting scarce attention, discovering new ways to manipulate users' behaviours is the mission of online platforms. Automation is implemented not only to remove but also organise and recommend content, thus influencing users' interactions. It would be enough to think about how the search results of Google or the Facebook newsfeed are not the same for each individual,[78] but they create what, at the beginning of this century, has already been defined as distinguished public spheres.[79]

The fragmentation of the public sphere is also driven by micro-targeting strategies which aim to limit the audience to certain content to increase the likelihood of capturing attention. While, like price discrimination, this is not an issue in the market field, it is instead when this practice is applied to the democratic debate that it shows how believing in a uniform public sphere in the information society could not be possible. Micro-targeting strategies intentionally focus just on certain groups giving the possibility to reach only those who are potentially interested in that content, no matter if the information is of commercial or political nature.[80] In this case, platforms become the arbiter of content online, including political speech.[81]

[76] Safiya U. Noble, *Algorithms of Oppression: How Search Engines Reinforce Racism* (New York University Press 2018).

[77] Leon Festinger, *A Theory of Cognitive Dissonance* (Stanford University Press 1957).

[78] Micheal A. DeVito, 'From Editors to Algorithms' (2017) 5(6) Digital Journalism 753.

[79] There is not a unitary notion of public sphere. See, e.g., Todd Gitlan, 'Public Sphere or Public Sphericules?' in Tamar Liebes and James Curran (eds.), *Media, Ritual and Identity* 168 (Routledge 2002); Micheal Warner, *Publics and Counterpublics* (MIT University Press 2002); Catherine R. Squires, 'Rethinking the Black Public Sphere: An Alternative Vocabulary for Multiple Public Spheres' (2002) 12(4) Communication Theory 446.

[80] Frederik J. Zuiderveen Borgesius and others, 'Online Political Microtargeting: Promises and Threats for Democracy' (2018) 14(1) Utrecht Law Review 82.

[81] Daniel Kreiss and Shannon C. Mcgregor, 'The "Arbiters of What Our Voters See": Facebook and Google's Struggle with Policy, Process, and Enforcement around Political

Although traditional media outlets could be accused of filtering relevant news or even manipulating information, they just provide unique platforms to discuss. On the opposite, online platforms create different places driven by business purposes for each user. Algorithms can indeed decide what deserves to be on top and what instead is best to hide. They choose who is a best friend rather than recommending that journal article or blog post to read. By processing a vast amount of information and data, artificial intelligence systems can select the relevant item to put in front of the user's eyes. The problem is that information that is relevant for the public debate is not defined by the exchange of views and opinions but machines. These systems are far from being perfect, leading to potential discriminatory bias or to exposure to objectionable content.[82]

Within this framework, content moderation contribute to generating intertwined public spheres whose sum then makes the single (and invisible) public sphere. This is also why, according to Schudson, the public sphere was never entirely based on agents' rational independency.[83] It has been always shaped by a form of intimate tribality governing the transmission of knowledge and ideas across society. What makes the public sphere is the sense of community or namely the function of communication towards building a global village,[84] where people consume information to underline their connection and define their place in the world.

Within this framework, users cannot access transparent information about what happens behind the screen. Between self-selected and pre-selected personalisation, also known as explicit or implicit personalisation,[85] the latter mostly prevail over the former.[86] In the

Advertising' (2019) 36(4) Political Communication 499; Shannon C. Mcgregor, 'Personalization, Social Media, and Voting: Effects of Candidate Self-Personalization on Vote Intention' (2017) 20(3) News Media & Society 1139.

[82] Muhammad Ali and others, 'Discrimination through Optimization: How Facebook's Ad Delivery Can Lead to Biased Outcomes' in *Proceedings of the ACM on Human-Computer Interaction* (ACM 2019); Reuben Binns and others, 'Like Trainer, Like Bot? Inheritance of Bias in Algorithmic Content Moderation' in Giovanni L. Ciampaglia, Afra Mashhadi and Taha Yasseri (eds.), *Social Informatics* 405 (Springer 2017).

[83] Micheal Schudson, 'Was There Ever a Public Sphere? If So, When? Reflections on the American Case' in John Calhoun (ed.), *Habermas and the Public Sphere* 143 (MIT Press 1992).

[84] Marshall McLuhan, *Understanding Media. The Extensions of Man* (MIT Press 1994).

[85] Neil Thurman and Steve Schifferes, 'The Future of Personalization at News Websites: Lessons from a Longitudinal Study' (2012) 13(5–6) Journalism Studies 775.

[86] Frederik J. Zuiderveen Borgesius and others, 'Should We Worry about Filter Bubbles?' (2016) 5(1) Internet Policy Review https://policyreview.info/node/401/pdf accessed 21 November 2021.

first case, users have more discretion in defining the criteria according to which online platforms organise their content through automated systems (i.e. selective exposure).[87] These options can include filters for certain types of content or topics rather than specific users or groups. This case is also relevant in the atomic world where individuals chose which kind of media outlets they wanted to rely on when buying a newspaper or watching television. This type of personalisation can also be beneficial for users since it leaves in the hands of individuals the possibility to choose their degree of exposure.[88] On the contrary, pre-selected personalisation is driven not only by online platforms but also exogenous factors as the goal to reach a new advertising strategy required by the market. Therefore, algorithmic accountability and transparency play a critical role in increasing users' autonomy and reduce the fragmentation of the public sphere.[89]

The challenges of content moderation could lead to the debasement of information pluralism in the digital environment. Instead of a democratic and decentralised society as defined at the end of the last century, an oligopoly of private entities has emerged, controlling information and determining how people exchange it.[90] Arendt described the public domain as a place 'where men exist not merely like other living or inanimate things, but to make their appearance explicitly' (i.e. the 'space of appearance').[91] Nonetheless, this space is not stable but highly dependent on the performance of deeds or the utterance of words. Indeed, 'unlike the spaces which are the work of our hands, it does not survive the actuality of the movement which brought it into being, but disappears not only with the dispersal of men – as in the case of great catastrophes when the body politic of a people is destroyed – but with the disappearance or arrest of the activities themselves'.[92]

The primary question is whether platform determinations shaping the public debate would lead to a qualitative arrest of human activities. Public actors are no longer the only source of concern in the (algorithmic) marketplace of ideas. The lack of transparency and accountability

[87] Natalie J. Stroud, 'Polarization and Partisan Selective Exposure' (2010) 60(3) Journal of Communication 556.

[88] Natalie Helberger, 'Diversity by Design' (2011) 1 Journal of Information Policy 441.

[89] Nikolas Diakopoulos, 'Algorithmic Accountability. Journalistic Investigation of Computational Power Structures' (2014) 3 Digital Journalism 398.

[90] Martin Moore and Damian Tambini (eds.), *Digital Dominance. The Power of Google, Amazon, Facebook, and Apple* (Oxford University Press 2018).

[91] Hannah Arendt, *The Human Condition* (University of Chicago Press 1998).

[92] Ibid., 199.

in online content moderation frustrates the exercise of freedoms in the public sphere encouraging to rethink the role of freedom of expression as a negative liberty in the algorithmic society. Platforms govern the flow of information online by defining, enforcing and balancing the right to freedom of expression online according to their business logics as the next subsection explains.

5.3.2 The Logic of Moderation

The shift from the free to the algorithmic marketplace of ideas can also be understood by focusing on the logic of moderation. Moderation can be defined as 'the screening, evaluation, categorization, approval or removal/hiding of online content according to relevant communications and publishing policies. It seeks to support and enforce positive communications behaviour online, and to minimize aggression and anti-social behaviour'.[93] By focusing on the virtues of moderation, Grimmelman has defined this process as 'the governance mechanisms that structure participation in a community to facilitate cooperation and prevent abuse'.[94] Content moderation decisions can be entirely automated, made by humans or a mix of them. While the activities of pre-moderation like prioritisation, delisting and geo-blocking are usually automated, post-moderation is usually the result of a mix between automated and human resources.[95] This activity usually implies the use of different kinds of automated systems to manage vast amounts of information in different phases.[96]

Moderation occurs before content is published (i.e. pre-moderation) or after publication (i.e. post-moderation). Precisely, post-moderation consists of the organisation of content, and it is implemented as a reactive measure to assess noticed content and as a proactive tool to actively monitor published content. Besides, removal is not the only way. For example, YouTube demonetises content by terminating any

[93] Terry Flew and others, 'Internet Regulation as Media Policy: Rethinking the Question of Digital Communication Platform Governance' (2019) 10(1) Journal of Digital Media & Policy 33, 40.

[94] James Grimmelmann, 'The Virtues of Moderation' (2015) 17 Yale Journal of Law and Technology 42, 47.

[95] Sarah T. Roberts, 'Content Moderation' in Laurie A. Schintler and Connie L. McNeely (eds.), *Encyclopedia of Big Data* (Springer 2017).

[96] Robert Gorwa, Reuben Binns and Christian Katzenbach, 'Algorithmic Content Moderation: Technical and Political Challenges in the Automation of Platform Governance' (2020) 7(1) Big Data & Society https://journals.sagepub.com/doi/pdf/10.1177/2053951719897945 accessed 19 November 2021.

revenue sharing agreement with the content provider. This process can be a powerful tool to silence certain speakers who rely on YouTube as a source of income. Another alternative to content removal is down-ranking or shadow banning. In this case, content is deprioritised in news feeds and other recommendation systems. This constitutes an editorial decision on the organisation of content affecting how public discourse is shaped online. Platforms can decide whether certain content is visible and, therefore, affect its potential reach and dissemination.

These considerations only partially explain why moderation is a need for social media. As observed by Gillespie, 'moderation is not an ancillary aspect of what platforms do. It is essential, constitutional, definitional. Not only can platforms not survive without moderation, they are not platforms without it'.[97] Moderation of online content is an almost mandatory step for social media not only to manage removal requests coming from governments or users but also to prevent that their digital spaces turn into hostile environments due to the spread, for example, of incitement to hatred. The implementation of these systems has become necessary as a filter to protect good expression from the massive presence of objectionable content.

However, the interest of platforms is not just focused on facilitating the spread of opinions and ideas across the globe to foster freedom of expression. They aim to create a digital environment where users feel free to share information and data that can feed commercial networks and channels and, especially, attract profits coming from advertising revenues.[98] Facebook, for instance, aims to maximise the amount of time users spend in their digital spaces to collect data and information.[99] Therefore, this approach leads to developing addictive technologies and capture users' attention, for instance, with inflammatory content and a low degree of privacy.[100] In other words, the activity of content moderation is performed to attract revenues by ensuring a healthy online community, protecting

[97] Tarleton Gillespie, *Custodians of the Internet. Platforms, Content Moderation, and the Hidden Decisions That Shape Social Media* 21 (Yale University Press 2018).

[98] Tarleton Gillespie, 'Regulation of and by Platforms' in Jean Burgess, Alice E. Marwick and Thomas Poell (eds.), *The SAGE Handbook of Social Media* 254 (Sage 2018).

[99] Adam Alter, *Irresistible: The Rise of Addictive Technology and the Business of Keeping us Hooked* (Penguin Press 2017).

[100] Emily Bell and Taylor Owen, 'The Platform Press: How Silicon Valley Reengineered Journalism' Tow Centre for Digital Journalism (29 March 2017) www.cjr.org/tow_center_reports/platform-press-how-silicon-valley-reengineered-journalism.php accessed 21 November 2021.

the corporate image and showing commitments to ethical values. Within this business framework, users' data are the central product of online platforms under a logic of accumulation.[101]

The story of moderation legally began in the aftermath of the Internet. The Big Bang of moderation can indeed be connected to the system of online intermediaries' liability based on a liberal regulatory approach adopted by the United States and EU as described in Chapter 2. As for the evolution of the universe, it took some phases to make the digital environment profitable. It has been only with the first experiments of processing users' information for advertising that digital capitalism understood the potentialities of the digital environment.[102]

At the end of the last century, there were no large corporations exercising powers in the digital environment. The political choice to follow a digital liberal path has led platforms to exploiting the legal framework to their advantage. According to Pasquale, online platforms try to avoid regulatory burdens by relying on the protection recognised by the First Amendment, while, at the same time, they claim immunities as passive conduits for third-party content.[103] Likewise, Citron and Norton observe how social media 'not only are free from First Amendment concerns as private actors, they are also statutorily immunized from liability for publishing content created by others as well as for removing that content'.[104] As Tushnet underlined, Section 230 'allows Internet intermediaries to have their free speech and everyone else's too'.[105]

This framework leads to the content moderation paradox. Notwithstanding several social media exploit rhetoric statements advocating to represent a global community and enhance free speech transnationally,[106] however, online platforms need to moderate

[101] Shoshana Zuboff, 'Big Other: Surveillance Capitalism and the Prospects of an Information Civilization' (2015) 30(1) Journal of Information Technology 75.

[102] Shoshana Zuboff, *The Age of Surveillance Capitalism: The Fight for a Human Future at the New Frontier of Power* (Public Affairs 2019).

[103] Frank Pasquale, 'Platform Neutrality: Enhancing Freedom of Expression in Spheres of Private Power' (2016) 17 Theoretical Inquiries in Law 487.

[104] Danielle Keats Citron and Helen L. Norton, 'Intermediaries and Hate Speech: Fostering Digital Citizenship for our Information Age' (2011) 91 Boston University Law Review 1436, 1439.

[105] Rebecca Tushnet, 'Power Without Responsibility: Intermediaries and the First Amendment' (2008) 76 The George Washington Law Review 986, 1002.

[106] Mark Zuckerberg, 'Building Global Community' Facebook (16 February 2017) www.facebook.com/notes/mark-zuckerberg/building-global-community/10154544292806634/ accessed 21 November 2021.

content to protect their business interests. As observed by Roberts, 'videos and other material have only one type of value to the platform, measured by their ability to either attract users and direct them to advertisers or to repel them and deny advertisers their connection to the user'.[107] An eventual escape of users due to the dissemination of content like terrorism and hate could severely harm advertising revenues. Other incentives are still linked to profit but come from concerns relating to corporate identity and reputation. For instance, online platforms aim to maintain control over the enforcement of their community guidelines and agreements to demonstrate that they act responsibly by complying with government requests relating to specific content like terrorist expressions.

At the same time, the grounding principle of content moderation is attracting profits by governing users' attention.[108] The frequency of interaction, emotional reactions or comments are just some examples of the information which platforms can extract from users' behaviours. This amount of information is then analysed to influence visibility and engagement which are usually fostered by matching similar content or standpoints according to micro-targeting strategies.[109] The numbers of likes or shares together with the analysis of users' similarities are then used for moderating information online and profiting from advertising revenues.[110] The revelations of platform's whistle-blowers have contributed to confirming how the system of moderation tends to be driven by the logic of virality through engagement among users,[111] and the Facebook Files have confirmed the failure of online platforms to behave responsibly when moderating online content.[112] The spread of hate in

107 Sarah T. Roberts, 'Digital Detritus: "Error" and the Logic of Opacity in Social Media Content Moderation' (2018) 23(3) First Monday https://firstmonday.org/ojs/index.php/fm/rt/printerFriendly/8283/6649 accessed 21 November 2021.

108 James G. Webster, 'User Information Regimes: How Social Media Shape Patterns of Consumption' (2010) 104 Northwestern University Law Review 593.

109 Philipp M. Napoli, *Social Media and the Public Interest: Media Regulation in the Disinformation Age* (Columbia University Press 2019).

110 Engin Bozdag, 'Bias in Algorithmic Filtering and Personalization' 15(3) Ethics and Information Technology 209.

111 Kari Paul and Dan Milmo, 'Facebook Putting Profit Before Public Good, Says Whistleblower Frances Haugen' The Guardian (4 October 2021) www.theguardian.com/technology/2021/oct/03/former-facebook-employee-frances-haugen-identifies-herself-as-whistleblower accessed 24 November 2021.

112 See, e.g., Jeff Horwitz, 'Facebook Says Its Rules Apply to All. Company Documents Reveal a Secret Elite That's Exempt' The Wall Street Journal (13 September 2021) www.wsj.com/articles/facebook-files-xcheck-zuckerberg-elite-rules-11631541353?mod=article_inline accessed 24 November 2021.

Myanmar, or the attack at the Capitol Hill in the United States, are examples of the pitfalls of content moderation and how platforms could contribute to producing harms beyond digital boundaries, without mentioning the possibility that social media become instruments to further harm through surveillance and computational propaganda.[113]

Therefore, content as data is 'food' for feeding the business model of social media using algorithms which tend to show users content which is related to their algorithmic profile. This is not entirely new but based on the tendency of humans to create relationships with people who share their ideas and values, what has been called the 'homophily of networks'.[114] This system also affects political speech by politicians or news media organisations.[115] According to Sajó, 'instead of creating a common space for democratic deliberation, the Internet and social media enabled fragmentation and segmentation. Discourse is limited to occur within self-selecting groups and there are tendencies of isolation. Views are more extreme and less responsive to external arguments and facts, resulting in polarization around alternative facts'.[116] The activity of content moderation indeed contributes to locking each user within personalised public spheres shaped by opaque business logics. Such a process turns online platforms into a manipulation machine.[117] Put another way, no matter what kind of speech, this is in the filtering hands of online platforms.

This content moderation paradox explains why, on the one hand, social media commit to protecting free speech, while, on the other hand, they moderate content regulating their communities for business purposes. Therefore, one of the primary issues concerns the compatibility between their private interests and public values.[118]

113 Zeynep Tufekci, 'Algorithmic Harms Beyond Facebook and Google: Emergent Challenges of Computational Agency' (2015) 13 Colorado Technology Law Journal 203.

114 Miller McPherson, Lynn Smith-Lovin and James M. Cook, 'Birds of a Feather: Homophily in Social Networks' (2001) 27 Annual Review of Sociology 415.

115 David Tewksbury and Jason Rittenberg, 'Online News Creation and Consumption: Implications for Modern Democracies' in Andrew Chadwick and Philipp N. Howard (eds.), *The Handbook of Internet Politics* 186 (Routledge 2008).

116 European Centre for Press and Media Freedom, 'Promoting Dialogue Between the European Court of Human Rights and the Media Freedom Community. Freedom of Expression and the Role and Case Law of the European Court of Human Rights: Developments and Challenges' (2017) www.ecpmf.eu/archive/files/ecpmf-ecthr_conference_e-book.pdf accessed 21 November 2021.

117 Siva Vaihyanathan, *Anti-Social Media* (Oxford University Press 2018).

118 José van Dijck, Thomas Poell, and Martijn de Waal, *The Platform Society: Public Values in a Connective World* (Oxford University Press 2018).

This situation is not only the result of the complexity of content moderation systems but also of the logic of opacity. Platforms are interested in pursuing their depoliticisation to escape from their social responsibilities coming from their key social functions. As argued by Roberts, platform tries to make the process obscure trying to denying 'the inherent gatekeeping baked in at the platform level by both its function as an advertising marketplace and the systems of review and deletion that have, until recently, been invisible to or otherwise largely unnoticed by most users'.[119]

To achieve this purpose, a critical piece of the moderation logic consists of the use of artificial intelligence systems. Platforms rely on automated technologies to cope with the amount of content uploaded by users whose non-automated management would require enormous costs in terms of human, technological and financial resources. Klonick has underlined the creation of a content moderation bureaucracy made of the work of humans and machines according to internal guidelines.[120] If, on the one hand, content moderation constitutes a valuable resource (and burden) for social media, on the other hand, the use of automated technologies for moderating content on a global scale challenges the protection of freedom of expression in the digital environment with effects extending far beyond domestic boundaries. The information uploaded by users is processed by automated systems that define (or at least suggest to human moderators) content to remove in a bunch of seconds according to non-transparent standards and providing the user access to limited remedies against a specific decision. It would not be possible to talk about content moderation online without considering to what extent algorithms are widely used for organising, filtering and removal procedures.[121]

The process (and the logic) of moderation is based on automated or semi-automated systems.[122] Decisions about users' expressions are left to the discretion of machines (and unaccountable moderators) operating on behalf of online platforms.[123] These procedures govern all the

[119] Roberts (n. 95).

[120] Klonick (n. 4).

[121] Jennifer M. Urban and others, *Notice and Takedown in Everyday Practice* (American Assembly 2016).

[122] Ben Wagner, *Global Free Expression: Governing the Boundaries of Internet Content* (Springer 2016).

[123] Paul M. Barrett, 'Who Moderates the Social Media Giants? A Call to End Outsourcing' NYU Stern (June 2020) https://static1.squarespace.com/static/5b6df958f8370af3217d4178/t/5ed9854bf618c710cb55be98/1591313740497/NYU+Content+Moderation+Report_June+8+2020.pdf> accessed 22 November 2021.

phases of content moderation in the platform environment from indexation, organisation, filtering, recommendation and, eventually, removal of expressions and accounts. The role of human intervention is also critical,[124] even if this could not be the solution for digital firms like Facebook due to the high amount of content to moderate.[125]

The pandemic has amplified these concerns and showed how the implementation of artificial intelligence to moderate content has contributed to spreading disinformation and to the blocking of accounts.[126] The decision of Google and Facebook to limit the employment of human moderation has affected the entire process with the result that different accounts and contents have been automatically suspended unnecessarily.[127] Notwithstanding the cooperative efforts of platforms to fight this situation,[128] the pandemic has underlined the limits of artificial intelligence in content moderation, particularly to tackle the spread of disinformation in a time where reliance over good health information has been critical.[129] This global health emergency has provided further clues concerning the role of online platforms as essential facilities or public utilities in the algorithmic society.[130]

124 Sarah T. Roberts, *Behind the Screen. Content Moderation in the Shadows of Social Media* (Yale University Press 2019); Paško Bilić, 'Search Algorithms, Hidden Labour and Information Control' (2016) 3(1) Big Data & Society 1.

125 Jessica Lessin, 'Facebook Shouldn't Fact Check' The New York Times (29 November 2016) www.nytimes.com/2016/11/29/opinion/facebook-shouldnt-fact-check.html accessed 21 November 2021.

126 Common position of European Commission and Consumer Protection Cooperation Network 20 March 2020 on stopping scams and tackling unfair business practices on online platforms in the context of the Coronavirus outbreak in the EU (20 March 2020) https://ec.europa.eu/info/sites/info/files/live_work_travel_in_the_eu/consumers/documents/cpc_common_position_covid19.pdf accessed 21 November 2021.

127 Elizabeth Dwoskin and Nitasha Tiku, 'Facebook Sent Home Thousands of Human Moderators due to the Coronavirus. Now the Algorithms are in Charge' The Washington Post (24 March 2020) www.washingtonpost.com/technology/2020/03/23/facebook-moderators-coronavirus/ accessed 21 November 2021.

128 See, e.g., joint industry statement of 17 March 2020 of Facebook, Google, LinkedIn, Microsoft, Reddit, Twitter and YouTube on working together to combat misinformation (16 March 2020) https://about.fb.com/news/2020/06/coronavirus/ accessed 21 November 2021.

129 Tobias R. Keller and Rosalie Gillett, 'Why Is It So Hard to Stop COVID-19 Misinformation Spreading on Social Media?' The Conversation (13 April 2020) https://theconversation.com/why-is-it-so-hard-to-stop-covid-19-misinformation-spreading-on-social-media-134396 accessed 21 November 2021.

130 K. Sabeel Rahman, 'The New Utilities: Private Power, Social Infrastructure, and the Revival of the Public Utility Concept' (2018) 39 Cardozo Law Review 1621.

Within this framework, it is worth stressing that content moderation is not only a necessity for online platforms but also a way for governments to enforce public policies online, and even for surveillance.[131] The case of India requiring Twitter to block more than 250 accounts of farmers protesting against a new farm law is just one example of how public authorities rely on online platforms to cope with dissent.[132] Governments could potentially enforce their policies online. Nonetheless, it is a matter of technical capabilities and resources. It is indeed easier to regulate or even rely on gatekeepers (e.g. telco or online platforms) to address illicit content across multiple jurisdictions, without considering that some of the alleged wrongdoers could also be artificial like bots. As examined in Chapter 3, governments and online platforms can profit much more from the benefits of an indivisible handshake rather than from regulation.[133] On the one hand, regulating content moderation would decrease the flexibility to use online platforms as instruments of public surveillance or collection of data, transforming digital spaces from areas fostering free expression in a cage for liberties. On the other hand, online platforms aim to maintain a cooperative approach to protect their freedoms to run their business and limit attempts to increase regulatory pressures, unless regulation can create legal barrier to enter the market, thus increasing their power by liming competition.

Therefore, the cooperation between public and private actors is inside the logic of moderation, even if it could seem irrelevant or even invisible at first glance. This relationship is also the reason why the regulation of online platforms has not changed until recently and just in Europe. Balkin has underlined that 'public/private cooperation – or cooptation – is a natural consequence of new-school speech regulation'.[134] Likewise, Reidenberg clarified that one of the systems to enforce public policies

131 Hannah Bloch Wehba, 'Content Moderation as Surveillance' (2021) 36 Berkeley Technology Law Journal 102.

132 Sangeeta Mahapatra, Martin Fertmann and Matthias C. Kettemann, 'Twitter's Modi Operandi: Lessons from India on Social Media's Challenges in Reconciling Terms of Service, National Law and Human Rights Law' Verfassungsblog (24 February 2021) https://verfassungsblog.de/twitters-modi-operandi/ accessed 23 November 2021.

133 Michael D. Birnhack and Niva Elkin-Koren, 'The Invisible Handshake: The Reemergence of the State in the Digital Environment' (2003) 8 Virginia Journal of Law & Technology 6.

134 Jack M. Balkin, 'Old-School/New-School Speech Regulation' (2014) 127 Harvard Law Review 2296, 2305.

online consists of not only regulating the architecture of the digital environment but also of relying on online intermediaries.[135] Within this framework, governing by proxy online could be almost a mandatory step for public actors to address unlawful content online even if it raises high risks for fundamental rights and liberties as the next subsections underline in the case of freedom of expression.

5.3.3 Private Enforcement of Freedom of Expression

The mix of digital liberalism and algorithmic technologies is one of the reasons for the troubling scenario of online speech in the digital environment. The legal immunity, mixed together with profiling technologies to moderate content, has constituted a green light for online platforms to freely choose the values they want to protect and promote, no matter if democratic or anti-democratic and authoritarian. This is a perfect environment to profit while escaping responsibility. Since online platforms are private businesses, given the lack of incentives, they would likely focus on minimising economic risks rather than ensuring a fair balance between fundamental rights in the digital environment. In other words, the system of immunity has indirectly entrusted online platforms with the role of moderating content and encouraged them to develop new profitable automated systems to organise, select and remove content based on a standard of protection of free speech influenced by business purposes.

The scope of platform power can be better understood by focusing on how these actors set and enforce their internal rules of moderation after balancing conflicting interests. When organising, recommending or removing, platforms make decisions on which kind of speech should be protected or fostered.[136] This is evident in the process of removal reflecting some characteristics of the powers traditionally vested in public authorities as underlined in Chapter 3. Human moderators refer to community guidelines or internal documents as a 'private legal basis' to remove content. Social media usually provide ToS and community guidelines where they explain to users the acceptable conducts and content, creating 'a complex interplay between users and platforms, humans and algorithms, and the social norms and regulatory structures of social media'.[137]

[135] Joel R. Reidenberg, 'States and Internet Enforcement' (2004) 1 University of Ottawa Law & Techonology Journal 213.

[136] Hannah Bloch-Webba, 'Global Platform Governance: Private Power in the Shadow of the State' (2019) 72 SMU Law Review 27.

[137] Kate Crawford and Tarleton Gillespie, 'What Is a Flag for? Social Media Reporting Tools and the Vocabulary of Complaint' (2016) 18 New Media & Society 410, 411.

However, these community rules do not necessarily represent the reality of content moderation. Facebook, for example, relies on internal guidelines which users cannot access and whose drafting process is unknown.[138] According to Klonick, Facebook's content moderation is 'largely developed by American lawyers trained and acculturated in American free-speech norms, and it seems that this cultural background has affected their thinking'.[139] Whatever American or European values are at stake, this process is far from being close to any democratic value. Besides, the use of internal guidelines which are not publicly disclosed, leads to looking at this process more as an authoritarian determination than a democratic expression.

The situation is even more complicated when internal standards are solely implemented by machines which translate top-down rules in an enforceable series of code, defining another layer of complexity in the moderation of expressions. From a technical perspective, the opacity of content moderation also derives from the implementation of machine learning techniques subject to the 'black box' effect.[140] On the one hand, algorithms can be considered as technical instruments facilitating the organisation of online content. Nevertheless, on the other hand, such technologies can constitute opaque self-executing rules, obviating any human control with troubling consequences for democratic values such as transparency and accountability.

This mix of human and machine definition of freedom of expression constitutes the basis for enforcing decisions which are the results of a balance between conflicting interests. Taking as an example the case of hate speech, this concept is then mediated by the private determinations of human moderators or machines. This process then leads to the hybridisation of freedom of expression where traditional dichotomies like public/private or human/machine merge into a unique soul.

[138] Max Fisher, 'Inside Facebook's Secret Rulebook for Global Political Speech' The New York Times (27 December 2018) www.nytimes.com/2018/12/27/world/facebook-moderators.html accessed 21 November 2021.

[139] Klonick (n. 4), 1622.

[140] Frank Pasquale, *The Black Box Society: The Secret Algorithms that Control Money and Information* (Harvard University Press 2015).

Within this framework, the lack of horizontal remedies leads online platforms to exercise the same discretion of an absolute power over its community. Despite the fundamental role of online platforms in establishing the standard of free speech and shaping democratic culture on a global scale,[141] the information provided by these companies about content moderation is opaque or lawless.[142] Online platforms are free to decide how to show and organise online content according to predictive analyses based on the processing of users' data. In other words, although at first glance social media foster freedom of expression by empowering users to share their opinions and ideas cross-border, however, the high degree of opacity and inconsistency of content moderation frustrates democratic values.

Content moderation does not only constitute an autonomous set of technical rules to control digital spaces but also contributes to defining the standard of protection of fundamental rights online, thus shaping the notion of public sphere and democracy. This situation leads towards computing legality as defined by a mere algorithmic calculation. The power of online platforms to shape the scope of protection of rights lies mostly in their ability to mathematically materialise abstract notions through digital means. Since artificial intelligence technologies are becoming more pervasive in online content moderation, the opacity of these technologies raises legal (and ethical) concerns for democracy.[143] Individuals are increasingly surrounded by technical systems influencing their decisions without the possibility to understand or control this phenomenon.[144] In other words, although the Internet has provided opportunities for users to access different types of information, the mediation of automated technologies leads to a process of hybridisation of freedom of expression becoming a mix of legal rules, platform guidelines and algorithmic determination. This trend towards computing abstract notions of law is a call for European digital constitutionalism to protect freedom of expression, and, more generally, constitutional values, in the algorithmic society.

[141] Marvin Ammori, 'The "New" New York Times: Free Speech Lawyering in the Age of Google and Twitter' (2014) 127 Harvard Law Review 2259.

[142] Nicolas Suzor, *Lawless: The Secret Rules That Govern Our Digital Lives* (Cambridge University Press 2019).

[143] Brent D. Mittelstadt and others, 'The Ethics of Algorithms: Mapping the Debate' (2016) 3(2) Big Data & Society https://journals.sagepub.com/doi/pdf/10.1177/2053951716679679 accessed 21 November 2021.

[144] Paul Nemitz, 'Constitutional Democracy and Technology in the Age of Artificial Intelligence' (2018) 376 Royal Society Philosophical Transactions A 89.

5.4 The First Reaction of European Digital Constitutionalism

In the process of content moderation, users are not only subject to the private determinations of online platforms on freedom of expression but, more importantly, they cannot generally rely on procedural safeguards in this process. In other words, as observed by Myers West, 'they are exactly the kinds of users who make up the kind of "town square", "global village", or "community" that these platforms themselves say they seek to cultivate – but current content moderation systems do not give them much opportunity to participate or grow as citizens of these spaces'.[145]

From an international perspective, both the Manila principles on intermediary liability and the best practises proposed by the IGF Dynamic Coalition on Platform Responsibility are just two examples of proposals towards the proceduralisation of content moderation.[146] Similarly, the Santa Clara principles on Transparency and Accountability in Content Moderation suggest the adoption of due process safeguards regarding how content moderation should be performed and what rights users can rely on in the context of this process.[147] Article 19 has proposed the creation of social media councils based on a self-regulatory and multistakeholder system of accountability for content moderation complying with international human rights' standards.[148] Likewise, in 2019, Facebook launched its oversight board.[149] At the same time, Twitter set an independent research group whose task is to develop standards for content moderation.[150]

[145] Sarah Myers West, 'Censored, Suspended, Shadowbanned: User Interpretations of Content Moderation on Social Media Platforms' (2018) 20(11) New Media & Society 4380. See, also, Trevor Puetz, 'Facebook: The New Town Square' (2014) 44 Southwestern Law Review 385.

[146] Manila Principles on Intermediary Liability (2017) https://manilaprinciples.org/index.html accessed 21 November 2021; the DCPR Best Practices on Platforms' Implementation on the Right to Effective Remedy www.intgovforum.org/multilingual/index.php?q=filedepot_download/4905/1550 accessed 20 November 2021.

[147] Santa Clara Principles on Transparency and Accountability in Content Moderation (2018) https://santaclaraprinciples.org/ 20 November 2021.

[148] Article 19, 'The Social Media Councils: Consultation Paper' (2019) www.article19.org/wp-content/uploads/2019/06/A19-SMC-Consultation-paper-2019-v05.pdf 20 November 2021.

[149] Kate Klonick, 'The Facebook Oversight Board: Creating an Independent Institution to Adjudicate Online Free Expression' (2020) 129 Yale Law Journal 2418; Evelyn Douek, 'Facebook's "Oversight Board:" Move Fast with Stable Infrastructure and Humility' (2019) 21(1) North Carolina Journal of Law & Technology 1.

[150] Katie Paul and Munsif Vengattil, 'Twitter Plans to Build "Decentralized Standard" for Social Networks' *Reuters* (11 December 2019) www.reuters.com/article/us-twitter

However, despite the relevance of these steps, users still have to deal with discretionary and voluntary mechanisms. The lack of any binding force of this system leaves online platforms free to decide whether to participate in this mechanism or formally comply with these standards while maintaining their internal rules of procedures. At the same time, the former UN Special Rapporteur for Freedom of Expression, David Kaye, underlined the increasing pressure on private actors to comply with international human rights law when moderating online content.[151] According to Kaye, since social media exercise regulatory functions in the digital environment, these private actors should refer to the existing international human rights law regime when setting their standard for content moderation.[152] International human rights law could help platforms apply a universal reference in their activities of content moderation, but there are still challenges concerning the promises of human rights law in content moderation.[153]

However, as already underlined, since online platforms are private actors, they are not obliged to respect human rights since international human rights law vertically binds only state actors with the result that the governance of online platforms is based on fragmented national and regional laws as well as soft-regulatory efforts.[154] The same consideration extends to fundamental rights since constitutional provisions bind only public actors to respect them even if there could be some cases where fundamental rights horizontally apply in the relationship between private actors.[155] Despite the role of self-regulation and

-content/twitter-plans-to-build-decentralized-standard-for-social-networks-idUSKBN1YF2EN accessed 21 November 2021.

151 David Kaye, *Speech Police: The Global Struggle to Govern the Internet* (Columbia Global Reports 2019).

152 Report of the Special Rapporteur to the Human Rights Council on online content regulation, A/HRC/38/35 (2018); See, also, Report of the Special Rapporteur on the Promotion and Protection of the Right to Freedom of Opinion and Expression, A/73/348 (2018); Guiding Principles on Business and Human Rights (2011).

153 Barrie Sander, 'Freedom of Expression in the Age of Online Platforms: The Promise and Pitfalls of a Human Rights based Approach to Content Moderation' (2020) 43(4) Fordham Journal of International Law 939.

154 Jennifer Grygiel and Nina Brown, 'Are Social Media Companies Motivated to Be Good Corporate Citizens? Examination of the Connection Between Corporate Social Responsibility and Social Media Safety' (2019) 43 Telecommunications Policy 445.

155 Some constitutions around the world (e.g. South Africa) horizontally extends the application of fundamental rights in the relationship between private actors. In other case, horizontal application is not the result of a direct constitutional provision but the result of judicial interpretation.

corporate social responsibility in building a shared global framework which could overcome any regulatory vacuum,[156] the remedies voluntarily provided by online platforms are highly fragmented and left to their discretion.[157] Moreover, the differences between (publicly available) community guidelines and (privately hidden) internal policy as well as the opacity about the use of automated systems in content moderation create a grey area of cases where organisation, recommendation and removal of content are set outside any democratic control.

While, in the US, the legal framework has not changed in the last twenty years, apart from some exception,[158] and the executive order on preventing online censorship adopted in 2020 which was then withdrawn by President Biden,[159] the Union has started to pave the way towards a new regulatory phase of online content moderation modernising the framework of the e-Commerce Directive.[160] The European objectives to protect constitutional values could be considered the political manifesto of the new European approach.[161] Such a shift towards wider responsibilities is not a mere political decision but the expression of the first steps of European digital constitutionalism.[162] As underlined in Chapter 2, the Directive on Copyright in the Digital Single Market,[163] the amendments to the Audiovisual Media Service

156 Rolf H. Weber, 'Corporate Social Responsibility As a Gap-Filling Instrument' in Andrew P. Newell (ed.). *Corporate Social Responsibility: Challenges, Benefits and Impact on Business* 87 (Nova 2014).

157 IGF Dynamic Coalition, 'Best Practices on Platforms' Implementation of the Right to an Effective Remedy' (2018) www.intgovforum.org/multilingual/content/dcpr-best-practices-on-due-process-safeguards-regarding-online-platforms'-implementation-of accessed 20 November 2021.

158 See the Stop Enabling Sex Traffickers Act (SESTA) and the Allow States and Victims to Fight Online Sex Trafficking Act (FOSTA) adopted in 2018.

159 Executive Order on Preventing Online Censorship (28 May 2020) www.federalregister.gov/documents/2020/06/02/2020-12030/preventing-online-censorship accessed 22 November 2021.

160 Directive 2000/31/EC of the European Parliament and of the Council of 8 June 2000 on certain legal aspects of information society services, in particular electronic commerce, in the Internal Market ('Directive on electronic commerce') (2000) OJ L 178/1.

161 Communication from the Commission to the European Parliament, the Council, the European Economic and Social Committee and the Committee of the Regions, Online Platforms and the Digital Single Market Opportunities and Challenges for Europe COM (2016) 288 final.

162 Ibid.

163 Directive (EU) 2019/790 of the European Parliament and of the Council of 17 April 2019 on copyright and related rights in the Digital Single Market and amending Directives 96/9/EC and 2001/29/EC (2019) OJ L 130/92.

Directive,[164] as well as the Regulation on terrorist content,[165] have constituted a first turning point in online content moderation, requiring online platforms to establish transparent and accountable mechanisms.

These measures are part of a broader strategy of the Union to foster accountability and transparency in online content moderation. Just to mention two examples, it would be enough to refer to the Code of Conduct on Countering Illegal Hate Speech Online and the Code of Practice on Online Disinformation,[166] resulting from the Communication on Tackling Online Disinformation and, especially, the Communication on tackling illegal content online,[167] then implemented in the Recommendation on measures to effectively tackle illegal content online.[168]

The approach of the Union in this field shows a shift from a liberal approach in online content moderation to transparency and accountability obligations and recommendations. Rather than just focusing on content regulation, the European approach focuses on introducing procedural safeguards to dismantle the logic of opacity.

In the meantime, in *Eva Glawischnig-Piesczek* v. *Facebook Ireland Limited*,[169] the ECJ has contributed to providing guidance in the process of content moderation in a case involving the removal of identical and equivalent content. The ECJ underlined the role of social media in promoting the dissemination of information online, including illegal content. In this case, a national judge's order of removing or blocking identical content does not conflict with the monitoring ban established

[164] Directive (EU) 2018/1808 of the European Parliament and of the Council of 14 November 2018 amending Directive 2010/13/EU on the coordination of certain provisions laid down by law, regulation or administrative action in Member States concerning the provision of audiovisual media services (Audiovisual Media Services Directive) in view of changing market realities (2018) OJ L 303/69.

[165] Regulation (EU) 2021/784 of the European Parliament and of the Council of 29 April 2021 on addressing the dissemination of terrorist content online OJ L 172/79.

[166] Code of Conduct on Countering Illegal Hate Speech Online (2016) http://ec.europa.eu/newsroom/just/item-detail.cfm?item_id=54300 accessed 21 November 2021; Code of Practice on Disinformation (2018) https://ec.europa.eu/digital-single-market/en/news/code-practice-disinformation accessed 21 November 2021.

[167] Communication from the Commission to the European Parliament, the Council, the European Economic and Social Committee and the Committee of the Regions, Tackling Illegal Content Online Towards an enhanced responsibility of online platforms COM(2017) 555 final.

[168] Recommendation of 1 March 2018 on measures to effectively tackle illegal content online (C(2018) 1177 final).

[169] Case C-18/18 *Eva Glawischnig-Piesczek* v. *Facebook Ireland Limited* (2019).

by the e-Commerce Directive.[170] As the Advocate General Szpunar underlines, an order to remove all identical information does not require 'active non-automatic filtering'.[171] The ECJ addressed the question concerning the removal of 'equivalent' content. According to the court, in order to effectively cease an illegal act and prevent its repetition, the order of the national judge has to be able to also extend to 'equivalent' content defined as 'information conveying a message the content of which remains essentially unchanged and therefore diverges very little from the content which gave rise to the finding of illegality'.[172] Otherwise, users would only access a partial remedy that could lead to resorting to an indefinite number of appeals to limit the dissemination of equivalent content.[173]

However, such an extension is not unlimited. The ECJ reiterated that the ban on imposing a general surveillance obligation established by the e-Commerce Directive is still the relevant threshold for Member States' judicial and administrative orders. If, on the one hand, the possibility of extending the orders of the national authorities to equivalent content aims to protect the victim's honour and reputation, on the other hand, such orders cannot entail an obligation for the hosting provider to generally monitor information to remove equivalent content. In other words, the ECJ defined a balance between, on the one hand, the freedom of economic initiative of the platform, and, on the other, the honour and reputation of the victim. The result of such a balance, therefore, leads to reiterate that the national orders of the judicial and administrative authorities have to be specific without being able to extend to the generality of content.

In order to balance these conflicting interests, the ECJ provided other conditions applying to equivalent content. Precisely, expressions have to contain specific elements duly identified by the injunction such as 'the name of the person concerned by the infringement determined previously, the circumstances in which that infringement was determined and equivalent content to that which was declared to be illegal'.[174] Under these conditions, the protection granted to the victim would not constitute an excessive obligation on the hosting provider

[170] Ibid., 37.

[171] Opinion of Advocate General in C-18/18 *Eva Glawischnig-Piesczek* v. *Facebook Ireland Limited*, 61.

[172] C-18/18 (n. 169), 39.

[173] Ibid., 41.

[174] Ibid., 45.

since its discretion is limited to certain information without leading to general monitoring obligation that could derive from an autonomous assessment of the equivalent nature of the content. If, on the one hand, the ECJ clarified how platforms should deal with users' requests for removal of identical and equivalent content, nonetheless, even in this case, the court did not define transparency and accountability safeguards in the process of content moderation.

These first steps of European digital constitutionalism have not solved the asymmetry of power in the field of content. Users and online platforms still face challenges raised by legal fragmentation in this field. There is not a unitary framework of users' rights or remedies, also considering that Member States enjoy margins of discretion in implementing such safeguards. Besides, safeguards in online content moderation have not been introduced horizontally to cover all content and situation. The Union has maintained a vertical approach based on specific categories of content (e.g. copyright content). The fragmentation of content moderation processes can lead to serious consequences for the freedom to conduct business of online platforms and, as a consequence, this uncertainty could produce chilling effects for users' freedom of expression. As analysed further in this chapter, the Digital Services Act provides an opportunity to complete this framework and provide a systematic horizontal approach to ensure more safeguards and remedies in the process of content moderation.[175]

Therefore, it is time to focus on how the new phase of European digital constitutionalism can provide instruments to address the imbalance of power between users and online platforms in the field of content. There are two ways addressed in the next sections, which look respectively at the horizontal effect doctrine and at the regulation of content moderation as also driven by the Digital Services Act.

5.5 Horizontal Effect Filling Regulatory Gaps

Within this troubling framework for democratic values in the algorithmic society, the question is whether European constitutional law already owns the instruments to react, even without regulatory

[175] Proposal for a Regulation of the European Parliament and of the Council on a Single Market for Digital Services (Digital Services Act) and amending Directive 2000/31/EC COM(2020) 825 final.

intervention. Whereas proposing a regulatory solution would be a largely traditional approach, it is necessary to step back and wonder about the role of constitutional law in content moderation. Even if, in Europe, lawmakers have seemed to be prone to regulate online platforms, on the one hand, the interest of public actors to monitor online activities and enforce public policies online should not be neglected. On the other hand, online platforms aim to maintain their freedom to conduct business outside regulatory interferences. This apparently unrelated but converging interest leads to an invisible cooperation between public and private actors, thus creating a powerful brake to regulatory intervention. Such a situation could lead to potential conflicts of interest since political power could not regulate online platforms to protect forms of unaccountable cooperation.

To overcome this political impasse, one of the few ways to move further is to look beyond political powers and, precisely, at judicial power. In other words, it may be possible to rely on courts, and their independence, to ensure that the protection of fundamental rights is not locked down between political and business interests but is interpreted within the evolving information society. This approach would lead to wondering to what extent the horizontal effect doctrine of fundamental rights in Europe could be a solution to remedy the imbalance of power between users and online platforms exercising private powers on online speech.

The horizontal doctrine may promise to go beyond the public/private division by extending constitutional obligations even to the relationship between private actors (i.e. platform/user). Unlike the liberal spirit of the vertical approach, this theory rejects a rigid separation where constitutional rules apply vertically only to public actors to ensure the liberty and autonomy of private actors. Put another way, the horizontal doctrine is concerned with the issue of whether and to what extent constitutional rights can affect the relationships between private actors. As observed by Gardbaum, '[t]hese alternatives refer to whether constitutional rights regulate only the conduct of governmental actors in their dealings with private individuals (vertical) or also relations between private individuals (horizontal)'.[176]

The horizontal effect can result from constitutional obligations on private parties to respect fundamental rights (i.e. direct effect) or their

[176] Stephen Gardbaum, 'The Horizontal Effect of Constitutional Rights' (2003) 102 Michigan Law Review 388.

application through judicial interpretation (i.e. indirect effect). Only in the first case, a private entity would have the right to rely directly on constitutional provisions to claim the violation of its rights vis-à-vis other private parties.[177] There is also a third (indirect) way through the positive obligations for states to protect human rights such as in the case of the Convention.[178]

The horizontal application of fundamental rights could constitute a limitation to the expansion of power by social systems. According to Teubner, the emergence of transnational regimes shows the limits of constitutions as means of regulation of the whole society since social subsystems develop their own constitutional norms.[179] Therefore, the horizontal effects doctrine can be considered as a limit to self-constitutionalising private regulation. As a result, if the horizontal effect of fundamental rights is purely considered a problem of political power within society, an approach which excludes its application would hinder the teleological approach behind this doctrine, the aim of which is to protect individuals against unreasonable violations of their fundamental rights vis-à-vis private actors. As Tushnet underlined, if the doctrine of horizontal effect is considered 'as a response to the threat to liberty posed by concentrated private power, the solution is to require that all private actors conform to the norms applicable to governmental actors'.[180]

Nonetheless, the horizontal application of fundamental rights does not apply in the same way across the Atlantic. Within the US framework, the Supreme Court has usually applied the vertical approach where the application of the horizontal approach, known in the US as the 'state action doctrine', would be considered the exception.[181] The First Amendment, and, more in general, US constitutional

[177] John H. Knox, 'Horizontal Human Rights Law' (2008) 102(1) American Journal of International Law 1.

[178] Daniel Augenstein and Lukasz Dziedzic, 'State Responsibilities to Regulate and Adjudicate Corporate Activities under the European Convention on Human Rights' (2017) EUI Working papers https://cadmus.eui.eu/bitstream/handle/1814/48326/LAW_2017_15.pdf?sequence=1&isAllowed=y accessed 21 November 2021.

[179] Gunther Teubner, 'The Project of Constitutional Sociology: Irritating Nation State Constitutionalism' (2013) 4 Transnational Legal Theory 44.

[180] Mark Tushnet, 'The Issue of State Action/Horizontal Effect in Comparative Constitutional Law' (2003) 1(1) International Journal of Constitutional Law 79.

[181] See *Shelley* v. *Kraemer* 334 U.S. 1 (1948). Mattias Kumm and Victor Ferreres Comella, 'What Is So Special about Constitutional Rights in Private Litigation? A Comparative Analysis of the Function of State Action Requirements and Indirect Horizontal Effect' in Andras Sajó and Renata Uitz (eds.), *The Constitution in Private Relations: Expanding*

rights,[182] lack horizontal effect not only *in abstracto* but also in relation to online platforms.

Even if scholars have tried to propose new ways to go beyond such a rigid verticality,[183] the Supreme Court has been clear about the limits of this doctrine when addressing the possibility that a non-profit corporation designated by New York City to run a public access television network limit users' speech.[184] In an ideological 5–4 ruling, the court rejected the idea that the TV station in question could be considered a state actor, and, therefore, there was no reason to focus on the violation of the First Amendment. Although this case concerned public access channels, the property-interest arguments could have a broad impact in the information society, precisely on the protection of speech over online platforms'. This would lead towards Balkin's warning about the limit of 'judge-made doctrines' of the First Amendment.[185]

The horizontal extension of fundamental rights is less rigid in the European environment,[186] and it is characterised by different models.[187] As already underlined in Chapter 1, one of the primary explanations for the extension of constitutional values beyond a vertical dimension lies in the roots of European constitutionalism, precisely in the protection of human dignity.[188] This approach is also reflected in the social democratic openness of Member States and the

Constitutionalism 265 (Eleven 2005); Mark Tushnet, 'Shelley v. Kraemer and Theories of Equality' (1988) 33 New York Law School Law Review 383.

182 The prohibition on slavery as provided for by the Thirteenth Amendment applies to public and private actors. Gardbaum (n. 176) 388; George Rutherglen, 'State Action, Private Action, and the Thirteenth Amendment' (2008) 24(6) Virginia Law Review 1367.

183 Jonathan Peters, 'The "Sovereigns of Cyberspace" and State Action: The First Amendment's Application (or Lack Thereof) to Third-Party Platforms' (2018) 32 Berkeley Technology Law Journal 988; Lyrissa B. Lidsky, 'Public Forum 2.0' (2011) Boston University Law Review 1975; Paul S. Berman, 'Cyberspace and the State Action Debate: The Cultural Value of Applying Constitutional Norms to "Private" Regulation' (2000) 71 University of Colorado Law Review 1263.

184 *Manhattan Community Access Corp.* v. *Halleck*, No. 17-1702, 587 U.S. ___ (2019).

185 Jack M. Balkin, 'The Future of Free Expression in a Digital Age' (2009) 36 Pepperdine Law Review 427, 443–4.

186 Regarding the horizontal effect of fundamental rights in the EU framework, see Eleni Frantziou, *The Horizontal Effect of Fundamental Rights in the European Union. A Constitutional Analysis* (Oxford University Press 2019); Sonya Walkila, *Horizontal Effect of Fundamental Rights in EU Law* (European Law Publishing 2016).

187 Aurelia Colombi Ciacchi, 'Judicial Governance in European Private Law: Three Judicial Cultures of Fundamental Rights Horizontality' (2020) 4 European Review of Private Law 931.

188 Catherine Dupré, *The Age of Dignity: Human Rights and Constitutionalism in Europe* (Hart 2015).

European area which is far from the liberal approach of the US framework. According to Tushnet, states which are more oriented to develop welfare systems and provide social rights in their constitutions more readily apply the horizontal effect doctrine. This position should not surprise since it is the natural consequence of how rights and freedoms are conceived in welfare states. The positive and programmatic nature of some constitutional rights leads to a broader role for lawmakers but, especially, for courts to define the limits of these rights. It is not by chance that, in the European framework, the doctrine of the horizontal effect has found an extensive application in the field of labour law.[189]

The European horizontal effect doctrine is far from being locked just in the field of social rights. Traditionally, the effects of the rights recognised directly under EU primary law have been capable of horizontal application. The ECJ has applied both the horizontal effect and the positive obligation doctrines regarding the four fundamental freedoms and general principles.[190] In the *Van Gend En Loos* case, the ECJ stated: 'Independently of the legislation of Member States, Community law not only imposes obligations on individuals but is also intended to confer upon them rights which become part of their legal heritage'.[191] This definition remained unclear until the court specified its meaning in *Walrave*,[192] which, together with *Bosman*[193] and *Deliege*,[194] can be considered the first acknowledgement of the horizontal effect of the EU fundamental freedoms.[195]

Likewise, since the Charter acquired the same legal value of a Treaty,[196] judicial activism has also been extended to the Charter.[197] Recently, in

[189] See Case 43/75 *Defrenne* v. *Sabena (No 2)* (1976) ECR 455. More recently, Case C-555/07 *Kücükdeveci* v. *Sweden* (2010) ECR I-365; Case C-144/04 *Mangold* v. *Rüdiger Helm* (2005) ECR I-9981. But see Case C-176/12 *Association de médiation sociale* v. *Union locale des syndicats CGT* (2014).

[190] Elena Gualco and Luisa Lourenço, '"Clash of Titans". General Principles of EU Law: Balancing and Horizontal Direct Effect' (2016) 1(2) European Papers 643.

[191] Case 26/62 *van Gend & Loos* v. *Netherlands Inland Revenue Administration* (1963) ECR 1.

[192] Case 36/74 *Walrave* v. *Association Union cycliste international* (1974) ECR 1405.

[193] Case C-415/93 *Union royale belge des sociétés de football association* v. *Bosman* (1995) ECR 4921.

[194] Case C-51/96 *Deliège* v. *Ligue francophone de judo et disciplines associées* (2000) ECR I-2549.

[195] Among the other decisions, see Case C-281/98 *Angonese* v. *Cassa di Risparmio di Bolzano* (2000) ECR I-2055; Case C-103/08 *Gottwald* v. *Bezirkshauptmannschaft Bregenz* (2009) ECR I-9117; Case C-223/09 *Dijkman* v. *Belgische Staat* (2010) ECR I-6649.

[196] Consolidated version of the Treaty on European Union (2012) OJ C 326/13, Art. 6(1). Grainne De Burca and Jo B. Aschenbrenner, 'The Development of European Constitutionalism and the Role of the EU Charter of Fundamental Rights' (2003) 9 Columbia Journal of European Law 355.

[197] Dorota Leczykiewicz, 'Horizontal Application of the Charter of Fundamental Rights' (2013) 38(3) European Law Review 479.

Egenberger,[198] the ECJ extended horizontal application to the right of non-discrimination and the right to an effective remedy and to a fair trial, respectively enshrined in Articles 21 and 47 of the Charter, in a case involving compensation for discrimination on the grounds of religion suffered in a recruitment procedure. Likewise, in *Bauer*,[199] the Court went even further. The ECJ did not only extend horizontal effects to the right to limitation of maximum working hours as fair and just working condition,[200] but also overcame its precedents in *Association de médiation sociale*, where it rejected horizontal effects to the workers' right to information and consultation.[201] In *Bauer*, the ECJ clarified that the narrow scope of Article 51(1) does not deal with whether individuals, or private actors, may be directly required to comply with certain provisions of the Charter.[202]

With regard to the right to freedom of expression as enshrined in the Charter,[203] the ECJ has not still provided its guidance. A literal interpretation of Article 11 of the Charter could constitute a barrier to any attempt to extend its scope of application. Likewise, Article 51(1) of the Charter seems to narrow down the scope of application of the Charter to EU institutions and Member States in their implementation of EU law.[204] Brkan warned about the risk for the system of European competences relating to the introduction of a positive obligation in the field of freedom of expression to fill the legislation gap.[205] Indeed, 'in creating such a positive obligation, the CJEU would not only have to observe the principles of conferral and subsidiarity, but also pay attention not to overstep its own competences by stepping into the shoes of a legislator'.[206] This issue, however, has not discouraged the ECJ to underline the

198 Case C-414/16 *Vera Egenberger* v. *Evangelisches Werk für Diakonie und Entwicklung e.V.* (2018).

199 Case C-569/16 *Stadt Wuppertal* v. *Maria Elisabeth Bauer* and *Volker Willmeroth* v. *Martina Broßonn* (2018).

200 Charter (n. 40), Art. 31(2).

201 C-176/12 (n. 189), 51.

202 C-569/16 (n. 199), 87.

203 Charter (n. 40), Art. 11.

204 Ibid. According to Art. 51(1): 'The provisions of this Charter are addressed to the institutions and bodies of the Union with due regard for the principle of subsidiarity and to the Member States only when they are implementing Union law. They shall therefore respect the rights, observe the principles and promote the application thereof in accordance with their respective power'.

205 Maja Brkan, 'Freedom of Expression and Artificial Intelligence: On Personalisation, Disinformation and (Lack Of) Horizontal Effect of the Charter' SSRN https://papers.ssrn.com/sol3/papers.cfm?abstract_id=3354180 accessed 21 November 2021.

206 Ibid.

relevance of the right to freedom of expression online in private litigations.[207] The court underlined that interferences with freedom of expression would not be justified in case the measures adopted by the provider are not 'strictly targeted, in the sense that they must serve to bring an end to a third party's infringement of copyright or of a related right but without thereby affecting internet users who are using the provider's services in order to lawfully access information'.[208]

The reasons for an alleged lack of horizontality are not only rooted in the separation between judicial and political power but also depend on the constitutive difference between negative liberties and positive rights. As Beijer underlined, in the Union framework, there is less pressure to rely on positive obligations based on the violation of fundamental rights since obligations are horizontally translated in acts of EU law.[209] The approach of the ECJ does not surprise since the field of labour law can be considered as one of the primary expressions of the welfare conception. The extension of such a rule to the principle of non-discrimination aims to ensure not only formal but also substantive equality between individuals. In this framework, the right to freedom of expression is instead conceived within the framework of negative liberties which only consider public actors as a threat. In other words, it is not just a matter of literal interpretation of Article 11 of the Charter but also of theoretical distance, even if the common matrix of human dignity in European constitutionalism could provide that constitutional ground to extend the (horizontal) effects to freedom of expression.

Besides, within the complexity of the horizontal effect doctrine,[210] it is worth highlighting at least a primary drawback, which can also be applied to content moderation. While the horizontal effect doctrine could be a constitutional instrument to generally mitigate the exercise of private powers on freedom of expression, nonetheless, the extension of obligations to respect constitutional rights to online platforms would raise several concerns. Applying this doctrine extensively could lead to negative effects for legal certainty. Every private conflict can virtually be represented as a clash between different fundamental rights. This

[207] Case C-314/12 *UPC Telekabel Wien GmbH* v. *Constantin Film Verleih GmbH and Wega Filmproduktionsgesellschaft mbH* (2014); Case C-484/14 *Tobias Mc Fadden* v. *Sony Music Entertainment Germany GmbH* (2016).

[208] *Telekabel* (n. 207), 56. See also *McFadden* (n. 207), 93.

[209] Malu Beijer, *The limits of Fundamental Rights Protection by the EU: The Scope for the Development of Positive Obligations* 297 (Intersentia 2017).

[210] Robert Alexy, *A Theory of Constitutional Rights* (Oxford University Press 2002).

approach could lead to the extension of constitutional obligations to every private relationship, thus hindering any possibility to foresee the consequences of a specific action or omission. Fundamental rights can be applied horizontally only ex post by courts through the balancing of the rights in question.

It cannot be excluded that this approach could be even more multifaceted in civil law countries where judges are not legally bound by precedents, but can take their own path to decide whether constitutional obligations apply to private litigations or not.[211] In Chapter 2, the judicial activism of the ECJ has already shown the role of courts in ensuring that the protection of fundamental rights is not frustrated in the digital environment. The further empowerment of judicial over political power could lead to increasing fragmentation and uncertainty about content moderation obligations, thus undermining the principle of the separation of powers and rule of law. This is not something far from reality. While, in the US, courts continue to ban any users' complaints against the removal of content,[212] some cases in Europe have shown how courts have already dealt with the horizontal extension of constitutional rights in private litigations between users and online platforms, also leading to different outcomes.[213]

These concerns around judicial power could be partially overcome by limiting the application of the horizontal effect only to those private actors exercising delgated public functions, as seen in Chapter 3. In the case of platforms, although these entities cannot be considered public actors per se, their delegated public functions to moderate content (e.g. obligation to remove illicit content in case of awareness) could be subject to the safeguards applying to the public

[211] The difference between common law and civil law should not be considered rigid. Nonetheless, the constitutive differences in the role of courts deserve to be mentioned when focusing on the limits of the horizontal effect doctrine. See, generally, Paul Brand and Joshua Getzler (eds.), *Judges and Judging in the History of the Common Law and Civil Law: From Antiquity to Modern Times* (Cambridge University Press 2015); Joseph Dainow, 'The Civil Law and the Common Law: Some Points of Comparison' (1966–7) 15(3) American Journal of Comparative 419.

[212] Niva Elkin Koren, Giovanni De Gregorio and Maayan Perel, 'Social Media as Contractual Networks: A Bottom up Check on Content Moderation' Iowa Law Review forthcoming; Daphne Keller, 'Who Do You Sue? State and Platform Hybrid Power over Online Speech' (2019) Aegis Series Paper No. 1902 (29 January 2019) www.hoover.org/sites/default/files/research/docs/who-do-you-sue-state-and-platform-hybrid-power-over-online-speech_0.pdf accessed 21 November 2021.

[213] See, e.g., Court of Rome, *CasaPound* v. *Facebook* (2019); German Federal Constitutional Court, *Der Dritte Weg* v. *Facebook Ireland Ltd.* (2019).

sector (e.g. transparency). In other words, constitutional law would extend its horizontal boundaries only where public actors entrust private actors with quasi-public functions through delegation of powers. Users have a legitimate expectation that, when public actors have entrusted private ones to pursue public tasks, the latter should be held accountable for violation of constitutional rights and freedoms. On the contrary, where platforms exercise autonomous powers, a broad extension of the horizontal effect doctrine would transform these entities into public actors by default. This approach would provide users with the right to bring claims related to violations of, for example, freedom of expression directly against platforms as entities performing delegated public functions.

At first glance, this mechanism would allow fundamental rights to become horizontally effective against the conduct or omission of actors evading their responsibilities under a narrative based on freedoms and liberties. However, a closer look could reveal how empowering users to challenge online platforms could lead to a compression of the freedom to conduct business of these actors. Such interference could not be tolerated under a European constitutional perspective. Freedom of expression is not an absolute right with the result that its protection cannot lead to the destruction of other constitutional interests.

Besides, requiring online platforms not to censor content or generally avoid interferences with freedom of expression (e.g. must-carry obligations) could affect the process of content moderation, thus making platforms' spaces more exposed to objectionable content. This situation would undermine not only the freedom to conduct business of online platforms which would lose advertising revenues but also democratic values online since users would be more exposed to harmful content, thus reducing their freedom to share opinions and ideas online.

Therefore, the horizontal effect doctrine cannot always provide a stable solution for the imbalances between public and private power in the algorithmic society. It could be a reactive remedy which would not be able to comprehensively mitigate the challenges of content moderation. This consideration does not imply that judges could not play a critical role in protecting constitutional values from technological annihilation.[214] On the one hand, this doctrine would perfectly

[214] Oreste Pollicino, *Judicial Protection of Fundamental Rights on the Internet: A Road Towards Digital Constitutionalism?* (Hart 2021).

match with the reactive side of European digital constitutionalism. On the other hand, it would fail to provide the other side of this constitutional phase, namely a normative framework based on the injection of democratic values online to deal with private powers in the long run.

There is also another chance for freedom of expression to mitigate and remedy the challenges of content moderation. By moving from a negative to a positive dimension, it is possible to look at freedom of expression not only as a negative liberty but also as a positive right. This is not a call to define the welfare of freedom of expression but to understand how to foster media pluralism in the digital environment. Likewise, this system would not just focus on directly empowering users to decide on the removal of content. As observed by Rosen, 'a user-generated system for enforcing community standards will never protect speech as scrupulously as unelected judges enforcing strict rules'.[215] The approach of European digital constitutionalism focuses on transparency and procedural safeguards to ensure more autonomy and diversity of online content.

The role of digital constitutionalism is not just to provide new solutions but also to reframe old categories into the evolving technological scenario. As the next section suggests, in order to limit the significant power of online platforms over constitutional rights and freedoms, it is not necessary to provide more access but to understand how to foster media pluralism in the algorithmic society by promoting diversity and transparency in content moderation.

5.6 Rethinking Media Pluralism in the Age of Online Platforms

The challenges of content moderation at the European level would require a more comprehensive strategy which is not only reactive but also promotes the development of a democratic public sphere. The fragmentation of substantive obligations and procedural safeguards and the limit of the horizontal effect does not seem to provide a stable framework to remedy platform power. Even if the first steps of European digital constitutionalism have led to a shift in the European approach to content moderation, still the lack of systemic remedies

[215] Jeffrey Rosen, 'The Deciders: The Future of Privacy and Free Speech in the Age of Facebook and Google' (2012) 80 Fordham Law Review 1525.

could increase uncertainty, thus undermining not only fundamental rights but also the principle of the rule of law. This consideration does not mean that the path of European digital constitutionalism has not designed a turning point, but the fragmentation of legal regimes influencing content moderation would introduce more risks than advantages, even for online platforms.

Consequently, it is worth wondering how European constitutional law can provide other ways to remedy the challenges to the right of freedom of expression in a public sphere which is characterised by opacity and lack of accountability. In the context of traditional media outlets, media pluralism would have been one of the primary ways to ensure more diversity and transparency, thus fostering the positive and passive dimension of the right to freedom of expression.[216] Together with media freedom, pluralism is a precondition for an open and dialectic debate in a democratic society. Granting access to vast and diversified sources of information increases individual exposure to different ideas and opinions contributing to a democratic public sphere. In the digital age, even if there are multiple definitions of media pluralism online,[217] and especially how to measure its effect,[218] users are exposed to content subject to the opaque governance of online platforms which do not provide users with any instruments to understand how their expressions are moderated online.

In order to fix the challenges of the algorithmic public sphere, it is worth understanding how to reframe media pluralism in the age of online platforms. In particular, ensuring access and diversity of information online contributes to ensuring that individuals are not just exposed to polarised information or harmful content. This approach is critical to ensure individual autonomy and dignity while promoting a dialectic relationship in a democratic society.

216 Damian Tambini, *Media Freedom* (Wiley 2021).

217 Judit Bayer and Sergio Carrera, 'A Comparative Analysis of Media Freedom and Pluralism in the EU Member States' (2016) Study for the LIBE Committee www.europarl.europa.eu/RegData/etudes/STUD/2016/571376/IPOL_STU(2016)571376_EN.pdf accessed 20 November 2021; Peter Barron and Simon Morrison, 'Pluralism after Acarcity: The Benefits of Digital Technologies' LSE Media Policy Project blog (18 November 2014) http://blogs.lse.ac.uk/mediapolicyproject/2014/11/18/pluralism-after-scarcity-the-benefits-of-digital-technologies/ accessed 20 November 2021.

218 Kari Karppinen, 'The Limits of Empirical Indicators: Media Pluralism As an Essentially Contested Concept' in Peggy Valcke and others (eds.), *Media Pluralism and Diversity: Concepts, Risks and Global Trends* 287 (Springer 2015).

Therefore, the point is about complementing the negative and active sides of freedom of expression with a positive and passive approach. In other words, rather than focusing on protecting users from public interferences (i.e. negative side) and allowing them to freely share ideas and opinion (i.e. active side), the question is about the role of public actors in providing users with tools to check and complain against private interferences (i.e. positive approach) and ensure information quality and diversity (i.e. passive approach). As examined by the next subsections, the two approaches are strictly interconnected. The positive and passive approaches to freedom of expression encourage public actors to regulate content moderation by injecting safeguards strengthening exposure and diversity.

5.6.1 The Positive Side of Freedom of Expression

Once again, European constitutional law owns the instruments to reach this aim. Serious threats for fundamental rights can be considered the triggers of the positive obligation of states to regulate private activities to protect fundamental rights as underlined by the Strasbourg Court,[219] also in relation to the right to be informed.[220] As the Council of Europe underlined, '[a]s the ultimate guarantors of pluralism, States have a positive obligation to put in place an appropriate legislative and policy framework to that end. This implies adopting appropriate measures to ensure sufficient variety in the overall range of media types, bearing in mind differences in terms of their purposes, functions and geographical reach'.[221] As the former UN special rapporteur on freedom of expression observed regarding the use of artificial intelligence technologies, 'human rights law imposes on States both negative obligations to refrain from implementing measures that interfere with the exercise

[219] See, e.g., *Von Hannover* v. *Germany* (2005) 40 EHRR 1; *Verein gegen Tierfabriken Schweiz (VgT)* v. *Switzerland* (2001) 34 EHRR 159. See Lech Garlicki, 'Relations between Private Actors and the European Convention on Human Rights' in Sajó and Uitz (n. 181), 129.

[220] See, e.g., *Österreichische Vereinigung zur Erhaltung, Stärkung und Schaffung* v. *Austria* (2013); *Youth Initiative for Human Rights* v. *Serbia* (2013); *Társaság a Szabadságjogokért* v. *Hungary* (2009); *Sdružení Jihočeské Matky* v. *the Czech Republic* (2006); *Bladet Tromsø and Stensaas* v. *Norway* (1999).

[221] Recommendation CM/Rec(2018)1 of the Committee of Ministers to Member States on media pluralism and transparency of media ownership (7 March 2018).

of freedom of opinion and expression and positive obligations to promote the rights to freedom of opinion and expression and to protect their exercise'.[222]

The Strasbourg Court has not only underlined the democratic role of the media,[223] or the prohibition for states to interfere with freedom of expression. It went even further by recognising that Article 10 can lead to positive obligations.[224] For instance, in *Dink* v. *Turkey*,[225] the court addressed a case concerning the protection of journalists' expressions clarifying that states have a positive obligation 'to create ... a favourable environment for participation in public debate by all the persons concerned enabling them to express their opinions and ideas without fear, even if they run counter to those defended by the official authorities or by a significant part of public opinion, or even irritating or shocking to the latter'.[226] More recently, in *Khadija Ismayilova* v. *Azerbaijan*,[227] the Strasbourg Court recognised that states are responsible for protecting investigative journalists. Besides, the protection of the right to freedom of expression under the Convention safeguards not only the right to inform but also the right to receive information.[228] The Strasbourg Court has further clarified the characteristics of such a positive obligation in *Appleby and Others* v. *UK*, precisely considering the nature of expression at stake and its role for public debates.[229]

With regard to the digital environment, the Strasbourg Court recognised the role of the Internet in 'enhancing the public's access to news and facilitating the dissemination of information in general',[230] underlining also that 'the internet has now become one of the principal means by which individuals exercise their right to freedom of expression and information, providing as it does essential tools for participation in activities and discussions concerning political issues

[222] Report of the Special Rapporteur on the promotion and protection of the right to freedom of opinion and expression (2018) https://undocs.org/A/73/348 accessed 21 November 2021.

[223] See, e.g., *Barthold* v. *Germany* (1985) 7 EHRR 383; *Lingens* v. *Austria* (1986) 8 EHRR 407.

[224] See, e.g., *Fuentes Bobo* v. *Spain* (2001) 31 EHRR 50; *Özgür Gündem* v. *Turkey* (2001) 31 EHRR 49.

[225] *Dink* v. *Turkey* (2010).

[226] Ibid., 137.

[227] *Khadija Ismayilova* v. *Azerbaijan* (2019).

[228] *Sunday Times* v. *the United Kingdom (No. 1)* (1979) 2 EHRR 245, 66 .

[229] *Appleby and Others* v. *UK* (2003).

[230] *Cengiz and Others* v. *Turkey* (2015), 49, 52.

and issues of general interest'.[231] Nonetheless, the court just addressed the problem of accessing information without scrutinising the criteria according to which information should be organised. Even if there are different views about how the introduction of artificial intelligence technologies in content moderation affects the right to receive information,[232] users still cannot access information about this process not only to understand the source and reliability of content they access but also remedy harms coming from the block of accounts or the removal of content.

In the European framework, positive obligations in the field of content moderation would also derive from the need to ensure users the right to access remedies against the violations of their fundamental rights. According to Article 13 ECHR, 'everyone whose rights and freedoms as set forth in this Convention are violated shall have an effective remedy before a national authority notwithstanding that the violation has been committed by persons acting in an official capacity', along with the requirements of Article 1 on the obligation to respect human rights and Article 46 on the execution of judgments of the Strasbourg Court. This provision requires contracting parties not just to protect the rights enshrined in the Convention but especially avoid that the protection of these rights is frustrated by lack of domestic remedies. As observed by the Strasbourg Court, 'where an individual has an arguable claim to be the victim of a violation of the rights set forth in the Convention, he should have a remedy before a national authority in order both to have his claim decided and, if appropriate, to obtain redress'.[233] Similarly, Article 47 of the Charter provides even broader protection of this right being recognised by a general principle of EU law.[234]

Moving from the Convention to the Charter, it is worth recalling that Article 11 does not only protect the negative dimension of freedom of expression, but also the positive dimension of media pluralism when it states that '[t]he freedom and pluralism of the media shall be respected'.[235] To achieve this purpose, Member States are required to

[231] *Ahmet Yıldırım* v. *Turkey* (2012), 54.

[232] Sarah Eskens and others, 'Challenged by News Personalisation: Five Perspectives on the Right to Receive Information (2017) 9(2) Journal of Media Law 259.

[233] *Leander* v. *Sweden* (1987), 77.

[234] Case 222/84 *Johnston* v. *Chief Constable of the Royal Ulster Constabulary* (1986) ECR 1651; Case 222/86 *Union nationale des entraîneurs et cadres techniques professionnels du football (Unectef)* v. *Georges Heylens and others* (1987) ECR 4097; Case C-97/91 *Oleificio Borelli SpA* v. *Commission of the European Communities* (1992) ECR I-6313.

[235] Charter (n. 40), Art. 11(2).

ensure not only that interferences with the right to freedom of expression are avoided (i.e. negative dimension), but also that diverse and plural access to content is guaranteed (i.e. positive dimension). In *Sky Österreich*,[236] the ECJ dealt with a case involving the protection of media pluralism relating to the financial conditions under which the provider is entitled to gain access to the satellite signal to make short news reports. In this case, the ECJ underlined the protection of the right to be informed or receive information guaranteed by Article 11 of the Charter as a limit to the freedom to conduct a business. In this case, by balancing the two fundamental rights in question, the ECJ gave priority to public access to information over contractual freedom. Nonetheless, once more, this case deals with access and not quality. It is also not clear whether the EU framework could be influenced by the positive obligations of the Convention. It is true that the Charter provides a bridge between the two systems by stating that 'the meaning and scope of [Charter's] rights shall be the same as those laid down by the said Convention'.[237]

Despite different interpretations, as observed by Kuczerawy, 'the duty to protect the right to freedom of expression involves an obligation for governments to promote this right and to provide for an environment where it can be effectively exercised without being unduly curtailed'.[238] In the field of algorithmic technologies, the Council of Europe has underlined the importance of ensuring different safeguards such as contestability and effective remedies in relation to public and private actors.[239] Precisely, states should ensure 'equal, accessible, affordable, independent and effective judicial and non-judicial procedures that guarantee an impartial review, in compliance with Articles 6, 13 and 14 of the Convention, of all claims of violations of Convention rights through the use of algorithmic systems, whether stemming from public or private sector actors'.[240]

[236] Case C-283/11 *Sky Österreich GmbH* v. *Österreichischer Rundfunk* (2013).

[237] Charter (n. 40), Art. 52(3).

[238] Aleksandra Kuczerawy, 'The Power of Positive Thinking. Intermediary Liability and the Effective Enjoyment of the Right to Freedom of Expression' (2017) 3 Journal of Intellectual Property, Information Technology and Electronic Commerce Law 182, 186–7.

[239] Recommendation CM/Rec(2020)1 of the Committee of Ministers to Member States on the human rights impacts of algorithmic systems (8 April 2020) www.statewatch.org/media/documents/news/2020/apr/coe-recommendation-algorithms-automation-human-rights-4-20.pdf accessed 21 November 2021.

[240] Ibid.

Therefore, the potential regulation of content moderation would not just result from the need to balance other constitutional interests. Injecting democratic safeguards in the process of content moderation would aim to enhance the effective protection of the right to freedom of expression rather than undermining it. Besides, it is not only the right to freedom of expression but also the freedom to conduct business which is limited by the prohibition of abuse of rights.[241] In other words, the positive obligations of public actors should lead to limit platform powers to define the protection of freedom of expression online, thus balancing constitutional rights and freedoms.

5.6.2 The Passive Side of Freedom of Expression

The logics of moderation limit the transparency and accountability of online platforms, thus marginalising users from understanding how content is processed in the digital environment. Since users cannot generally rely on horizontal and general rights vis-à-vis online platforms, this situation leaves these actors free to decide how to balance and enforce fundamental rights online without any public guarantee. Since the liberal approach to free speech (i.e. the free marketplace of ideas) has led to collateral effects in the digital environment, the protection of the negative side of this freedom is not enough to protect constitutional rights any longer. Therefore, in order to reduce the power of online platforms moderating content on a global scale, it is worth proposing a positive dimension of freedom of expression, triggering a new regulatory intervention towards the adoption of substantive rights and procedural safeguards. This approach contributes to filling the gap of safeguards in content moderation.

At first glance, addressing this issue could lead to changing the liability system of online platforms to increase their degree of responsibility in online content moderation. Nevertheless, this kind of regulatory approach could undermine the economic freedoms of online platforms, which would be overwhelmed by disproportionate obligations. Moreover, changing the safe harbour system would not solve the issue of transparency and accountability in online content moderation. Increasing legal pressure on online platforms by introducing monitoring obligations would result in 'overly aggressive, unaccountable self-policing, leading to arbitrary and

[241] Convention (n. 41), Art. 17; Charter (n. 40), Art. 54.

unnecessary restrictions on online behavior'.[242] This risk, known as collateral censorship, could have strong effects on democracy, thus requiring regulators to avoid threatening online platforms for failing to correctly police content.[243] Due to the ability to govern their digital spaces through content moderation, governments find themselves stuck in cooperating with online platforms.

Apart from the risks of surveillance, even the best-equipped public body would be overwhelmed when handling all the content that platforms moderate. It is true that, in a perfect world, decisions about rights and freedoms should be covered by safeguards and guaranteed by independent public bodies. Nonetheless, reality shows that the fight against illegal content would be hard without online platforms. This consideration does not mean that constitutional democracies should renounce protecting constitutional values but that they should recognise the limits of public enforcement in the digital environment. Therefore, as underlined in Chapter 7, the match is not between private and public enforcement but it is about how to put together the two systems by injecting democratic safeguards in the relationship between public and private actors.

The aim of this new positive and passive approach is not to make platforms liable for their conducts, but responsible for protecting democratic values through more transparent and user-driven procedures. A solution could consist of regulating diversity.[244] Some algorithms can be designed to increase diversity and operate adversarial to profiling. In other words, algorithms could also be a support to ensure pluralism and fight the process of targeting based on users' interaction and network (e.g. echo chambers), thus reaching serendipity.[245] The European Commission's Code of Practice on Disinformation has encouraged platforms to conduct a process of dilution to tackle

[242] Milton Mueller, 'Hyper-Transparency and Social Control: Social Media as Magnets for Regulation' (2016) 39(9) Telecommunications Policy 804, 809.

[243] Jack M. Balkin, 'Free Speech and Hostile Environments' (1999) 99 Columbia Law Review 2295.

[244] Maria Luisa Stasi, 'Ensuring Pluralism in Social Media Markets: Some Suggestions' (2020) EUI Working Paper RSCAS 2020/05 https://cadmus.eui.eu/bitstream/handle/1814/65902/RSCAS_2020_05.pdf?sequence=1&isAllowed=y accessed 20 November 2021.

[245] Judith Möller and other, 'Do not Blame it on the Algorithm: An Empirical Assessment of Multiple Recommender Systems and their Impact on Content Diversity' (2018) 21(7) Information, Communication & Society 959.

disinformation by improving the findability of trustworthy content. This solution would be a way to frame the role of algorithms not only as a risk but also as a support for democratic values.[246] In other words, such a new positive framework of freedom of expression would address the process of moderation without regulating content or changing platform immunities.

Therefore, the issue to solve is not just that relating to the liability of online intermediaries but also that concerning the injection of transparency obligations and procedural safeguards.[247] Here, the proposal for a positive framework of freedom of expression is focused on the proceduralisation of content moderation which would not affect platform immunity. The Council of Europe stressed the relevance of the positive obligation to ensure the protection of rights and freedoms through the horizonal effect of human rights and the introduction of regulatory measures. In this case, 'due process guarantees are indispensable, and access to effective remedies should be facilitated vis-à-vis both States and intermediaries with respect to the services in question'.[248]

Without regulating online content moderation, it is not possible to expect that platforms will turn their business interests driven by profit maximisation to a constitutional oriented approach. New substantive rights and procedural rules would provide users with a set of remedies against the potential violation of their fundamental rights resulting from discretionary decisions by platforms concerning online content while providing proportionate obligations in the field of content moderation.

Besides, this positive approach to freedom of expression could also advantage online platforms. A harmonised regulatory framework of content moderation would reduce the costs of compliance while

[246] Brigit Stark and others, 'Are Algorithms a Threat to Democracy? The Rise of Intermediaries: A Challenge for Public Discourse' Algorithm Watch (26 May 2020) https://algorithmwatch.org/wp-content/uploads/2020/05/Governing-Platforms-communications-study-Stark-May-2020-AlgorithmWatch.pdf accessed 22 November 2021.

[247] Aleksandra Kuczerawy, 'Safeguards for Freedom of Expression in the Era of Online Gatekeeping' (2018) 3 Auteurs & Media 292; Kate Crawford and Jason Schultz, 'Big Data and Due Process: Toward a Framework to Redress Predictive Privacy Harms' (2014) 55 Boston College Law Review 93; Danielle K. Citron and Frank Pasquale, 'The Scored Society: Due Process for Automated Predictions' (2014) 89 Washington Law Review 1.

[248] Recommendation CM/Rec(2018)2 of the Committee of Ministers to Member States on the roles and responsibilities of internet intermediaries (2018).

enhancing legal certainty and their freedom to conduct business. The liability regime established by the e-Commerce Directive could be replaced by a uniform system of rules and safeguards to increase harmonisation in the internal market. It should not be forgotten that the market is not made only of large online platforms able to comply with any regulation. Therefore, the regulation of content moderation should provide a layered scope of application which takes into consideration small and medium-sized businesses. Otherwise, the risk is to create a legal barrier in the market, fostering the power of some online platforms over the others. A new set of rules on procedural transparency and accountability would reduce the challenges raised by regulatory fragmentation and legal uncertainty which platforms face when moderating content. Even the complementary introduction of a 'Good Samaritan' clause could increase legal certainty by breaking the distinction between active and passive providers and encourage platforms to take voluntary measures. Nonetheless, the solution of European digital constitutionalism would lead to increasing transparency and accountability in the process of content moderation, and maintaining the exception of liability of online platforms.

Therefore, the regulation of online content moderation should be based on four general principles: ban of general monitoring obligation; transparency and accountability; proportionality; availability of human intervention. Precisely, according to the first principle, Member States should not oblige platforms to generally moderate online content. This ban is crucial to safeguard fundamental rights such as freedom to conduct business, privacy, data protection and, last but not least, freedom of expression.[249] Secondly, content moderation rules should be assessed and explained to users ex ante in a transparent and user-friendly way and ex post when content is removed or blocked. In this case human rights impact assessment and transparent notice including the guidelines and criteria used by online platforms to moderate content can ensure that risks for fundamental rights are mitigated and decisions are as predictable as possible. The third principle aims to strike a fair balance between the rights of users and the obligations of platforms. Although the lack of transparent and accountable procedures relegates users in a position of *subjectionis*, the enforcement of users'

[249] See, for example, Case C-70/10 *Scarlet Extended SA* v. *Société belge des auteurs, compositeurs et éditeurs SCRL (SABAM)* (2011) ECR I-11959; Case C-360/10 *Belgische Vereniging van Auteurs, Componisten en Uitgevers CVBA (SABAM)* v. *Netlog NV* (2012).

rights should not nonetheless lead to a disproportionate limitation of the right and freedom of online platforms to perform their business, especially if we want to protect new or small platforms. The fourth principle is based on introducing the principle of human-in-the-loop in content moderation. The role of humans in this process could be an additional safeguard allowing users to rely on a human translation of the procedure subject to specific conditions.

5.6.3 The Digital Services Act

The adoption of the Digital Services Act constitutes a primary step towards the normative framework supported by the rise of European digital constitutionalism. The Digital Services Act is just a piece of a broader European strategy reviewing the objectives of the Digital Single Market to shape the European digital future.[250] As examined in Chapter 7, the proposal for a regulation on artificial intelligence technologies is another example of this European strategy which aims to face the challenges of the algorithmic society.[251]

The adoption of the Digital Services Act can be considered a milestone of the European constitutional strategy. In order to face the challenges raised by platform power, together with the Digital Markets Act,[252] the Digital Services Act plays a critical role in providing a supranational and horizontal regime to mitigate the challenges raised by the power of online platforms in content moderation. This legal package promises to update a regulatory framework that dates to the e-Commerce Directive by providing a comprehensive approach to increase transparency and accountability of online platforms in content moderation. Also, the Digital Services Act takes into account the different sizes of online providers by establishing that its scope extends to micro or small enterprises pursuant to the annex to Recommendation 2003/361/EC.[253] Besides, it will provide a horizontal framework for a series of other

[250] Communication from the Commission to the European Parliament, the Council, the European Economic and Social Committee and the Committee of the Regions, Shaping Europe's digital future, COM(2020) 67 final.

[251] Proposal for a Regulation of the European Parliament and of the Council Laying Down Harmonised Rules on Artificial Intelligence (Artificial Intelligence Act) and Amending Certain Union Legislative Acts COM(2021) 206 final.

[252] Proposal for a Regulation of the European Parliament and of the Council on contestable and fair markets in the digital sector (Digital Markets Act) COM(2020)842 final.

[253] Commission Recommendation of 6 May 2003 concerning the definition of micro, small and medium-sized enterprises C(2003) 1422.

measures adopted in recent years which are instead defined as *lex specialis* like the Copyright Directive or the AVMS Directive.[254]

The title of the proposal reveals how the Digital Services Act will affect the regulatory framework envisaged by the e-Commerce Directive. While maintaining the exemption of liability for online platforms,[255] and the ban for Member States to impose general monitoring obligations,[256] the Digital Services Act overcomes the issue of neutrality by adopting a Good Samaritan clause. This approach contributes to overcoming the legal uncertainty relating to the definition of passive providers. Online platforms will be free to take 'voluntary own initiative investigations or other activities aimed at detecting, identifying and removing, or disabling of access to, illegal content' without fearing to be sanctioned for failing to comply with their exemption of liability.[257] Nonetheless, the Digital Services Act is different from the Communications Decency Act since it limits platform power by providing substantial obligations and procedural safeguards which require platforms to disclose information, assess the risk for fundamental rights and provide redress mechanisms. Additionally, it also maintains (and clarifies) the role of courts or administrative authorities, by requiring an intermediary service provider to terminate or prevent a specific infringement by proceduralising the process to follow for orders to act against illicit content,[258] or provide information.[259]

Even if the proposal maintains the rules of exemption of liability for online intermediaries and extends their freedom to take voluntary measures, it introduces some (constitutional) adjustment which aims to increase the level of transparency and accountability of online platforms. Since the first Recitals, the Digital Services Act complements the goals of the internal market with a constitutional-oriented approach. In particular, it clarifies that providers of intermediary services shall behave responsibly and diligently to allow Union citizens and other persons to exercise their fundamental rights guaranteed in the Charter of Fundamental Rights of the European Union, in particular

[254] Caroline Cauffman and Catalina Goanta, 'A New Order: The Digital Services Act and Consumer Protection' (2021) European Journal of Risk Regulation 1.
[255] Digital Services Act (n. 175), Arts. 3–5.
[256] Ibid., Art. 7.
[257] Ibid., Art. 6.
[258] Ibid., Art. 8.
[259] Ibid., Art. 9.

the freedom of expression and information and the freedom to conduct a business, and the right to non-discrimination.[260]

To achieve this purpose, the Digital Services Act introduces transparency requirements and provides users with the possibility to access redress mechanisms.[261] In other words, without regulating content, it requires online platforms to comply with procedural safeguards, thus making the process of content moderation more transparent and accountable. These obligations lead online platforms to consolidating their bureaucracy of online content which designs the administrativisation of content moderation. The procedural rules on the notice-and-takedown or on reasons about content removal are just two primary examples of how the Union is trying to require online platforms to be more transparent and accountable.

This approach however has not been enough since the Digital Services Act provides additional obligations which only apply to those platforms falling within the notion of 'very large online platforms'.[262] In this case, the proposal sets a higher standard of due diligence, transparency and accountability. These platforms are required to develop appropriate tools and resources to mitigate the systemic risks associated with their activities. And to make this system more effective, the Digital Services Act introduces sanctions applying to all the intermediaries up to 6 per cent of turnover on a global scale in the previous year.[263]

This framework underlines how the Commission aims to provide a new legal framework for digital services that is capable of strengthening the Digital Single Market while protecting the rights and values of the Union which are increasingly challenged by the governance of online platforms in the information society. This approach should not surprise since it perfectly fits within the path of European digital constitutionalism whose roots, based on human dignity, do not tolerate the exercise of private power threatening fundamental rights and democratic values while escaping public oversight.

The Digital Services Act shows the resilience of the European constitutional model reacting to the threats of private powers to freedom of expression. Even if some of these rules could be improved during the process of adoption, it is possible to underline that this proposal

260 Ibid., Recital 3.
261 Ibid., Arts. 12–24.
262 Ibid., Arts. 25–33.
263 Ibid., Art. 42.

provides a horizontal regulatory framework to limit platform power in the field of content, thus showing the positive and passive side of European freedom of expression. This new phase should not be seen merely as a turn towards regulatory intervention or as an imperialist extension of European constitutional values. It is more a normative reaction of European digital constitutionalism promoting the positive and passive side of freedom of expression to address the challenges of the algorithmic society.

5.7 Expressions and Personal Data

The relevance of European constitutional law in the field of content moderation should be unveiled at this time. While constitutional provisions have been conceived as limits to the coercive power of the state, in the algorithmic society an equally important and pernicious threat for freedom of expression comes from online platforms making decisions on expression based on their ethical, economic and self-regulatory framework. This situation leads European constitutional law to react to protect constitutional rights and liberties, thus designing a strategy in the long run. This approach does not mean that public actors' interferences with the right to freedom of expression are not relevant any longer, but that it is necessary to look at the limitations to the exercise of freedoms as the result of platform power.

The current opacity of content moderation constitutes a challenge for democratic societies. If individuals cannot understand the reasons behind decisions involving their rights, primarily when automated decision-making systems are involved, the pillars of autonomy, transparency and accountability on which democracy is based are destined to fall. While, in the past, the liberal approach to free speech fitted with the purpose to safeguard democratic values in the digital environment, today, the emergence of new powers governing the flow of information may require a shift from a negative dimension to a positive approach by regulating content moderation. The liberal approach transplanted in the Union from the western side of the Atlantic in the aftermath of the Internet has led online platforms to impose their authoritative regime on content based on a mix of technological and contractual instruments. The result of this situation has led users in a status of *subjectionis* where they find themselves forced to comply with standards of freedom of expression autonomously determined by online platforms.

Within this framework, the Union has started to focus on introducing mechanisms of transparency and accountability in online content moderation. For example, the rights to obtain motivation or human intervention are still unripe but important steps towards a more democratic digital environment. These user rights should not be considered only as instruments to improve transparency and accountability but also as tools to limit the discretion of online platforms operating as private powers outside any constitutional boundary. Nevertheless, it is necessary to observe that Union efforts are still not enough to ensure a path towards the democratisation of the digital environment. The multiple legal regimes regulating online content moderation are increasingly intertwined. This approach could also affect the platform freedom to conduct business since it requires these actors to set different regimes of content moderation.

Nonetheless, the approach of the Union underlines the talent of European digital constitutionalism to react against new forms of powers undermining democratic values. As in the field of data, as examined in Chapter 6, the Union has started to pave the way towards the regulation of platform powers, thus leading to an increasing convergence of safeguards in the field of data and content. In other words, the Union's approach can be considered a first crucial step towards a new approach to content moderation where online platforms are required to operate as responsible actors in light of their gatekeeping role in the digital environment.

Still, the challenges to freedom of expression are not isolated. They are intimately intertwined with the protection of privacy and personal data. Content and data are the two sides of the same coin of digital capitalism. For example, this relationship is evident in content moderation where the content shared by users is also processed as data to provide tailored advertising services. More generally, the challenge concerns the intimate relationship between algorithmic technologies and the processing of (personal) data. Therefore, it is time to focus on the field of data to underline the role of European digital constitutionalism in protecting fundamental rights and democracy.

6 Digital Constitutionalism, Privacy and Data Protection

6.1 Data in the Algorithmic Society

The evolution of the algorithmic society has shed light on the relevance of data in daily life. Algorithms are becoming more pervasive, providing new opportunities for the private sector,[1] and even for the performance of public tasks.[2] The possibilities raised by automated technologies have led to defining data as the raw materials of digital capitalism driving the fourth industrial revolution.[3] These systems are not just drivers of economic growth. Their implementation by public and private actors is increasingly influencing individual decisions without the possibility to understand or control how the processing of personal data affects rights and freedoms.

The organisation and dissemination of information in the digital environment, the profiling of consumers based on credit scores or new techniques in predictive law enforcement are only some examples of the answers which automated decision-making systems can provide and of how such technologies can raise concerns not only from the perspective of individual rights and freedoms but also for democracy. [4] As in the case of freedom of expression, the implementation of algorithms challenges democratic systems due to the lack of transparency

[1] Julie E. Cohen, *Between Truth and Power: The Legal Constructions of Informational Capitalism* (Oxford University Press 2019).

[2] Marion Oswald, 'Algorithm-Assisted Decision-making in the Public Sector: Framing the Issues Using Administrative Law Rules Governing Discretionary Power' (2018) 376 Philosophical Transaction Royal Society A.

[3] Viktor Mayer-Schönberger and Kenneth Cukier, *Big Data: A Revolution That Will Transform How We Live, Work, and Think* (Houghton Mifflin Harcourt 2013).

[4] Paul Nemitz, 'Constitutional Democracy and Technology in the age of Artificial Intelligence' (2018) Royal Society Philosophical Transactions A.

and accountability in decision-making affecting fundamental rights and freedoms. As Regan underlined, the value of privacy is not just related to the individual dimension and human dignity. It is also a critical safeguard for society.[5]

Orwell's dystopian scenario is not still the rule, but there is an increasing tendency in monitoring and classifying human behaviours in every moment of daily life.[6] From home application to biometric surveillance in public spaces, there are fewer private spaces where individuals can escape from the eyes of public and private actors. Nonetheless, this situation does not concern only the individual private sphere but also the impossibility to scrutinise data collection and use. Individuals tend to adapt their behaviours to a new societal form of surveillance or fear to express themselves, and new information asymmetries do not allow individuals to understand what is happening behind the scenes.[7]

The result is that digital technologies become an instrument for social control. Individuals are increasingly transparent operating in a virtual world which is increasingly opaque. In 2010, Zuckerberg underlined 'The age of privacy is over'.[8] From this perspective, algorithmic technologies are incompatible with data protection which is seen as an obsolete instrument of compliance limiting the datafication of human life for business purposes. This process increasingly makes privacy public while the processing of personal data opaque. These threats do not just involve the private sphere of rights and freedoms but also autonomy and awareness undermined by the lack of transparency and accountability. The case of Cambridge Analytica has been a paradigmatic example of the asymmetry of power in the data field, underlining how the role of microtargeting of voters for electoral purposes challenges fairness and transparency.[9]

[5] Priscilla M. Regan, *Legislating Privacy, Technology, Social Values and Public Policy* 321 (University of North Carolina Press 1995).

[6] George Orwell, *1984* (Penguin Books 2008).

[7] Shoshana Zuboff, *The Age of Surveillance Capitalism: The Fight for a Human Future at the New Frontier of Power* (Public Affairs 2018).

[8] Marshall Kirkpatrick, 'Facebook's Zuckerberg Says the Age of Privacy is Over' The New York Times (10 January 2010) www.nytimes.com/external/readwriteweb/2010/01/10/10readwriteweb-facebooks-zuckerberg-says-the-age-of-privac-82963.html?source=post_page accessed 21 November 2021.

[9] Brittany Kaiser, *Targeted: The Cambridge Analytica Whistleblower's Inside Story of How Big Data, Trump, and Facebook Broke Democracy and How It Can Happen Again* (Harper Collins 2019).

The large exploitation of data from public and private actors put the protection of personal information under pressure. This is why the reaction of digital constitutionalism does not just involve the right to freedom of expression. The threats of the algorithmic society and digital capitalism affect other two pillars on which liberty and democracy are based in the 'onlife' dimension, in particular the right to privacy and data protection.[10] The latter complements the protection of the former against the threats coming from profiling and, more generally, the computation of human life. Privacy and data protection share a common objective, precisely that of protecting individual autonomy as a precondition to fully participate in a democratic society.

Therefore, data protection in the algorithmic society aims to provide safeguards for individuals while maintaining control of their data. In this sense, data protection represents the 'positive' side of the rights to privacy against interference with the individual freedom to be let alone. Without rules governing the processing of personal data, individuals could not rely on guarantees protecting their privacy and autonomy against the discretionary processing of personal information. Without accountability and transparency safeguards, it is not possible to mitigate the asymmetry of power nor to mitigate the effects of automated decisions on fundamental rights as well as on democratic values.

The constitutional values underpinning privacy and data protection can play a critical role in shaping the exercise of powers in the algorithmic society. While, with respect to content, the primary issue concerns the adoption of procedural safeguards to foster transparency and accountability, the field of data is more mature. Nonetheless, even if the consolidation of the positive dimension of privacy in the right to data protection culminated with the adoption of the GDPR,[11] European data protection law would require further steps forward to address the challenges of the algorithmic society.

Within this framework, this chapter aims to underline how, even in the field of data, European digital constitutionalism provides a normative framework to protect fundamental rights and democratic values while limiting platform power. This process is not based on

[10] Luciano Floridi (ed.), *The Onlife Manifesto Being Human in a Hyperconnected Era* (Springer 2015).

[11] Regulation (EU) 2016/679 of the European Parliament and of the Council of 27 April 2016 on the protection of natural persons with regard to the processing of personal data and on the free movement of such data, and repealing Directive 95/46/EC (General Data Protection Regulation) (2016) OJ L 119/1.

introducing new safeguards but providing a teleological interpretation of the GDPR unveiling its constitutional dimension. In other words, protecting privacy and data protection in the European framework would not lead to searching for new rules and instruments to mitigate private powers but interpreting the GDPR under the lens of European digital constitutionalism.

In order to achieve this purpose, the first part of this chapter focuses on the rise and consolidation of data protection in the European framework. This part explains how and to what extent personal data have started to be protected in the algorithmic society. The second part addresses the rise of the big data environment and the constitutional challenges introduced by automated decision-making technologies, thus underlining how the implementation of algorithmic technologies challenges the boundaries of privacy and data protection. The third part focuses on the GDPR underlining the opportunities and challenges of European data protection law concerning artificial intelligence. This part aims to highlight to what extent the system of the GDPR can ensure the protection of the right to privacy and data protection in relation to artificial intelligence technologies. The fourth part underlines the constitutional values underpinning the GDPR to provide a constitutional interpretation of how European data protection, as one of the mature expressions of European digital constitutionalism, can mitigate the rise of unaccountable powers in the algorithmic society.

6.2 From the Right to Be Let Alone . . .

In the field of data, the role of digital constitutionalism in the algorithmic society could be observed by directly focusing on the GDPR. However, such an approach would provide just a limited picture of the underpinning constitutional principles on which the right to data protection is based in Europe. Therefore, understanding which values characterise data protection is critical to provide a constitutional-oriented interpretation of the GDPR. European data protection law is not just the result of regulatory but also historical reasons and constitutional values linked to the evolution of new technologies, precisely automated systems.

The European path towards the constitutional recognition of data protection as a fundamental right began from the evolution of the concept of privacy in the US framework. This right, referred to as 'the right to be let alone' by Warren and Brandeis at the end of the nineteenth century,[12] was conceived as a negative liberty safeguarding the individual's private life against potential external interferences.[13] Also in the European framework, privacy has been conceived as a negative liberty. The Strasbourg Court underlined the right to privacy as the right to live far from publicity,[14] or away from unwarranted attention.[15] This right also extends to online anonymity,[16] thus enabling individuals to live peacefully in the online and offline environment. Nevertheless, the Strasbourg Court has not only underlined the right to privacy as a right to be let alone but also as a condition to development and fulfilment of personality, as well as personal autonomy and identity,[17] intimately connected with the right to human dignity in the European constitutional framework.

However, this historical framework is not enough to explain the reasons triggering the positive evolution of data protection from the negative matrix of privacy. From a merely negative perspective (i.e. the right to be let alone), characterised by predominant liberal imprinting, the right to privacy in Europe has evolved towards a positive dimension consisting of the right to the protection of personal data. This development can be mainly attributed to the increasing role of information to perform public tasks and the evolution of new technologies. It firstly resulted from the increase in data usage and processing, primarily from the progress of the welfare state, the consolidation of new channels of communication (e.g. the telephone) and automated processing techniques like databases.[18] In *Malone* v. *The United Kingdom*, profiling citizens by the public authorities was highlighted as a dangerous trend

[12] Samuel D. Warren and Louis D. Brandeis, 'The Right to Privacy' (1890) 4 Harvard Law Review 193.

[13] Daniel J. Solove, 'A Brief History of Information Privacy Law' (2006) Proskauer on Privacy; Alan Westin, *Privacy and Freedom* (Athenum 1967).

[14] *X.* v. *Iceland* (1976) ECHR 7.

[15] *Smirnova* v. *Russia* (2004) 39 EHRR 22.

[16] *Delfi AS* v. *Estonia* (2015).

[17] *Reklos and Davourlis* v. *Greece* (2009) EMLR 290; *Burghartz* v. *Switzerland* (1994) ECHR 22.

[18] Jeffrey A. Meldman, 'Centralized Information Systems and the Legal Right to Privacy' (1969) 52 Marquette Law Review 335; Richard Ruggles, John de J. Pemberton Jr. and Arthur R. Miller, 'Computers, Data Banks, and Individual Privacy' (1968) 53 Minnesota Law Review 211; Arthur R. Miller, 'Personal Privacy in the Computer Age: The Challenge of a New Technology in an Information-Oriented Society' (1969) 67 Michigan Law Review 1089.

threatening democratic society.[19] Computing (or information) technologies have introduced new possibilities for storage and organisation of data with lower costs. Nonetheless, this new framework has also introduced new risks related to the automated processing of personal data.[20]

These developments affected the autonomy of individuals. The lack of control and safeguards against the massive collection and processing of data has enabled governmental authorities and private companies to take decisions without explaining which data have been used, for which purposes and duration. In 1983, the German federal constitutional court invalidated a federal law allowing the collection and sharing of census information between national and regional authorities.[21] The case involved the automated collection of personal data by public authorities for the performance of a public task. This decision, known as the *Volkszählungsurteil*, paved the way towards a right to 'informational self-determination' resulting from the constitutional interpretation of enshrining a general right to personality,[22] and the protection of human dignity.[23] This landmark decision highlighted the need to protect personal data from the interferences of automation and its connection with the autonomy and dignity of individuals. The court did not deny that data play a critical role for the development of public policies and the pursuit of public tasks in industrialised countries. At the same time, it shed light on the lack of individual awareness about the processing of personal data for public tasks in the field of tax or social security. This case has provided a first clue of the different characterisation of the right to privacy on the eastern side of the Atlantic and the role of a positive right to data protection aimed to protect the right to self-determination and human dignity.

This European focus on the individual is not by chance. When looking at the eastern side of the Atlantic, different underpinning values have guided the evolution and consolidation of the right to privacy and the

[19] *Malone* v. *the United Kingdom* (1984) 7 EHRR 14.

[20] Council of Europe, 'Convention no. 108/1981 – Explanatory Report' https://rm.coe.int/CoERMPublicCommonSearchServices/DisplayDCTMContent?documentId=09000016800ca434 accessed 21 November 2021.

[21] BVerfG 15 December 1983, 1 BvR 209/83, *Volkszählung*.

[22] German Basic Law, Art. 2(1).

[23] Ibid., Art. 1(1). See Gerrit Hornung and Christoph Schnabel, 'Data Protection in Germany I: The Population Census Decision and the Right to Informational Self-Determination' (2009) 25 Computer Law & Security Review 84.

rise of data protection.[24] As in the case of freedom of expression, the right to privacy in Europe was conceived as a negative freedom but based on different constitutional premises. The European experience has been traumatised by the Second World War where even the right to privacy completely vanished.[25] The increasing amount of data collected for identifying people for creating government records based on data like ethnicity, political ideas and gender is a paradigmatic sample of how such a liberty was compressed. On the other hand, the US has experienced less interferences on privacy and less misuse of personal information, which encouraged a laissez-faire approach based on individual liberty. According to Whitman, Europe would be the dignity side of the Atlantic while the US would represent a model of privacy based on liberty.[26]

The reality is more nuanced, but it cannot be neglected that the grounding values of the right to privacy across the Atlantic are different.[27] This distance is evident indeed when focusing on the evolution of the protection of personal data. In the United States, the protection of privacy is not linked to the individual but to a sectorial approach and the mosaic theory which considers each individual as not relevant per se without the other tiles of the mosaic.[28] In other words, the personalistic characterisation of European data protection law cannot be found on the other side of the Atlantic whose protection is centred on the sectorial and aggregated effects of certain processing of personal information, even if recently privacy and data protection are capturing more attention in the US framework.[29]

It is not by chance that, in that period, some Member States had introduced data protection regulations even before the advent of the Internet,[30] and anticipating the Data Protection Directive. Until 1995, at

[24] Gloria Gonzalez Fuster, *The Emergence of Personal Data Protection as a Fundamental Right of the EU* (Springer 2014).

[25] Elizabeth Harvey and others (eds.), *Private Life and Privacy in Nazi Germany* (Cambridge University Press 2019).

[26] James Q. Whitman, 'The Two Western Cultures of Privacy: Dignity Versus Liberty' (2004) 113(6) Yale Law Journal 1151.

[27] Paul M. Schwartz and Karl-Nikolaus Peifer, 'Transatlantic Data Privacy' (2017) 106 Georgetown Law Journal 115.

[28] Orin S. Kerr, 'The Mosaic Theory of the Fourth Amendment' (2012) 111 Michigan Law Review 311.

[29] Woodrow Hartzog and Neil Richards, 'Privacy's Constitutional Moment and the Limits of Data Protection' (2020) 61 Boston College Law Review 1687.

[30] See the *Datenschutzgesetz* adopted on 7 October 1970 in Germany; *Datalagen* adopted on 11 May 1973 in Sweden; Loi n. 78–17 6 January 1978 in France; Data Protection Act 1984 12 July 1984 in UK.

a supranational level, data protection has been primarily addressed within the framework of the Council of Europe through the judicial interpretation of Article 8 of the Convention by the Strasbourg Court.[31]

Together with the Convention, the Council of Europe has specifically focused on the challenges of automation for the right to privacy. In 1968, the Parliamentary Assembly of the Council of Europe proposed to establish a committee of experts to examine whether 'the national legislation in the member States adequately protects the right to privacy against violations which may be committed by the use of modern scientific and technical methods'.[32] This acknowledgement of the role of new data processing techniques is also the reason for the adoption of Convention No. 108 on the protection of individuals with regard to automatic processing of personal data adopted already in 1981.[33] This international instrument was the first to recognise the concerns relating to automated processing when neither the Internet nor artificial intelligence technologies had proven yet that they were the source of new challenges to the protection of personal data. Ensuring the protection of personal data taking account of the increasing flow across frontiers of personal data undergoing automatic processing was the first aim of this document which was subsequently modernised in 2018.[34] As a result, it is possible to underline the role played by automation in founding the constitutional basis for the new fundamental right of data protection whose aim is to protect 'every individual'.[35]

If, at that time, the Council of Europe could be considered the promoter of the constitutional dimension of personal data, this consideration can be extended only partially to the European Union. In this case, the Data Protection Directive regulated the processing of personal data

[31] European Convention on Human Rights (1950). See *Leander* v. *Sweden* (1987) 9 EHRR 433; *Amann* v. *Switzerland* (2000) 30 EHRR 843; *S. and Marper* v. *The United Kingdom* (2008) 48 EHRR 50; *M.M.* v. *UK A no 24029* (2012) ECHR 1906. The ECtHR has justified such approach providing a definition of the Convention as a 'living instrument'. See, also, *Mamatkulov and Askarov* v. *Turkey* (2005).

[32] Parliamentary Assembly of the Council of Europe, 'Recommendation 509 (1968) – Human Rights and Modern Scientific and Technological Developments' https://assembly.coe.int/nw/xml/XRef/Xref-XML2HTML-EN.asp?fileid=14546&lang=en accessed 21 November 2021.

[33] Convention for the Protection of Individuals with regard to Automatic Processing of Personal Data (1981).

[34] Amending protocol to the Convention for the Protection of Individuals with Regard to the Processing of Personal Data, adopted by the Committee of Ministers at its 128th Session in Elsinore on 18 May 2018.

[35] Ibid., Art. 1.

only in 1995 and before the adoption of the Charter of Nice in 2000,[36] which recognised data protection as a fundamental right,[37] albeit without any binding character until the entry into force of the Lisbon Treaty in 2009.[38] As already underlined in Chapter 2, it would be enough to look at the Recitals of the Data Protection Directive highlighting the functional (and non-fundamental) nature of the protection of personal data for the consolidation and proper functioning of the single market,[39] and, consequently, as an instrument to guarantee the fundamental freedoms of the Union.[40] This scenario based on the prevalence of the economic-functional dimension of the protection of personal data, the recognition of the binding nature of the Charter and the inclusion in EU primary law have contributed to codifying the constitutional dimension of the right to data protection in the Union.[41] This change of paradigm has led the ECJ to extend the boundaries of protection of these fundamental rights, thus triggering a positive regulatory outcome with the adoption of the GDPR.

Data protection in the European framework constitutes a relatively new right developed as a response to technological evolution.[42] European data protection law is an example of the shift from a mere negative liberty (i.e. privacy) to a positive right (i.e. data protection) to face the threats coming from the unaccountable exercise of powers through the processing of personal data. The advent of the Internet has not only lowered this cost but has also increased the speed for transferring large sets of information and connecting single nodes into a network for sharing data.[43] Thanks to the evolution of data management systems, the public and private sector benefited from

[36] Charter of Fundamental Rights of the European Union (2012) OJ C 326/391.

[37] Ibid., Art. 8.

[38] Consolidated version of the Treaty on European Union (2012) OJ C 326/13, Art. 6.

[39] Directive 95/46/EC of the European Parliament and of the Council of 24 October 1995 on the protection of individuals with regard to the processing of personal data and on the free movement of such data (1995) OJ L 281/31.

[40] Data Protection Directive (n. 39). According Recital 3: 'Whereas the establishment and functioning of an internal market in which, in accordance with Article 7a of the Treaty, the free movement of goods, persons, services and capital is ensured require not only that personal data should be able to flow freely from one Member State to another, but also that the fundamental rights of individuals should be safeguarded'.

[41] Hielke Hijmans, *The European Union as Guardian of Internet Privacy. The Story of Art 16 TFEU* (Springer 2016).

[42] Orla Lynskey, *The Foundations of EU Data Protection Law* (Oxford University Press 2015). Gonzalez Fuster (n. 24).

[43] Helen Nissenbaum, 'Protecting Privacy in a Information Age: The Problem of Privacy in Public' (1998) 17 Law and Philosophy 559.

the new possibilities of the data-driven economy. The broad protection of privacy and personal data in Europe limits the possibility to develop and implement technologies escaping transparency and accountability. It is not by chance that the right to privacy in Europe has been defined as the US First Amendment.[44] Besides, as observed by the ECJ, data protection needs to be ensured, primarily when automated processing is involved, thus recognising a specific threat coming from automation and, *a fortiori*, on artificial intelligence technologies.[45]

If the right to privacy was enough to meet the interests of individual protection against public interferences, in the algorithmic society, the widespread processing of personal data through automated means has meant that it is no longer enough to protect only the negative dimension of this fundamental right. It has been the role of digital technologies to trigger the rise of data protection as the positive side of the right to privacy and as a new and autonomous fundamental right in the European framework. Therefore, the next section focuses on examining the rise of Big Data analytics to understand the limits of European data protection law given the lack of an interpretative lens unveiling its constitutional dimension.

6.3 ... To Privacy and Data Protection in the Age of Big Data

'Data is the new oil'.[46] This is one of the most common expressions to describe the role of data in the information society where algorithmic processing contributes to the extraction and creation of value. Nonetheless, data do not exactly fit within this definition, precisely because of their immateriality. Unlike oil, data can be reused multiple times, for different purposes and in non-rivalrous ways, without being consumed or losing their value. While oil is refined and consumed, the use of data is potentially perpetual.

[44] Bilyana Petkova, 'Privacy as Europe's First Amendment' (2019) 25(2) European Law Journal 140.

[45] Cases C-293/12 and C-594/12, *Digital Rights Ireland Ltd* v. *Minister for Communications, Marine and Natural Resources and Others and Kärntner Landesregierung and Others* (2014) 54 and 55; Case C-362/14, *Maximillian Schrems* v. *Data Protection Commissioner* (2015), 91. See, also, as regards Article 8 ECHR, *S. and Marper* v. *the United Kingdom* (2008) 103, and *M. K.* v. *France* (2013), 35.

[46] 'The World's Most Valuable Resource is no Longer Oil, but Data' The Economist (6 May 2017) www.economist.com/leaders/2017/05/06/the-worlds-most-valuable-resource-is-no-longer-oil-but-data accessed 21 November 2021.

The idea of data as oil however could be considered accurate when looking at the ability of data to generate value. Like oil for the industrial economy, the processing of a vast amount of data becomes a primary and endless source of values in the algorithmic society. As with other expressions in the field of digital technologies, the term 'Big Data' has become a metaphor.[47] In 2011, the term was used by the McKinsey Global Institute, which defined Big Data as data sets whose size exceeds a database's ability to acquire, store, manage and analyse data and information.[48]

At the beginning of this century, Laney's three-dimensional model on data management based on Volume, Variety and Velocity already anticipated the premises of Big Data analytics.[49] These three Vs were developed in the context of e-commerce to generally describe the increase in the amount of data deriving from homogeneous and heterogeneous sources such as, for example, online accounts and sensors (i.e. Volume). Along with an exponential increase in the quantity of data, the sources have multiplied. If, on the one hand, the increase in volume constitutes one of the primary characteristics, on the other hand, the heterogeneity of the sources and types of data constitutes a fundamental element to fully understand the phenomenon of Big Data (i.e. Variety). In the past, the processing of data was characterised by structured data, namely information stored in databases organised according to rigid schemes. The development of new analytics techniques has allowed the exploitation of the so-called unstructured data or data that is not placed under any pattern or scheme.[50] The third element of growth is the rapid creation and sharing of data (i.e. Velocity). This model was then enriched by (at least) two other characteristics, namely Veracity and Value,[51] even if these elements reflect a different logic from Laney's model based on incremental growth.

47 Cornelius Puschmann and Jean Burgess, 'Big Data, Big Questions. Metaphors of Big Data' (2014) 8 International Journal of Communication 1690.

48 James Manyika and others, 'Big Data: The Next Frontier for Innovation, Competition, and Productivity' McKinsey Global Institute (2011) www.mckinsey.com/business-functions/mckinsey-digital/our-insights/big-data-the-next-frontier-for-innovation accessed 21 November 2021.

49 Doug Laney, '3D Data Management: Controlling Data Volume, Velocity and Variety' (2001) Application Delivery Strategies.

50 Rob Kitchin and Tracey P. Lauriault, 'Small Data, Data Infrastructures and Big Data' (2014) 80(4) GeoJournal 463.

51 Chun-Wei Tsai and others, 'Big Data Analytics: A Survey' (2015) 2 Journal of Big Data 21.

When looking at these characteristics in the context of the protection of privacy and personal data, the techniques used for processing purposes constitute a critical factor in the processing of personal data. It is no coincidence that Big Data analytics have been defined as 'the storage and analysis of large and or complex data sets using a series of techniques including, but not limited to: NoSQL, Map Reduce and machine learning'.[52] The mix of these techniques is used for general value or to derive new information from apparently heterogeneous data. From traditional forms of data processing based on deterministic rules, Big Data analytics rely on new forms of processing using unstructured or semi-structured data such as multimedia content and social media accounts.[53] Content, blog posts, comments or accounts leave online traces revealing large parts of personal information. This issue is also relevant when considering the information collected after visiting webpages (e.g., cookies) or using online applications which track users passively.

Therefore, the combination between quantitative and qualitative data makes Big Data a 'new generation of technologies and architectures, designed to economically separate value from very large volumes of a wide variety of data, by enabling high-velocity capture, discovery and analysis'.[54] This definition can complement the idea of Boyd and Crawford who identified three criteria: technology, analysis and mythology.[55] By technology, they mean the mix of computing power and algorithmic methods capable of leading to the collection and analysis of large clusters of data. The analysis phase consists of identifying and predicting models that could have economic, social or legal effects. Mythology refers to the belief that new levels of forecast and knowledge can be obtained using these processing techniques. In light of these considerations, it is possible to define the phenomenon of Big Data as the collection and analysis of a large volume of structured and unstructured data through computational skills or algorithms to discover

[52] John S. Ward and Adam Barker, 'Undefined By Data: A Survey of Big Data Definitions' ArXiv http://arxiv.org/abs/1309.5821 accessed 21 November 2021.

[53] Richard Cumbley and Peter Church, 'Is Big Data Creepy?' (2013) 29 Computer Law and Security Review 601.

[54] Priyank Jain, Manasi Gyanchandani and Nilai Khare, 'Big Data Privacy: A Technological Perspective and Review' (2016) 3 Journal of Big Data.

[55] Danah Boyd and Kate Crawford, 'Critical Questions for Big Data: Provocations for a Cultural, Technological, and Scholarly Phenomenon' (2015) 15 Information Communication and Society 662.

models and correlations that can lead to predictive analysis or automated decisions.

The relevance of the processing explains why attention has been paid to the phase of analytics, namely the processing techniques (e.g. data mining) to define models or find correlations between structured and unstructured data sets.[56] The scope of this processing is different from the traditional search for information based on causal relationships. The implementation of algorithms in the phase of analytics has moved the focus from causality to probabilities and correlations. Traditional systems of processing are not enough to deal with the vast amount of data, thus encouraging the implementation of statistical methods. This shift from causality to probability is not neutral but raises concerns about the reliance on the outcome of these technologies.

This new framework has captured the European attention due to the challenges in protecting privacy and personal data. The WP29 underlined the growing expansion both in the availability and in the automated use of data analysed through automated systems. As underlined, 'Big data can be used to identify more general trends and correlations but ... big data may also pose significant risks for the protection of personal data and the right to privacy'.[57] The European Data Protection Supervisor has also intervened in this field by underlining how modern data collection and analytics techniques represent challenges for the protection of privacy and personal data.[58] Even the Council of Europe has adopted a definition that highlights the relevance of the new methods of data processing since, as regards the protection of privacy,

[56] According to the European Union Agency for Cybersecurity (ENISA), Big Data analytics refers to 'the whole data management lifecycle of collecting, organizing and analysing data to discover patterns, to infer situations or states, to predict and to understand behaviours'. Giuseppe D'Acquisto and others, 'Privacy by Design in Big Data. An Overview of Privacy Enhancing Technologies in the Era of Big Data Analytics', ENISA (December 2015) www.enisa.europa.eu/publications/big-data-protection accessed 21 November 2021.

[57] Working Party Article 29, 'Opinion 03/2013 on Purpose Limitation' (April 2013) https://ec.europa.eu/justice/article-29/documentation/opinion-recommendation/files/2013/wp203_en.pdf accessed 21 November 2021.

[58] According to the EDPS, Big Data refers to 'the practice of combining huge volumes of diversely sourced information and analysing them, using more sophisticated algorithms to inform decisions. Big data relies not only on the increasing ability of technology to support the collection and storage of large amounts of data, but also on its ability to analyse, understand and take advantage of the full value of data'. European Data Protection Supervisor, 'Opinion 7/2015, Meeting the challenges of Big Data' (November 2015) https://edps.europa.eu/sites/edp/files/publication/15-11-19_big_data_en.pdf accessed 21 November 2021.

the focal issues consist not just of the quantity and variety of the data processed but especially their analysis leading to predictive and decisional results.[59] In other words, the processing phase is the critical moment for the purposes of privacy and the protection of personal data since it does not only influence the collection of data but also the predictive and decision-making output. The phase of analytics can be considered, on the one hand, the step from which value is extracted from the analysis of different categories of data. On the other hand, it is also the phase leading to the algorithmic output producing the most relevant effect for individuals and society.

This challenge is particularly relevant when considering that public and private actors increasingly rely on algorithms for decision-making and predictive models. Although data constitute a crucial economic asset in the algorithmic society due to the value generated by its processing and marketing, at the same time, data can be closely linked to the individual identity and private sphere, thus leading to discrimination and interferences with the right to privacy. In other words, on the one hand, Big Data analytics can stimulate innovation of digital services by ensuring private economic initiatives and the free flow of information. On the other hand, these technologies can lead to disproportionate interferences with fundamental rights and democratic values while contributing to the consolidation of unaccountable powers.

6.4 The Constitutional Challenges of Big Data

The constitutional dimension of Big Data is hidden behind the opacity of algorithmic technologies. At first glance, algorithms could be considered as neutral and independent systems capable of producing models and answers useful for dealing with social changes and market dynamics. From a technical point of view, algorithms are mathematical methods expressing results within a limited amount of space and time and in a defined formal language, transforming inputs, consisting of data, into outputs based on a specified calculation process. Nonetheless, from a social point of view, these technologies constitute decision-making processes designed by programmers and developers. The human contribution in the development of these technologies leads to

[59] Consultative Committee of the Convention for the Protection of Individuals with Regard to Automatic Processing of Personal Data, Guidelines on the protection of individuals with regard to the processing of personal data in a world of Big Data, T-PD (2017)01.

the translation of personal interests and values into algorithmic processes.[60] In other words, algorithms express results which, although determined by their code, constitute subjective determinations provided by automated systems. This underlines how algorithms are not the exclusive source of challenges in the digital age. Behind these technologies, there are actors developing and implementing these systems to pursue their public and private interests.

In this scenario, if algorithms are tools to extract value from data, then, moving to a social perspective, these technologies constitute automated decision-making processes influencing the rights of individuals and society at large. The processing of a vast amount of data allows to obtain information about the behaviours, preferences and lifestyles of data subjects.[61] The implementation of automated decision-making, especially based on machine-learning techniques, raises challenges not only for privacy and data protection but also for the potential discriminatory and biased results coming from inferential analytics.[62]

If this scenario may not look less problematic at first glance, however, the same processing acquires a different value when the categorisation of the individual in a group rather than in another one leads to a decision affecting individuals' rights.[63] Profiling and automated decisions are processes whose implicit purpose is to divide groups of individuals into different categories based on common characteristics and make decisions based on the membership of a specific group, raising question beyond data protection.[64] Besides, profiling and automated decision-making do not focus only on the individual, but also on

[60] Philip A. E. Brey and Johnny Soraker, *Philosophy of Computing and Information Technology* (Elsevier 2009); Norbert Wiener, *The Human Use of Human Beings: Cybernetics and Society* (Da Capo Press 1988).

[61] Danielle Keats Citron and Frank Pasquale, 'The Scored Society: Due Process for Automated Predictions' (2014) 89 Washington Law Review 1; Tal Zarsky, 'Understanding Discrimination in the Scored Society' (2014) 89 Washington Law Review 1375; Frederike Kaltheuner and Elettra Bietti, 'Data Is Power: Towards Additional Guidance on Profiling and Automated Decision-Making in the GDPR' (2018) 2(2) Journal of Information Rights, Policy and Practice https://jirpp.winchesteruniversitypress.org/articles/abstract/10.21039/irpandp.v2i2.45/ accessed 21 November 2021.

[62] Solon Barocas and Andrew D. Selbst, 'Big Data's Disparate Impact' (2016) 104 California Law Review 671.

[63] Brent D. Mittelstadt and Luciano Floridi, 'The Ethics of Big Data: Current and Foreseeable Issues in Biomedical Contexts' (2016) 22 Science and Engineering Ethics 303.

[64] Raphaël Xenidis, 'Tuning EU equality law to algorithmic discrimination: Three pathways to resilience' (2021) 27(6) Maastricht Journal of European and Comparative Law 736.

clusters or groups based on common characteristics.[65] This automatic classification can lead to discrimination and serious effects on individual fundamental rights and freedoms.[66] The case of algorithmic discrimination by search engines can be considered a paradigmatic example of the implications of these technologies across society.[67]

This trend is increasingly relevant in the algorithmic society where the role of (personal) data plays a critical role in the public and private sector. As underlined by the GDPR, technology allows both private companies and public authorities to make use of personal data on an unprecedented scale to pursue their business goals. Natural persons increasingly make personal information available publicly and globally.[68]

Everything is transforming into digital data. At the beginning of this century, the dematerialisation and digitisation of different products have contributed to increasing the amount of information flowing online. Music, videos and texts are nothing else than data. In the algorithmic society, the dematerialisation concerns the individual and its identity which is increasingly subject to datafication. In this case, data controllers can obtain even intimate information concerning private life.

These considerations only provide some examples of why constitutional law is relevant in the case of algorithmic systems processing personal data. Big Data analytics provide opportunities for data analysis leading to insights into social, economic or political matters. At the same time, the probabilistic and statistic approach makes these outcomes problematic since correlation does not per se imply causation. If correlation overcomes causation, legal systems are exposed to risks coming from determinations whose degree of error or inaccuracy is

[65] Alessandro Mantelero, 'From Group Privacy to Collective Privacy: Towards a New Dimension of Privacy and Data Protection in the Big Data Era' in Linnet Taylor and others (eds.), *Group Privacy* (Springer 2017).

[66] Maddalena Favaretto, Eva De Clercq and Bernice Simone Elger, 'Big Data and Discrimination: Perils, Promises and Solutions. A Systematic Review' (2019) 6 Journal of Big Data 12; Talia B. Gillis and Jann L. Spiess, 'Big Data and Discrimination' (2019) 86 The University of Chicago Law Review 459; Monique Mann and Tobias Matzner, 'Challenging Algorithmic Profiling: The Limits of Data Protection and Anti-Discrimination in Responding to Emergent Discrimination' (2019) 6(2) Big Data & Society https://journals.sagepub.com/doi/pdf/10.1177/2053951719895805 accessed 21 November 2021.

[67] Safiya U. Noble, *Algorithms of Oppression: How Search Engines Reinforce Racism* (New York University Press 2018).

[68] GDPR (n. 11), Recital 6.

the natural result of a probabilistic logic. Within this framework, data protection plays a critical role in the algorithmic society since the datafication of society makes this fundamental right functional (or even necessary) to protect the right to privacy. Without ensuring that data are processed according to safeguards based on transparency and accountability, it is not possible to protect the unlawful processing of personal data and mitigate the interferences with the right to privacy. In other words, artificial intelligence technologies underline the critical role of data protection as a shield of individual self-determination and dignity against the new challenges raised by digital capitalism.[69]

Furthermore, the role of data protection in the algorithmic society acquires a critical position not only to protect individual privacy but also as a safeguard for democratic values. The effective protection of privacy allows people to exercise their individual autonomy. In a democratic society, protecting privacy enables citizens to develop their beliefs, freely exchange opinions and express their identities. In order to promote autonomy and self-determination, it is critical that individuals can control their identity and how their personal information is processed.[70] One of the primary challenges for democracy comes from regimes of public and private surveillance which, based on the processing of personal data, can lead to different profiling or targeting of users. This process can affect not only the right to privacy but also freedom of expression, with clear effects on democratic values. Therefore, liberal arguments based on 'anything to hide' fails to represent how people adapt their behaviours when they are observed or identifiable.[71]

Informational privacy is therefore critical for democracy,[72] but could not be enough without data protection law. Data protection does not only protect individuals against surveillance but also fosters transparency and accountability to mitigate the asymmetries of powers that threaten democratic values. The processing of vast amounts of data would lead to clear interferences with the possibility to understand how personal data are processed and according to which criteria. This

[69] Anne de Hing, 'Some Reflections on Dignity as an Alternative Legal Concept in Data Protection Regulation' (2018) 19(5) German Law Journal 1270.

[70] Charles Fried, 'Privacy: A Moral Analysis' (1968) 77 Yale Law Journal 475.

[71] Daniel Solove, *Nothing to Hide: The False Tradeoff Between Privacy and Security* (Yale University Press 2013).

[72] Volker Boehme-Neßler, 'Privacy: A Matter of Democracy. Why Democracy Needs Privacy and Data Protection' (2016) 6(3) International Data Privacy Law 222.

is why data protection is a necessary piece of the democratic puzzle in the algorithmic society.[73] It allows citizens to make informed decisions (i.e. decisional privacy),[74] while protecting their private sphere. As a result, a democratic digital society would fail not only without privacy but also without data protection.

Besides, the increasing reliance on automated decision-making could lead democratic values to lose their attraction. Zuboff has described some examples of how big tech corporations have built a surveillance capitalism based on the users' addiction to friendly technologies and under the logic of accumulation.[75] The neoliberal charm using efficiency and innovation as a justification to massively implement automated decision-making technologies could lead to a process of dehumanisation where the logic of the market guide not only business interests but imbues even the activities of public authorities. The mix of public and private values is a primary challenge for protecting the human dimension of the algorithmic society.

Within this framework, data protection plays a primary role to foster transparency and accountability against opaque processing, thus promoting the right to privacy and self-determination as pillars for democracy while limiting powers. Although, at first glance, the GPDR, as a milestone of European digital constitutionalism, aims to foster the protection of personal data in the Union, the application of data protection rules to the algorithmic environment is far from being straightforward. The implementation of artificial intelligence promises to provide new phases of growth for the internal market and foster fundamental freedoms while, at the same time, the massive processing of personal data through algorithmic technologies questions the basic foundation of data protection law and challenges the protection of fundamental rights and freedoms. This is primarily because there is an intimate connection between (constitutional) law and technology in this case due to the relevance of (personal) data in the algorithmic society.[76]

[73] Antoinette Rouvroy and Yves Poullet, 'The Right to Informational Self-Determination and the Value of Self-Development: Reassessing the Importance of Privacy for Democracy' in Serge Gutwirth and others (eds.), *Reinventing Data Protection?* 45 (Springer 2009).

[74] Neil M. Richards, 'The Information Privacy Law Project' (2006) 94 Georgetown Law Journal 1087.

[75] Shoshana Zuboff, 'Big Other: Surveillance Capitalism and the Prospects of an Information Civilization' (2015) 30(1) Journal of Information Technology 75.

[76] Christopher Kuner and others, 'Machine Learning with Personal Data: Is Data Protection Law Smart Enough to Meet the Challenge?' (2017) 7(1) International Data Privacy Law 1.

As underlined by the next subsection, the implementation of algorithmic technologies highly challenges the boundaries of European data protection law. This issue requires the examination of the relationship between the GDPR and Big Data analytics, particularly focusing on the notion of personal data, the general principles of the GDPR and automated decision-making processes.

6.4.1 The Blurring Boundaries of Personal Data

The scope of application of the GDPR is firmly dependent on the notion of personal data. As already observed, such a personalistic approach characterises the European legal framework of protection in the field of data. In the algorithmic society, the economic value of Big Data comes from the processing of personal and non-personal data. Therefore, in order to trigger the machine of European data protection law, it is necessary to understand when the link between information and individuals leads to defining data as 'personal'.

The GDPR only applies to the processing of 'personal data' as 'any information concerning an identified or identifiable natural person'.[77] While the notion of 'identified natural person' does not raise particular concerns for defining personal data, the notion of identifiability deserves more attention, especially when artificial intelligence technologies are involved. The GDPR provides a comprehensive approach concerning the identifiability of the data subject which can be identified by 'all means … which the data controller or a third party can reasonably use to identify said natural person directly or indirectly'.[78] The assessment concerning the reasonableness of these means should be based on objective factors 'including the costs and the time required for identification, taking into account both the technologies available at the time of treatment and the technological developments'.[79]

Within this framework, the ECJ has extensively interpreted the notion of personal data extending its boundaries also to information apparently outside this definition. For instance, in *YS*,[80] the ECJ clarified that the data relating to an applicant for a residence permit contained in an administrative document, and the data in the legal analysis contained

[77] GDPR (n. 11), Art. 4(1)(1).

[78] Ibid., Recital 26.

[79] Working Party Article 29, 'Opinion 4/2007 on the Concept of Personal Data' (June 2007) https://ec.europa.eu/justice/article-29/documentation/opinion-recommendation/files/2007/wp136_en.pdf accessed 21 November 2021.

[80] Joined Cases C-141/12 and C-372/12, *YS* v. *Minister voor Immigratie* (2014).

in that document, are personal data, while the analysis per se cannot be considered within this notion. Likewise, in *Digital Rights Ireland*,[81] the ECJ recognised the relevance of metadata as personal data since they could make it possible 'to know the identity of the person with whom a subscriber or registered user has communicated and by what means, and to identify the time of the communication as well as the place from which that communication took place'.[82] Therefore, the ECJ extended the notion of personal data considering also the risk of identification deriving from the processing of certain information.

The same approach was adopted in *Breyer*.[83] The dispute concerned the processing and storing of dynamic IP addresses of visitors to institutional websites by the German federal institutions to prevent cyber-attacks. The domestic court asked the ECJ whether the notion of personal data also included an IP address which an online media service provider stores if a third party (an access provider) has the additional knowledge required to identify the data subject. In *Scarlet*,[84] the ECJ had already found that static IP addresses should be considered personal data since they allow users to be identified. In this case, the attention is on dynamic IP addresses that cannot independently reveal the identity of a subject as they are provisional and assigned to each Internet connection and replaced in the event of other accesses. Therefore, the primary question focused on understanding whether the German administration, as the provider of the website, was in possession of additional information that would allow the identification of the user. The ECJ identified such means in the legal instruments allowing the service provider to contact, precisely in case of cyber-attacks, the competent authority, so that the latter takes the necessary steps to obtain this information from the former to initiate criminal proceedings. As a result, firstly, this case shows that, for the purpose of the notion of personal data, it is not necessary that information allows the identification of the data subject per se. Secondly, the information allowing identification could not be in the possession of a single entity.

The ECJ addressed another case enlarging the scope of the notion of personal data in *Novak*.[85] The case concerned the Irish personal data authority's refusal to guarantee access to the corrected copy of

[81] Cases C-293/12 and C-594/12 (n. 45).

[82] Ibid., 26.

[83] Case C-582/14, *Patrick Breyer* v. *Bundesrepublik Deutschland* (2016).

[84] Case C-70/10, *Scarlet Extended SA* v. *Société belge des auteurs, compositeurs et éditeurs SCRL (SABAM)* (2011) ECR I-11959.

[85] Case C-434/16, *Peter Nowak* v. *Data Protection Commissioner* (2017).

an examination test due to the fact that the information contained therein did not constitute personal data. After reiterating that the notion of personal data includes any information concerning an identified or identifiable natural person, the ECJ observed that, in order to answer the question raised by the national court, it is necessary to verify whether the written answers provided by the candidate during the examination and any notes by the examiner relating to them constitute information falling within the notion of personal data. The ECJ observed that the content of those answers reflects the extent of the candidate's knowledge and competence in a given field and, in some cases, his intellect, thought processes and judgment as well as graphological information. The collection of these responses also has the function of assessing the candidate's professional skills and their suitability to exercise the profession in question. Finally, the use of such information, which translates into the success or failure of the candidate for the exam in question, can have an effect on their rights and interests, as it can determine or influence, for example, their ability to access the desired profession or job. Likewise, with regard to the examiner's corrections, the content of these annotations reflects the examiner's opinion or evaluation on the candidate's individual performance during the examination, and, precisely, on their knowledge and skills in the field in question. Together with *Breyer*, this case shows an extensive approach to the notion of personal data with the result that it is not possible to foresee in any case when information should be considered 'personal' but it is necessary to examine the context through a case-by-case analysis.

In the algorithmic society, this overall picture would lead to consider *a fortiori* how the dichotomy between personal and non-personal data looks less meaningful. Even if the processing of personal data through artificial intelligence technologies does not always involve personal data such as, for example, climatic and meteorological data, the potentiality of artificial intelligence technologies to find correlation through a mix of related and unrelated as well as personal and non-personal data, broadens the cases in which the scope of application of the GDPR covers the processing of information which would not fall within the notion of personal data at first glance. For instance, big data analytics aims to identify correlations based on originally unrelated data.[86] It is

[86] GDPR (n. 11), Recital 30. According to this Recital: 'Natural persons may be associated with online identifiers provided by their devices, applications, tools and protocols, such as internet protocol addresses, cookie identifiers or other identifiers such as radio frequency identification tags. This may leave traces which, in particular when

the processing of different types of data that could lead to discovering or redefining data or information as personal.[87] Therefore, it could be impossible to find information that cannot be potentially transformed into personal data,[88] precisely because the economic value of Big Data encourage to process vast amounts of personal and non-personal data.

This consideration could be extended even to the process of anonymisation of personal data. The GDPR does not apply to anonymous data or information that does not refer to an identified or identifiable natural person or to personal data made sufficiently anonymous to prevent or disallow the identification of the data subject. Consequently, anonymised data would not fall within the scope of application of the GDPR. However, it could be easy to define the cases in which the anonymisation process is not reversible or apparently anonymous data are instead personal when mixed with other information. Therefore, there is no single definition of anonymous data, but this notion should be considered in the framework in which the data controller operates, taking into account 'all objective factors, such as the costs of and the amount of time required for identification, taking into consideration the available technology at the time of the processing and technological developments'.[89]

The primary criterion to assess whether data are anonymous comes from a mix of factors and refers to the reasonable usability of the available means to reverse the process of anonymisation referring precisely to 'all the means reasonably likely to be used, such as singling out, either by the controller or by another person to identify the natural person directly or indirectly'.[90] According to Finck and Pallas, this complexity is linked both to technical and legal factors. On the one hand, '[f]rom a technical perspective, the increasing availability of data points as well as the continuing sophistication of data analysis algorithms and performant hardware makes it easier to link datasets and infer personal information from ostensibly non-personal data'. On the other hand, '[f]rom a legal

combined with unique identifiers and other information received by the servers, may be used to create profiles of the natural persons and identify them'.

87 Paul Schwartz and Daniel Solove, 'The PII Problem: Privacy and a New Concept of Personally Identifiable Information' (2011) 86 NYU Law Review 1814.

88 Nadezhda Purtova, 'The Law of Everything. Broad Concept of Personal Data and Future of EU Data Protection Law' (2018) 10(1) Law, Innovation and Technology 40.

89 GDPR (n. 11), Recital 26.

90 Ibid.

perspective, it is at present not obvious what the correct legal test is that should be applied to categorise data under the GDPR.[91]

Therefore, even data that would lead to the identification of individuals could be considered anonymous, due to the absence of reasonable means to obtain personal data from that information. Nonetheless, as underlined by Stalla-Bourdillon and Knight, the approach to anonymisation would be idealistic and impractical.[92] This is because the phase of analytics plays a crucial role in the anonymisation of personal data. It is possible to observe how the quantity and quality of elements identifying personal data influence the number of resources needed for anonymisation. There is a point where the resources available no longer allow the identification due to the number of data to be anonymised. The anonymisation process is effective when it can prevent anyone using reasonable means from obtaining personal data from anonymised data consisting of irreversible de-identification.[93] According to the WP29, 'the outcome of anonymisation as a technique applied to personal data should be, in the current state of technology, as permanent as erasure, i.e. making it impossible to process personal data'.[94] The concept of anonymous data still creates 'the illusion of a definitive and permanent contour that clearly delineates the scope of data protection laws'.[95] Anonymising data could not mean that we are not dealing with personal data any longer. Even when the data controller makes it almost impossible to identify the data subject, evidence shows that the risk of re-identification is concrete.[96] The WP29 has already underlined that the advance of new technologies makes anonymisation increasingly difficult to achieve. Researchers

[91] Michele Finck and Frank Pallas, 'They Who Must Not Be Identified – Distinguishing Personal from Non-Personal Data under the GDPR' (2020) 10(1) International Data Privacy Law 11, 11.

[92] Sophie Stalla-Bourdillon and Alison Knight, 'Anonymous Data v. Personal Data – A False Debate: An EU Perspective on Anonymisation, Pseudonymisation and Personal Data' (2017) 34 Wisconsin International Law Journal 284.

[93] Working Party Article 29, 'Opinion 05/2014 on Anonymisation Techniques' (2014), 6 https://ec.europa.eu/justice/article-29/documentation/opinion-recommendation/files/2014/wp216_en.pdf accessed 21 November 2021.

[94] Ibid., 6.

[95] Khaled El Emam and Cecilia A. lvarez, 'A Critical Appraisal of the Article Working Party Opinion 05/2014 on Data Anonymization Techniques' (2015) 5 International Data Privacy Law 73, 81–2.

[96] Michael Veale, Reuben Binns and Jef Ausloos, 'When Data Protection by Design and Data Subject Rights Clash' (2018) 8 International Data Privacy Law 105.

have underlined the fallacies of anonymisation in different fields,[97] especially when Big Data analytics are involved.[98]

Furthermore, even when focusing on pseudonymisation, the GDPR still applies.[99] Pseudonymisation consists of 'the processing of personal data so that personal data can no longer be attributed to a specific data subject without the use of additional information, provided that such additional information is stored separately and subject to technical and organizational measures intended to ensure that such personal data is not attributed to an identified or identifiable natural person'.[100] The GDPR explicitly promotes the use of this technique as a risk-management measure but not as an exception to its scope of application. Unlike anonymisation, the data controller can reverse pseudonymised data, and this is why this information falls within the scope of personal data.

Pseudonymisation consists just of the replacement of data with equally univocal, but not immediately, intelligible information. Therefore, on the one hand, as long as data can be considered anonymous, this information can be processed freely by using Big Data analytics techniques, provided that, as already underlined, the processing does not lead to the identification of the data subject. On the other hand, in the case of pseudonymisation, the discipline of the GDPR applies and, as a result, the data controller is responsible for assessing the risks of this processing and relying on the appropriate legal basis. Furthermore, even if it cannot be excluded that, in some cases, pseudonymised data could be close to the notion of anonymity, they could fall under the processing of the GDPR allowing the data controller not to maintain, acquire or process additional information if the purposes for which a controller processes personal data do not or do no longer require the identification of data subjects.[101]

97 Arvind Narayanan and Vitaly Shmatikov, 'Myths and Fallacies of Personally Identifiable Information' (2010) 53 Communications of the ACM 24, 26; Luc Rocher, Julien M. Hendrickx and Yves-Alexandre de Montjoye, 'Estimating the Success of Re-identifications in Incomplete Datasets Using Generative Models' (2019) 10 Nature Communications 3069.

98 Paul Ohm, 'Broken Promises of Privacy: Responding to the Surprising Failure of Anonymization' (2010) 57 UCL Law Review 1701.

99 Miranda Mourby and others, 'Are "Pseudonymised" Data Always Personal Data? Implications of the GDPR for Administrative Data Research in the UK' (2018) 34 Computer Law & Security Review 222.

100 GDRP (n. 11), Art. 2(5).

101 Ibid., Art. 11. In this case, the data controller is not required to comply with Arts. 15–20 GDPR unless the data subject provides additional information enabling their identification for the purposes of exercising these rights.

Therefore, on the one hand, the GDPR would increase the protection of data subjects by extending the scope of the notion of personal data. The more the notion of personal data is broadly interpreted, the more the processing of data through artificial intelligence technologies falls under data protection laws and, therefore, the processing of information through these technologies is subject to the GDPR's safeguards. However, the impossibility to foresee when this technique could lead to the reidentification of data undermines legal certainty, thus constituting a brake to the development of digital technologies in the internal market.

6.4.2 Clashing General Principles

The implementation of artificial intelligence technologies to process personal information does not just contribute to blurring the gap between non-personal and personal data but also to broadly challenge the general principles governing the GDPR. Once information falls within the category of personal data, the relationship between the GDPR and algorithmic processing is far from being exhausted. The challenges concern not only the scope of application of European data protection law but also its founding principles. It would be enough to look at the Charter underlining that 'data must be processed fairly for specified purposes and on the basis of the consent of the person concerned or some other legitimate basis laid down by law'.[102] Together with other grounding values, the GDPR has introduced these principles representing the expression of the constitutional dimension of privacy and data protection as fundamental rights of the Union.

The GDPR's general principles can be considered the horizontal translation of constitutional values guiding data controllers when ensuring the compliance with data protection rules and the protection of the data subject's rights. General principles play a crucial role in avoiding that the processing of personal data leads to serious interference with the data subjects' fundamental rights. At the same time, they constitute axiological limits to the exercise of powers based on the discretionary processing of personal data.

Generally, the analysis of large quantities of data through opaque processing leading to outputs that are not always predictable are just some elements to consider when assessing the compatibility of Big Data analytics with the general principles of European data protection law.

[102] Charter (n. 36), Art. 8(2).

Such a multifaceted analysis of data for multiple purposes raises serious concerns about, but not limited to, the principles of lawfulness, fairness and transparency. These principles require natural persons to be made 'aware of risks, rules, safeguards and rights in relation to the processing of personal data and how to exercise their rights in relation to such processing'.[103] The obligations for the data controller to inform data subjects about the processing of their personal data,[104] or the legal basis for processing personal data, are just two examples expressing (or implementing) the general principles.[105] As observed by Gutwirth and De Hert, while the right to privacy is an instrument of opacity for the protection of the individual, data protection plays the role of a transparency tool.[106]

These principles are challenged by algorithmic processings whose decision-making processes are often opaque.[107] These techniques do not always allow to explain to data subjects the consequences of processing their personal data through such systems. For example, Big Data analytics often involve the re-use of data and lead to the creation of other information through inferences.[108] Therefore, it would not always be possible to predict from the beginning all the types of data processed and potential uses.[109] Therefore, the process of mandatory disclosure required by the GDPR would de facto fail before the characteristics of these technologies. It is no coincidence that Richard and King have defined this situation as a 'transparency paradox'.[110] On the one hand, Big Data analytics promise new levels of knowledge by defining models and predictions. On the other, the mechanisms by which these

[103] GDPR (n. 11), Recital 39.

[104] Ibid., Arts. 14–15.

[105] Ibid., Arts. 6, 9.

[106] Serge Gutwirth and Paul De Hert, 'Regulating Profiling in a Democratic Constitutional States' in Mireille Hildebrandt and Serge Gutwirth (eds.), *Profiling the European Citizen* 271 (Springer 2008).

[107] Frank Pasquale, *The Black Box Society: The Secret Algorithms That Control Money and Information* (Harvard University Press 2015); Matteo Turilli and Luciano Floridi, 'The Ethics of Information Transparency' (2009) 11(2) Ethics and Information Technology 105; Tal Zarsky, 'Transparent Predictions' (2013) 4 University of Illinois Law Review 1507.

[108] Sandra Wachter and Brent D. Mittelstadt, 'A Right to Reasonable Inferences: Re-Thinking Data Protection Law in the Age of Big Data and AI' (2019) Columbia Business Law Review 494.

[109] Ira S. Rubinstein, 'Big Data: The End of Privacy or a New Beginning?' (2013) 3(2) International Data Privacy Law 74.

[110] Neil M. Richards and Jonathan H. King, 'Three Paradoxes of Big Data' (2013) 66 Stanford Law Review Online 41.

systems reach a new degree of knowledge are obscure. In other words, the price to access more knowledge is accepting a certain degree of data ignorance.

The information asymmetry between the data subject and data controller leads to questioning not only the principle of transparency but also those of lawfulness and fairness. The lack of transparency in the processing may not always allow the data subject to express a valid consent.[111] Artificial intelligence technologies challenge how data subjects express their free and informed consent. In this situation, where the data controller cannot explain the potential use of data transparently, the data subject is not aware of the risks when giving their consent to access products and services. Such information asymmetry is even more problematic when the data subject needs, for example, to access public services which are provided by a data controller or the data controller in a position of monopoly or oligopoly. According to the GDPR, the legal basis of consent should not be valid for processing personal data where there is a clear imbalance between the data subject and the data controller.[112]

Besides, the principle of lawfulness is undermined not only by the low level of transparency in the field of artificial intelligence but also by how information about the processing of personal data is shared with data subjects through privacy policies. This issue is not only relating to the use of long and complex explanations about the processing of personal data undermining de facto the possibility for data subjects to really understand how their personal data are used and for which purposes.[113] Another primary issue concerns the spread of daily life applications (i.e. Internet of Things) collecting personal data in public and private places without the awareness of data subjects.[114] The strict rules to obtain consent and the burden of

[111] Alessandro Mantelero, 'The Future of Consumer Data Protection in the EU Re-Thinking the "Notice and Consent" Paradigm in the New Era of Predictive Analytics' (2014) 30(6) Computer Law & Security Review 643.

[112] GDPR (n. 11), Recital 43.

[113] Aleecia M. Mcdonald and Lorrie F. Cranor, 'The Cost of Reading Privacy Policies' (2008) 4(3) I/S: A Journal of Law and Policy for the Information Society 543.

[114] Carsten Maple, 'Security and Privacy in Internet of Things' (2017) 2 Journal of Cyber Policy 155; Scott R. Peppet, 'Regulating the Internet of Things: First Steps Toward Managing Discrimination, Privacy, Security, and Consent' (2014) 93 Texas Law Review 85; Rolf H. Weber, 'Internet of Things – New Security and Privacy Challenges' (2010) 26 (1) Computer Law & Security Review 23.

proof can prevent discretionary determinations over personal data but also encourage data controllers to rely on other legal bases beyond consent.[115]

This trend could be problematic for the principle of lawfulness also because the legal bases for the processing of personal data do not apply when the data controller processes particular categories of data, namely 'those personal data that reveal racial or ethnic origin, political opinions, religious beliefs or philosophical, or union membership, as well as genetic data, biometric data intended to uniquely identify a natural person, data relating to the health or sexual life or sexual orientation of the person'.[116] As already observed, the analysis of a vast amount of data from heterogeneous datasets can lead to the discovering of new data (i.e. inferences) which could require a different legal basis to process them.[117]

In the algorithmic society, the rationale behind the distinction between 'ordinary' and 'particular' categories of data tends to be nullified by the way in which the data are processed for at least two reasons. Firstly, Big Data analytics are based on a high volume of structured and unstructured data, which usually do not rely on the distinction between categories of data. Secondly, data on health, race or sexual orientation can be obtained from the processing of unstructured data. For example, the content of a social network account can reveal health or racial origin data that inevitably become part of the analysis process that leads to profiling or an automated decision. In other words, even non-particular categories of data can constitute a vehicle for the deduction of information of a particular nature. As noted by Zarsky, 'the rise of big data substantially undermines the logic and utility of applying a separate and expansive legal regime to special categories'.[118]

Such a consideration also shows how artificial intelligence technologies challenge the principle of purpose limitation, precisely due to the multiple and unpredictable re-use of data.[119] It would not be by chance

115 GDPR (n. 11), Recital 42.

116 Ibid., Art. 9.

117 Wachter and Mittelstadt (n. 108).

118 Tal Zarsky, 'Incompatible: The GDPR in the Age of Big Data' (2017) 47 Seton Hall Law Review 1014.

119 Nikolaus Forgó and others, 'The Principle of Purpose Limitation and Big Data' in Marcelo Corrales and others (eds.), *New Technology, Big Data and the Law. Perspectives in Law, Business and Innovation* 17 (Springer 2017).

if the WP29 focused on the need to respect this principle in the field of Big Data by ensuring that the purposes for which the data is processed can be known or foreseen by the data subjects.[120] In order to comply with the principle of purpose limitation, it is necessary to inform the data subject of the processings whose purposes differ from the initial ones at the time of data collection and analysis. Therefore, the aim of this principle is to protect data subjects against the unforeseeable extension of processing purposes. The general use of Big Data analytics implies that data is not just held and used by a certain and predetermined number of third parties for a specific purpose. On the contrary, as observed by Mittelstadt, data 'travels with the person between systems and affects future opportunities and treatment at the hands of others'.[121]

Besides, the relevance of the principle of purpose limitation deserves to be examined not only by looking at the protection of data subjects' rights but also by considering the effects that such a principle can produce on the internal market. It could constitute a barrier to the development of monopolies and dominant situations in the context of data analysis by limiting the possibility for data controllers to use data for any contingent purpose. Nevertheless, as Hildebrandt observed, a narrow interpretation of this principle could limit the potentialities of analytics which, usually, rely on creating models and previsions based on unrelated data and purposes.[122] The principle of purpose limitation can indeed constitute a barrier to data-driven innovation, especially for data sharing. However, what is defined as 'purpose limitation' could be more precisely described as 'non-incompatibility'.[123] Since it is not possible in some cases to foresee all the potential uses, the principle of purpose limitation would apply only in relation to that processing which is incompatible with those disclosed to the data subject.

Nonetheless, the challenges to the principles of transparency, lawfulness and fairness do not exhaust the concerns about the relationship between algorithmic technologies and the GDPR's general principles.

[120] Working Party Article 29, 'Statement of the WP29 on the Impact of the Development of Big Data on the Protection of Individuals with Regard to the Processing of their Personal Data in the EU' (2014) https://ec.europa.eu/justice/article-29/documentation/opinion-recommendation/files/2014/wp221_en.pdf accessed 21 November 2021.

[121] Brent Mittelstadt, 'From Individual to Group Privacy in Big Data Analytics' (2017) 30(4) Philosophy and Technology 475, 482.

[122] Mireille Hildebrandt, 'Slaves to Big Data. Or Are We?' (2013) 17 IDP Revista de Internet Derecho y Política 7.

[123] Working Party Article 29 (n. 57).

The collection and analysis of vast amounts of data can affect the principle of data minimisation. Bygrave has described this principle as an instrument to ensure proportionality and necessity without exceeding the quantity of data to be processed.[124] Unlike the processing of data through analogical means, new automated processing techniques allow extracting value even from apparently unrelated data. This feature has been facilitated by the possibility of storing and analysing increasing amounts of data according to the so-called 'N = all' model according to which the collection and analysis of information are not based just on relevant data but on the whole.[125] The processing and accumulation of a vast amount of data also threaten the principles of integrity and confidentiality due to the increasing risks in handling large volumes of information to be managed.[126] The more data are processed and stored, the more the risk of facing serious data breaches will be amplified. Likewise, the trend towards data accumulation could also clash with the principle of data retention and security.[127] Dealing with large amounts of data processed for multiple purposes could make retention policies complex to implement and security measures subject to increasing layers of risks because of the amount of information involved.

Likewise, the principle of accuracy also plays a primary role because the result of automated decision-making is strongly influenced by the quality of data. Data mining techniques rely on various sources such as social media and other third-party sources that are known for not always being accurate. The pluralism of data sources increases the risk of dealing with inaccurate data.[128] This problem does not only occur ex ante when collecting and analysing data but also ex post due to the distorted effects that inaccurate data can have on the outputs.[129] According to Tene and Polonetsky, 'in a big data world, what calls for scrutiny is often the accuracy of the raw data but rather the accuracy of the inferences drawn from the data'.[130]

124 Lee A. Bygrave, *Data Protection Law: Approaching Its Rationale, Logic and Limits* (Wolter Kluwer 2002).

125 Hildebrandt (n. 122).

126 GDPR (n. 11), Art. 4(f).

127 Ibid., Arts. 5(1)(e), 5(1)(f).

128 Boyd and Crawford (n. 55).

129 Ibid., 662.

130 Omer Tene and Jules Polonetsky, 'Big Data for All: Privacy and User Control in the Age of Analytics' (2013) 11 Northwestern Journal of Technology and Intellectual Property 239.

All these principles should be read in light of the principle of the data controller's accountability, which is the ground upon which the GDPR's risk-based approach is built. The data controller should be able to prove compliance with general principles. The meaning of the principle of accountability can be better understood when focusing on the dynamic definition of the controller's responsibility based on the nature, scope, context and purposes of processing as well as the risks of varying likelihood and severity for the rights and freedoms of natural persons.[131]

On this basis, the data controller is required to implement appropriate technical and organisational measures to guarantee, and be able to demonstrate, that the processing is carried out in accordance with the GDPR and, especially, its principles. According to the principle of privacy by design and by default,[132] the data controller is required to set adequate technical and organisational measures, such as pseudonymisation, to implement the principles of data protection effectively and to provide the necessary guarantees by design and ensure that, by default, only the personal data necessary for each specific purpose are processed. For example, as far as the principles of transparency or purpose limitation are concerned, data processing should allow the data subject to be aware of the modality of processing even when artificial intelligence technologies are involved, thus requiring these technologies to take into consideration the requirement established by the GDPR. In other words, these principles would require data controllers to ensure ex ante that the implementation of technologies processing personal data complies with the general principles of European data protection law. However, there is a tension with general principles when data controllers rely on algorithmic technologies to process personal data.

These considerations could be enough to explain the clash between artificial intelligence and European data protection. Nevertheless, the implementation of algorithmic technologies for processing personal data is also relevant for the protection of data subjects' rights, precisely when these systems lead to significant legal effects on their rights and freedoms.

6.4.3 The Freedom from Algorithmic Processing

One of the primary constitutional challenges for privacy and data protection in the age of Big Data consists exactly of dealing with the lack of transparency and accountability in automated decision-making

[131] Ibid., Art. 24.
[132] GDPR (n. 11), Art. 25.

processes and their effects on individual fundamental rights and freedoms as well as democratic values. As already stressed, the involvement of algorithmic processing for purposes of profiling and automated decision-making challenges privacy and data protection.[133]

Automated decision-making could be defined as the process of making decisions without human intervention. According to the GDPR, this process consists of a decision based solely on automated processing.[134] Usually, these processes involve the use of artificial intelligence technologies. These techniques can lead to binding decisions also depriving individuals of legal rights such as accessing credit.[135] It is in this case that the GDPR aims to introduce safeguards to protect individuals against the discretionary use of personal data for purposes of automated decision-making. In order to empower data subjects to maintain control over their data and mitigate the asymmetry between the data controller and subject, the GDPR provides the so-called data subjects' rights.[136]

The GDPR is particularly concerned by profiling which consists of 'any form of automated processing of personal data consisting in the use of such personal data to evaluate certain personal aspects relating to a natural person, precisely, to analyse or foresee aspects concerning professional performance, the situation economic, personal health, preferences, interests, reliability, behaviour, location or movements'.[137] Against such processing, the data subject has the right to object at any time, for reasons connected with their particular situation. However, this right is not absolute since it can only be exercised when the processing is necessary for the performance of a task carried out in the public interest or in the exercise of official authority vested in the controller,[138] or for the purposes of the legitimate interests pursued by the controller or by a third party, except where such interests are overridden by the interests or fundamental rights and freedoms of the data subject.[139] Therefore, the scope of such a right is narrow and does not apply when profiling occurs

[133] Bart W. Schermer, 'The Limits of Privacy in Automated Profiling and Data Mining' (2011) 27(1) Computer Law & Security Review 45.

[134] GDPR (n. 11), Art. 22.

[135] Tal Zarsky, 'The Trouble with Algorithmic Decisions: An Analytic Road Map to Examine Efficiency and Fairness in Automated and Opaque Decision Making' (2016) 41 Science, Technology, & Human Values 118.

[136] GDPR (n. 11), Arts. 15–22.

[137] Ibid., Art. 4(4).

[138] Ibid., Art. 6(1)(e).

[139] Ibid., Art. 6(1)(f).

based on the consent of the data subject or any other legal basis provided for by the GDPR.

Once the right to object has been exercised, the data controller cannot process personal data unless it demonstrates the existence of legitimate reasons prevailing over the interests, rights and freedoms of the interested party or to ascertain, exercise or defend a right in court. Furthermore, if personal data is processed for direct marketing purposes, the data subject has the right to object at any time to the processing of personal data for these purposes, including profiling. In both cases, the data controller is explicitly required to present this information clearly and separately from any other information at the time of the first communication with the data subject.

Such a right aims to empower users who can complain about the processing of their personal data when it is made by a public authority or it is the result of the choice of data controllers to rely on the legitimate interests as a legal basis of the processing, which, in any case, needs to balance the interest of the controller with the fundamental rights of the data subject. In this case, the right to object allows users to intervene in this balancing which, otherwise, would be left in the hands of data controllers. In this case, the right to object protects data subjects against profiling by artificial intelligence technologies, even if the scope of this right is narrow.

Together with this safeguard, under the GDPR, individuals can rely on their right not to be subject to a decision based solely on automated processing, including profiling, which produces legal effects that concern him or her, or that significantly affects his or her person.[140] The WP29 has clarified that the reference to the expression 'right' not to be subject to a decision based exclusively on automated processing does not imply that this guarantee only applies when the subject invokes this right, since 'individuals are automatically protected from the potential effects this type of processing may have'.[141] As pointed out by Mendoza

[140] Stephan Dreyer and Wolfgang Schulz, 'The General Data Protection Regulation and Automated Decision-Making: Will It Deliver?: Potentials and Limitations in Ensuring the Rights and Freedoms of Individuals, Groups and Society as a Whole' (2019) Bertelsmann Stiftung www.bertelsmann-stiftung.de/doi/10.11586/2018018 accessed 21 November 2021; Isak Mendoza and Lee A. Bygrave, 'The Right Not to Be Subject to Automated Decisions Based on Profiling' in Tatiani Synodinou and other (eds.), EU *Internet Law: Regulation and Enforcement* 77 (Springer 2017).

[141] Working Party Article 29, 'Guidelines on Automated individual decision-making and Profiling for the purposes of Regulation 2016/679' (2018), 20 https://ec.europa.eu/newsroom/article29/item-detail.cfm?item_id=612053 accessed 21 November 2021.

and Bygrave, it is more appropriate to think of this safeguard as a prohibition rather than a right.[142] In this context, the principle of transparency would require the data controller to provide information to the data subject 'on the logic used, as well as the importance and the expected consequences of this treatment for the data subject', regardless of whether the data is collected by the data subject,[143] in line with the spirit of the GDPR which requires a high level of transparency in the processing of personal data.

By arguing *a contrario*, the lack of such a right would produce negative effects not only for individuals but also for democratic values since it would leave data controllers to fully rely on artificial intelligence technologies to make decisions affecting the rights of data subjects without providing any safeguards such as transparency and accountability for these outcomes. The lack of these safeguards is particularly evident when looking, for instance, at the framework of content moderation as examined in Chapter 5. This freedom can be considered as the positive translation of constitutional rights within the legal regimes of data protection and, therefore, it applies to private actors without the need to rely on the horizontal application of fundamental rights. In this sense, the right not to be subject solely to automated decision-making processes increases the possibility for data subjects to receive information about the automated decisions involving them and, therefore, fosters the level of transparency and accountability.

Therefore, even if the relevance of this right within the framework of the GDPR is clear, the remaining question concerns the degree of transparency which the data controller should ensure. According to the GDPR, the data controller should provide meaningful information about the logics involved in the decision-making process.[144] In order to ensure transparency and fairness, these logics should take into account the circumstances and context of the processing, implementing appropriate mathematical or statistical procedures for the profiling, technical and organisational measures appropriate to minimise errors and inaccuracies, as well as safe procedures for personal data to prevent, inter alia, discriminatory effects.[145]

The right not to be subject solely to automated decision-making has triggered a debate on whether the GDPR provides an effective legal basis

142 Mendoza and Bygrave (n. 140).
143 GDPR (n. 11), Art. 13(2)(f), Art. 14(2)(g), Art. 15(1)(h).
144 Ibid., Recital 71.
145 Ibid.

for data subjects to avoid potentially harmful consequences deriving from the implementation of algorithms, most notably by relying on a 'right to explanation' in respect of automated decision-making processes.[146] Some argue that the GDPR introduces it.[147] Others underline that such a right fosters qualified transparency over algorithmic decision-making,[148] deny the existence of such a right,[149] or doubt that the GDPR provisions provide a concrete remedy to algorithmic decision-making processes.[150]

It is not by chance that transparency is one of the most debated issues when focusing on algorithmic technologies.[151] The threats to individuals are intimately, even if not exclusively, connected with the impossibility to ensure transparent outcomes of automated decision-making processes.[152] Despite the criticisms of the process of mandatory disclosure,[153] these obligations constitute a first step to mitigate the asymmetries between data subjects and data controllers. The GDPR aims to empower data subjects by mitigating the technical opacity of automated decision-making.[154] The data controller should not only disclose the data used and the purposes of the processing, but it has

[146] See Bryce Goodman and Seth Flaxman, 'European Union Regulations on Algorithmic Decision-making and a "Right to Explanation"' (2016) 38(3) AI Magazine 50.

[147] Mendoza and Bygrave (n. 140); Andrew D. Selbst and Julia Powles, 'Meaningful Information and the Right to Explanation' (2017) 7 International Data Privacy Law 233; Bryan Casey, Ashkon Farhangi and Roland Vogl, 'Rethinking Explainable Machines: The GDPR's "Right to Explanation" Debate and the Rise of Algorithmic Audits in Enterprise' (2019) 34 Berkeley Technology Law Journal 143.

[148] Margot E. Kaminski, 'The Right to Explanation, Explained' (2019) 34 Berkley Technology Law Journal 189.

[149] Sandra Wachter and others, 'Why a Right to Explanation of Automated Decision-Making Does Not Exist in the General Data Protection Regulation' (2017) 7 International Data Privacy Law 76.

[150] Lilian Edwards and Michael Veale, 'Slave to the Algorithm? Why a "Right to an Explanation" Is Probably Not the Remedy You Are Looking For' (2017) 16 Duke Law & Technology Review 18.

[151] See, e.g., Daniel Neyland, 'Bearing Accountable Witness to the Ethical Algorithmic System' (2016) 41 Science, Technology & Human Values 50; Mariarosaria Taddeo, 'Modelling Trust in Artificial Agents, a First Step Toward the Analysis of E-Trust' (2010) 20 Minds and Machines 243.

[152] Jenna Burrell, 'How the Machine "Thinks": Understanding Opacity in Machine Learning Algorithms' (2016) 3(1) Big Data & Society https://journals.sagepub.com/doi/full/10.1177/2053951715622512 accessed 21 November 2021; Mireille Hildebrandt, 'The Dawn of a Critical Transparency Right for the Profiling Era' in Jacques Bus and others (eds.), *Digital Enlightenment Yearbook* (IOS Press 2012).

[153] Bert-Jaap Koops, 'The Trouble with European Data Protection Law' (2014) 4(4) International Data Privacy Law 250.

[154] Edwards and Veale (n. 150).

also the duty to inform the data subjects about the use of automated decision-making and explain the logic of this process. These safeguards constitute a shield against potential predetermined and discretionary decisions against which the data subject would not have any remedy.

A further guarantee for data subjects against automated decision-making is provided by the limitation to the processing of particular categories of data provided for by the GDPR, without prejudice to the cases of explicit consent of the data subject and if the processing is necessary for reasons of significant public interest on the basis of Union or Member State law, which must be proportionate to the aim pursued, respect the essence of the right to data protection and provide for appropriate and specific measures to protect the fundamental rights and interests of the data subject.[155] In the field of Big Data analytics, profiling aims to create clusters of individuals based on their characteristics. Often, processing telephone numbers or names and surnames would not be enough to develop predictive models since profiling focuses on the individual characteristics which constitute particular categories of data such as health information, political ideas or even biometric data. Even in these cases, adequate measures have to be in force to protect the rights, freedoms and legitimate interests of the data subject.

Nevertheless, this data subjects' right is not absolute. The general notion of 'legal or similarly significant effects' limits its general applicability.[156] The WP29 has also specified that this freedom applies just in cases of 'serious impactful effects' and when the automated decision could 'significantly affect the circumstances, behaviour or choices of the individuals concerned; have a prolonged or permanent impact on the data subject; or at its most extreme, lead to the exclusion or discrimination of individuals'.[157] For example, this provision would apply when the data subject is applying for a credit card as well as accessing to education or health services.

Moreover, several exceptions limit the scope of data protection safeguards. Unlike the case of the notion of personal data and general principles, the GDPR provides a clearer set of exceptions to the application of this data subjects' right against automated decision-making processes. This liberty does not apply when the automated decision is

155 GDPR (n. 11), Arts. 9(2)(a), 9(2)(g).
156 Ibid.
157 Ibid.

necessary for the conclusion or execution of a contract between the interested party and a data controller as well as when it is authorised by Union or Member State law to which the data controller is subject, which also specifies appropriate measures to protect the rights, freedoms and legitimate interests of the data subject. Moreover, this safeguard also does not apply when the processing is based on the explicit consent of the data subject. However, when the processing is based on a contract or the explicit consent of the data subject, the data controller is required to implement suitable measures to safeguard the data subject's rights and freedoms and legitimate interests. In this case, this prohibition turns into a right when the GDPR recognises that the data subject should at least have the right to obtain human intervention on the part of the controller, to express his or her point of view and to contest the decision. This data subject's safeguard cannot lead to 'fabricating human involvement' since human involvement and oversight should be meaningful.

Furthermore, the data controller may limit the boundary of the right to explanation by invoking its interest to protect the trade secrets and intellectual property rights,[158] or, more generally, its freedom of economic initiative that would be frustrated by complying with transparency obligations requiring unreasonable resources.[159] For instance, when the techniques of data analysis through machine learning are involved, it is possible to highlight the so-called black box effect consisting of the impossibility to reconstruct the steps from the beginning of the processing up to the final output.[160] Bathaee underlined that this issue 'poses an immediate threat to intent and causation tests that appear in virtually every field of law'.[161]

This scenario is made even more opaque and fragmented by the limits that Member States establish to these data subjects' rights.[162] Member States can restrict such rights to the extent that limitations are established by EU law or the Member State, provided that this restriction respects the essence of fundamental rights and freedoms and a necessary and proportionate measure in a democratic society to

158 Luciano Floridi, *The Fourth Revolution: How the Infosphere is Reshaping Human Reality* (Oxford University Press 2014).

159 GDPR (n. 11), Recital 63.

160 Pasquale (n. 107).

161 Yavar Bathaee, 'The Artificial Intelligence Black Box and the Failure of Intent and Causation' (2018) 31(2) Harvard Journal of Law & Technology 890.

162 GDPR (n. 11), Art. 23.

safeguard interests such as, for example, national security.[163] Therefore, on the one hand, the rights to data subjects against automated processing can mitigate the interferences coming from processing of personal data through algorithmic technologies. On the other hand, the scope of these rights could undermine the concrete enforcement of this safeguard, thus increasing the possibility for data controllers to rely on automated decision-making technologies to process personal data. Besides, the lack of legal certainty around the scope of this safeguard could also affect the consistent application of this safeguard as also demonstrated by the complexity of multi-state profiling.[164]

Within this framework, the challenges raised by automated decision-making processes are another example of the clash between algorithmic technologies and the protection of fundamental rights and democratic values. This case is another example of how European digital constitutionalism is called to reframe the role of European data protection in the algorithmic society.

6.5 The Constitutional Reframing of the GDPR

The analysis of the constitutional challenges of algorithmic technologies has underlined the limits of European data protection law in relation to the exercise of powers in the field of data. A stand-alone reading of the GDPR can only provide a partial view which could not solve the tension with the principle of the rule of law. The constitutional dimension of Big Data leads to examining the role of European digital constitutionalism in providing an interpretative angle reframing the GDPR in the algorithmic society.

As examined in Chapter 2, in the field of data, the constitutionalisation of the Union has played a critical role in shifting the attention from an economic perspective to a fundamental rights system. Moving from the field of the law in the books to that of the law in action, the ECJ played a fundamental role in consolidating the right to data protection. From the first recognition of data protection as a fundamental right in

[163] Gianclaudio Malgieri, 'Automated Decision-Making in the EU Member States: The Right to Explanation and Other "Suitable Safeguards" in the National Legislations' (2019) 35(5) Computer Law & Security Review 105327.

[164] Reuben Binns and Michael Veale, 'Is that Your Final Decision? Multi-stage Profiling, Selective Effects, and Article 22 of the GDPR' (2021) International Data Privacy Law https://academic.oup.com/idpl/advance-article/doi/10.1093/idpl/ipab020/6403925?login=true accessed 21 November 2021.

the *Promusicae* case,[165] even without emancipating this right from the safeguard of private life,[166] the ECJ reinforced its protection as it appears particularly clear in the decisions on digital privacy which followed the entry into force of the Lisbon Treaty.[167] The constitutional path of the protection of personal data reached a further step not only in the aftermath of Lisbon, but also with the adoption of the GDPR whose first aim is to ensure the right to protection of personal data as data subjects' fundamental rights.[168]

The codification of a new approach in the GDPR is not enough to assess the degree of protection in the European context but needs to be framed within the European constitutional matrix. Both judicial emancipation and legislative consolidation have led the protection of the fundamental rights to privacy and data protection to be a global model on which the European fortress of personal data is based as examined in Chapter 7. This is why the mere analysis of the GDPR can just provide a short answer about the role of European data protection. Here, European digital constitutionalism can provide the normative lens guiding European data protection which, despite its positive dimension, still needs to be constitutionally framed to face the asymmetry of power in the field of data.

The GDPR can be considered as the expression of a new societal *pactum*. It is no more enough to look at such fundamental rights in a negative vertical perspective, thus binding only public actors to individuals, but it is also necessary to look at them as triggers of a positive responsibility to intervene at the horizontal level to remedy the asymmetry of power fostered by the algorithmic society. In other words, by translating constitutional values in legal principles and rights, the GDPR is an expression of the new phase of European digital constitutionalism. The GDPR breaks the vertical nature of fundamental rights, recognising that individuals need to be protected by automated

[165] C-275/06 *Productores de Música de España (Promusicae) v. Telefónica de España SAU* (2008) ECR I-271. Paul De Hert and Serge Gutwirth, 'Data Protection in the Case Law of Strasbourg and Luxembourg: Constitutionalisation in Action' in Serge Gutwirth and others (eds.), *Reinventing Data Protection* 3 (Springer 2009).

[166] *Promusicae*, ibid. According to para. 63: 'However, the situation in respect of which the national court puts that question involves, in addition to those two rights, a further fundamental right, namely the right that guarantees protection of personal data and hence of private life'.

[167] Oreste Pollicino, *Judicial Protection of Fundamental Rights on the Internet: A Road Towards Digital Constitutionalism?* (Hart 2021).

[168] GDPR (n. 11), Recitals 1–2.

decision-making not only when performed by public actors but also when performed by powerful private companies such as online platforms.

When applying these considerations to data protection law, it is necessary to look at the European constitutional framework, precisely the constitutional values underpinning the GDPR. The primary purpose of data protection law is to protect autonomy while ensuring transparency and accountability. As a result, the following subsections provide a teleological interpretation of the GDPR under the lens of European digital constitutionalism. This approach would shed light on the constitutional values underpinning the GDPR and on how they can contribute to providing a constitutional-oriented interpretation mitigating the exercise of powers in the algorithmic society.

6.5.1 Recentring Human Dignity

The evolution of the algorithmic society has contributed to underlining the relevance of data as a personal piece of information. Increasingly, public and private actors rely on machines to make decisions on individual rights and freedoms based on the processing of data. While public actors trust algorithmic technologies to improve public services and perform public tasks such as biometric surveillance, private actors implement automated decision-making to process data to attract revenues following the logic of digital capitalism.[169] Within this framework, as underlined by Gutwirth and De Hert, 'humans have become detectable, (re)traceable and correlatable'.[170] Personal data disseminated in daily lives are raw materials for artificial intelligence systems which then are trained to cluster this data based on correlation. Nonetheless, since, in the age of Big Data, even generic pieces of information could be considered personal, clustering data also mean profiling individuals.

In Europe, personal data are 'personal' since they are connected to the individual. This focus is not only because the notion of personal data extends far beyond the notion of identified natural persons but also because data protection law without personal data would lose its constitutional meaning within the European framework. It is not by chance

[169] Jathan Sadowski, 'When Data Is Capital: Datafication, Accumulation, and Extraction' (2019) 6 Big Data & Society 1.
[170] Gutwirth and De Hert (n. 106), 287.

that the scope of the GDPR does not extend to legal persons or deceased,[171] or non-personal data.[172] This characteristic underlines how, in Europe, personal data are not only relevant for the circulation of information or the extraction of value. As stressed in Chapter 3, the rise of European digital constitutionalism has shed light on the constitutional dimension of privacy and data protection complementing the internal market goals.

This constitutional framework is the reason why personal data cannot be seen just as an object of property rights but also as data 'extra commercium'.[173] The 'propertisation' of personal data contributes to their commodification under the logic of digital capitalism with the result that any data would be considered as tradable as goods and not as a piece of individual identity. It is true that the circulation and exchange of personal data constitute the pillars of the algorithmic society. Nonetheless, the unaccountable and discretionary commodification of personal data would lead to considering consumer protection or contract law as the primary instrument to deal with the commercial exploitation of data.[174] However, these concurring regimes would fail to protect personal data as an expression of the individual and, therefore, this is also why personal data 'cannot be considered as a commodity'.[175] Likewise, the EDPS has underlined that personal data cannot be conceived as mere economic assets.[176] As Floridi underlined, '"My" in my data is not the same as "my" in my car, but it is the same as

[171] Bart van der Sloot, 'Do Privacy and Data Protection Rules Apply to Legal Persons and Should They? A Proposal for a Two-tiered System' (2015) 31 Computer Law and Security Review 26.

[172] Regulation (EU) 2018/1807 of the European Parliament and of the Council of 14 November 2018 on a framework for the free flow of non-personal data in the European Union OJ L 303/59.

[173] Václav Janeček and Gianclaudio Malgieri, 'Data Extra Commercium' in Sebastian Lohsse, Reiner Schulze and Dirk Staudenmayer (eds.), *Data as Counter-Performance – Contract Law 2.0?* 93 (Hart 2020).

[174] Yves Poullet, 'Data Protection Between Property and Liberties. A Civil Law Approach' in Henrik W. K. Kaspersen and Anja Oskamp (eds.), *Amongst Friends in Computers and Law. A Collection of Essays in Remembrance of Guy Vandenberghe* 160 (Kluwer Law International 1990); Nadezhda Purtova, *Property Rights in Personal Data: A European Perspective* (Kluwer Law International 2011).

[175] Directive (EU) 2019/770 of the European Parliament and of the Council of 20 May 2019 on certain aspects concerning contracts for the supply of digital content and digital services (2019) OJ L 136/1, Recital 24.

[176] European Data Protection Supervisor, 'Opinion 8/2016 on Coherent Enforcement of Fundamental Rights in the Age of Big Data' (23 September 2016) https://edps.europa.eu/sites/edp/files/publication/16-09-23_bigdata_opinion_en.pdf accessed 21 November 2021.

"my" in my hand'.[177] Therefore, protecting the right to privacy should be considered as a matter of personal identity and integrity since it determines the evolution of human personality and therefore of human dignity. In a different way, the right to be forgotten exactly showed this face of the right to privacy even before the rise of online platforms, and the *Google Spain* case.[178]

Even if human dignity is almost invisible in the GDPR,[179] the human-centric approach in European data protection law comes from the ability of human dignity to permeate in the core of European fundamental rights.[180] The Charter opens up the catalogue of rights stating 'human dignity is inviolable. It must be respected and protected'.[181] The central position of this value within the Charter is not a formal recognition of constitutionality,[182] but it plays the role of a pillar for the entire system of fundamental rights. This approach mirrors the Universal Declaration of Human Rights which enshrines human dignity in its preamble.[183] Therefore, as stressed in Chapter 1, human dignity should not be seen as a clashing value but as the core of each fundamental right laid down in the Charter. Human dignity therefore is a necessary piece of the puzzle to be considered and safeguarded in the balancing process. This is part of the European constitutional roots which look at dignity as the pillar against any human annihilation.

Therefore, the mission of data protection law would be to ensure that its human imprinting does not fall apart while ensuring democratic values of transparency and accountability. Even in this case, the role of dignity could be considered as a primary trigger for the consolidation of data protection as the positive dimension of the right to privacy,

177 Luciano Floridi, 'On Human Dignity as a Foundation for the Right to Privacy' (2016) 29 Philosophy of Technology 307, 308.

178 Franz Werro, 'The Right to Inform v. the Right to be Forgotten: A Transatlantic Crash' in Aurelia Colombi Ciacchi and others (eds.), *Liability in the Third Millennium, Liber Amicorum Gert Bruggemeier* 285 (Nomos 2009).

179 GDPR (n. 11), Art. 88. This provision requires Member States to ensure the protection of the rights and freedoms in respect of the processing of personal data in the employment context 'to safeguard the data subject's human dignity, legitimate interests and fundamental rights'.

180 Stefano Rodotà, *Vivere la democrazia* (Laterza 2019); Catherine Dupré, *The Age of Dignity Human Rights and Constitutionalism in Europe* (Hart 2015).

181 Charter (n. 36), Art. 1.

182 Case C-377/98 *Netherlands* v. *European Parliament and Council* (2001) ECR I-7079, 70–77.

183 Universal Declaration of Human Rights (1948): 'Whereas recognition of the inherent dignity and of the equal and inalienable rights of all members of the human family is the foundation of freedom, justice and peace in the world'.

similarly to how human dignity could contribute to fostering the positive dimension of the right to freedom of expression to address the challenges of content moderation as examined in Chapter 5. According to the EDPS, '[p]rivacy is an integral part of human dignity, and the right to data protection was originally conceived in the 1970s and 80s as a way of compensating the potential for the erosion of privacy and dignity through large scale personal data processing'.[184]

The notion of personal data is not the only point showing the role of human dignity in the GDPR. Individual consent is the primary pillar of European data protection law, thus representing the centrality of individual self-determination.[185] As mentioned in Chapter 1, the first decision of the German Constitutional Court on data protection has shed the light on the role of dignity in the processing of personal data. It is indeed the autonomous choice of the data subject which would allow the data controller to legally process personal data. This is why, even if imbalances of power question the meaning of consent in European data protection law, the GDPR still focus on consent as a primary legal basis defined as 'any freely given, specific, informed and unambiguous indication of the data subject's wishes by which he or she, by a statement or by a clear affirmative action, signifies agreement to the processing of personal data relating to him or her'.[186]

Likewise, the distinction between personal data and particular categories of data provides another clue about the human-centric approach of European data protection law. This double track of protection for personal data aims to protect personal information which can reveal intimate aspects of human lives. Such a difference, already introduced in the Data Protection Directive, has been fostered by the GDPR which has not only extended the categories of data falling under the scope of such a special regime but also provides a general ban of the processing of this type of data even though it foresees conditions of lawfulness as exceptions.[187] For instance, biometrics and DNA data have been included within the broader protection of particular categories of data, being it information able to represent humans as they are.

[184] European Data Protection Supervisor, 'Opinion 4/2015. Towards a new Digital Ethics' (11 September 2015) https://edps.europa.eu/sites/edp/files/publication/15-09-11_data_ethics_en.pdf accessed 21 November 2021.

[185] Yves Poullet, 'Data Protection Legislation: What is at Stake for our Society and Democracy' (2009) 25 Computer Law & Security Review 211.

[186] GDPR (n. 11), Art. 4(11).

[187] Ibid., Art. 9.

Precisely, in a phase where biometric technologies are expanding and intertwining with artificial intelligence to pursue different tasks,[188] such a safeguard reflects the need to avoid that personal data are subject to automated decisions without the 'explicit consent' of data subjects. In this case, it is not enough to rely on the conditions for processing personal data, but it is necessary to ground the processing on specific legal bases.[189] Even in this case, the core of the entire system is the data subject's consent, which, in this case, has to be 'explicit'.

Such a personalistic approach also affects the framework of automated decision-making processing. The GDPR does not expressly clarify the constitutional values underpinning its structure. Therefore, a literal or systemic interpretation of data protection law could not provide a full picture of the values which the prohibition to subject individuals to these systems would protect. Dreyer and Schulz have underlined that the goal of this rule is beyond the mere protection of personal data.[190] Even if not exclusively, the primary goal of this rule is the protection of human dignity. The right not to be subject to automated decision-making deals with the ability of machines to make determinations about human lives. Even in this case, the rise of the Internet has underlined how digital technologies can perform activities in a more efficient way than humans. The same is true for algorithmic technologies that are able to see correlations that humans do not perceive, or predict the future which is one of the abilities that humans have always tried to reach.

What does not actually change is the risk of error. Even if machines were more efficient than humans, they could still fail and reproduce the biases of their programmers. At first glance, algorithms would appear as neutral technologies which can extract values from information that are useful for businesses and society. However, from a technical perspective, algorithms are far from being neutral. They are not just mathematical models providing outcomes in a certain form based on the processing of information.[191] Algorithms transform inputs into outputs, thus expressing a value judgement. Automated decision-making

[188] Els J. Kindt, *Privacy and Data Protection Issues of Biometric Applications. A Comparative Legal Analysis* (Springer 2013).
[189] GDPR (n. 11), Art. 9(2).
[190] Dreyer and Schulz (n. 140).
[191] Tarleton Gillespie, 'The Relevance of Algorithms' in Tarleton Gillespie, Pablo J. Boczkowski and Kristen A. Foot (eds.), *Media Technologies: Essays on Communication, Materiality, and Society* 167 (MIT Press 2014).

systems are therefore value-laden.[192] The human role in the programming and development of these technologies contributes to reflecting the biases and values of programmers into the technological design.[193] This issue is not a novelty since all technologies are the result of certain design choices. Reidenberg and Lessig have already clarified how much the architecture of technology is a critical piece of the regulatory jigsaw.[194] In the case of algorithms, the role of design is even more critical since these technologies can produce decisions on which humans ground their activities, or even largely rely.[195]

Besides, machines are still not entirely able to interpret real dynamics and exactly understand contexts and emotions,[196] or translating legal concept into machine determinations.[197] This limit also explains why so frequently the implementation of artificial intelligence technologies has led to discrimination.[198] The right to equality can be considered another expression of human dignity. Without being considered equal, there are multiple layers of protection for different categories of 'humans'. The right to non-discrimination is one of the fundamental principles of European constitutional law. The right to equality is the basic pillar of democratic constitutionalism as shown by its relevance in the Charter and the Convention.[199] Discriminatory outcomes of

[192] Brent D. Mittelstadt and others, 'The Ethics of Algorithms: Mapping the Debate' (2016) 3(2) Big Data & Society https://journals.sagepub.com/doi/pdf/10.1177/2053951716679679 accessed 22 November 2021.

[193] Pasquale (n. 107).

[194] Lawrence Lessig, *Code: And Other Laws of Cyberspace. Version 2.0* (Basic Books 2006); Joel R. Reidenberg, 'Lex Informatica: The Formulation of Information Policy Rules through Technology' (1997–8) 76 Texas Law Review 553.

[195] John Zerilli and others, 'Algorithmic Decision-Making and the Control Problem' (2019) 29 Minds and Machines 555.

[196] Andrew McStay and Lachlan Urquhart, 'This Time with Feeling? Assessing EU Data Governance Implications for Out of Home Emotional AI' (2019) 24(10) First Monday https://firstmonday.org/ojs/index.php/fm/article/download/9457/8146 accessed 21 November 2021.

[197] Simon Deakin and Christopher Markou, 'Ex Machina Lex: Exploring the Limits of Legal Computability' in Simon Deakin and Christopher Markou (eds.), *Is Law Computable? Critical Perspectives on Law and Artificial Intelligence* (Hart Publishing 2020).

[198] Sandra Wachter, Brent Mittelstadt, Chris Russell, 'Why Fairness cannot be Automated: Bridging the Gap between EU Non-discrimination Law and AI' (2021) 41 Computer Law & Security Review 105567; Andrea Romei and Salvatore Ruggieri, 'A Multidisciplinary Survey on Discrimination Analysis' (2014) 29 The Knowledge Engineering Review 582; Bart Custers and others (eds.), *Discrimination and Privacy in the Information Society* (Springer 2013); Kevin Macnish, 'Unblinking Eyes: The Ethics of Automating Surveillance' (2012) 14 Ethics and Information Technology 151.

[199] Charter (n. 36), Art. 20; Convention (n. 31), Art. 14.

algorithmic processing can originate from the low level of data quality or embedded bias in the programming phase like in the case of discrimination based on ethnicity.[200]

Therefore, the GDPR shields data subjects against the interference to their legal rights coming from the errors automated decision-making can produce. This prohibition recognises that machines cannot be fully trusted. In other words, such a rule clarifies that efficiency cannot prevail over fundamental rights and freedoms. At the same time, artificial intelligence technologies can also foster fundamental rights, thus allowing humans to escape from paths of marginalisation. Even in this case, the GDPR has not introduced a general ban for this type of processing but has tried to limit the serious effects that these technologies can produce on data subjects. Likewise, the GDPR has introduced the so-called human-in-the-loop principle to ensure that human decisions are not affected by decisions taken just by unaccountable systems. This approach is firmly connected with the acknowledgement that machines err and are (still) not able to distinguish the complexity of human lives. The attempts to digitise human lives to a mere calculation would annihilate the role of humans, leading towards a process of dehumanisation. In other words, the human being is *dignus*. Any attempt to digitise humanity would clash with the nature of human beings.

Within this framework, human dignity constitutes the primary beacon for data controllers and courts when focusing on the challenges of automated decision-making. This focus does not mean that this right should confer privacy and data protection a quasi-absolute protection in any case. On the opposite, privacy and data protection would acquire a predominant role when there is the need to ensure that individual rights are not so compressed that autonomy and self-determination are effectively compromised. The limit established by the GDPR to the processing of personal data through automated decision-making processes is not a mere data subject right which can be overcome easily by ensuring security measures or opaque forms of explanation. It is an instrument of freedom against the techno-determinism established by predominant private and public actors.[201] This rule horizontally connects human dignity, as the

200 Raphaële Xenidis and Linda Senden, 'EU Non-discrimination Law in the Era of Artificial Intelligence: Mapping the Challenges of Algorithmic Discrimination' in Ulf Bernitz and others (eds.), *General Principles of EU law and the EU Digital Order* 151 (Kluwer Law International 2020).

201 Antoniette Rouvroy, 'Technology, Virtuality and Utopia: Governmentality in an Age of Autonomic Computing' in Mireille Hildebrandt and Antoniette Rouvroy, *Law, Human*

basic pillar of European constitutionalism, with algorithmic technologies, thus making the promises of a more constitutional sustainable innovation. The focus on human dignity would be the primary reference for lawmakers and judges in approaching this safeguard, thus implying a strict interpretation of the exceptions and limitations to this 'human' right.

6.5.2 Conflicting Positions and Proportionality

Human dignity is the primary but not the only underpinning value of the GDPR. Another constitutional principle grounding European data protection is proportionality which can be considered the foundation of the risk-based approach based on the principle of accountability. As in the case of human dignity, different angles can show how this value is expressed by the GDPR.

Proportionality is a pillar of democratic constitutionalism.[202] Even if this principle is declined in different ways on a global scale,[203] proportionality expresses the need to internally limit the exercise of public and private powers, thus safeguarding individuals against excessive interferences.[204] The structure of European data protection is a paradigmatic example of the principle of proportionality. As already stressed, personal data enjoy a broad margin of protection in the Union.

Although the ECJ has recognised a high degree of protection to personal data, there is not a rigid hierarchy between fundamental rights and freedoms. Data protection is not an absolute right even when focusing on legitimate interests according to the tests established by the Convention and the Charter. The protection of this fundamental right cannot lead to the destruction of other constitutional interests such as freedom to conduct business as enshrined in the Charter.[205]

Therefore, when interpreting the obligations of the GDPR, it is crucial not to forget that the interests of the data controller and of the data

Agency and Autonomic Computing: The Philosophy of Law Meets the Philosophy of Technology (Routledge 2011).

202 Stephen Gardbaum, 'Proportionality and Democratic Constitutionalism' in Grant Huscroft and others (eds.), *Proportionality and the Rule of Law. Rights, Justification, Reasoning* 259 (Cambridge University Press 2014).

203 Alec Stone Sweet and Jud Mathews, *Proportionality Balancing and Constitutional Governance. A Comparative and Global Approach* (Oxford University Press 2019).

204 Vicki C. Jackson and Mark Tushnet (eds.), *Proportionality: New Frontiers, New Challenges* (Cambridge University Press 2017); Aharon Barak, *Proportionality Constitutional Rights and their Limitations* (Cambridge University Press 2012); Robert Alexy, *A Theory of Rights* (Oxford University Press 1985).

205 Charter (n. 37), Art. 16.

subject represent nothing but the constitutional clash between the protection of personal data with other fundamental rights and freedoms or legitimate interests in the case of public authorities. In other words, the general principles, safeguards and obligations of the GDPR need to be framed within such a context of balancing rather than axiology. It is not by chance that the ECJ has relied on the principle of proportionality since its first cases on data protection,[206] and this balancing logic is at the core of the GDPR's structure.

Moving from the constitutional level to the GDPR, the principle of accountability of the data controller could be considered the constitutional translation of a risk-based approach based on the notion of balancing. This principle requires the controller to prove compliance with the GDPR's principles by establishing safeguards and limitations based on the specific context of the processing, primarily the risks for data subjects.[207] The Data Protection Directive had already tried to introduce such an approach focused on the risk of processing, for instance, concerning the implementation of security measures. Likewise, the WP29 stressed the role of a risk-based approach in data protection underlining how risk management is not a new concept in data protection law.[208] Even the Council of Ministers of the Organisation for Economic Co-operation and Development implemented a risk-based approach when revising the Guidelines Governing the Protection of Privacy and Transborder Flows of Personal Data, first adopted in 1980.[209]

From a formal perspective, despite the open clauses, the move from minimum to full harmonisation has been a powerful boost for legal certainty in the internal market. Such a move has not only led to strengthening the protection of privacy and personal data as fundamental rights of the Union but has also allowed a more balanced approach between rights and obligations. The principle of accountability reflects such a mix between certainty and proportionality. The data controller

206 Charlotte Bagger Tranberg, 'Proportionality and Data Protection in the Case Law of the European Court of Justice' (2011) 1 International Data Privacy Law 239.

207 Raphael Gellert, *The Risk-Based Approach to Data Protection* (Oxford University Press 2020).

208 Working Party Article 29, 'Statement on the Role of a Risk-Based Approach in Data Protection Legal Frameworks' (30 May 2014) https://ec.europa.eu/justice/article-29/documentation/opinion-recommendation/files/2014/wp218_en.pdf accessed 21 November 2021.

209 OECD, 'Guidelines Governing the Protection of Privacy and Transborder Flows of Personal Data' (2013) www.oecd.org/sti/ieconomy/oecd_privacy_framework.pdf accessed 21 November 2021.

has been considered responsible (and not only liable) to ensure that the protection of data subject's privacy and data protection are ensured and protected. And this role comes from the respect not only of the GDPR's obligations but also of general principles.

The GDPR modulates the obligations of the data controller according to the specific context in which the processing takes place, namely 'taking into account the nature, scope, context and purposes of processing as well as the risks of varying likelihood and severity for the rights and freedoms of natural person'.[210] For instance, when looking at legitimate interest as a condition for lawfully processing personal data, the GDPR provides a limitation balancing 'the interests or fundamental rights and freedoms of the data subject which require protection of personal data, in particular where the data subject is a child'.[211] This focus extends also to the principle of privacy by design and by default as an expression of the general principle of accountability.[212] As observed by Macenaite, 'risk becomes a new boundary in the data protection field when deciding whether easily to allow personal data processing or to impose additional legal and procedural safeguards in order to shield the relevant data subjects from possible harm'.[213] It would be enough to focus on the norms concerning the Data Protection Impact Assessment or the appointment of the Data Protection Officer to understand how the GDPR has not introduced mere obligations to comply but a flexible risk-based approach which leads to defining different margins of responsibility on each data controller depending on the context at stake.[214]

[210] GDPR (n. 11), Art. 24(1).

[211] Ibid., Art. 6(1)(f).

[212] Ibid., Art. 25. Ira S. Rubinstein, 'Regulating Privacy by Design' (2012) 26 Berkeley Technology Law Journal 1409; Ugo Pagallo, 'On the Principle of Privacy by Design and its Limits: Technology, Ethics and the Rule of Law' in Serge Gutwirth and others (eds.), *European Data Protection: In Good Health?* 331 (Springer 2012).

[213] Milda Macenaite, 'The "Riskification" of European Data Protection Law through a Two-Fold Shift' (2017) 8(3) European Journal of Risk Regulation 506.

[214] Working Party Article 29, 'Guidelines on Data Protection Impact Assessment (DPIA) and Determining Whether Processing is "Likely to Result in a High Risk" for the Purposes of Regulation 2016/679' (4 October 2017) http://ec.europa.eu/newsroom/document.cfm?doc_id=47711 accessed 21 November 2021. See Ruben Binns, 'Data Protection Impact Assessment: A Meta-Regulatory Approach' (2017) 7(1) International Data Privacy Law 22; Paul De Hert, 'A Human Rights Perspective on Privacy and Data Protection Impact Assessments' in David Wright and Paul De Hert (eds), *Privacy Impact Assessment* 33 (Springer 2012).

Fundamental rights are the parameters on which the risk-based approach, as a system where data controllers' responsibility is assessed on a case-by-case basis, is grounded. This system represents nothing but the expression of a principle of proportionality reflecting the lack of a rigid axiology in the European constitutional framework. The risk-based approach reflects nothing else than the balancing of the conflicting interests of data subjects and controllers. In other words, the GDPR has led to the merge of a rights-based approach where the fundamental rights of data subjects play the role of a beacon for compliance.

From the perspective of data controllers, the high standard of compliance required by the GDPR could however affect small or medium controllers which can be required to adopt higher safeguards, primarily when data processing operations could lead to high risks for the data subjects. This approach could affect the freedom to conduct business and development of the internal market. Even if the GDPR's approach could favour multinational corporations in the process of compliance,[215] nevertheless, it introduces a mechanism which does not focus only on rigid obligations but also on the concrete framework of the processing. This margin of discretion could promote the development of artificial intelligence technologies while protecting individual fundamental rights. This shift from theory to practice introduces certain flexibility allowing the data controller to determine the measures to apply according to the risks connected to data processing, while maintaining the duty to justify the reasons for these decisions. The GDPR would increase the discretion of the data controller in determining which safeguards apply to the data collected and processed in a certain context.

Likewise, from the data subjects' standpoint, the risk-based system is complemented by a rights-based system coming from the broad extension of fundamental rights in the European framework. Individuals have the right to access and limit the processing of their data, ask about their erasure or portability based on the conditions established by the GDPR for each data subject's right. Scholars have underlined that 'from the user perspective, the impact of data portability is evident both in terms of control of personal data (and in general in the sense of empowerment of control rights of individuals), and in terms of a more user-centric interrelation between services. At the same time, it is

[215] Michal S. Gal and Oshrit Aviv, 'The Competitive Effects of the GDPR' (2020) 16(3) Journal of Competition Law and Economics 349.

a challenge to third data subjects' rights'.[216] This approach underlines how the GDPR does not provide users with absolute rights. While empowering data subjects would increase the control over the processing of data, the implementation of their rights is a burden requiring data controllers to invest resources and define procedures to implement them.

When framing such considerations in the field of artificial intelligence, the GDPR does not establish an absolute prohibition in relation to automated decision-making, even if it bans the processing of particular categories of data except for the case where the data subject has given his or her explicit consent. The GDPR introduces exceptions according to which, despite potential legal or similarly significant consequences, data subjects cannot rely on this right. Their presence should not come as a surprise when focusing on the characteristics of European constitutionalism which, as already stressed, does not recognise absolute protection to fundamental rights. The ECJ underlined that the right to the protection of personal data does not enjoy absolute protection but is subject to balancing with other interests.[217] In any case, limitations shall be strictly necessary to genuinely meet the objectives of general interest pursued, subject to the principle of proportionality.[218] Moreover, Member States can introduce exceptions to limit the right not to be subject to automated decision-making processes.[219] In any case, the protection of fundamental rights cannot lead to the annihilation of any other rights and freedoms recognised in this Charter.

Therefore, the principle of accountability is not only a burden for data controllers but also a threatening delegation of responsibility concerning the protection of fundamental rights and freedoms. This way, the GDPR leads data controllers to become the arbiters of privacy and data protection. The limit to the exercise of this power is the principle of proportionality which, together with human dignity, are guidance for lawmakers and judges when addressing the balancing between the accountability of data controllers and the fundamental rights of data subjects. Therefore, the principle of accountability can play an important role in the development of the internal market without leaving

216 Paul De Hert and others, 'The Right to Data Portability in GDPR: Towards User-Centric Interoperability of Digital Services' (2018) 34(2) Computer Law & Security Review 193, 197.

217 Joined cases C-92/09 and C-93/09, *Volker und Markus Schecke GbR and Hartmut Eifert* (2010) ECR I-11063. See GDPR (n. 11), Recital 4.

218 Charter (n. 36), Art. 52.

219 GDPR (n. 11), Art. 23.

fundamental rights behind. As a general principle, the more the discretion exercised by the data controller, the more the data subjects should be protected. This principle would leave data controllers to perform their activities considering that their beacon of compliance is not simply represented by the GDPR's material and organisational requirements but also coincides with the protection of individuals, precisely their dignity.

Therefore, the principle of human dignity is relevant within the framework of proportionality. Although the GDPR's exceptions to data subjects' rights and freedoms may find their legitimation in the need to balance conflicting interests, however, justifying exceptions to data subjects' rights against automated decision-making processes would betray the aim to protect human dignity. It would be worth wondering how exceptions could be tolerated in this case if these technologies could lead to a process of dehumanisation in the long run. The answer to such a concern can be found by looking at due process safeguards which would aim to preserve human dignity while promoting a sustainable solution to foster innovation.

6.5.3 Enhancing Due Process

The question is therefore how human dignity can be protected against potential disbalances in the exercise of conflicting rights and freedoms. Limitations to individual rights reflecting the principle of proportionality should not be considered as a threat to human dignity when due process safeguards are in place. The possibility to rely on procedural safeguards would mitigate disproportionate effects resulting from the exercise of public powers or private determinations. Due process would play a crucial role even beyond the boundaries of public powers.[220]

Together with the personalistic principle, European data protection law is an example of due process safeguards. Since the adoption of the Data Protection Directive, European data protection law has primarily provided substantive obligations and procedural safeguards regulating the entire process of data processing from analysis of risks (e.g. DPIA), to rules on notice (e.g. mandatory disclosure), collection (e.g. consent), processing (e.g. purpose limitation), safeguards (e.g. data subject rights) and remedies (e.g. judicial enforcement). These norms represent the expression of the right to self-determination of individuals who,

[220] Giacinto Della Cananea, *Due Process of Law Beyond the State: Requirements of Administrative Procedure* (Oxford University Press 2016).

without knowing how data are processed, cannot be aware of the processing of their personal data. These ex ante safeguards increase transparency and accountability, thus making the individual more aware of how personal data are used to make even automated decisions which could affect their legal rights. Put another way, such an approach would meet that principle of self-determination which makes humans *dignus* rather than subject to public and private determinations.

By promoting transparency and accountability in automated decision-making processes through procedural safeguards, the GDPR fosters human dignity. Therefore, due process is an essential tile of the constitutional mosaic of the GDPR. This constitutional architecture is also evident when focusing on the safeguards relating to artificial intelligence technologies. The data controller is required to inform data subjects about the existence of a process of automated decision-making, its logic, significance and consequences,[221] while the data subject has the right to ask the data controller to access their personal data.[222] In the case of the right not to be subject to automated decision-making, the GDPR recognises a procedural safeguard consisting of the right 'to require human intervention, to express her point of view and to contest the decision'.[223] Therefore, apart from when the processing is authorised by Union or Member State law to which the controller is subject and which also lays down suitable measures to safeguard the data subject's rights and freedoms and legitimate interests, individuals have the right to ask for human intervention to assess the machine's outcome.[224]

The principle of human-in-the-loop in the context of algorithmic decision-making is a paradigmatic attempt to introduce procedural safeguards. Minimal due process becomes a precondition to mitigate the asymmetry of powers between individuals and data controllers in the context of automated decision-making.[225] In this sense, due process

221 GDPR (n. 11), Art. 13.

222 Ibid., Art. 15.

223 GDPR (n. 11), Art. 22(3). See Ben Wagner, 'Liable, but Not in Control? Ensuring Meaningful Human Agency in Automated Decision-Making Systems' (2019) 11(1) Policy & Internet 104; Fabio M. Zanzotto, 'Viewpoint: Human-in-the-loop Artificial Intelligence' (2019) 64 Journal of Artificial Intelligence Research 243.

224 Meg L. Jones, 'Right to a Human in the Loop: Political Constructions of Computer Automation and Personhood' (2017) 47 Social Studies of Science 216.

225 Danielle K. Citron and Frank Pasquale, 'The Scored Society: Due Process for Automated Predictions' (2014) 89 Washington University Law Review 1; Kate Crawford and Jason Schultz, 'Big Data and Due Process: Toward a Framework to Redress Predictive Privacy Harms' (2014) 55 Boston College Law Review 93; Danielle K. Citron, 'Technological Due Process' (2008) 85 Washington University Law Review 1249.

is an inalienable right in the algorithmic society,[226] or why individuals should have a right to contest artificial intelligence systems.[227] This constitutional value raised within the realm of state actor is horizontally extended to the private actors through the obligation to ensure human intervention. It is not by chance that this principle is stated only when the processing involved automated decision-making technologies. This is because algorithmic decisions can produce serious effects on individual rights and freedoms. To remedy the lack of transparency oversight on algorithmic technologies, the GDPR requires that this processing deserves to be complemented by an adversarial principle and redress mechanism based on human intervention.

By recognising this right, the GDPR also seems to suggest that the last word over individual rights and freedoms should be human. A machine should not play this function without the support of humans that need to be in the loop. This is what the Commission already underlined in 1992 when stating that 'human judgment must have its place'.[228] Therefore, due process safeguards can protect human dignity complementing the general prohibition of full automated decision-making systems for the processing of personal data. This principle does not just recognise the role of humans in automated decision-making but also the primacy of human assessment over the efficiency of machines. Paradoxically, the inefficiency and irrationality of human beings is the last safeguard against the true interpretation of its nature.

The principle of human-in-the-loop cannot be considered as a general solution for the challenges raised by artificial intelligence. By looking at such a principle under the lens of proportionality, it can be observed that, while enhancing due process safeguards, it could potentially disregard other interests requiring protection. A broad extension of this rule can undermine the freedom to conduct business of private actors or the performance of public tasks. Besides, as already stressed, relying on human intervention as a procedural safeguard does not always ensure better decision-making.

226 Frank Pasquale, 'Inalienable Due Process in an Age of AI: Limiting the Contractual Creep toward Automated Adjudication' in Hans-W Micklitz and others (eds.), *Constitutional Challenges in the Algorithmic Society* (Cambridge University Press 2021).

227 Margot E. Kaminski and Jennifer M. Urban, 'The Right to Contest AI' (2021) 121(7) Columbia Law Review 1957.

228 Amended Proposal for a Council Directive on the Protection of Individuals with Regard to the Processing of Personal Data and on the Free Movement of Such Data COM(92)422 final, 26–7.

These drawbacks are just a small price to pay to ensure that humans are not marginalised by opaque algorithmic technologies and asymmetries of powers. These concerns are compensated by the critical role which due process plays against the unaccountable development of artificial intelligence technologies and the rise of private powers in the algorithmic society. The development of automated systems is not always driven by public purposes but usually by business interests focused on profit maximisation. Design choices could be not neutral and answer to opaque business logics which transform human life in technical norms of processing and extraction of values. In other words, the definition of transnational standards of automated systems outside any public scrutiny contributes to creating a para-constitutional environment competing with public values. This situation is not only relevant for due process, but also for the principle of the rule of law. If legal norms are replaced by technological standards, there will be no space for democratic constitutionalism to ensure the protection of public values against the rise of unaccountable technologies expressing private powers. Within this framework, the principle of human-in-the-loop is a shield not only as a due process safeguard, but also to protect democratic values.

The GDPR is fostering the principle of rule of law when the processing of personal data involves automated decision-making. This way, the GDPR bans any discretionary use of automated decision-making to process personal data. The principle of the rule of law is of a critical value to reduce the gap between the public and private sector involved in processing personal data. In the lack of any legal obligations, private actors are not required to give reasons justifying their policies or actions. While public actors are required to comply with constitutional principles, the private sector is not bound by constitutional principles and norms without a positive translation as it occurred with the GDPR. In the algorithmic society, private companies have demonstrated their abilities to acquire dominant positions in the market of data by extracting value from them. Within this framework, the data subject could be considered as a vulnerable actor whose protection of rights and freedoms should not only find its ground in the substantive rights but also in procedural safeguards to remedy the imbalance of power.

Within this framework, enhancing due process complements the relevance of human dignity and proportionality as expression of the constitutional values underpinning the GDPR. In this case, the GDPR obligations should not be seen as a mere instrument for requiring data controllers to comply with certain rules but as the constitutional expression of procedural safeguards aimed to avoid a disproportionate exercise of powers in the balancing between conflicting interests. In this sense, the obligations of the GDPR should be constitutionally interpreted as a means to ensure that human dignity and democratic values are not annihilated by the lack of transparency and accountability in the exercise of powers in the field of data.

6.6 Constitutional Values in the Algorithmic Society

The implementation of algorithmic technologies in the processing of personal data has increased the concerns for individuals, who are subject to ubiquitous forms of control and surveillance, and democratic values. The role of algorithmic technologies for the fourth industrial revolution is not only relevant for the potentialities of these technologies but, as for the Internet at the end of the last century, also for its dissemination in society and commodification.[229] These technologies are no longer closed to the domain of academics or specific business sectors, but are spreading as expressions of powers thus reaching consumers, especially because of the need to gather data and information to train artificial intelligence technologies which can provide new models and predictive answers. One of the primary promises of these technologies is to help humans decide, for example, by replacing or solving complex questions through data analytics.[230]

Nonetheless, the massive implementation of these technologies does not always seem to bring positive effects, especially when looking at the protection of fundamental rights and democratic values. The challenges relating to the exercise of powers in the field of data challenges the right to privacy once again, thus requiring a positive approach to protect fundamental rights and democratic values. This is the result of the European process of constitutionalisation leading the protection of individual fundamental rights to be the beacon of data protection law. The rise and consolidation of European data protection has been a first

[229] Brandon Allgood, 'The Commoditization of AI and The Long-Term Value of Data' Forbes (10 April 2017) www.forbes.com/sites/forbestechcouncil/2017/04/10/the-commoditization-of-ai-and-the-long-term-value-of-data/#74c71abd159c accessed 21 November 2021.

[230] Brian Cantwell Smit, *The Promise of Artificial Intelligence. Reckoning and Judgment* (MIT Press 2019).

answer to the challenges of automation. The constitutional evolution of data protection in the European framework shows the relevance of this fundamental right for safeguarding democratic values in a society which has strongly digitised in the last forty years. The ECJ has underlined a shift from the functional dimension of the Data Protection Directive, linked to the growth of the internal market, to a constitutional approach which has led to the adoption of the GDPR. Still, the modernisation of European data protection law fails to achieve the goal of protecting privacy and personal data in the lack of constitutional guidance.

The characteristics of European digital constitutionalism can provide an interpretative path to understand the role of data protection in the algorithmic society. The constitutional-oriented interpretation of the GDPR shows the horizontal underpinning values of the protection of privacy and data protection as fundamental rights, precisely human dignity, proportionality and due process. These values guiding European data protection can contribute to safeguarding the right of privacy and self-determination while breaking the asymmetries of powers threatening democratic values.

Therefore, the rise and consolidation of European data protection has not only led to an evolution of the constitutional paradigm but also to a translation of vertical constitutional values into horizontal principles and operational norms. This approach may protect the centrality of human dignity against the opaque and unaccountable processing of personal data in the hands of powerful actors, such as online platforms, while ensuring a proportionate approach to the conflicting rights at stake also thanks to due process safeguards.

Within this framework, the role of digital constitutionalism is far from being exhausted. Constitutional values have just started to imbue the algorithmic society and the European constitutional path is still at the beginning. A new phase of digital constitutionalism is likely around the corner.

7 The Road Ahead of European Digital Constitutionalism

7.1 The Consolidation of European Digital Constitutionalism

The European path towards digital constitutionalism has led to a shift of paradigm. The liberal goals of the internal market have met democratic values, thus building a new (digital) constitutional approach. As examined in Chapter 2, European constitutional values have enriched the digital liberal approach adopted at the end of the last century, which has been slowly complemented by a democratic strategy. This shift has been possible thanks to the consolidation of the European constitutional order in the aftermath of the Lisbon Treaty and the ECJ's judicial lessons, which have paved the way towards the constitutional reaction characterising the third (constitutional) phase opposing the troubling rise and evolution of private powers in the algorithmic society.

At the dawn of a new digital constitutional phase in Europe, it is worth wondering in which direction the Union will orient its strategy in the fourth revolution.[1] The Union has already demonstrated its commitment to be an active part of global dynamics of the digital age.[2] In her political guidelines, Commission president von der Leyen underlined the two political branches guiding the Union in the next decades to ensure the transition to a healthy planet and a new digital world which are

[1] Luciano Floridi, *The Fourth Revolution: How the Infosphere is Reshaping Human Reality* (Oxford University Press 2014).

[2] Communication from the Commission to the European Parliament, the Council, the European Economic and Social Committee and the Committee of the Regions, Commission Work Programme 2020. A Union that strives for more, COM(2020) 37 final.

considered as complementary areas.[3] The mix between environment and technology is critical,[4] as also highlighted by the UN Sustainable Development Goals.[5] The Data Strategy aims to establish the creation of a 'single European data space'.[6] It consists of ten sectoral common European data spaces which are relevant for the twin purposes of green and digital transitions. Shaping the digital future is based on the balancing between the interests in ensuring innovation in the internal market and protecting fundamental rights and democratic values.[7] The Data Governance Act is a leading example of this approach.[8] Likewise, the White paper on artificial intelligence is another piece of the European constitutional strategy,[9] as then translated in the proposal for the Artificial Intelligence Act.[10]

The focus on the digital future of the Union fits exactly within the global rush to build a position of standard maker in the algorithmic society. China is approaching being the world leader in the field of artificial intelligence technologies by 2030.[11] Whereas the US tech giants dominate digital markets and continue to extend their power to other sectors.[12] The role of digital technologies, particularly artificial intelligence, for the fourth industrial revolution does not only relate to

[3] Luciano Floridi, 'The Green and the Blue: Naïve Ideas to Improve Politics in a Mature Information Society' in Carl Öhman and David Watson, *The 2018 Yearbook of the Digital Ethics Lab* 183 (Springer 2018).

[4] Communication from the Commission to the European Parliament, the Council, the European Economic and Social Committee and the Committee of the Regions, The European Green Deal, COM(2019) 640 final.

[5] UN General Assembly, Resolution adopted by the General Assembly on 25 September 2015 A/RES/70/1 (2015).

[6] Communication from the Commission to the European Parliament, the Council, the European Economic and Social Committee and the Committee of the Regions – A European strategy for data, COM(2020) 66 final.

[7] Communication from the Commission to the European Parliament, the Council, the European Economic and Social Committee and the Committee of the Regions, Shaping Europe's digital future, COM(2020) 67 final.

[8] Proposal for a Regulation of the European Parliament and of the Council on European Data Governance COM(2020) 767 final.

[9] White paper, 'On Artificial Intelligence – A European Approach to Excellence and Trust' COM(2020) 65 final.

[10] Proposal for a Regulation of the European Parliament and of the Council Laying Down Harmonised Rules on Artificial Intelligence (Artificial Intelligence Act) and Amending Certain Union Legislative Acts COM(2021) 206 final.

[11] Will Knight, 'China Plans to Use Artificial Intelligence to Gain Global Economic Dominance by 2030' MIT Technology Review (21 July 2017) www.technologyreview.com/2017/07/21/150379/china-plans-to-use-artificial-intelligence-to-gain-global-economic-dominance-by-2030/ accessed 21 November 2021.

[12] Nick Srnicek, *Platforms Capitalism* (Polity Press 2016).

the potentialities of these technologies but also to their dissemination in the society and to commodification.[13] These technologies are no longer closed to the domain of academics or specific business sectors, but are spreading in daily lives, gathering data and information, which then contribute to training artificial intelligence technologies promising new opportunities based on predictive models and answers.[14] This process could play a critical role for the expansion of the internal market and in keeping it competitive in the international arena. At the same time, if, on the one hand, artificial intelligence is likely to provide new opportunities for the Union and Member States, on the other hand, they also pose relevant challenges for society,[15] especially concerning fundamental rights and democratic values.[16]

The previous chapters have underlined how the evolution of the digital environment have led constitutional democracies to adopting a liberal approach to protect innovation, thus leading to the rise of new digital powers. Against these challenges, the rise of digital constitutionalism has provided a first reaction laying the foundations to build a European strategy in the next years to avoid constitutional values slowly fading away in the name of innovation or business purposes outside democratic channels. However, as stressed in Chapters 5 and 6, the path has just started. The Digital Services Act and the GDPR have been just the first answers of the European constitutional strategy in the field of content and data.[17] This is why the rise of digital constitutionalism looks far from being

[13] Brandon Allgood, 'The Commoditization of AI and The Long-Term Value of Data' Forbes (10 April 2017) www.forbes.com/sites/forbestechcouncil/2017/04/10/the-commoditization-of-ai-and-the-long-term-value-of-data/#74c71abd159c accessed 21 November 2021.

[14] Brian Cantwell Smit, *The Promise of Artificial Intelligence. Reckoning and Judgment* (MIT Press 2019).

[15] Sue Newell and Marco Marabelli, 'Strategic Opportunities (and Challenges) of Algorithmic Decision-making: A Call for Action on The Long-Term Societal Effects of 'Datification' (2015) 24 The Journal of Strategic Information Systems 3.

[16] Mireille Hildebrandt, 'The Artificial Intelligence of European Union Law' (2020) 21 German Law Journal 74; Paul Nemitz, 'Constitutional Democracy and Technology in the Age of Artificial Intelligence' (2020) 376 Philosophical Transaction A.

[17] Proposal for a Regulation of the European Parliament and of the Council on a Single Market for Digital Services (Digital Services Act) and amending Directive 2000/31/EC, COM(2020) 825 final; Regulation (EU) 2016/679 of the European Parliament and of the Council of 27 April 2016 on the protection of natural persons with regard to the processing of personal data and on the free movement of such data, and repealing Directive 95/46/EC (General Data Protection Regulation), 2016 OJ (L 119) 1.

a point of arrival or the last step of the European constitutional path in the algorithmic society.

It is already possible to examine some trends leading the European constitutional strategy before dilemmas or trade-offs which could lead to polarisation. Firstly, automated decision-making technologies developed by transnational actors are promising new opportunities for growth and innovation. Like at the end of the last century, this promising scenario could trigger neoliberal approaches, thus contributing to the the path of digital capitalism. At the same time, these technologies have already highlighted the challenges for the protection of fundamental rights and freedoms, thus raising questions about safeguarding human dignity. Therefore, the first dilemma is a matter of values driving the algorithmic society (i.e. digital humanism versus digital capitalism).

Secondly, it is worth focusing on the governance of these values. The mix of public authority and private ordering contributes to shaping the evolution and implementation of digital technologies. Both public and private powers propose models for governing technology which do not always lead to cooperation but sometimes also to competition, thus blurring the boundaries between different normativities. The dilemma between hard- and self-regulation is one of the primary challenges for constitutional democracies which are still following diverging strategies in the algorithmic society (i.e. public authority versus private ordering).

Thirdly, the global spread of algorithmic technologies leads to focusing on the scope of these values and their governance at the intersection between public and private actors. While the traditional characteristics of sovereign powers would limit the application of rights and freedoms to a certain territory, private actors enjoy more flexibility in extending their standards on a global scale. As a result, public actors are encouraged to make the protection of fundamental rights extraterritorial to mitigate the influence of global standards developed by unaccountable private entities or other external interferences by other states. At the same time, the limits to the exercise of sovereign powers beyond territorial boundaries could encourage constitutional democracies to look at global phenomena with scepticism while fearing the consequences of reciprocity. Illiberal regimes could take the extraterritorial application of rights and freedoms as a model to support the extension of their illiberal agenda beyond their boundaries. This trend could trigger a protectionist reaction by constitutional democracies to shield constitutional values from the interferences of global private standards and illiberal public values (i.e., constitutional imperialism versus constitutional protectionism).[18]

Within this framework, this chapter argues that the characteristics of European digital constitutionalism defines a third way escaping polarisation. The primary goal of this chapter is to underline how the talent of European digital constitutionalism promotes a sustainable growth of the internal market and the protection of fundamental rights and democratic values in the long run. The first part of this chapter focuses on the relationship between digital humanism and digital capitalism underlining the potential path characterising the European approach to artificial intelligence technologies. The second part examines how European digital constitutionalism would lead to a third way between public authority and private ordering. The third part underlines to what extent the Union would likely extend the scope of its constitutional values to address the global challenges of artificial intelligence technologies. Once this chapter addresses the potential road ahead of European digital constitutionalism, the fourth part summarises the primary findings of this research.

7.2 Values: Digital Humanism versus Digital Capitalism

The development of artificial intelligence technologies has triggered a new wave of opportunities for economic growth. The processing of vast amounts of data have become an integral part of the public and private sector. While, in the last century, the lack of a vast amount of interconnected data has led to the so-called AI winters,[19] today, the evolution of global communication technologies allowing the storing and exchange of information seems to promise a different path.

The availability of large data sets has led to a sharp increase in the number of intelligent products and services. Although most of the automated systems are still in the phase of 'narrow AI', significant improvements have been achieved, for example, in the analysis and prediction of human behaviour and characteristics, or in the field of

[18] James Tully, 'The Imperialism of Modern Constitutional Democracy' in Martin Loughlin and Neil Walker (eds.), *The Paradox of Constitutionalism: Constituent Power and Constitutional Form* (Oxford University Press 2008).

[19] Luciano Floridi, 'AI and Its New Winter: From Myths to Realities' (2020) 33 Philosophy & Technology 1.

robotics.[20] From banking and insurance to the medical sector, automated decision-making technologies offer new possibilities of prediction and interpretation of reality based on different degrees of determinism like neural networks. One example consists of biometric technologies where voice and facial recognition are not only implemented by public authorities for the performance of public tasks like border control,[21] but also by the private sector, primarily to profile individuals for business purposes.[22]

This is why artificial intelligence is one of the primary drivers of the fourth industrial revolution. Data are the fundamental asset for the digital economy due to their capacity to generate value. At the same time, the previous chapters have shown how automated technologies have highly challenged the protection of fundamental rights and democratic values. Discriminatory results, biased decisions, censoring speech or subject users to forms of surveillance are only some examples of these concerns.[23] Health and security, privacy and self-determination, speech and discrimination, are just examples of the values involved in processes of decision-making outside human judgment or oversight. This scenario leads to a crossroads between a model where individual rights and freedoms are shielded against the appeal and promise of new technologies (i.e. digital humanism) and a neoliberal view looking at the new opportunities of artificial intelligence technologies as a potential engine for economic growth and individual autonomy (i.e. digital capitalism).

This would not be the first time that constitutional democracies face this dilemma. Turning back and looking at the last twenty years, the Union has already addressed this question moving from a digital liberal approach coming from the US neoliberal paradigm to a constitutional approach which takes into high consideration the protection of fundamental rights and democratic values in the algorithmic society. At the end of the last century, there were not so

[20] Ryan Calo, 'Artificial Intelligence Policy: A Primer and Roadmap' (2017) 51 UC Davis Law Review 399.

[21] Paul De Hert, 'Biometrics and the Challenge to Human Rights in Europe. Need for Regulation and Regulatory Distinctions' in Patrizio Campisi (ed.), *Security and Privacy in Biometrics* 369 (Springer 2013).

[22] Lauren Stewart, 'Big Data Discrimination: Maintaining Protection of Individual Privacy Without Disincentivizing Businesses' Use of Biometric Data to Enhance Security' (2019) 60 Boston College Law Review 347.

[23] David Lyon, *The Culture of Surveillance: Watching as a Way of Life* (Polity Press 2018).

many clues to look at the rise of digital capitalism as a potential challenge for constitutional democracies. Nonetheless, this liberal approach has been exactly the constitutional ground for the evolution of digital powers against which European digital constitutionalism has reacted. Chapters 5 and 6 have underlined the role of European constitutionalism, and precisely human dignity, in promoting new positive approaches in the fields of content and data. The rise of a new phase of digital constitutionalism can be considered a natural European reaction to the threats of digital capitalism.

Therefore, human dignity is increasingly raising as the last resort to mitigate the potential threats of tecno-determinist solutions that could lead to processes of dehumanisation and gradually the vanishing of democratic values. According to the European Data Protection Supervisor, '[The] respect for, and the safeguarding of, human dignity could be the counterweight to the pervasive surveillance and asymmetry of power which now confronts the individual. It should be at the heart of a new digital ethics'.[24] The consolidation of the algorithmic society brings with it ethical and legal concerns like the autonomy of robots, online censorship and trust in automated decision-making processes.[25] Digital ethics is at the centre of the European policy response to the challenges raised by artificial intelligence technologies in terms of liability, safety, the Internet of Things (IoT), robotics, algorithmic awareness, consumer and data protection.

It should not come as a surprise that a human-centred approach is the core of the European strategy to artificial intelligence. In 2018, the Commission appointed a new High-Level Expert Group on Artificial Intelligence which published its artificial intelligence ethical guidelines.[26] The group underlined the importance of adopting a pan-human approach to these technologies which looks at human dignity as the common foundation of European fundamental rights and values according to which 'the human being enjoys a unique and inalienable moral status of primacy in the civil, political, economic and social fields'.[27]

[24] European Data Protection Supervisor, 'Opinion 4/2015. Towards a new Digital Ethics' (11 September 2015) https://edps.europa.eu/sites/edp/files/publication/15-09-11_data_ethics_en.pdf accessed 21 November 2021.

[25] Mark Coeckelbergh, *AI Ethics* (MIT Press 2020); Michael Kearns and Aaron Roth, *The Ethical Algorithm: The Science of Socially Aware Algorithm Design* (Oxford University Press 2019).

[26] High-Level Expert Group, 'Ethics Guidelines for Trustworthy AI' (8 April 2019) https://ec.europa.eu/newsroom/dae/document.cfm?doc_id=60419 accessed 21 November 2021.

[27] Ibid., 10.

The same approach is also reflected in the strategy of the Union on artificial intelligence.[28] The white paper on artificial intelligence expressly clarifies that '[g]iven the major impact that AI can have on our society and the need to build trust, it is vital that European AI is grounded in our values and fundamental rights such as human dignity and privacy protection'.[29] The Council of Europe also underlined to be aware of the positive and negative impact that the application of algorithmic systems 'has on the exercise, enjoyment and protection of all human rights and fundamental freedoms, and of the significant challenges, also for democratic societies and the rule of law, attached to the increasing reliance on algorithmic systems in everyday life'.[30]

From this perspective, the Union seems to define a precise path towards digital humanism. A closer look can reveal how the Union has not entirely closed its doors to digital capitalism. It is true that protecting rights and democratic values against a reckless race to innovation towards dehumanisation is one of the aims of European digital constitutionalism. Nonetheless, the situation is more nuanced than it could appear at first glance. The European constitutional safeguards could be considered as limits to the development of digital technologies and, therefore, be a competitive disadvantage vis-à-vis other global technological poles, like China or the US.

As examined in Chapter 5, the Union has adopted a more restrictive approach to the power of online platforms over content. Precisely, the European strategy has focused on shaping the boundaries of online platform responsibilities in Europe. A first positive reaction of the Union has led to remedying the discretionary interferences coming from platform power by introducing transparency and accountability safeguards in content moderation. Likewise, Chapter 6 has underlined the role of data protection in counterbalancing and preventing disproportionate interferences with individual personal data and, therefore, autonomy and dignity. In this sense, the GDPR can be considered as the horizontal translation of a mix of constitutional values characterising European constitutionalism.

[28] COM(2020) 65 (n. 9).

[29] Ibid., 2.

[30] Recommendation CM/Rec(2020)1 of the Committee of Ministers to member States on the human rights impacts of algorithmic systems (8 April 2020) www.statewatch.org/media/documents/news/2020/apr/coe-recommendation-algorithms-automation-human-rights-4–20.pdf%3E"www.statewatch.org/media/documents/news/2020/apr/coe-recommendation-algorithms-automation-human-rights-4–20.pdf%3E accessed 21 November 2021.

These limits to safeguard fundamental rights and democratic values would not raise concerns if the Union was the only actor participating in the run towards artificial intelligence technologies around the world. Even if these safeguards aim to protect constitutional values, they could also slow down the smooth development of digital technologies. Granting extensive protection to fundamental rights over innovation could lead the Union to become a 'standard-taker' rather than a 'standard-maker' in the fourth industrial revolution. It would be enough to focus the broad constitutional protection recognised to personal data in the European context to argue, at least apparently, a competitive disadvantage of the Union vis-à-vis other countries where the safeguards in the field of content and data are not equivalent. Since granting 'extensive protection of data privacy rights restrains the use of AI's most useful features: autonomy and automation',[31] one of the most important challenges for the Union in the fourth industrial revolution is to understand where to draw a line between innovation and risk.

Considering the role of artificial intelligence for the fourth industrial revolution, this is not a trivial constitutional issue. A lower degree of guarantees and safeguards can constitute a competitive advantage in the algorithmic society. This situation could trigger a rush to the bottom in the protection of fundamental rights in order not to suffer a competitive disadvantage. It cannot be excluded that the fight in the international arena for becoming the standard-maker in the field of artificial intelligence could lead to a dangerous reduction in democratic and constitutional safeguards in the name of innovation. The extensive protection of individual fundamental rights and democratic values could lead the Union in a position of technological *subjectionis* driven by the extension of technological paradigms of protection coming from areas of the world which do not ensure adequate safeguards for users and society at large. Put another way, this constitutional disadvantage could lead Europe to dealing with a situation of de facto technological disadvantage compared to areas of the world where the lack of restrictions allow the development of technologies becoming market standards. The need to be competitive in a global market would lead the

[31] Matthew Humerick, 'Taking AI Personally: How the E.U. Must Learn to Balance the Interests of Personal Data Privacy & Artificial Intelligence' (2018) 34 Santa Clara High Technology Law Journal 393, 412.

Union to accepting the extension of external paradigms of protection, thus influencing European values.

Within this multifaceted framework, the primary challenge concerns what kind of innovation the Union wants to achieve and whether this choice is based on a liberal approach reducing the scope of safeguards in the name of innovation. Therefore, the question would be whether, in this bipolar system made of opportunities and threats, European digital constitutionalism could provide a third way precluding neoliberal approaches or illiberal agenda from taking the lead of the algorithmic society.

The position of the Union in this field is peculiar due to the role of the two technological poles, precisely China and the US, which are currently leading the fourth industrial revolution.[32] In this geopolitical scenario, the Union has shown its intent to be a crucial player in this match,[33] as also underlined by the proposal for the Artificial Intelligence Act. Although the Union is aware of the potentialities of these technologies and the need to be competitive in the international arena, the protection of fundamental rights, such as personal data, together with the compelling need to protect democratic values against the threats raised by artificial intelligence technologies could constitute a 'constitutional brake' limiting the flourishing of these technologies.

Despite this consideration, the Union has not totally abandoned its economy roots.[34] It should not come as a surprise if the Union agenda already demonstrated a commitment to build a Digital Single Market.[35] To benefit from the full potentialities of this new technological

[32] Klaus Schwab, *The Fourth Industrial Revolution* (Crown 2016); Daniel Araya, 'Governing The Fourth Industrial Revolution' Forbes (12 May 2019) www.forbes.com/sites/danielaraya/2019/03/12/governing-the-fourth-industrialrevolution/#4eea13a14b33 accessed 21 November 2021.

[33] See, e.g., Communication from the Commission to the European Parliament, the European Council, the Council, the European Economic and Social Committee and the Committee of the Regions: Artificial Intelligence for Europe, COM(2018) 237 final; Communication from the Commission to the European Parliament, the European Council, the Council, the European Economic and Social Committee and the Committee of the Regions, Coordinated Plan on Artificial Intelligence COM(2018) 795 final.

[34] Sophie Robin-Olivier, 'The 'Digital Single Market' and Neoliberalism: Reflections on Net Neutrality' in Margot E. Salomon and Bruno De Witte (eds.), *Legal Trajectories of Neoliberalism: Critical Inquiries on Law in Europe* 45 (RSCAS 2019).

[35] Communication from the Commission to the European Parliament, the Council, the European Economic and Social Committee and the Committee of the Regions. A Digital Single Market Strategy for Europe COM(2015) 192 final.

framework, it is necessary to invest resources and ensure the smooth development of these technologies without hindering innovation. In the mid-term review of the Digital Single Market strategy, the Commission highlighted the relevance of being in a leading position in the development of artificial intelligence technologies.[36] It underlined the importance for the Union to benefit from the opportunities of these technologies through a three-pronged approach: increasing public and private investment; preparing for socio-economic changes brought about by artificial intelligence; and ensuring an appropriate ethical and legal framework.

The Union has underlined its intention not only to limit platform power and mitigate the threats of digital capitalism but also to become a standard-maker rather than a mere follower of other technological poles. The Digital Services Act aims not only to increase responsibilities of online platforms and certainty in the moderation of content but also to ensure fair competition and promote the development of small- and medium-sized businesses.[37] Moving to the field of data, while the GDPR increases the degree of protection for individual fundamental rights, other aspects promote the processing of personal data in the business sector and leave some areas of governance to the private sector. In this case, the GDPR can be considered a regulation of surveillance capitalism which does not impede tech giants to collect and process data but regulates this process.

Likewise, the proposal for the Artificial Intelligence Act could provide an example of this hybrid approach. At first glance, this proposal does not focus on individual protection but provides top-down standards defined by the Commission to mitigate the risk coming from artificial intelligence technologies. In other words, rather than a piece in the puzzle of digital constitutionalism, the proposal looks far from the structure of the GDPR or the Digital Services Act. Nonetheless, the objective of the proposal is not only to promote the development of artificial intelligence technologies in Europe to foster the development of the internal market but also to avoid that misuse of technologies producing risks for public interests and rights that would 'contradict Union values of respect for human dignity, freedom, equality, democracy and the rule of law and Union fundamental rights, including the right to non-discrimination, data protection

[36] COM(2018) 237 final (n. 33).
[37] COM(2020) 825 final (n. 17).

and privacy and the rights of the child'.[38] This duality of goals is precisely the characterisation of the European approach at the intersection between digital humanism and digital capitalism.

This mix between innovation and the protection of individual fundamental rights is not just the result of regulatory choices but reflects the characteristics of European constitutionalism where the need to balance different fundamental rights could not lead digital humanism or digital capitalism to entirely prevail over each other. The constitutional protection of freedom of expression, privacy and personal data requires to take into consideration not only how to safeguard fundamental rights but also other conflicting interests such as the freedom to conduct business. At the same time, the freedom to conduct business or the aim to achieve the goals of the internal market cannot lead to the annihilation of fundamental rights and freedoms. European constitutional law is not prone to recognise an absolute protection to constitutional values which would lead to the destruction of other conflicting interests.

Therefore, European digital constitutionalism would lead towards a hybrid approach between digital humanism and capitalism. This European 'third way' should not be considered just a political choice but the result of the natural tendency of European constitutionalism not to take a polarised position but merge the different pieces of the puzzle in a dialectic form. The Union does not aim to leave private actors free to develop technologies under a neoliberal scheme such as in the US or strongly intervene in the market to support the development of new technologies and businesses as is the case of China. As we will underline in the next sections, the Union is rising as a global regulator driven by a balanced constitutional approach whose beacon is represented by the principle of human dignity. This approach belongs to the nature of the Union since it is 'founded on the values of respect for human dignity, freedom, democracy, equality, the rule of law and respect for human rights, including the rights of persons belonging to minorities'.[39]

In front of the crossroads between digital humanism and capitalism, the Union seems to have chosen a path towards the development of a sustainable artificial intelligence environment rather than focusing just on fostering innovation to exploit the potentialities of these

[38] COM(2021) 206 final (n. 10), Recital 15.

[39] Consolidated version of the Treaty on European Union (2012) OJ C 326/13, Art. 2.

technologies or merely impeding their development. Although the Union approach could be subject in the short term to a competitive disadvantage in the field of artificial intelligence, in the long term, the European approach could promote a human-centric development of artificial intelligence technologies. As stressed by the Commission, '[g]iven the major impact that AI can have on our society and the need to build trust, it is vital that European AI is grounded in our values and fundamental rights such as human dignity and privacy protection'.[40] Put another way, against a fierce global competition in the field of artificial intelligence and considering its relevance for the future of Europe, the Union has chosen to promote the development of these technologies without forgetting the protection of rights and freedoms.

The definition of this European strategy cannot be understood without examining the governance of these values. It is worth wondering how the Union would concretely put in place its strategy at the intersection between digital humanism and digital capitalism. In order to ensure that technology does not order society and human beings, but is functional to the evolution of mankind, it is critical to wonder about the relationship between the exercise of public authority and private ordering, precisely between the role of hard regulation and self-regulation.

Choosing between public authority or private ordering in the algorithmic society is not a neutral choice. As underlined in the previous chapters, the private governance of content and data in the digital environment left individuals at the margins and subject to private ubiquitous systems influencing their decisions without being able to understand or control the technologies and, therefore, to participate consciously in a democratic society. Therefore, the primary challenge is how citizens can ensure that constitutional values underpinning their social contract are not left to unaccountable determinations outside democratic circuits.

This is a question concerning the governance of values in the algorithmic society. As underlined by the Council of Europe, 'ongoing public and private sector initiatives intended to develop ethical guidelines and standards for the design, development and ongoing deployment of algorithmic systems, while constituting a highly welcome recognition of the risks that these systems pose for normative values, do not relieve Council of Europe Member States of their obligations as primary

40 COM(2020) 65 final (n. 9), 2.

guardians of the Convention'.[41] Rather than proposing a self-regulatory approach, the consolidation of European digital constitutionalism would increasingly lead public actors to be gatekeepers of democratic values, thus defining the framework of values guiding the development of artificial intelligence technologies. The next subsection underlines how finding a point of balance between the exercise of public authority and private ordering would be critical to promote a sustainable and democratic development of artificial intelligence technologies in Europe.

7.3 Governance: Public Authority versus Private Ordering

'People are entitled to technology that they can trust. What is illegal offline must also be illegal online. While we cannot predict the future of digital technology, European values and ethical rules and social and environmental norms must apply also in the digital space'.[42] This political statement underlines the importance of the European values in the development of digital technologies. However, defining values is just one step. The positive consequences of the spread of artificial intelligence firmly clashes with the troubling opacity of 'algocracy'.[43] Individuals are increasingly surrounded by ubiquitous systems whose values are governed by public and private actors. Leaving algorithmic technologies without any democratic safeguard would lead to open the way to a form of technodeterminism, allowing not only public authorities but also private actors to govern algorithmic technologies to autonomously determine the standard of protection of rights and freedoms on a global scale. The Council of Europe underlined the importance of 'bearing in mind that digital technologies hold significant potential for socially beneficial innovation and economic development, and that the achievement of these goals must be rooted in the shared values of democratic societies and subject to full democratic participation and oversight'.[44] Therefore, in order to protect democratic values while promoting innovation, defining the governance of artificial

[41] CM/Rec(2020)1 (n. 30).
[42] COM(2020) 67 final (n. 7), 10.
[43] John Danaher, 'The Threat of Algocracy: Reality, Resistance and Accommodation' (2016) 29 Philosophy & Technology 245.
[44] CM/Rec(2020)1 (n. 30).

intelligence technologies is a critical piece of the puzzle. Put another way, the Union's choice at the intersection between digital humanism and digital capitalism may be effective only if the Union will adopt a system of governance which can ensure the effective implementation of the European democratic approach to the algorithmic society.

As examined in Chapter 3, transnational private actors have consolidated delegated and autonomous areas of powers while privately ordering the fields of content and data. The rise of European digital constitutionalism can also be read as a reaction against the power of online platforms to set their values on a global scale on a discretionary basis. Content moderation and individual profiling are just two examples of how private actors have been able to rely on a self-regulatory framework driven by business logics rather than by public values. While, at the end of the last century, the primary concern was not overwhelming the private sector with regulatory burdens, now, the Union is showing to be concerned about the dramatic shift from public values to private determinations driven by profit maximisation. The rise of digital capitalism is nothing else than the fruit of a digital liberal approach which has not considered how leaving private actors without a framework of safeguards and oversight could affect society at large and lead to a concentration of digital private powers.

The Union has already expressed its commitment not to be subject to the logics of digital capitalism. According to Vestager, 'platforms [. . .] can have an enormous impact on the way we see the world around us. And that's a serious challenge for our democracy. . . . So we can't just leave decisions which affect the future of our democracy to be made in the secrecy of a few corporate boardrooms'.[45]

The European orientation to digital ethics underlines that the market cannot autonomously prevail over the need to safeguard fundamental rights and democracy. Ethics could play a critical role in the making of artificial intelligence governance.[46] Nonetheless, an extensive reliance

[45] Margrethe Vestager, 'Algorithms and Democracy' Algorithmic Watch (30 October 2020) https://ec.europa.eu/commission/commissioners/2019-2024/vestager/announcements/algorithms-and-democracy-algorithmwatch-online-policy-dialogue-30-october-2020_en accessed 21 November 2021.

[46] Coeckelbergh (n. 25); Virginia Dignum, *Responsible Artificial Intelligence* (Springer 2019); Luciano Floridi and others, 'AI4People – An Ethical Framework for a Good AI Society: Opportunities, Risks, Principles, and Recommendations' (2018) 28(4) Minds and Machines 689.

on solutions based on ethics and self-regulation could not solve the current situation of asymmetry of power in the algorithmic society. The predominance of ethics over the law could build a neoliberal narrative diluting the role of regulation over self-regulation, thus leading the private sector to define what is good behaviour or, more precisely, what is an objectionable conduct online. Even if companies share their commitment to ethical values or refer to their responsibilities in relation to human rights, they are still free to establish their business purposes which, in the lack of incentives, are usually not oriented to public interests as much as to profit maximisation.

When looking outside the Union, there are other examples which are trying to govern the values underpinning the evolution of tomorrow's digital environment. In the US, the neoliberal approach in the last twenty years would represent a different form of digital constitutionalism. The executive order on preventing online censorship is an interesting example to understand the characteristics of US digital constitutionalism,[47] even if the order was withdrawn in May 2021,[48] and courts had already blocked users' complaints.[49] The presidential move resulted in a constitutional paradox.[50] Beyond the constitutional issues involving the separation of powers between the executive and legislative powers, as the former has no power to amend the work of the latter, the order is incoherent when looking at how the First Amendment has protected online intermediaries in the last twenty years,[51] as also demonstrated by the legislative attempts to amend the Communication Decency Act.

[47] Executive Order on Preventing Online Censorship (28 May 2020) www.federalregister.gov/documents/2020/06/02/2020-12030/preventing-online-censorship accessed 21 November 2021.

[48] 'Executive Order on the Revocation of Certain Presidential Actions and Technical Amendment' (14 May 2021) www.whitehouse.gov/briefing-room/presidential-actions/2021/05/14/executive-order-on-the-revocation-of-certain-presidential-actions-and-technical-amendment/ accessed 21 November 2021.

[49] *Gomez* v. *Zuckenburg*, 2020 U.S. Dist. LEXIS 130989 (N.D.N.Y. July 23, 2020).

[50] Giovanni De Gregorio and Roxana Radu, 'Trump's Executive Order: Another Tile in the Mosaic of Governing Online Speech' MediaLaws (6 June 2020) www.medialaws.eu/trumps-executive-order-another-tile-in-the-mosaic-of-governing-online-speech/ accessed 21 November 2021.

[51] Daphne Keller, 'Who Do You Sue? State and Platform Hybrid Power Over Online Speech' (2019) Hoover Institution, Aegis Series Paper No. 1902 www.hoover.org/sites/default/files/research/docs/who-do-you-sue-state-and-platform-hybrid-power-over-online-speech_0.pdf accessed 21 November 2021.

Likewise, moving from the legislative to judicial power, the order was also not in line with the recent orientation of the US Supreme Court. Without going into the details of national case law like *Lewis* v. *YouTube*,[52] Chapter 5 has already underlined how the Supreme Court defined social media as the vast democratic forum of the Internet in *Packingham* v. *North Carolina*.[53] The order also refers to *Pruneyard Shopping Center* v. *Robins* to argue that, although social media platforms are private actors, they provide a public forum online. Nonetheless, these cases deal with the banning of national law introducing a prior restraint over free speech.[54] These cases should have been enough to impede the public interferences to free speech that this executive order introduces. Besides, in a 2019 decision, *Manhattan Community Access Corp.* v. *Halleck*,[55] the Supreme Court closed the door to a potential extension of the state action doctrine when it decided that private actors, precisely cable tv companies operating public access channels, do not serve as a public actor (i.e. the city of New York) and are thus not bound to protect free speech rights. The relevance of this decision can be understood when looking at the national case law which has already relied on this decision to ban interference with platform freedoms such as in *PragerU* v. *YouTube*.[56]

This liberal framework characterising US digital constitutionalism will likely constitute the perfect environment for the consolidation of private ordering in the following years. Online platforms have started a process of institutionalisation by attracting legitimation for their functions and proposing alternative models to the traditional exercise of public powers. The Facebook Oversight board is a paradigmatic example of this process. No matter whether it may be considered as independent or as a supreme court, this process shows how platforms enforce human rights standards not only as instrument of scrutiny over the decisions of Facebook based on their community guidelines but also represent a model of private adjudication in the algorithmic society which, de facto, competes with the model of justice and procedures proposed by public authorities.

On the other pole, China is following a different strategy. Rather than adopting a neoliberal approach to the digital environment, China has always exercised sovereign powers over the Internet to control online

52 *Lewis* v. *YouTube*, 197 Cal. Rptr. 3d 219 (Cal. Ct. App. 2015).
53 *Packingham* v. *North Carolina*, 582 U.S. ___ (2017).
54 *Pruneyard Shopping Center* v. *Robins*, 447 U.S. 74 (1980).
55 *Manhattan Community Access Corp.* v. *Halleck*, No. 17-1702, 587 U.S. ___ (2019).
56 *Prager University* v. *Google LLC*, No. 18-15712 (9th Cir. 2020).

activities.[57] The case of the social credit system is an example of the control that China can exercise in the algorithmic society.[58] In these years, after firstly excluding other digital companies like US tech giants through the Great Firewall,[59] China has ensured a walled market environment allowing its businesses to grow outside competition under the Huawei model.[60] This approach has led to the creation of a Chinese digital political economy focused on surveillance and market intervention.

Within this framework, the Union is going towards a different path. Rather than adopting a mere neoliberal approach or supporting the development of its model of the Internet, it is emerging at the intersection between the two models. The governance of values in the algortihmic society is not left either to private determinations through self-regulation or market intervention. The Union is consolidating a co-regulatory approach characterised by the definition of the value framework within which the private sector operates. Therefore, European constitutional values are not simply shaped by private determinations or by unaccountable forces, but are protected by a common regulatory framework injecting constitutional values in self-regulation. This result is not by chance but derives from the path of European digital constitutionalism.

Despite its economic history, as analysed in Chapter 2, the rise of an increasing relevant dimension of European constitutional law has mitigated the goals of the internal market and the predominance of self-regulation. The European orientation to dignity explains why the rise of private powers is seen as a threat to fundamental rights and democratic values. Unlike the US, the Union's dimension oriented to welfare goals does not allow capitalistic logics to prevail over the social dimension of the European market. This could provide clues about the failure of the European model to promote the creation of businesses able to compete with US tech giants. At the same time, the need to ensure competition in the internal market blocks the

57 Jonathan Zittrain and Benjamin Edelman, 'Empirical Analysis of Internet Filtering in China' (2003) Harvard Law School Public Law Research Paper No. 62.

58 Genia Kostka, 'China's Social Credit Systems and Public Opinion: Explaining High Levels of Approval' (2019) 21(7) New Media & Society 1565; Fan Liang and others, 'Constructing a Data-Driven Society: China's Social Credit System as a State Surveillance Infrastructure' (2018) 10(4) Policy & Internet 415.

59 Yu Hong, *Networking China: The Digital Transformation of the Chinese Economy* (University of Illinois Press 2017).

60 Madison Cartwright, 'Internationalising State Power through the Internet: Google, Huawei and Geopolitical Struggle' (2020) 9(3) Internet Policy Review https://policyreview.info/node/1494/pdf accessed 21 November 2021.

creation of large corporations while limiting the possibility for Member States' aid to their businesses. Furthermore, the democratic constitutional basis of the Union precludes any attempt to increase surveillance over the Internet while leaving the doors open to online platforms operating on a transnational scale.

Therefore, even in this case, the path of European digital constitutionalism suggests a third way at the intersection between public authority and private ordering. The Union has not shown either its intention to leave the market free to determine the values of the algorithmic society or the interest in intervening in the market to support internal businesses in the rush for becoming a standard-maker in the algorithmic society. Even if the Artificial Intelligence Act provides a top-down approach where the Commission is at the forefront in defining the degree of risk, thus without apparently leaving spaces for self-regulation or collaboration, it is possible to consider how the Digital Services Act Package and the GDPR show how the Union is struggling to find a proportionate balance between hard and self-regulation. The Digital Services Act is not just a new legal framework to strengthen the internal market and foster the development of digital services, thus promoting innovation.[61] As in the case of the GDPR, it could be considered another way to rise as a global model for regulating transnational powers while protecting democratic values. The two pillars of this package consist of proposing clear rules for framing digital services responsibilities and ex ante rules applying to large online platforms acting as gatekeepers, which now set the rules of the game for their users and their competitors.[62]

Likewise, the GDPR can be considered a hybrid solution between regulation and self-regulation. As stressed in Chapter 6, the GDPR is a peculiar legal instrument. The risk-based approach leaves margins of discretion for public and private actors when implementing their data processing. In a certain sense, the Union's approach can be considered as an attempt to regulate digital capitalism at the intersection between market logics and democratic values. Put another way, it constitutes

[61] COM(2020) 37 final (n. 2).

[62] See Digital Services Act package: deepening the Internal Market and clarifying responsibilities for digital services European Commission, Inception impact assessment - Ares(2020)2877686; Digital Services Act package: Ex ante regulatory instrument for large online platforms with significant network effects acting as gate-keepers in the European Union's internal market Inception impact assessment - Ares(2020)2877647.

a hybrid approach defining that value framework of principles and rules whose boundaries are left to the implementation of transnational businesses under the oversight of judicial power and independent competent authorities.

The European approach increasingly tends to promote a governance approach where online platforms are considered regulated centres of collaboration or digital utilities. As underlined in Chapter 3, the ability of these actors to govern content and data is not only a risk but also an opportunity to enforce public policies online. The pandemic has fostered this trend where online platforms have shown their predominant role. This situation has underlined the relevance of digital technologies for remote activities and delivery services.[63] For instance, without controlling moderation of content, disinformation and hate speech would spread online. Besides, in the field of data, the example of contact tracing apps is paradigmatic of how Google and Apple have been able to provide a global tracking application, thus capturing the attention of governments.[64]

Some platforms perform a role beyond the mere provision of services. While it may be argued that they have an editorial role which should be shielded by the protection of the right to free speech,[65] other scholars underline their role as information or privacy fiduciaries,[66] or as public utilities like infrastructures.[67] The primary challenge is not to oppose

[63] Daisuke Wakabayashi and others, 'Big Tech Could Emerge from Coronavirus Crisis Stronger Than Ever' The New York Times (23 March 2020) www.nytimes.com/2020/03/23/technology/coronavirus-facebook-amazon-youtube.html accessed 21 November 2021.

[64] Oreste Pollicino, 'Contact tracing and COVID-19: Commission and Member States agree on specifications' EU Law Live (16 June 2020) https://eulawlive.com/contact-tracing-and-covid-19-commission-and-member-states-agree-on-specifications/ accessed 21 November 2021.

[65] Eric Goldman, 'Of Course the First Amendment Protects Google and Facebook (and It's Not a Close Question)' Knight First Amendment Institute (February 2018) https://knightcolumbia.org/content/course-first-amendment-protects-google-and-facebook-and-its-not-close-question accessed 21 November 2021.

[66] Jack M. Balkin, 'The Fiduciary Model of Privacy' (2020) 134(1) Harvard Law Review Forum 11; Jack M. Balkin, 'Information Fiduciaries and the First Amendment' (2016) 49 UC Davis Law Review 1183.

[67] Jean-Christophe Plantin and others, 'Infrastructure studies meet platform studies in the age of Google and Facebook' (2018) 20(1) New Media & Society 293; K. Sabeel Rahman, 'Monopoly Men' Boston Review (11 October 2017) http://bostonreview.net/science-nature/k-sabeel-rahman-monopoly-men accessed 21 November 2021; Cale Guthrie Weissman, 'Maybe It's Time to Treat Facebook Like a Public Utility' Fast Company (1 May 2017) www.fastcompany.com/40414024/maybe-its-time-to-treat-facebook-like-a-public-utility accessed 21 November 2021; Danah Boyd, 'Facebook Is a Utility; Utilities Get Regulated' Apophenia (15 May 2010) www.zephoria.org/thoughts/archives/

their bigness but rather to regulate their power coming from a governance of social infrastructure. As underlined by Rahman, 'where private actors accumulate outsized control over those goods and services that form the vital foundation or backbone of our political economy – social infrastructure – this control poses dangers'.[68] The Council of Europe highlighted the increasing privatisation of public functions, particularly observing that '[w]hen such systems are then withdrawn for commercial reasons, the result can range from a decrease in quality and/or efficiency to the loss of services that are considered essential by individuals and communities'. In these cases, '[s]tates should put contingencies in place to ensure that essential services remain available irrespective of their commercial viability, particularly in circumstances where private sector actors dominate the market in ways that place them in positions of influence or even control'.[69]

Within this framework, the concept of public utilities could lead to a solution to find a balanced approach between public authority and private ordering. The increasing control over large parts of political, economic and social life leads online platforms to be critical and essential infrastructures.[70] This consolidation of power is relevant not only for individuals but also for the market. The services provided by Google or Facebook play an important role in the success of online content providers like traditional media outlets or influencers. The dominance of these actors is not limited to consumer retail sales but also the power over other business sectors relying on their services. It is not by coincidence that the Union has adopted a legal instrument to increase fairness and transparency for business users of online intermediation services.[71]

However, there is much more beyond economic power. The power of platforms to influence policy-makers and users' behaviours is a dangerous trend for constitutional democracies. In the US framework, Crawford underlines common carriage concerns would lead to overcoming First Amendment protection without requiring undue speech

2010/05/15/facebook-is-a-utility-utilities-get-regulated.html accessed 21 November 2021.

68 K. Sabeel Rahman, 'The New Utilities: Private Power, Social Infrastructure, and the Revival of the Public Utility Concept' (2018) 39 Cardozo Law Review 1621, 1625.

69 CM/Rec(2020)1 (n. 30).

70 Nikolas Guggenberger, 'Essential Platforms' (2021) 24 Stanford Technology Law Review 237.

71 Regulation (EU) 2019/1150 of the European Parliament and of the Council of 20 June 2019 on promoting fairness and transparency for business users of online intermediation services (2019) OJ L 186/57.

restraints.[72] Similarly, in the field of search engines, Pasquale underlined the threats beyond individual privacy including a range of biased and discriminatory information results.[73] A framework of public utilities would lead online platforms to perform their business while increasing oversight and fairness. Facebook could be encouraged to ensure more diversity in the organisation of content while Amazon could be required to treat all retailers equally. The idea is not to oppose these social infrastructures which are increasingly critical in daily lives but to preclude their social power from overcoming the protection of constitutional values underpinning a democratic society. From services in the market, online platforms have increasingly acquired a foundational or infrastructural role in the algorithmic society. Therefore, the power of online platforms coming from the governance of digital infrastructures would deserve a regulatory framework to protect democratic values in the long run.

This new approach to digital utilities would not push constitutional democracies back to the end of the last century and lead to following a neoliberal perspective based on unaccountable cooperation between the public and private sector. Unlike at the advent of the Internet, the Union can rely on a precedent showing the challenges of going back to digital liberalism at the dawn of artificial intelligence technologies. The new phase of European digital constitutionalism shows that the Union is aware of this situation. Therefore, the primary challenge for the Union in the algorithmic society is how to ensure that the values underpinning these technologies are not entirely determined by unaccountable powers but shaped by democratic processes based on transparent and accountable procedures. This would not mean intervening in the market but providing a common regulatory frame of values and principles based on which private actors may perform their businesses. The overarching value of human dignity can limit the consolidation of powers which abuse constitutional rights.

To ensure that European values at the intersection between digital humanism and capitalism are not left to the determination of private actors, the Union is relying on a mix of hard and co-regulatory strategies. As underlined by Marsden, co-regulation entails that 'the regulatory regime is made up of a complex interaction of general legislation

[72] Susan Crawford, 'First Amendment Common Sense' (2014) 127 Harvard Law Review 2343.

[73] Frank Pasquale, 'Internet Nondiscrimination Principles: Commercial Ethics for Carriers and Search Engines' (2008) University of Chicago Legal Forum 263.

and a self-regulatory body'.[74] Put another way, the European governance strategy is oriented towards avoiding the autonomous constitutionalisation of self-regulation.[75] As clarified in the white paper on artificial intelligence, '[i]t is also essential to make sure that the private sector is fully involved in setting the research and innovation agenda and provides the necessary level of co-investment. This requires setting up a broad-based public private partnership, and securing the commitment of the top management of companies'.[76] The Council of Europe has stressed that states should establish appropriate levels of transparency with regard to the public procurement, use, design and basic processing criteria and methods of algorithmic systems implemented by and for them, or by private sector actors. Even more importantly, it underlined that 'the legislative framework for intellectual property or trade secrets should not preclude such transparency, nor should States or private parties seek to exploit them for this purpose'.[77] To face the adverse human rights impacts of artificial intelligence, it is worth working on 'ethics labels or seals for algorithmic systems to enable users to navigate between systems',[78] while ensuring 'particularly high standards as regards the explainability of processes and outputs'.[79]

Co-regulation implemented through different systems like public-private partnerships or public utilities regulation would be the third way that digital constitutionalism would be promoted in the European framework. Between granting a a hard regulation of the digital environment and leaving the private sector to establish the predominant values, the Union is defining a constitutional framework in between where it provides the values guiding private actors. This form of co-regulation would lead online platforms not to exercise discretionary powers on fundamental rights and democratic values, but as regulated entities driven by a mix of profit maximisation and public purposes. The focus of the Council of Europe, and also the ad-hoc committee on artificial intelligence, known as CAHAI,[80] on the introduction of algorithmic

[74] Christopher Marsden, *Internet Co-Regulation: European Law, Regulatory Governance and Legitimacy in Cyberspace* (Cambridge University Press 2011).
[75] Julia Black, 'Constitutionalising Self-Regulation' (1996) 59 Modern Law Review 24.
[76] COM(2020) 65 final (n. 9).
[77] CM/Rec(2020)1 (n. 30).
[78] Ibid.
[79] Ibid.
[80] CAHAI, 'Feasibility Study on a Legal Framework on AI Design, Development and Application based on Council of Europe's Standards' (17 December 2020)

impact assessment is an evident example of the European way to increase the accountability of the public and private sector when implementing artificial intelligence technologies.[81] As observed by the Council of Europe, '[p]rivate sector actors engaged in the design, development, sale, deployment, implementation and servicing of algorithmic systems, whether in the public or private sphere, must exercise due diligence in respect of human rights'.[82]

Considering the global reach and dissemination of algorithmic technologies, this framework would increasingly underline the role of the Union as a global regulator. Put another way, rather than governing or neglecting market dynamics, the Union is tailoring its role between public authority and private ordering. Nonetheless, being a global regulator would clash with traditional territorial limits to the exercise of sovereign powers. Even if the Union is proposing its approach to algorithmic technologies on a global scale, still the hybrid approach between hard and self-regulation meets constitutional limits. Therefore, the next subsection addresses the third trade-off focusing on whether digital constitutionalism increases the tendency towards extraterritoriality of European values or, instead, promotes a phase of constitutional protectionism to avoid external interferences undermining fundamental rights and democratic values.

7.4 Scope: Constitutional Imperialism versus Constitutional Protectionism

The transnational dimension characterising the values and governance of the algorithmic society leads to focusing on how far European digital constitutionalism could extend its influence to protect fundamental rights and democratic values. If, on the one hand, the Union has proven to be oriented towards a sustainable development of algorithmic technologies and adopting a hybrid governance strategy between public values and private ordering, being a global regulator entails dealing with the external limits of sovereign powers. Territory is the natural limitation of state

www.coe.int/en/web/artificial-intelligence/-/the-feasibility-study-on-ai-legal-standards-adopted-by-cahai accessed 21 November 2021.

[81] Ibid.

[82] Ibid.

sovereignity. Inside that space, citizens are expected to comply with the applicable law in that area while, outside this framework, they would be subject to the influence of other sovereign powers.

As stressed in Chapter 3, the Internet, as an expression of globalisation, has challenged the traditional model to exercise sovereign powers. At the same time, the global reach of digital technologies does not necessarily leave states unarmed against overseas interferences. The cases of China and Russia show how these countries propose alternatives for governing digital technologies which tend to reflect their values.[83] Such influence has not only been domestic but also international. Together with the approach of Russia,[84] China has already tried to dismantle the western multi-stakeholder model by proposing to move Internet governance within the framework of the International Telecommunications Union in 2012.[85]

In the fight for digital sovereignty,[86] countries are following different strategies also in relation to platform power. On the one hand, still the First Amendment provides a shield against any public interference leading US companies to extend their powers and standards of protection beyond its territory. Despite some attempts to deal with platform power at the federal level,[87] and even at the local,[88]

[83] Dennis Broeders and others, 'Coalition of the Unwilling? Chinese and Russian Perspectives on Cyberspace' The Hague Program for Cyber Norms Policy Brief (November 2019) www.thehaguecybernorms.nl/research-and-publication-posts/a-coalition-of-the-unwilling-chinese-and-russian-perspectives-on-cyberspace accessed 21 November 2021; Stanislav Budnitsky and Lianrui Jia, 'Branding Internet Sovereignty: Digital Media and the Chinese–Russian Cyberalliance' (2018) 21(5) European Journal of Cultural Studies 594.

[84] Eva Claessen, 'Reshaping the Internet – The Impact of the Securitisation of Internet Infrastructure on Approaches to Internet Governance: The Case of Russia and the EU' (2020) 5(1) Journal of Cyber Policy 140.

[85] Julia Bader, 'To Sign or Not to Sign. Hegemony, Global Internet Governance, and the International Telecommunication Regulations' (2019) 15(2) Foreign Policy Analysis 244.

[86] Julia Pohle, 'Digital Sovereignty' (2020) 9(4) Internet Policy Review https://policyreview.info/pdf/policyreview-2020-4-1532.pdf accessed 21 November 2021. Stephane Couture and Sophie Toupin. 'What Does the Notion of "Sovereignty" Mean When Referring to the Digital?' (2019) 21(10) New Media & Society 2305. See also Milton L. Mueller, 'Against Sovereignty in Cyberspace' (2020) 22(4) International Studies Review 779; Benjamin H. Bratton, *The Stack. On Software and Sovereignty* (MIT University Press 2016).

[87] See, e.g., the Platform Accountability and Consumer Transparency (PACT) Act (2020).

[88] See, e.g., Sofia Andrade, 'Florida's New Pro-Disney, Anti-Facebook and Twitter Law' Slate (25 May 2021) https://slate.com/technology/2021/05/florida-stop-social-media-censorship-act-disney.html accessed 21 November 2021.

nonetheless, such a liberal approach does not only foster private ordering but also hides an indirect and omissive way to extend constitutional values beyond territorial boundaries. Rather than intervening in the market, the US has not changed its role while observing its rise as a liberal hub of global tech giants. As stressed in Chapter 3, regulating online platforms in the US could affect the smooth development of the leading tech companies in the world while also increasing the transparency of the cooperation between the governments and online platforms in certain sector like security, thus unveiling the invisible handshake.[89] Snowden's revelations have already underlined how far public authorities rely on Internet companies to extend their surveillance programme and escape accountability.[90] Put another way, the US digital sovereignty would benefit from private ordering and the invisible cooperation between public and private actors.

On the other hand, China has always controlled its market from external interferences rather than adopting a liberal approach or exporting values through international economic law. China is only imitating the western conception of the Internet while maintaining control over its businesses. Baidu, Alibaba and Tencent, also known as BAT, are increasingly competing with the dominant power of Google, Apple, Facebook, Amazon, or GAFA. The international success of TikTok is an example of how China aims to attract a global audience of users while supporting its business sector.[91] Besides, the adoption of the Digital Silk Road increasingly makes China a relevant player beyond territorial boundaries. The Huawei model is based on exporting technological power supplying digital infrastructure even in peripheral areas. Put another way, China is only partially opening to digital globalisation while it is maintaining control over the network architecture. This twofold approach is part of what has been called the Beijing effect.[92]

89 Michael Birnhack and Niva Elkin-Koren, 'The Invisible Handshake: The Reemergence of the State in the Digital Environment' (2003) 8(2) Virginia Journal of Law & Technology 1.

90 David Lyon, *Surveillance after Snowden* (Polity Press 2015).

91 Michael Keane and Haiqing Yu, 'A Digital Empire in the Making: China's Outbound Digital Platforms' (2019) 13 International Journal of Communication 4624.

92 Matthew S. Erie and Thomas Streinz, 'The Beijing Effect: China's "Digital Silk Road" as Transnational Data Governance' SSRN (2021) https://papers.ssrn.com/sol3/papers.cfm?abstract_id=3810256 accessed 21 November 2021.

The Union has already shown its ability to influence global dynamics, so that scholars have named such an attitude the 'Brussels effect'.[93] The Union is increasingly aware of its ability to extend its 'regulatory soft power', influencing the policy of other areas of the world in the field of digital technologies. It should not surprise that the Union has also started to build its narrative about digital sovereignty.[94] As underlined by the Commission, 'European technological sovereignty starts from ensuring the integrity and resilience of our data infrastructure, networks and communications' aimed to mitigate 'dependency on other parts of the globe for the most crucial technologies'.[95] This approach does not entail closing European boundaries towards a form of constitutional protectionism but to ensure Europe's ability to define its rules and values in the digital age. Indeed, 'European technological sovereignty is not defined against anyone else, but by focusing on the needs of Europeans and of the European social model',[96] and, as a result, 'the EU will remain open to anyone willing to play by European rules and meet European standards, regardless of where they are based'.[97] These statements suggest that the Union is taking its path towards a leading role in regulating the digital environment and artificial intelligence technologies. Rather than focusing just on promoting the European industry, the Union approach is oriented towards rising as a global standard-maker. Its narrative is not adversarial but cooperative towards external actors while, at the internal level, it is not possible to foresee how digital sovereignty will be articulated at the supranational level or driven by Member States' single actions. This is also why the fight for digital sovereignty is particularly relevant on the external and internal level, especially for the Union.[98]

The GDPR shows the intention of the Union to act as a global regulator. The long arm of European data protection law has been already highlighted in the framework of the Data Protection Directive,[99]

[93] Anu Bradford, *The Brussels Effect. How the European Union Rules the World* (Oxford University Press 2020). See also Joanne Scott, 'Extraterritoriality and Territorial Extension in EU Law' (2018) 62 American Journal of Comparative Law 87.

[94] COM(2020) 67 final (n. 7), 2.

[95] Ibid., 2.

[96] Ibid.

[97] Ibid.

[98] Luciano Floridi, 'The Fight for Digital Sovereignty: What It Is, and Why It Matters, Especially for the EU' (2020) 33 Philosophy and Technology 369.

[99] Lokke Moerel, 'The Long Arm of EU Data Protection Law: Does the Data Protection Directive Apply to Processing of Personal Data of EU Citizens by Websites Worldwide?' (2011) 1(1) International Data Privacy Law 28.

defining the 'global reach of EU law'.[100] The European framework of data protection is finding its path on a global scale,[101] while raising as a model for other legislations across the world.[102] The UN secretary-general has welcomed the European approach by underlining how this measure is inspiring for other countries and encouraged the Union and its Member States to follow this path.[103] Furthermore, the adoption of the GDPR has led a growing number of companies to voluntarily comply with some of the rights and safeguards even for data subjects outside the territory of the Union because protecting privacy and personal data has become a matter of reputation.[104] The recent spread of the pandemic has shown the relevance of data protection safeguards for constitutional democracies when dealing with contact tracing applications or other forms of public surveillance.[105]

Besides, the GDPR has not only become a model at the global level but also provides a scope of application which would extend beyond the European territory. Precisely, even though the data controller is established outside the Union, European data protection law is nevertheless applicable if the processing of personal data implies the provision of products or services to data subjects who are in the Union, and the processing activities are related either to the offering of goods and services in the EU, or to the monitoring of the behaviour of data subjects in the EU.[106] By extending the scope of application of the GDPR also outside the EU framework, the Union adopts a form of constitutional imperialism by imposing its own legal standard of protection on a global scale.

[100] Christopher Kuner, 'The Internet and the Global Reach of EU Law' in Marise Cremona and Joanne Scott (eds.), *EU Law Beyond EU Borders: The Extraterritorial Reach of EU Law* (Oxford University Press 2019).

[101] Paul Schwartz, 'Global Data Privacy: The EU Way' (2019) 94 NYU Law Review 771.

[102] Graham Greenleaf, 'Global Data Privacy Laws 2019: 132 National Laws & Many Bills' (2019) 157 Privacy Laws & Business International Report 14.

[103] Address of the UN Secretary-General to the Italian Senate, 18 December 2019 www.un.org/press/en/2019/sgsm19916.doc.htm accessed 21 November 2021.

[104] Cisco, 'Consumer Privacy Study. The Growing Imperative of Getting Data Privacy Right (November 2019) www.cisco.com/c/dam/en/us/products/collateral/security/cybersecurity-series-2019-cps.pdf accessed 21 November 2021.

[105] Oreste Pollicino, 'Fighting COVID-19 and Protecting Privacy under EU Law. A Proposal Looking at the Roots of European Constitutionalism' EU Law Live (16 May 2020) https://eulawlive.com/weekend-edition/weekend-edition-no17/ accessed 21 November 2021.

[106] GDPR (n. 17), Art. 3(2).

Nonetheless, while it is true that the GDPR is rising as a global model for the protection of privacy and personal data, it is not driven by a mere goal of extraterritoriality or imperialism. Rather, it shows that the Union aims to ensure that formal territorial limitations do not undermine the protection of fundamental rights of privacy and data protection and the related democratic values in the Union. The extraterritorial reach of European data protection law and, in general, of the GDPR can be considered as an 'anti-circumvention mechanism'.[107] The ECJ has contributed to explaining the need to extend European rules to ensure the effective protection of fundamental rights. The GDPR territorial scope of application has codified the doctrine of establishment developed by the ECJ in *Weltimmo* and *Google Spain*.[108] In *Weltimmo*, the ECJ adopted a broad interpretation of the concept of 'establishment' avoiding any formalistic approach linked to the place registration of companies. Likewise, in *Google Spain*, the ECJ underlined this flexible interpretation '[i]n the light of the objective pursued by Directive 95/46, consisting in ensuring effective and complete protection of the fundamental rights and freedoms of natural persons, and in particular their right to privacy, with respect to the processing of personal data'.[109] The consequence of such a rule is twofold. On the one hand, this provision involves jurisdiction. The GDPR's territorial scope of application overcomes the doctrine of establishment developed by the ECJ's case law, since even those entities that are not established in the EU will be subject to the GDPR. On the other hand, the primary consequence of such an extension of territoriality is that of extending European constitutional values globally.

The intention to overcome territorial formalities also drove the ECJ in the *Schrems* case,[110] when it invalidated the Commission's adequacy decision,[111] known as the 'safe harbour agreement', concerning the transfer of personal data from the EU to the United States. In this case, it is possible to observe another manipulation of data protection law

[107] Svetlana Yakovleva and Kristina Irion, 'Toward Compatibility of the EU Trade Policy with the General Data Protection Regulation' (2020) 114 AJIL Unbound 10.

[108] C-230/14 *Weltimmo s.r.o.* v. *Nemzeti Adatvédelmi és Információszabadság Hatóság* (2015).

[109] C-131/12 *Google Spain SL and Google Inc. v Agencia Española de Protección de Datos (AEPD) and Mario Costeja González* (2014).

[110] Case C-362/14 *Maximillian Schrems* v. *Data Protection Commissioner* (2015).

[111] Commission Decision of 26 July 2000 pursuant to Directive 95/46/EC of the European Parliament and of the Council on the adequacy of the protection provided by the safe harbour privacy principles and related frequently asked questions issued by the US Department of Commerce (2000) OJ L 215/7.

extending its boundaries across the Atlantic. Although the Data Protection Directive required US data protection law to ensure an 'adequate' level of protection,[112] the ECJ went beyond this boundary by stating that the safeguards should be 'equivalent' to those granted by EU law to ensure the effective protection of the fundamental rights to privacy and data protection as enshrined in the Charter.[113]

However, this decision did not exhaust the concerns about the safeguards in the transfer of personal data across the Atlantic. The ECJ invalidated the new adequacy decisions (i.e. Privacy Shield),[114] in light of the protection of fundamental rights as also translated into the new framework for personal data transfer introduced by the GDPR.[115] The ECJ went even further assessing the Standard Contractual Clauses (SCCs) framework. Even without invalidating the Commission Decision on the use of these clauses,[116] the ECJ underlined that the equivalent level of protection applies even to this legal instrument. The court expressly underlined the limits of EU law in relation to third countries since SSCs are not capable of binding the authorities of that third country.[117] Therefore, the ECJ recognised the role of the controller established in the Union and the recipient of personal data to check and monitor whether the third country involved ensures an essentially equivalent degree of protection.[118] When this is not the case, the ECJ does not preclude the transfer but underlines the need to set additional safeguards to ensure that degree of protection.[119]

This system has recognised the freedom of business actors to define the standard of protection of personal data across the Atlantic. Besides,

[112] Directive 95/46/EC of the European Parliament and of the Council of 24 October 1995 on the protection of individuals with regard to the processing of personal data and on the free movement of such data (1995) OJ L 281/31, Art. 25.

[113] Oreste Pollicino and Marco Bassini, 'Bridge Is Down, Data Truck Can't Get Through . . . A Critical View of the Schrems Judgment in the Context of European Constitutionalism' (2017) 16 The Global Community Yearbook of International Law and Jurisprudence 245.

[114] Commission Implementing Decision (EU) 2016/1250 of 12 July 2016 pursuant to Directive 95/46/EC of the European Parliament and of the Council on the adequacy of the protection provided by the EU-U.S. Privacy Shield (2016) OJ L 207/1.

[115] C-311/18 *Data Protection Commissioner* v. *Facebook Ireland Limited and Maximillian Schrems* (2020).

[116] Commission Decision of 5 February 2010 on standard contractual clauses for the transfer of personal data to processors established in third countries under Directive 95/46/EC of the European Parliament and of the Council (2010) OJ L 39/5.

[117] Ibid., 136.

[118] Ibid., 135, 137, 142.

[119] Ibid., 133.

Daskal underlined the limits of the entire system since 'there is no guarantee that the companies will win such challenges; they are, after all, ultimately bound by U.S. legal obligations to disclose. And even more importantly, there is absolutely nothing that companies can do to provide the kind of back-end judicial review that the Court demands'.[120]

While these questions are still open, it cannot be excluded that this over-reaching scope of protection beyond European boundaries could affect free speech and the financial interests of other countries and their citizens,[121] and decrease the degree of legal certainty leading to a binary approach which is not scalable.[122] The GDPR has also been criticised for its 'privacy universalism'.[123] Proposing the GDPR as a global model entails exporting a western conception of privacy and data protection that could clash with the values of other areas of the world, especially in peripheral areas of the world, thus opening a new phase of (digital) colonialism together with the US and China.[124]Although other scholars do not share the same concerns, they have observed that 'when a law is applicable extraterritorially, the individual risks being caught in a network of different, sometimes conflicting legal rules requiring simultaneous adherence. The result - conflicts of jurisdiction - may put an excessive burden on the individual, confuse him or her, and undermine the individual's respect for judicial proceedings and create loss of confidence in the validity of law'.[125]

The ECJ has recently highlighted these challenges in the decision *Google* v. *CNIL* where the core of the preliminary questions raised by the French judge aimed to clarify the boundaries of the right to be

[120] Jennifer C. Daskal, 'What Comes Next: The Aftermath of European Court's Blow to Transatlantic Data Transfers' Just Security (17 July 2020) www.justsecurity.org/71485/what-comes-next-the-aftermath-of-european-courts-blow-to-transatlantic-data-transfers/ accessed 21 November 2021.

[121] Dan J. B. Svantesson, 'A "Layered Approach" to the Extraterritoriality of Data Privacy Laws' (2013) 3(4) International Data Privacy Law 278, 1.

[122] Christoper Kuner, 'Extraterritoriality and Regulation of International Data Transfers in EU Data Protection Law' (2015) 5(4) International Data Privacy Law 235.

[123] Payal Arora, 'GDPR - A Global Standard? Privacy Futures, Digital Activism and Surveillance Cultures in the Global South' (2019) 17(5) Surveillance & Society 717.

[124] Micheal Kwet, 'Digital Colonialism: US Empire and the New Imperialism in the Global South' (2019) 60(4) Race & Class 3; Danielle Coleman, 'Digital Colonialism: The 21st Century Scramble for Africa through the Extraction and Control of User Data and the Limitations of Data Protection Laws' (2019) 24 Michigan Journal of Race & Law 417.

[125] Paul De Hert and Michal Czerniawski, 'Expanding the European Data Protection Scope Beyond Territory: Article 3 of the General Data Protection Regulation in its Wider Context' (2016) 6(3) International Data Privacy Law 230, 240.

forgotten online, especially its global scope.[126] Within this framework, the ECJ ruled on a preliminary reference concerning the territorial scope of the right to be forgotten online.

The court observed that the scope of the Data Protection Directive and the GDPR is to guarantee a high level of protection of personal data within the Union and, therefore, a de-referencing covering all the domains of a search engine (i.e. global delisting) would meet this objective. This is because the role of search engines in disseminating information is relevant on a global scale since users can access links to information 'regarding a person whose centre of interests is situated in the Union is thus likely to have immediate and substantial effects on that person within the Union itself'.[127]

Nevertheless, the ECJ underlined the limits of this global approach. Firstly, states around the world do not recognise the right to delist or provide different rules concerning the right to be forgotten online.[128] Even more importantly, since the right to privacy and data protection are not absolute rights, they need to be balanced with other fundamental rights,[129] among which the right to freedom of expression.[130] The protection of these fundamental rights (and, therefore, their balance) is not homogenous around the world. The GDPR does not aim to strike a fair balance between fundamental rights outside the territory of the Union.[131] Before this crossroads, rather than extending the boundaries of data protection law to the global scale, the ECJ followed the opinion of Advocate General Szpunar,[132] thus observing that neither the Data Protection Directive nor the GDPR recognises the right of data subjects to require a search engine like Google to delist content worldwide.[133]

Therefore, although Google falls under the scope of European data protection law, it is not required to delist information outside the territory of Member States. Nonetheless, Member States still maintain the possibility to issue global delisting orders according to their legal framework. The ECJ specified that if, on the one hand, EU law does not require search

[126] Case C-507/17, *Google Inc. v. Commission nationale de l'informatique et des libertés (CNIL)* (2019).

[127] Ibid., 57.

[128] Ibid., 58.

[129] Ibid., 59.

[130] See Cases C-92/09 and C-93/09, *Volker und Markus Schecke GbR and Hartmut Eifert* v. *Land Hessen* (2010) ECR I-11063, 48; Opinion 1/15 EU-Canada PNR Agreement (2017), 136.

[131] GDPR (n. 17) Art. 17(3)(a).

[132] Opinion of Advocate General in C-507/17 (n. 126), 63.

[133] C-507/17 (n. 126), 64.

engines to remove links and information globally, on the other hand, it does not ban this practice. It is for Member States to decide whether extending the territorial scope of judicial and administrative order according to their constitutional framework of protection of privacy and personal data balances with the right to freedom of expression.[134]

The ECJ also explained that the impossibility to require search engines to delist information on a global scale is the result of the lack of cooperation instruments and mechanisms in the field of data protection. The GDPR only provides the supervisory authorities of the Member States with internal instruments of cooperation to come to a joint decision based on weighing a data subject's right to privacy and the protection of personal data against the interest of the public in various Member States in having access to information.[135] Therefore, such instruments of cooperation cannot be applied outside the territory of the Union.

Regarding the second question, concerning the territorial scope of delisting within the territory of the Union, the ECJ observed that the adoption of the GDPR aims to ensure a consistent and high level of protection of personal data in all the territory of the Union and, therefore, delisting should be carried out in respect of the domain names of all Member States.[136] Nonetheless, the ECJ acknowledged that, even within the Union, the interest to accessing information could change between Member States as also shown by the degree of freedom Member States enjoy in defining the boundaries of processing in the field of freedom of expression and information pursuant to Article 85 of the GDPR.[137] In other words, the ECJ underlined not only that freedom of expression does not enjoy the same degree of protection at the international level but also, in Europe, it can vary from one Member State to another. Therefore, it is not possible to provide a general obligation to delist links and information applying to all Member States.

To answer this issue, the court left this decision to national supervisory authorities which through the system of cooperation established by the GDPR should, inter alia, reach 'a consensus and a single decision which is binding on all those authorities and with which the controller must ensure compliance as regards processing activities in the context of all

[134] Case C-617/10, *Åklagaren* v. *Hans Åkerberg Fransson* (2013), 29; C-399/11, *Stefano Melloni* v. *Ministerio Fiscal* (2013), 60.

[135] GDPR (n. 17), Arts. 56, 60–6.

[136] C-507/17 (n. 126), 66.

[137] Ibid., 67.

its establishments in the Union'.[138] Likewise, also with respect to geo-blocking techniques, the ECJ did not interfere with Member States' assessment about these measures but simply recalled, by analogy, that 'these measures must themselves meet all the legal requirements and have the effect of preventing or, at the very least, seriously discouraging Internet users in the Member States from gaining access to the links in question using a search conducted on the basis of that data subject's name'.[139] By distancing itself from Advocate General Szpunar's view on this point,[140] the ECJ decided not to recognise a general removal obligation at the European level but relied on the mechanism of cooperation of national authorities as well as on the discretion of Member States concerning preventive measures.

Just one week later, in *Glawischnig-Piesczek* v. *Facebook*,[141] the court addressed the territorial extension of national injunctions concerning the removal of content. The ECJ observed that the e-Commerce Directive does not provide for any limitation to the territorial scope of the measures that Member States can adopt and, consequently, EU law does not prevent a national order from extending its scope application globally. As a general limit, the ECJ specified that Member States should take into consideration their international obligations given the global dimension of the circulation of content, without either specifying which rules of international law would apply in this case.

With regard to the territorial extension of national orders, the ECJ did not clarify to which rules of international law the Member States should refer to assess the territorial scope of removal orders. Some perspectives on this point can be found in the decision *Google* v. *CNIL*. In this case, the ECJ expressly refers to the potential contrast of a global delisting order with the protection of rights at an international level. Therefore, national competent authorities can strike a fair balance between individuals' right to privacy and data protection with the right to freedom of information. However, the different protection of freedom of expression at a global level would limit the application of the balancing results. Advocate General Szpunar reaches the same conclusion in the Facebook case, explaining that, although EU law leaves Member States

[138] Ibid., 68.

[139] Ibid., 70. See, inter alia, Case C-484/14, *Tobias McFadden* v. *Sony Music Entertainment Germany GmbH* (2016), 96.

[140] Opinion of Advocate General in C-507/17 (n. 126), 78.

[141] Case C-18/18, *Eva Glawischnig-Piesczek* v. *Facebook* (2019).

free to extend the territorial scope of their injunctions outside the territory of the Union, national courts should limit their powers to comply with the principle of international comity.[142]

This trend towards local removal is based not only on the status quo of EU law at the time of the decisions but also on the effects that a general extension of global remove can produce in the field of content and data. As observed by Advocate General Szpunar, a worldwide de-referencing obligation could initiate a 'race to the bottom, to the detriment of freedom of expression, on a European and worldwide scale'.[143] In other words, the ECJ's legitimacy could start a process of cross-fertilisation, thus leading other countries to extend their removal order on a global scale. This could be particularly problematic when looking at authoritarian or illiberal regimes which could exploit this decision to extend their orders, or, more generally, the scope of their system beyond their territories.

Moreover, in *Google* v. *CNIL*, the ECJ explained that the limit for global removal also comes from the lack of intention to confer an extraterritorial scope to the right to erasure established by the GDPR.[144] The lack of cooperation mechanisms between competent authorities extending outside the territory of the Union would confirm this argument. Nevertheless, by supporting this position, the ECJ did not consider that, more generally, the GDPR establishes a broad territorial scope of application covering processing activities related to the offering of goods or services, irrespective of whether a payment of the data subject is required, to such data subjects in the Union; or the monitoring of their behaviour as far as their behaviour takes place within the Union.[145]

Nonetheless, it is worth underlining that the Union has not closed the doors to the possibility of extending the territorial scope of removal orders beyond EU borders. At first glance, the ECJ seems to express an opposite view in the two cases regarding the territorial scope of national orders. On the one hand, in *Google* v. *CNIL*, the ECJ stated that EU law does not require search engines to carry out the delisting of information and links on a global scale. In *Glawischnig-Piesczek* v. *Facebook*, on the other hand, the ECJ explained that there are no obstacles to global removal, but also leaves the evaluation to Member States.

142 Opinion of Advocate General in C-18/18 (n. 141), 100.
143 Ibid., 61.
144 C-507/17 (n. 126), 62.
145 GDPR (n. 17), Art. 3(2).

Although the two judgments may seem opposite, they lead to the same result, namely that EU law does not either impose nor preclude national measures whose scope extends worldwide. This is a decision which rests with Member States which are competent to assess their compliance with international obligations. The e-Commerce Directive does not provide a specific territorial scope of application and the ECJ has not gone further. Otherwise, 'it would have trespassed within the competencies of Member States, which under EU law retain primary legislative power on criminal law matters'.[146] Besides, the reasons for this different approach can be attributed to the different degree of harmonisation of the protection of personal data and defamation as observed by Attorney General Szpunar.[147] Therefore, it is not just an issue concerning public international law but also private international law contributes to influencing the territorial scope of removal orders.[148]

Despite the relevance of this point, leaving Member States free to determine when a national order should be applied globally could lead to different national approaches which would fragment harmonisation goals. This situation is particularly relevant in the framework of the GDPR since it provides a new common framework for Member States in the field of data. While the content framework still relies on the e-Commerce Directive, leaving margins of discretion to Member States, this approach in the field of data is more problematic. On the one hand, the GDPR extends its scope of application to ensure a high degree of protection of fundamental rights of the data subjects. On the other hand, such a framework can be questioned by the autonomy of Member States to decide the reach of the right to be forgotten online. As Zalnieriute explains, '[b]y creating the potential for national data protection authorities to apply stronger protections than those afforded by the GDPR, this decision could be seen as another brick in the "data privacy wall" which the ECJ has built to protect EU citizens'.[149]

[146] Elda Brogi and Marta Maroni, 'Eva Glawischnig-Piesczek v Facebook Ireland Limited: A New Layer of Neutrality' CMPF (7 October 2010) https://cmpf.eui.eu/eva-glawischnig-piesczek-v-facebook-ireland-limited-a-new-layer-of-neutrality/ accessed 21 November 2021.

[147] Opinion Advocate General in C-18/18 (n. 141), 79.

[148] Paolo Cavaliere, 'Glawischnig-Piesczek v Facebook on the Expanding Scope of Internet Service Providers' Monitoring Obligations' (2019) 4 European Data Protection Law 573, 577.

[149] Monika Zalnieriute, 'Google LLC v. Commission Nationale de l'Informatique et des Libertés (CNIL)' (2020) 114(2) American Journal of International Law 261.

Furthermore, even in this case, the ECJ has not focused on the peculiarities of platform activities and the consequences of these decisions on the governance of freedom of expression in the digital space. In *Glawischnig-Piesczek* v. *Facebook*, a local removal order would not eliminate the possibility of accessing the same content – identical or equivalent – through the use of other technological systems or outside the geographical boundaries envisaged by the removal order. This problem is particularly relevant in *Google* v. *CNIL* since it is possible to access different Google domain names around the world easily. The interest in the protection of reputation could also require an extension beyond the borders of the Union to avoid relying just on partial or ineffective remedies. The ECJ recognised that access to the referencing of a link referring to information regarding a person in the Union is likely to have 'immediate and substantial effects on the person'.[150] Therefore, even if this statement is just one side of the balancing activity with the protection of international law on the other side, it leads to contradictory results frustrating data subjects' right to be forgotten due to the potential access to search engines' domain names. Furthermore, to comply with geographical limits, geo-blocking and other technical measures would require an additional effort for platforms, thus increasing the risk of censorship on a global scale and creating a technological barrier for small-medium platforms.

It is possible to observe how one of the consequences of this approach is to increase the regulatory burdens for those entities which, although not established in the Union territory, offer goods and services or monitor the behaviour of data subjects in the Union. In other words, the Union is trying to ensure that formal geography could not constitute a shield to avoid compliance with any regulation. Rather than a European constitutional imperialism, this approach would aim to protect individual fundamental rights,[151] while avoiding businesses escaping from complying with EU law just by virtue of a formal criterion of establishment. Otherwise, the primary risk is to encourage a disproportionate imbalance between businesses operating physically in the territory of a state, and other entities which, by processing data and offering other digital services, would avoid complying with the law of the states in which they perform their business.

[150] C-507/17 (n. 126), 57.

[151] De Hert and Czerniawski (n. 125).

Therefore, the extraterritorial effects of European data protection law does not express a form of constitutional imperialism or protectionism. The need to ensure the protection of fundamental rights in a globalised world leads the Union to exercise a global influence which, at first glance, would be the opposite of constitutional protectionism. At the same time, the Union is aware of the consequences of the extension of constitutional values on the global scale which, according to the ECJ case law, seems to appear an exceptional resort based on Member States' assessment.

The proposal for the Artificial Intelligence Act is an example of this European approach. On the one hand, the scope of the proposal would extend to 'providers placing on the market or putting into service AI systems in the Union, irrespective of whether those providers are established within the Union or in a third country', thus providing a broader territorial coverage which aims to ensure that European standards are taken seriously on a global scale. On the other hand, this instrument can be considered an expression of constitutional protectionism. The top-down approach of the Union, which aims to leave small margins to self-regulation, would be an attempt to protect the internal market from technological standards which would not comply with the European standard of protection, whose beacon, even if less evidently in this case, is the protection of European values and, therefore, fundamental rights and democracy. Rather than making operators accountable for developing and implementing artificial intelligence systems, the regulation aims to prevent the consolidation of standards which, even if far from European constitutional values, could however find a place in the internal market.

This way, the Union is rising as global regulator proposing a transnational model to limit interferences coming from oppressive models of governance based on a wide liberal approach or oppressive public control. In other words, rather than adopting an extraterritorial or protectionist approach, the Union seems to have chosen a third way once again. As in the case of values and governance, the Union has shown its intent to take a third way proposing its role as a global regulator rather than a liberal or authoritarian hub for tech giants. The European constitutional standard would not only promote the sustainable development of artificial intelligence in the long term but also, in the short term, limit and mitigate the competitive advantage of other States.

Such a third way is the result of the role of European digital constitutionalism which, in these years, has demonstrated how rights and freedoms cannot be frustrated just by formal doctrines based on territory and establishment. At the same time, European digital constitutionalism does not express imperialist or protectionist goals but rather proposes a different political and normative model to protect fundamental rights and democratic values on a global scale.

7.5 Conclusions: The Constitutional Lesson Learnt and the Digital Road Ahead

The rise of European digital constitutionalism has shown to what extent the consolidation of the algorithmic society has affected constitutional values underpinning the social contract. The evolution of digital technologies has provided invaluable opportunities for the exercise of fundamental rights and democratic values while unveiling the opaque side of a new system of values and governance which aims at imposing itself globally, notwithstanding the fact that constitutional values are still rooted and fragmented in local traditions.

The unitary state and its laws is slowly replaced by the fragmentation of new institutions expressing their principles and values on a global scale. The traditional notion of the law, as an expression of public authority, seems to be increasingly nuanced and competing with norms (auto)produced by other subsystems. Put another way, from 'law and territory', this research has underlined how the relationship between 'norms and space' is increasingly relevant in the algorithmic society. Non-state actors, private corporations and supranational governance institutions contribute to defining their rules and codes of conduct whose global reach overlaps with the traditional expression of national sovereign power. This scenario should not come as a surprise. It is the inevitable result of globalisation leading to an intertwined scenario made of norms and values at the global level. Such a parallel production of standards and norms for the digital environment inevitably meets local constitutional values. States rely on the possibility to express sovereign powers enjoying the exclusive monopoly on the use of force. International organisations develop standards for the digital environment, while transnational private actors, precisely online platforms, privately determine the boundaries to moderate content and process data, thus rising as social infrastructures. In this process of mutual influence between global and local dynamics, constitutional values are just a small piece of the jigsaw.

This research has demonstrated how, in this framework of legal pluralism defining interrelated normativities, the talent of European constitutionalism has provided a first reaction oriented to the protection of fundamental rights and democratic values in the algorithmic society. The answer to the first research question, 'what are the reasons for the rise of European digital constitutionalism?', has focused on underlining the path leading the Union to move from digital liberalism to a democratic constitutional approach. Vis-à-vis the constitutionalisation of global systems, the Union has entered into a new digital constitutional phase. Chapter 2 analysed how, at the end of the last century, the Union adopted a digital liberal approach oriented to trust in the ability of the internal market to grow thanks to the development of new digital products and services. The fear of overwhelming the market and slowing down the development of this promising technological framework governed the European approach at the end of the last century. The strict regulation of the online environment would have damaged the growth of the internal market, exactly when new technologies were going to revolutionise the entire society and promise new opportunities. The minimum harmonisation adopted in the field of content and data can be considered two examples of the neoliberal approach characterising the first phase of the Union's approach to the digital environment.

The end of this phase was the result of two events which, at the very least, have led to the end of the first (liberal) phase and trigger a new phase of the European path characterised by the role of the ECJ in paving the way towards digital constitutionalism through judicial activism. Precisely, the emergence of the Nice Charter as a bill of rights and the increasing relevance of globalised dynamics and the consolidation of private powers in the digital environment have played a critical role to move the perspective of the Union from economic freedoms to fundamental rights and democratic values. The rise of digital constitutionalism in Europe has been characterised by two primary characteristics. Firstly, the codification of the ECJ's efforts to extend the protection of fundamental rights in the digital environment has translated judicial activism into a regulatory outcome. Secondly, within the framework of the Digital Single Market strategy, the Union also clarified its intentions to limit platform powers by fostering the degree of transparency and accountability of online platforms and asking these actors to protect core values. This phase of European digital constitutionalism has shown the talent of European constitutional law in providing a first reaction not only against public interferences but also against the exercise of digital powers by transnational private actors.

Nonetheless, the reaction of European digital constitutionalism to the challenges of the algorithmic society is not enough to explain the characteristics of digital powers. This is why the second question of this work focused on answering 'what are the characteristics and the limits to platform powers in the digital environment?'. As examined in Chapter 3, the liberal approach adopted at the end of last century has empowered online intermediaries to enforce public policies. Requiring online intermediaries to remove 'illegal' content based on their awareness is an example of delegation to the private sector of functions traditionally vested in public authorities, namely the definition of content legality. This delegation of functions has not been guided by public safeguards like due process, thus leaving online platforms to set their own procedure to moderate content and process personal data on a global scale. This way, platforms have been free to remove content or block accounts without any accountability, no matter if they affected speech on a global scale. Similar considerations can be extended to the field of data where the possibility to easily acquire or even overcome consent and the risk-based approach have recognised data controllers ample margins of discretion in defining the degree of safeguards of personal data in a certain context, thus becoming the arbiters of data protection.

Additionally, the lack of safeguards, mixed with the opportunities offered by the development of algorithmic processing technologies, has led these actors to being able to complement such delegated powers with autonomous ones. Indeed, such a new form of (digital) power is also the result of the capability to extract value from the processing of data and organisation of content through the implementation of artificial intelligence technologies. The private development of digital and automated decision-making technologies has not only challenged the protection of individual fundamental rights such as freedom of expression and data protection. This new technological framework has also empowered online platforms to perform quasi-public functions in the transnational context. It is because of this political, legal and technological framework that the freedom to conduct business has turned into power. Focusing just on the delegation of powers does not provide a clear picture of the power which online platforms exercise when discretionarily setting and enforcing rules driven by private determinations rather than constitutional values. Online platforms vertically order the relationship with users while autonomously setting the rules to enforce and balance users' fundamental rights by using automated decision-making processes without any constitutional safeguard.

These considerations are still not enough to explain the characteristics of digital powers in the algorithmic society. Another critical piece of the constitutional puzzle is at the intersection of the legal regimes of content and data. As examined in Chapter 4, it is possible to understand the consolidation of platform powers by looking at the blurring boundaries of the legal regimes of expression and data in the algorithmic society which, in the phase of digital liberalism, have been conceived on parallel tracks. This choice, which could seem neutral at the end of the last century when online intermediaries performed passive activities, is now questioned by a digital environment made of active providers whose business model is based on the extraction of value from information.

When looking at online platforms, precisely social media and search engines, it is possible to understand the technological intersection between the legal regimes of content and data. These actors operate as data controllers when deciding the means and the purposes of processing personal data while they can also be considered processors for the data they host. On the other hand, platforms actively organise content according to the data they collect from users even if they can rely on an exemption of liability for hosting and organising third-party illicit content. The mix of content and data liability regimes makes it easier for online platforms to shield their activities in the blurring lines between the two systems. The organisation of users' content and the processing of data are part of a unique framework even if the legal regimes of content and data have been conceived on parallel tracks. In other words, the technological divergence between content and data at the end of the last century has converged towards overlapping layers of protection.

This situation leads to wondering whether European digital constitutionalism could provide a solution to the exercise of unaccountable powers in the algorithmic society. In order to unveil the normative side of this phase, the third question of this research aims to examine: 'which remedies can European constitutionalism provide to solve the imbalances of power in the algorithmic society and mitigate the risks for fundamental rights and democratic values?' The rise of digital constitutionalism has been just a first step. The talent of European constitutional law has not just led to a reaction against the rise of digital powers but also proposes a normative framework for protecting democratic values in the long run. Still, the primary issues in the field of content and data led to thinking about the role of European constitutional law in addressing the primary challenges for fundamental rights and democracy in the algorithmic society.

As underlined in Chapter 5, protecting freedom of expression just as a liberty cannot be enough to ensure an effective protection of this fundamental right in the algorithmic society. The process of content moderation has shown how online platforms, as private actors, exercise their powers on freedom of expression on a global scale while maintaining their immunity. Despite the step forward made within the framework of the Digital Single Market strategy, users cannot rely on a clear set of transparency and accountability safeguards in the process of content moderation. They do not usually know the criteria or the logic based on which their expressions are organised and filtered or even removed. The lack of any safeguard and remedy against online platform discretion in moderating content leads to thinking about the instruments that constitutional law may provide to remedy this situation. While the horizontal application of freedom of expression could not be a general solution but just a reactive approach, rethinking media pluralism online could be another way to rely on the states' obligations to ensure not only the negative but also the positive side of freedom of expression. This shift of view would be primarily encouraged by the constitutional humus of the Union whose overarching principle of dignity would limit abuses of power annihilating the protection of other constitutional values. In this case, European constitutional law could promote a uniform regulatory framework of the procedures to moderate content. Such a normative approach would not aim to dismantle the system of platform liability nor regulate speech. Instead, as shown by the Digital Services Act, it consists of limiting platform discretion and introducing procedural safeguards in content moderation.

When moving to the field of data, the normative side of European digital constitutionalism looks slightly different. Unlike in the case of content, individuals can rely on a positive framework of safeguards which aims to mitigate private powers through instruments of transparency and accountability. The GDPR is a paradigmatic example of this approach. Nonetheless, this result does not mean that digital constitutionalism has achieved its purpose. As analysed in Chapter 6, the reactive approach of digital constitutionalism has not been enough to address the challenges of the algorithmic society to privacy and data protection. The GDPR leaves broad margins of discretion by adopting a risk-based approach where the data controller becomes the arbiter of personal data protection. For this reason, in order to preclude such a freedom from turning into forms of power, the normative side of European digital constitutionalism in the field of data consists of providing constitutional guidance. The GDPR includes values underpinning European constitutionalism. Precisely, the principles of human dignity, proportionality and due process are the core driving values of European data protection law. These values can provide the normative interpretation on which lawmakers and courts can rely to scrutinise and mitigate data controllers' discretion, thus maintaining their accountability without overwhelming the private sector with further obligations.

The talent of European constitutionalism in reacting and proposing a normative framework to remedy the exercise of digital powers is only a starting point vis-à-vis the challenges of the algorithmic society. The fourth research question was oriented to understand: 'which paths could the consolidation of European digital constitutionalism open to the Union in the next years?' The previous sections of this chapter have underlined how digital constitutionalism could find its 'third way' to address the challenges of the algorithmic society. In front of the regulatory crossroad of the fourth industrial revolution, the Union seems to have chosen a path towards the development of a sustainable artificial intelligence environment rather than focusing simply on fostering innovation to exploit the potentialities of these technologies or merely impeding their development to protect fundamental rights and democratic values. Likewise, in order to limit autonomous determinations of public values by the private sector, the Union is rising as a global regulator whose approach is based on co-regulation. The challenges raised by self-regulation and the risk of hard regulation have led the Union to choose a third way also in this case by proposing a hybrid system of governance based on a common framework of public values guiding the determinations of the private sector. The scope of this system is another tile of the mosaic. The need to protect fundamental rights and democratic values from global challenges has not led the Union to enter into a phase of constitutional imperialism or protectionism. It has raised a balanced approach which limits the extraterritoriality of European constitutional values while narrowing the scope of formal justifications based on territorial boundaries which could substantially undermine the protection of fundamental rights and democratic values.

These challenges have led the Union to learn an important constitutional lesson. Neoliberal approaches refraining the role of public actors in protecting fundamental rights and democratic values may clash with the characteristics of European constitutionalism. Fundamental rights and democratic values cannot be left in the hands of unaccountable powers which, even if private, make decisions affecting daily lives outside democratic circuits. Against the threats coming from a ubiquitous automation which pushes the role of humans aside, European digital constitutionalism can rely on a set of safeguards and guarantees among which human dignity plays a critical role as a constitutional guidance. These characteristics would reveal the mission of European digital constitutionalism: rising as a shield against the discretionary exercise of powers which puts humans under a new *status subjectionis* driven by the logics of digital capitalism. European constitutions do not consider human beings and their identity based on capitalistic logics. European constitutionalism protects dignity even when humans do not meet the expectation of a capitalist system to protect them from its consequences, such as poverty and inequality. Within this framework, European digital constitutionalism would constitute a limit to a process of dehumanisation driven by digital capitalism. Even if the challenges of the algorithmic society cannot be compared to the horror of the last century, constitutional democracies should be concerned about the rise and consolidation of powers outside any control.

A fourth phase or a more mature expression of digital constitutionalism would aim to oppose techno-determinist solutions and contribute to promoting European values as a sustainable constitutional model for the development of automated technologies in the global context. Therefore, the primary goal of digital constitutionalism in the algorithmic society is to promote and safeguard constitutional values from the rise of unaccountable digital powers. The road ahead of digital constitutionalism is far from being straight but the path already made so far seems to be promising.

Bibliography

Abrams F., *The Soul of the First Amendment* (Yale University Press 2017).

Ackerman B., *We The People: Transformations* (Belknap Press 1998).

Alexy R., *A Theory of Constitutional Rights* (Oxford University Press 2002).

Alexy R., *A Theory of Rights* (Oxford University Press 1985).

Ali M. and others, 'Discrimination through Optimization: How Facebook's Ad Delivery Can Lead to Biased Outcomes' in *Proceedings of the ACM on Human-Computer Interaction* (ACM 2019).

Allgood B., 'The Commoditization of AI and The Long-Term Value of Data' Forbes (10 April 2017) www.forbes.com/sites/forbestechcouncil/2017/04/10/the-commoditization-of-ai-and-the-long-term-value-of-data/#74c71abd159c.

Alter A., *Irresistible: The Rise of Addictive Technology and the Business of Keeping us Hooked* (Penguin Press 2017).

Ammori M., 'The "New" New York Times: Free Speech Lawyering in the Age of Google and Twitter' (2014) 127 Harvard Law Review 2259.

Andrade S., 'Florida's New Pro-Disney, Anti-Facebook and Twitter Law' Slate (25 May 2021) https://slate.com/technology/2021/05/florida-stop-social-media-censorship-act-disney.html.

Araya D., 'Governing The Fourth Industrial Revolution' Forbes (12 May 2019) www.forbes.com/sites/danielaraya/2019/03/12/governing-the-fourth-industrialrevolution/#4eea13a14b33.

Arendt H., *The Human Condition* (University of Chicago Press 1998).

Arora P., 'GDPR – A Global Standard? Privacy Futures, Digital Activism and Surveillance Cultures in the Global South' (2019) 17(5) Surveillance & Society 717.

Augenstein D. and Dziedzic L., 'State Responsibilities to Regulate and Adjudicate Corporate Activities under the European Convention on Human Rights' (2017) EUI Working papers https://cadmus.eui.eu/bitstream/handle/1814/48326/LAW_2017_15.pdf?sequence=1&isAllowed=y.

Bader J., 'To Sign or Not to Sign. Hegemony, Global Internet Governance, and the International Telecommunication Regulations' (2019) 15(2) Foreign Policy Analysis 244.

Bagger Tranberg, C., 'Proportionality and Data Protection in the Case Law of the European Court of Justice' (2011) 1 International Data Privacy Law 239.

Balkin J. M., 'Digital Speech and Democratic Culture: A Theory of Freedom of Expression for the Information Society' (2004) 79 New York University Law Review 1.

Balkin J. M., 'Free Speech and Hostile Environments' (1999) 99 Columbia Law Review 2295.

Balkin J. M., 'Free Speech in the Algorithmic Society: Big Data, Private Governance, and New School Speech Regulation' (2018) 51 U.C. Davis Law Review 1151.

Balkin, J. M., 'Information Fiduciaries and the First Amendment' (2016) 49 UC Davis Law Review 1183.

Balkin J. M., 'Old-School/New-School Speech Regulation' (2014) 127 Harvard Law Review 2296.

Balkin J. M., 'The Fiduciary Model of Privacy' (2020) 134(1) Harvard Law Review Forum 11.

Balkin J. M., 'The Future of Free Expression in a Digital Age' (2009) 36 Pepperdine Law Review 427.

Barak A., *Proportionality Constitutional Rights and their Limitations* (Cambridge University Press 2012).

Barata J., 'New EU Proposal on the Prevention of Terrorist Content Online', CIS Stanford Law (2018) https://cyberlaw.stanford.edu/files/publication/files/2018.10.11.Comment.Terrorism.pdf.

Barber N., The Principles of Constitutionalism (Oxford University Press 2018).

Barendt E., 'Balancing Freedom of Expression and Privacy' (2009) 1(1) Journal of Media Law 49.

Barendt E., *Freedom of Speech* (Oxford University Press 2017).

Barkan J., 'Law and the Geographic Analysis of Economic Globalization' (2011) 35(5) Progress in Human Geography 589.

Barlow J. P., 'The Economy of Ideas: Selling Wine Without Bottles on the Global Net' in Peter Ludlow (ed.), *High Noon on the Electronic Frontier: Conceptual Issues in Cyberspace* (MIT Press 1999).

Barocas S. and others, 'Governing Algorithms: A Provocation Piece', SSRN (4 April 2013) https://ssrn.com/abstract=2245322.

Barocas S. and Selbst A. D., 'Big Data's Disparate Impact' (2016) 104 California Law Review 671.

Barocas S., Hood S. and Ziewitz M., 'Governing Algorithms: A Provocation Piece' (2013) https://ssrn.com/abstract=2245322.

Barron P. and Morrison S., 'Pluralism after Scarcity: The Benefits of Digital Technologies' LSE Media Policy Project blog (18 November 2014) http://blogs.lse.ac.uk/mediapolicyproject/2014/11/18/pluralism-after-scarcity-the-benefits-of-digital-technologies/.

Bartole S., *The Internationalisation of Constitutional Law* (Hart 2020).

Barzilai-Nahon K., 'Toward a Theory of Network Gatekeeping: A Framework for Exploring Information Control' (2008) 59(9) Journal of the American Society for Information Science and Technology 1493.

Bassini M., 'Fundamental Rights and Private Enforcement in the Digital Age' (2019) 25(2) European Law Journal 182.

Bassini M., 'Mambo Italiano: The Italian Perilous Way on ISP Liability' in Tuomas Ojanen and Byliana Petkova (eds), *Fundamental Rights Protection Online: The Future Regulation of Intermediaries* (Edward Elgar 2020).

Bathaee Y., 'The Artificial Intelligence Black Box and the Failure of Intent and Causation' (2018) 31(2) Harvard Journal of Law & Technology 890.

Bayer J. and Carrera S., 'A Comparative Analysis of Media Freedom and Pluralism in the EU Member States' (2016) Study for the LIBE Committee www.europarl.europa.eu/RegData/etudes/STUD/2016/571376/IPOL_STU(2016)571376_EN.pdf.

Becchi P., 'Human Dignity in Europe: Introduction' in Paolo Becchi and Klaus Mathis (eds.), *Handbook of Human Dignity in Europe* (Springer 2019).

Beijer M., *The Limits of Fundamental Rights Protection by the EU: The Scope for the Development of Positive Obligations* 297 (Intersentia 2017).

Bell E. and Owen T., 'The Platform Press: How Silicon Valley Reengineered Journalism' Tow Centre for Digital Journalism (29 March 2017) www.cjr.org/tow_center_reports/platform-press-how-silicon-valley-reengineered-journalism.php.

Belli L., Francisco P. A. and Zingales N., 'Law of the Land or Law of the Platform? Beware of the Privatisation of Regulation and Police' in Luca Belli and Nicolo Zingales (eds.), *How Platforms Are Regulated and How They Regulate Us* (FGV Rio 2017).

Belli L. and Venturini J., 'Private Ordering and the Rise of Terms of Service as Cyber-Regulation' (2016) 5(4) Internet Policy Review https://policyreview.info/node/441/pdf.

Ben-Shahar O. and Schneider C. E., *More than You Wanted to Know: The Failure of Mandated Disclosure* (Princeton University Press 2016).

Benkler Y., 'Degrees of Freedom Dimension and Power' (2016) 145 Daedalus 18.

Benkler Y., *The Wealth of Networks: How Social Production Transforms Markets and Freedom* (Yale University Press 2006).

Berman P. S., 'Cyberspace and the State Action Debate: The Cultural Value of Applying Constitutional Norms to "Private" Regulation' (2000) 71 University of Colorado Law Review 1263.

Berman P. S., Global Legal Pluralism: A Jurisprudence of Law beyond Borders (Cambridge University Press 2012).

Bilić P., 'Search Algorithms, Hidden Labour and Information Control' (2016) 3(1) Big Data & Society 1

Binns R., 'Data Protection Impact Assessment: A Meta-Regulatory Approach' (2017) 7 (1) International Data Privacy Law 22.

Binns R. and Veale M., 'Is that Your Final Decision? Multi-stage Profiling, Selective Effects, and Article 22 of the GDPR' (2021) International Data Privacy

Law https://academic.oup.com/idpl/advance-article/doi/10.1093/idpl/ipab020/6403925?login=true.

Binns R. and others, 'Like Trainer, Like Bot? Inheritance of Bias in Algorithmic Content Moderation' in Giovanni L. Ciampaglia, Afra Mashhadi and Taha Yasseri (eds.), *Social Informatics* (Springer 2017).

Birnhack M. and Elkin-Koren N., 'The Invisible Handshake: The Reemergence of the State in the Digital Environment' (2003) 8 Virginia Journal of Law and Technology 6.

Black J., 'Constitutionalising Self-Regulation' (1996) 59 Modern Law Review 24.

Bloch-Webba H., 'Global Platform Governance: Private Power in the Shadow of the State' (2019) 72 SMU Law Review 27.

Blocher J., 'Institutions in the Marketplace of Ideas' (2008) 57(4) Duke Law Journal 820.

Boehme-Neßler V., 'Privacy: A Matter of Democracy. Why Democracy Needs Privacy and Data Protection' (2016) 6(3) International Data Privacy Law 222.

Bognetti G., 'The Concept of Human Dignity in European and U.S. Constitutionalism' in Georg Nolte (ed.), *European and US Constitutionalism* (Cambridge University Press 2005).

Bollinger L. C. and Stone G. R. (eds.), *The Free Speech Century* (Oxford University Press 2019).

Bond S., 'Google and Facebook Build Digital Duopoly' Financial Times (14 March 2017) ft.com/content/30c81d12-08c8-11e7-97d1-5e720a26771b.

Boyd D., 'Facebook Is a Utility; Utilities Get Regulated' Apophenia (15 May 2010) www.zephoria.org/thoughts/archives/2010/05/15/facebook-is-a-utility-utilities-get-regulated.html.

Boyd D. and Crawford K., 'Critical Questions for Big Data: Provocations for a Cultural, Technological, and Scholarly Phenomenon' (2015) 15 Information Communication and Society 662.

Boyle J., 'A Nondelegation Doctrine for the Digital Age?' (2000) 50 Duke Law Journal 5.

Boyle J., 'Foucault in Cyberspace: Surveillance, Sovereignty, and Hardwired Censors' (1997) 66 University of Cincinnati Law Review 177.

Bozdag E., 'Bias in Algorithmic Filtering and Personalization' 15(3) Ethics and Information Technology 209.

Bradford A., *The Brussels Effect. How the European Union Rules the World* (Oxford University Press 2020).

Brand P. and Getzler J. (eds.), *Judges and Judging in the History of the Common Law and Civil Law: From Antiquity to Modern Times* (Cambridge University Press 2015).

Brandeis L. D., 'The Curse of Bigness' in Osmond K. Fraenkel (ed.), *The Curse of Bigness: Miscellaneous Papers of Louis D. Brandeis* (Viking Press 1934).

Brauneis R. and Goodman E. P., 'Algorithmic Transparency for the Smart City' (2018) 20 Yale Journal of Law and Technology 103.

Brey P. A. E. and Soraker J., *Philosophy of Computing and Information Technology* (Elsevier 2009).

Brietzke P. H., 'How and Why the Marketplace of Ideas Fails' (1997) 31(3) Valparaiso University Law Review 951.

Brison J., 'The Artificial Intelligence of the Ethics of Artificial Intelligence: An Introductory Overview for Law and Regulation' in Markus D. Dubber, Frank Pasquale and Sunit Das (eds.), *The Oxford Handbook on Ethics of AI* (Oxford University Press 2020).

Brkan M., 'Freedom of Expression and Artificial Intelligence: On Personalisation, Disinformation and (Lack Of) Horizontal Effect of the Charter' SSRN (17 March 2019) https://papers.ssrn.com/sol3/papers.cfm?abstract_id=3354180.

Broeders D. and others, 'Coalition of the Unwilling? Chinese and Russian Perspectives on Cyberspace' The Hague Program for Cyber Norms Policy Brief (November 2019) www.thehaguecybernorms.nl/research-and-publication-posts/a-coalition-of-the-unwilling-chinese-and-russian-perspectives-on-cyberspace.

Brogi E. and Maroni M., 'Eva Glawischnig-Piesczek v Facebook Ireland Limited: A New Layer of Neutrality' CMPF (7 October 2010) https://cmpf.eui.eu/eva-glawischnig-piesczek-v-facebook-ireland-limited-a-new-layer-of-neutrality/.

Brown I. and Marsden C., *Regulating Code: Good Governance and Better Regulation in the Information Age* (MIT Press 2013).

Bucher T., 'Want to Be on the Top? Algorithmic Power and the Threat of Invisibility on Facebook' (2012) 14(7) New Media & Society 1164.

Budnitsky S. and Jia L., 'Branding Internet Sovereignty: Digital Media and the Chinese–Russian Cyberalliance' (2018) 21(5) European Journal of Cultural Studies 594.

Burrell J., 'How the Machine "Thinks": Understanding Opacity in Machine Learning Algorithms' (2016) 3 Big Data & Society https://journals.sagepub.com/doi/full/10.1177/2053951715622512.

Burris S, Drahos P. and Shearing C., 'Nodal Governance' (2005) 30 Australian Journal of Law and Policy 30.

Busch C. and others, 'The Rise of the Platform Economy: A New Challenge for EU Consumer Law?' (2016) 5 Journal of European Consumer and Market Law 3.

Bygrave L. A., *Data Protection Law: Approaching Its Rationale, Logic and Limits* (Wolters Kluwer 2002).

Bygrave L. A., *Internet Governance by Contract* (Oxford University Press 2015).

Calo R., 'Artificial Intelligence Policy: A Primer and Roadmap' (2017) 51 UC Davis Law Review 399.

Calliess G. and Zumbansen P., *Rough Consensus and Running Code: A Theory of Transnational Private Law* (Hart 2010).

Cantwell Smit B., *The Promise of Artificial Intelligence. Reckoning and Judgment* (MIT Press 2019).

Cartabia M., 'Europe and Rights: Taking Dialogue Seriously' (2009) 5 European Constitutional Law Review 5.

Cartwright M., 'Internationalising State Power through the Internet: Google, Huawei and Geopolitical Struggle' (2020) 9(3) Internet Policy Review https://policyreview.info/node/1494/pdf.

Casey B., Farhangi A. and Vogl R., 'Rethinking Explainable Machines: The GDPR's "Right to Explanation" Debate and the Rise of Algorithmic Audits in Enterprise' (2019) 34 Berkeley Technology Law Journal 143.

Castells M., *Networks of Outrage and Hope: Social Movements in the Internet Age* (Polity Press 2012).

Castells M., *The Rise of the Network Society: The Information Age: Economy, Society, and Culture* (Blackwell 2009).

Cauffman C. and Goanta C., 'A New Order: The Digital Services Act and Consumer Protection' (2021) European Journal of Risk Regulation 1.

Cavaliere P., 'Glawischnig-Piesczek v Facebook on the Expanding Scope of Internet Service Providers' Monitoring Obligations' (2019) 4 European Data Protection Law 573.

Celeste E., 'Digital Constitutionalism: A New Systematic Theorization' (2019) 33 (1) International Review of Law, Computers and Technology 76.

Celeste E., 'Terms of Service and Bills of Rights: New Mechanisms of Constitutionalisation in the Social Media Environment?' (2018) 33(2) International Review of Law, Computers & Technology 122.

Chander A., 'Facebookistan' (2012) 90 North Carolina Law Review 1807.

Chander A. and P Le U., 'Data Nationalism' (2015) 64(3) Emory Law Journal 677.

Chenou J. M., 'From Cyber-Libertarianism to Neoliberalism: Internet Exceptionalism, Multi-stakeholderism, and the Institutionalisation of Internet Governance in the 1990s' (2014) 11(2) Globalizations 205.

Chenou J. M. and Radu R., 'The "Right to Be Forgotten": Negotiating Public and Private Ordering in the European Union' (2017) 58 Business & Society 74.

Christou G., and Simpson S., 'The Internet and Public–Private Governance in the European Union' (2006) 26(1) Journal of Public Policy 43.

Citron D. K., 'Technological Due Process' (2008) 85 Washington University Law Review 1249.

Citron D. K. and Norton H. L., 'Intermediaries and Hate Speech: Fostering Digital Citizenship for our Information Age' (2011) 91 Boston University Law Review 1436.

Citron D. K. and Pasquale F., 'The Scored Society: Due Process for Automated Predictions' (2014) 89 Washington University Law Review 1.

Citron D. K. and Wittes B., 'The Internet Will Not Break: Denying Bad Samaritans § 230 Immunity' (2017) 86 Fordham Law Review 401.

Civil M. da Internet, Law no. 12.965 (2014); Dichiarazione dei diritti in Internet (2015).

Claessen E., 'Reshaping the Internet – The Impact of the Securitisation of Internet Infrastructure on Approaches to Internet Governance: The Case of Russia and the EU' (2020) 5(1) Journal of Cyber Policy 140.

Clark J. and others, 'The Shifting Landscape of Global Internet Censorship' (2017) Berkman Klein Center for Internet & Society Research Publication https://dash.harvard.edu/handle/1/33084425.

Coase R., 'Markets for Goods and Market for Ideas' (1974) 64(2) American Economic Review 1974.

Cobbe J. and Bietti E., 'Rethinking Digital Platforms for the Post-COVID-19 Era' CIGI (12 May 2020) www.cigionline.org/articles/rethinking-digital-platforms-post-covid-19-era.

Coeckelbergh M., *AI Ethics* (MIT Press 2020).

Cohen J., *Between Truth and Power: The Legal Constructions of Informational Capitalism* (Oxford University Press 2019).

Cohen J., 'Intellectual Privacy and Censorship of the Internet' (1998) 8(3) Seton Hall Constitutional Law Journal 693.

Cohen J. E., 'What Privacy Is For' (2013) 126 Harvard Law Review 1904.

Cohen M. R., 'Property and Sovereignty' (1927) 13 Cornell Law Review 8.

Colombi Ciacchi A., 'Judicial Governance in European Private Law: Three Judicial Cultures of Fundamental Rights Horizontality' (2020) 4 European Review of Private Law 931.

Craig P., 'EU Accession to the ECHR: Competence, Procedure and Substance' (2013) 35 Fordham International Law Journal 111.

Couture S. and Toupin S. 'What Does the Notion of "Sovereignty" Mean When Referring to the Digital?' (2019) 21(10) New Media & Society 2305.

Crawford K. and Gillespie T., 'What Is a Flag for? Social Media Reporting Tools and the Vocabulary of Complaint' (2016) 18 New Media & Society 410.

Crawford K. and Schultz J., 'Big Data and Due Process: Toward a Framework to Redress Predictive Privacy Harms' (2014) 55 Boston College Law Review 93.

Crawford S., 'First Amendment Common Sense' (2014) 127 Harvard Law Review 2343.

Cumbley R. and Church P., 'Is Big Data Creepy?' (2013) 29 Computer Law and Security Review 601.

Custers B. and others (eds.), *Discrimination and Privacy in the Information Society* (Springer 2013).

D'Acquisto G. and others, 'Privacy by Design in Big Data. An Overview of Privacy Enhancing Technologies in the Era of Big Data Analytics', ENISA (December 2015) www.enisa.europa.eu/publications/big-data-protection.

D'Arcus B., 'Extraordinary Rendition, Law and the Spatial Architecture of Rights' (2014) 13 ACME: An International E-Journal for Critical Geographies 79.

Dainow J., 'The Civil Law and the Common Law: Some Points of Comparison' (1966–7) 15(3) American Journal of Comparative 419.

Daly A., *Private Power, Online Information Flows and EU Law. Mind the Gap* (Hart 2016).

Danaher J., 'The Threat of Algocracy: Reality, Resistance and Accommodation' (2016) 29 Philosophy & Technology 245.

Daskal J., 'What Comes Next: The Aftermath of European Court's Blow to Transatlantic Data Transfers' Just Security (17 July 2020) www.justsecurity.org/71485/what-comes-next-the-aftermath-of-european-courts-blow-to-transatlantic-data-transfers/.

Daskal J. C., 'Borders and Bits' (2018) 71 Vanderbilt Law Review 179.

de Burca G., 'The Road Not Taken: The EU as a Global Human Rights Actor' (2011) 105(4) American Journal of International Law 649.
de Burca G. and Aschenbrenner J. B., 'The Development of European Constitutionalism and the Role of the EU Charter of Fundamental Rights' (2003) 9 Columbia Journal of European Law 355.
de Búrca G. and Weiler J. H. H. (eds.), *The Worlds of European Constitutionalism* (Cambridge University Press 2012).
de Burca G., 'After the EU Charter of Fundamental Rights: The Court of Justice as a Human Rights Adjudicator?' (2013) 20(2) Maastricht Journal of European and Comparative Law 168.
De Gregorio G., 'From Constitutional Freedoms to Powers: Protecting Fundamental Rights Online in the Algorithmic Society' (2019) 11(2) European Journal of Legal Studies 65.
De Gregorio G. and Radu R., 'Trump's Executive Order: Another Tile in the Mosaic of Governing Online Speech' MediaLaws (6 June 2020) www.medialaws.eu/trumps-executive-order-another-tile-in-the-mosaic-of-governing-online-speech/.
De Gregorio G. and Stremlau N., 'Internet Shutdowns and the Limits of Law' (2020) 14 International Journal of Communication 4224.
De Gregorio G., Pollicino O. and Perotti E., 'Flexing the Muscles of Information Power: On the Australian News Media Mandatory Bargaining Code' (2021) Verfassungsblog (26 February 2021) https://verfassungsblog.de/facebook-flexing/.
De Hert P., 'A Human Rights Perspective on Privacy and Data Protection Impact Assessments', in David Wright and Paul De Hert (eds.), *Privacy Impact Assessment* (Springer 2012).
De Hert P., 'Biometrics and the Challenge to Human Rights in Europe. Need for Regulation and Regulatory Distinctions' in Patrizio Campisi (ed.), *Security and Privacy in Biometrics* (Springer 2013).
De Hert P. and Czerniawski M., 'Expanding the European Data Protection Scope Beyond Territory: Article 3 of the General Data Protection Regulation in its Wider Context' (2016) 6(3) International Data Privacy Law 230.
De Hert P. and Gutwirth S., 'Data Protection in the Case Law of Strasbourg and Luxembourg: Constitutionalisation in Action' in Serge Gutwirth and others (eds.), *Reinventing Data Protection* (Springer 2009).
De Hert P. and Kloza D., 'Internet (Access) as a new Fundamental Right. Inflating the Current Rights Framework?' (2012) 3(2) European Journal of Law and Technology www.ejlt.org/index.php/ejlt/article/view/123/268.
De Hert P. and others, 'The Right to Data Portability in GDPR: Towards User-Centric Interoperability of Digital Services' (2018) 34(2) Computer Law & Security Review 193.
de Hing A., 'Some Reflections on Dignity as an Alternative Legal Concept in Data Protection Regulation' (2018) 19(5) German Law Journal 1270.
De Nardis L., *The Internet in Everything: Freedom and Security in a World with No Off Switch* (Yale University Press 2020).

De Secondat C., *L'esprit des loi* (1748).

De Witte B. and Imanovic S., 'Opinion 2/13 on Accession to the ECHR: Defending the EU Legal Order against a Foreign Human Rights Court' (2015) 5 European Law Review 683.

Deakin S. and Markou C., 'Ex Machina Lex: Exploring the Limits of Legal Computability' in Simon Deakin and Christopher Markou (eds.), *Is Law Computable? Critical Perspectives on Law and Artificial Intelligence* (Hart Publishing 2020).

Deibert R. and others, *Access Denied: The Practice and Policy of Global Internet Filtering* (MIT Press 2008).

Delaney D. 'Legal Geography I: Constitutivities, Complexities, and Contingencies' (1996) 39(1) Progress in Human Geographies 96.

Della Cananea G., *Due Process of Law Beyond the State: Requirements of Administrative Procedure* (Oxford University Press 2016).

Devins C. and others, 'The Law and Big Data' (2017) 27 Cornell Journal of Law & Public Policy 357.

DeVito M. A., 'From Editors to Algorithms' (2017) 5(6) Digital Journalism 753.

Diakopoulos N., 'Algorithmic Accountability. Journalistic Investigation of Computational Power Structures' (2014) 3 Digital Journalism 398.

Dignum V., *Responsible Artificial Intelligence* (Springer 2019).

Dinwoodie G. B. (ed.), *Secondary Liability of Internet Service Providers* (Springer 2017).

Douek E., 'Facebook's "Oversight Board:" Move Fast with Stable Infrastructure and Humility' (2019) 21(1) North Carolina Journal of Law & Technology 1.

Douglas-Scott S., 'A Tale of Two Courts: Luxembourg, Strasbourg and the Growing European Human Rights Acquis' (2006) 43 Common Market Law Review 629.

Douglas-Scott S., 'The European Union and Human Rights after the Treaty of Lisbon' (2011) 11(4) Human Rights Law Review 645.

Douglas-Scott S., 'The Relationship between the EU and the ECHR Five Years on from the Treaty of Lisbon' in Sybe De Vries, Ulf Bernitz and Stephen Weatherill (eds.), *The EU Charter of Fundamental Rights as a Binding Instrument: Five Years Old and Growing* (Hart 2015).

Dreyer S. and Schulz W., 'The General Data Protection Regulation and Automated Decision-Making: Will It Deliver?: Potentials and Limitations in Ensuring the Rights and Freedoms of Individuals, Groups and Society as a Whole' (2019) Bertelsmann Stiftung www.bertelsmann-stiftung.de/doi/10.11586/2018018.

Dupré C., *The Age of Dignity Human Rights and Constitutionalism in Europe* (Hart 2015).

Dworkin R., *Freedom's Law: The Moral Reading of the American Constitution* (Oxford University Press 1999).

Dwoskin E. and Tiku N., 'Facebook Sent Home Thousands of Human Moderators due to the Coronavirus. Now the Algorithms are in Charge' The Washington

Post (24 March 2020) www.washingtonpost.com/technology/2020/03/23/face book-moderators-coronavirus/.

Dylko I. and others, 'The Dark Side of Technology: An Experimental Investigation of the Influence of Customizability Technology on Online Political Selective Exposure' (2017) 73 Computers in Human Behavior 181.

Easterbrook F. H., 'Cyberspace and the Law of the Horse' (1996) University of Chicago Legal Forum 207.

Edwards L., 'Privacy, Security and Data Protection in Smart Cities: A Critical EU Law Perspective' (2016) 1 European Data Protection Law 26.

Edwards L., 'The Problem of Intermediary Service Provider Liability' in Lilian Edwards (ed.), *The New Legal Framework for E-Commerce in Europe* (Hart 2005).

Edwards L. and Veale M., 'Slave to the Algorithm? Why a "Right to an Explanation" Is Probably Not the Remedy You Are Looking For' (2017) 16 Duke Law & Technology Review 18.

Eichensehr K. E., 'Digital Switzerlands' (2018) 167 University Pennsylvania Law Review 665.

El Emam K. and lvarez C. A., 'A Critical Appraisal of the Article Working Party Opinion 05/2014 on Data Anonymization Techniques' (2015) 5 International Data Privacy Law 73.

Elkin Koren N., De Gregorio G. and Perel M., 'Social Media as Contractual Networks: A Bottom up Check on Content Moderation' Iowa Law Review, forthcoming.

Elkin-Koren N. and Haber E., 'Governance by Proxy: Cyber Challenges to Civil Liberties' (2017) 82(1) Brooklyn Law Review 105.

Elkin-Koren N. and Perel M., 'Guarding the Guardians: Content Moderation by Online Intermediaries and the Rule of Law' in Giancarlo Frosio (ed.), *Oxford Handbook of Online Intermediary Liability* (Oxford University Press 2020).

Erdos D., 'From the Scylla of Restriction to the Charybdis of Licence? Exploring the Scope of the "Special Purposes" Freedom of Expression Shield in European Data Protection' (2015) 52 Common Market Law Review 119.

Erdos D., 'Intermediary Publishers and European Data Protection: Delimiting the Ambit of Responsibility for Third-Party Rights through a Synthetic Interpretation of the EU Acquis' (2018) 26 International Journal of Law and Information Technology 189.

Erie M. S. and Streinz T., 'The Beijing Effect: China's "Digital Silk Road" as Transnational Data Governance' SSRN (23 March 2021) https://papers .ssrn.com/sol3/papers.cfm?abstract_id=3810256.

Evans D. S., 'Governing Bad Behavior by Users of Multi-Sided Platforms' (2012) 27 Berkeley Technology Law Journal 1201.

Fabbrini F., 'The European Court of Justice Ruling in the Data Rentention Case and its Lessons for Privacy and Surveillance in the U.S.' (2015) 28 Harvard Human Rights Journal 65.

Favaretto M., De Clercq E. and Elger B. S., 'Big Data and Discrimination: Perils, Promises and Solutions. A Systematic Review' (2019) 6 Journal of Big Data 12.

Feather J., *The Information Society: A Study of Continuity and Change* (American Library Association 2013).

Feeley M., 'EU Internet Regulation Policy: The Rise of Self-Regulation' (1999) 22 (1) Boston College International and Comparative Law Review 159.

Festinger L., *A Theory of Cognitive Dissonance* (Stanford University Press 1957).

Fichera M., *The Foundations of the EU as a Polity* (Edward Elgar 2018).

Finck M. and Pallas F., 'They who Must not be Identified – Distinguishing Personal from Non-Personal Data under the GDPR' (2020) 10(1) International Data Privacy Law 11, 11.

Fisher M., 'Inside Facebook's Secret Rulebook for Global Political Speech' New York Times (27 December 2018) www.nytimes.com/2018/12/27/world/facebook-moderators.html.

Fitzgerald B., 'Software as Discourse – A Constitutionalism for Information Society' (1999) 24 Alternative Legal Journal 144.

Fleishmandec G., 'Cartoon Captures Spirit of the Internet' The New York Times (14 December 2000) www.nytimes.com/2000/12/14/technology/cartoon-captures-spirit-of-the-internet.html.

Fletcher R. and Nielsen R. K., 'Are News Audiences Increasingly Fragmented? A Cross-National Comparative Analysis of Cross-Platform News Audience Fragmentation and Duplication' (2017) 67(4) Journal of Communication 476.

Flew T. and others, 'Internet Regulation as Media Policy: Rethinking the Question of Digital Communication Platform Governance' (2019) 10(1) Journal of Digital Media & Policy 33.

Floridi L., 'AI and Its New Winter: From Myths to Realities' (2020) 33 Philosophy & Technology 1.

Floridi L., 'On Human Dignity as a Foundation for the Right to Privacy' (2016) 29 Philosophy & Technology 307.

Floridi L., 'The Fight for Digital Sovereignty: What It Is, and Why It Matters, Especially for the EU' (2020) 33 Philosophy and Technology 369.

Floridi L., *The Fourth Revolution How the Infosphere Is Reshaping Human Reality* (Oxford University Press 2014).

Floridi L., 'The Green and the Blue: Naïve Ideas to Improve Politics in a Mature Information Society' in Carl Öhman and David Watson (eds.), *The 2018 Yearbook of the Digital Ethics Lab* (Springer 2018).

Floridi L. (ed.), *The Onlife Manifesto Being Human in a Hyperconnected Era* (Springer 2015).

Floridi L. and others, 'AI4People—An Ethical Framework for a Good AI Society: Opportunities, Risks, Principles, and Recommendations' (2018) 28(4) Minds and Machines 689.

Foucault M., *Discipline and Punish: The Birth of a Prison* (Penguin 1991).

Foer F., 'Facebook's War on Free Will' The Guardian (19 September 2017) www.theguardian.com/technology/2017/sep/19/facebooks-war-on-free-will.

Forgó N. and others, 'The Principle of Purpose Limitation and Big Data' in Marcelo Corrales and others (eds.), *New Technology, Big Data and the Law. Perspectives in Law, Business and Innovation* (Springer 2017).

Franklin M., *Digital Dilemmas: Power, Resistance, and the Internet* (Oxford University Press 2013).

Frantziou E., *The Horizontal Effect of Fundamental Rights in the European Union. A Constitutional Analysis* (Oxford University Press 2019).

Frantziou E., 'The Horizontal Effect of the Charter of Fundamental Rights of the EU: Rediscovering the Reasons for Horizontality' (2015) 21(5) European Law Journal 657.

Fraser N., 'Rethinking the Public Sphere: A Contribution to the Critique of Actually Existing Democracy' (1990) 25/26 Social Text 56.

Freeman J. and Minow M. (eds.), *Government by Contract Outsourcing and American Democracy* (Harvard University Press 2009).

Fried C., 'Privacy: A Moral Analysis' (1968) 77 Yale Law Journal 475.

Froomkin A. M., 'The Death of Privacy?' (2000) 52 Stanford Law Review 1461.

Froomkin A. M., 'The Internet as a Source of Regulatory Arbitrage' in Brian Kahin and Charles Nesson (eds.) *Coordinating the Internet* (MIT Press 1997).

Froomkin A. M., 'Wrong Turn in Cyberspace: Using ICANN to Route Around the APA and the Constitution' (2000) 50 Duke Law Journal 17.

Frosio G., 'The Death of "No Monitoring Obligations": A Story of Untameable Monsters' (2017) 8(3) Journal of Intellectual Property, Information Technology 212.

Frosio G. and Mendis S., 'Monitoring and Filtering: European Reform or Global Trend?' in Giancarlo Frosio (ed.), *The Oxford Handbook of Online Intermediary Liability* (Oxford University Press 2020).

Gal M. S. and Aviv O., 'The Competitive Effects of the GDPR' (2020) 16(3) Journal of Competition Law and Economics 349.

Gardbaum S., 'Proportionality and Democratic Constitutionalism' in Grant Huscroft and others (eds.), *Proportionality and the Rule of Law. Rights, Justification, Reasoning* (Cambridge University Press 2014).

Gardbaum S., 'The Horizontal Effect of Constitutional Rights' (2003) 102 Michigan Law Review 388.

Garlicki L., 'Relations between Private Actors and the European Convention on Human Rights' in Andra Sajó and Renata Uitz (eds.), *The Constitution in Private Relations: Expanding Constitutionalism* (Eleven 2005).

Gates B., *The Road Ahead* (Viking Press 1995).

Geiger S., 'Does Habermas Understand the Internet? The Algorithmic Construction of the Blogo/Public Sphere' (2009) 10(1) Gnovis: A Journal of Communication, Culture, and Technology www.gnovisjournal.org/2009/12/22/does-habermas-understand-internet-algorithmic-construction-blogopublic-sphere/.

Gellert R., *The Risk-Based Approach to Data Protection* (Oxford University Press 2020).

Gellert R., 'Understanding the Notion of Risk in the General Data Protection Regulation' (2018) 34 Computer Law & Security Review 279.

Geradin D., 'What Should EU Competition Policy do to Address the Concerns Raised by the Digital Platforms' Market Power?' (2018) TILEC Discussion Paper No. 2018-041 https://papers.ssrn.com/sol3/papers.cfm?abstract_id=3011188.

Gillespie T., *Custodians of the Internet. Platforms, Content Moderation, and the Hidden Decisions That Shape Social Media* (Yale University Press 2018).

Gillespie T., 'Regulation of and by Platforms' in Jean Burgess, Alice E. Marwick and Thomas Poell (eds.), *The SAGE Handbook of Social Media* (Sage 2018).

Gillespie T., 'The Relevance of Algorithms' in Tarleton Gillespie, Pablo J. Boczkowski and Kirsten A. Foot (eds.), *Media Technologies: Essays on Communication, Materiality, and Society* (MIT Press 2014).

Gillespie T., 'The Politics of Platforms' (2010) 12(3) News Media & Society 347.

Gillis T. B. and Spiess J. L., 'Big Data and Discrimination' (2019) 86 The University of Chicago Law Review 459.

Ginsburg T. and Simpser A. (eds.), *Constitutions in Authoritarian Regimes* (Cambridge University Press 2014).

Ginsburg T., Huq A. Z. and Versteeg M., 'The Coming Demise of Liberal Constitutionalism?' (2018) 85(2) The University of Chicago Law Review 239.

Gitlan T., 'Public Sphere or Public Sphericules?' in Tamar Liebes and James Curran (eds.), *Media, Ritual and Identity* (Routledge 2002).

Goel V., 'Facebook Tinkers with Users' Emotions in News Feed Experiment, Stirring Outcry' The New York Times (29 June 2014) www.nytimes.com/2014/06/30/technology/facebook-tinkers-with-users-emotions-in-news-feed-experiment-stirring-outcry.html.

Goldman A. I. and Cox J. C., *Speech, Truth, and the Free Market for Ideas* (Cambridge University Press 1996).

Goldman E., 'Of Course the First Amendment Protects Google and Facebook (and It's Not a Close Question)' Knight First Amendment Institute (February 2018) https://knightcolumbia.org/content/course-first-amendment-protects-google-and-facebook-and-its-not-close-question.

Goldsmith J. and Wu T., *Who Controls the Internet? Illusions of a Borderless World* (Oxford University Press 2006).

Goldsmith J. L., 'Against Cyberanarchy' (1998) 65 University of Chicago Law Review 1199.

Goldsmith J. L., 'The Internet and the Abiding Significance of Territorial Sovereignty' (1998) 5 Indiana Journal of Global Legal Studies 474.

Goldsmith J. L., 'The Internet, Conflicts of Regulation and International Harmonization', in Christoph Engel (ed.), *Governance of Global Networks in the Light of Differing Local Values* (Nomos 2000).

Golia A. Jr. and Teubner G., 'Networked Statehood: An Institutionalised Self-contradiction in the Process of Globalisation?' (2021) 12(1) Transnational Legal Theory 7.

Golia A. Jr. and Teubner G., 'Societal Constitutionalism: Background, Theory, Debates'. Max Planck Institute for Comparative Public Law & International

Law (MPIL) Research Paper No. 2021-08 https://papers.ssrn.com/sol3/papers.cfm?abstract_id=3804094.

Gonzalez Fuster G., *The Emergence of Personal Data Protection as a Fundamental Right of the EU* (Springer 2014).

Goodman B. and Flaxman S., 'European Union Regulations on Algorithmic Decision-making and a "Right to Explanation"' (2016) 38(3) AI Magazine 50.

Gorwa R., Binns R. and Katzenbach C., 'Algorithmic Content Moderation: Technical and Political Challenges in the Automation of Platform Governance' (2020) 7(1) Big Data & Society https://journals.sagepub.com/doi/pdf/10.1177/2053951719897945.

Graber C. B., 'Bottom-Up Constitutionalism: The Case of Net Neutrality' (2017) 7 Transnational Legal Theory 524.

Graef I., *EU Competition Law, Data Protection and Online Platforms: Data as Essential Facility: Data as Essential Facility* (Wolters Kluwer 2016).

Greene L., *Silicon States: The Power and Politics of Big Tech and What It Means for Our Future* (Counterpoint 2018).

Greenleaf G., 'An Endnote on Regulating Cyberspace: Architecture vs Law?' (1998) 2(2) University of New South Wales Law Journal 593.

Greenleaf G., 'Global Data Privacy Laws 2019: 132 National Laws & Many Bills' (2019) 157 Privacy Laws & Business International Report 14.

Gregg A. and Greene J., 'Pentagon Awards Controversial $10 Billion Cloud Computing Deal to Microsoft, Spurning Amazon' Washington Post (26 October 2019) www.washingtonpost.com/business/2019/10/25/pentagon-awards-controversial-billion-cloud-computing-deal-microsoft-spurning-amazon/.

Grimm P., *Constitutionalism. Past, Present and Future* (Oxford University Press 2016).

Grimmelmann J., 'Speech Engines' (2014) 98 Minnesota Law Review 868.

Grimmelmann J., 'The Virtues of Moderation' (2015) 17 Yale Journal of Law and Technology 42.

Grimmelmann J., 'Virtual World Feudalism' (2009) 118 Yale Law Journal Pocket Part 126.

Grygiel J. and Brown N., 'Are Social Media Companies Motivated to Be Good Corporate Citizens? Examination of the Connection Between Corporate Social Responsibility and Social Media Safety' (2019) 43 Telecommunications Policy 445.

Gualco E. and Lourenço L., '"Clash of Titans". General Principles of EU Law: Balancing and Horizontal Direct Effect' (2016) 1(2) European Papers 643.

Guggenberger N., 'Essential Platforms' (2021) 24 Stanford Technology Law Review 237

Guimarães G. C., *Global Technology and Legal Theory: Transnational Constitutionalism, Google and the European Union* (Routledge 2019).

Guthrie Weissman C., 'Maybe It's Time to Treat Facebook Like a Public Utility' Fast Company (1 May 2017) www.fastcompany.com/40414024/maybe-its-time-to-treat-facebook-like-a-public-utility.

Gutwirth S. and De Hert P., 'Regulating Profiling in a Democratic Constitutional States' in Mireille Hildebrandt and Serge Gutwirth (eds.), *Profiling the European Citizen* (Springer 2008).

Habermas J., *Between Facts and Norms* (MIT Press 1998).

Habermas J., 'Political Communication in Media Society: Does Democracy Still Enjoy an Epistemic Dimension? The Impact of Normative Theory on Empirical Research' (2006) 16(4) Communication Theory 411.

Habermas J., *The Structural Transformation of the Public Sphere: An Inquiry into a Category of Bourgeois Society* (MIT Press 1991).

Haggart B., Tusikov N. and Scholte J. A. (eds.), *Power and Authority in Internet Governance Return of the State?* (Routledge 2021).

Halpin E. and Simpson S., 'Between Self-Regulation and Intervention in the Networked Economy: The European Union and Internet Policy' (2002) 28(4) Journal of Information Science 285.

Hartmut R., *Social Acceleration: A New Theory of Modernity* (Columbia University Press 2013).

Hartzog W. and Richards N., 'Privacy's Constitutional Moment and the Limits of Data Protection' (2020) 61 Boston College Law Review 1687.

Hartzog W., 'Website Design as Contract' (2011) 60(6) American University Law Review 1635.

Hartzog W., Melber A. and Salinger E., 'Fighting Facebook: A Campaign for a People's Terms of Service' Center for Internet and Society (22 May 2013) http://cyberlaw.stanford.edu/blog/2013/05/fighting-facebook-campaign-people%E2%809699s-terms-service.

Harvey E. and others (eds.), *Private Life and Privacy in Nazi Germany* (Cambridge University Press 2019).

Helberger N., 'Diversity by Design' (2011) 1 Journal of Information Policy 441.

Helberger N., 'On the Democratic Role of News Recommenders' (2019) 7(8) Digital Journalism 993.

Helberger N. and others, 'Governing Online Platforms: From Contested to Cooperative Responsibility' (2018) 34(1) The Information Society 1.

Helmond A., 'The Platformization of the Web: Making Web Data Platform Ready' (2015) 1(2) Social Media + Society 1.

Hijmans H., *The European Union as Guardian of Internet Privacy. The Story of Art 16 TFEU* (Springer 2016).

Hildebrandt M. and Gutwirth S. (eds.), *Profiling the European Citizen. Cross-Disciplinary Perspectives* (Springer 2008).

Hildebrandt M. and O'Hara K. (eds.), *Life and the Law in the Era of Data-Driven Agency* (Edward Elgar 2020).

Hildebrandt M., 'Slaves to Big Data. Or Are We?' (2013) 17 IDP Revista de Internet Derecho y Política 7.

Hildebrandt M., *Smart Technologies and the End(s) of Law* (Edward Elgar 2016).

Hildebrandt M., 'The Artificial Intelligence of European Union Law' (2020) 21 German Law Journal 74.

Hildebrandt M., 'The Dawn of a Critical Transparency Right for the Profiling Era' in Jacques Bus and others (eds.), *Digital Enlightenment Yearbook* (IOS Press 2012).

Hirsch D. D., 'The Law and Policy of Online Privacy: Regulation, Self-Regulation, or Co-Regulation?' (2011) 34 Seattle University Law Review 439.

Hirschl R. and Shachar A., 'Spatial Statism' (2019) 17(2) International Journal of Constitutional Law 387.

Ho D. E. and Schauer F., 'Testing the Marketplace of Ideas' (2015) 90 New York University Law Review 1161.

Hong Y., *Networking China: The Digital Transformation of the Chinese Economy* (University of Illinois Press 2017).

Horwitz, J., 'Facebook Says Its Rules Apply to All. Company Documents Reveal a Secret Elite That's Exempt' The Wall Street Journal (13 September 2021) www.wsj.com/articles/facebook-files-xcheck-zuckerberg-elite-rules-11631541353?mod=article_inline.

Humerick M., 'Taking AI Personally: How the E.U. Must Learn to Balance the Interests of Personal Data Privacy & Artificial Intelligence' (2018) 34 Santa Clara High Technology Law Journal 393.

Husovec M., *Injunctions against Intermediaries in the European Union. Accountable but Not Liable?* (Cambridge University Press 2017).

Husovec M., 'Holey Cap! CJEU Drills (yet) Another Hole in the e-Commerce Directive's Safe Harbours' (2017) 12(2) Journal of Intellectual Property Law and Practice 115.

Husovec M., 'How Europe Wants to Redefine Global Online Copyright Enforcement' in Tatiana E. Synodinou (ed.), *Pluralism or Universalism in International Copyright Law* (Wolters Kluwer 2019).

Ingram M., 'How Google and Facebook Have Taken Over the Digital Ad Industry' Fortune (4 January 2017) https://fortune.com/2017/01/04/google-facebook-ad-industry/.

Ip E. C., 'Globalization and the Future of the Law of the Sovereign State' (2010) 8 (3) International Journal of Constitutional Law 636.

Jackson V. C. and Tushnet M. (eds.), *Proportionality: New Frontiers, New Challenges* (Cambridge University Press 2017).

Jaffe L., 'Law Making by Private Groups' (1937) 51 Harvard Law Review 201.

Jain P., Gyanchandani M. and Khare N., 'Big Data Privacy: A Technological Perspective and Review' (2016) 3 Journal of Big Data.

Jančiūtė L., 'EU Data Protection and "Treaty-base Games": When Fundamental Rights are Wearing Market-making Clothes' in Ronald Leenes and others (eds.), *Data Protection and Privacy. The Age of Intelligent Machine* (Hart 2017).

Janeček V. and Malgieri G., 'Data Extra Commercium' in Sebastian Lohsse, Reiner Schulze and Dirk Staudenmayer (eds.), *Data as Counter-Performance—Contract Law 2.0?* (Hart 2020).

Jenkins H., *Convergence Culture: Where Old and New Media* Collide (New York University Press 2006).

Johnson D. R. and Post D., 'And How Shall the Net be Governed?' in Brian Kahin and James Keller (eds.) *Coordinating the Internet* (MIT Press 1997).

Johnson D. R. and Post D., 'Law and Borders: The Rise of Law in Cyberspace' (1996) 48(5) Stanford Law Review 1371.

Johnston L. and Shearing C., *Governing Security. Explorations in Policing and Justice* (Routledge 2003).

Jones M. L., 'Right to a Human in the Loop: Political Constructions of Computer Automation and Personhood' (2017) 47 Social Studies of Science 216.

Jozwiak M., 'Balancing the Rights to Data Protection and Freedom of Expression and Information by the Court of Justice of the European Union. The Vulnerability of Rights in an Online Context' (2016) 23(3) Maastricht Journal of European and Comparative Law 404.

Kaiser B., *Targeted: The Cambridge Analytica Whistleblower's Inside Story of How Big Data, Trump, and Facebook Broke Democracy and How It Can Happen Again* (Harper Collins 2019).

Kaltheuner F. and Bietti E., 'Data Is Power: Towards Additional Guidance on Profiling and Automated Decision-Making in the GDPR' (2018) 2(2) Journal of Information Rights, Policy and Practice.

Kaminski M. E., 'Binary Governance: Lessons from the GDPR's Approach to Algorithmic Accountability' (2019) 92 Southern California Law Review 1529.

Kaminski M. E. and Urban J. M., 'The Right to Contest AI' (2021) 121(7) Columbia Law Review 1957.

Kaminski M. E., 'The Right to Explanation, Explained' (2019) 34 Berkley Technology Law Journal 189.

Kaplan C. S., 'A Kind of Constitutional Convention for the Internet' The New York Times (23 October 1998) www.nytimes/com/library/tech/98/10/cyber/cyberlaw/23law.html.

Karapapa S. and Borghi M., 'Search Engine Liability for Autocomplete Suggestions: Personality, Privacy and the Power of the Algorithm' (2015) 23 International Journal of Law & Information Technology 261.

Karppinen K., 'The Limits of Empirical Indicators: Media Pluralism as an Essentially Contested Concept' in Peggy Valcke and others (eds.), *Media Pluralism and Diversity: Concepts, Risks and Global Trends* (Springer 2015).

Kaye D., *Speech Police: The Global Struggle to Govern the Internet* (Columbia Global Reports 2019).

Keane M. and Yu H., 'A Digital Empire in the Making: China's Outbound Digital Platforms' (2019) 13 International Journal of Communication 4624.

Kearns M. and Roth A., *The Ethical Algorithm: The Science of Socially Aware Algorithm Design* (Oxford University Press 2019).

Keller D., 'The Right Tools: Europe's Intermediary Liability Laws and the Eu 2016 General Data Protection Regulation' (2018) 33 Berkeley Technology Law Journal 297.

Keller D., 'Who Do You Sue? State and Platform Hybrid Power Over Online Speech' (2019) Hoover Institution, Aegis Series Paper No. 1902 www.hoover.org/sites/default/files/research/docs/who-do-you-sue-state-and-platform-hybrid-power-over-online-speech_0.pdf.

Keller T. R. and Gillett R., 'Why Is It So Hard to Stop COVID-19 Misinformation Spreading on Social Media?' The Conversation (13 April 2020) https://theconversation.com/why-is-it-so-hard-to-stop-covid-19-misinformation-spreading-on-social-media-134396.

Kerr O. S., 'The Mosaic Theory of the Fourth Amendment' (2012) 111 Michigan Law Review 311.

Kessler F., 'Contract of Adhesion - Some Thoughts about Freedom of Contract' (1943) 43 Columbia Law Review 629.

Kettemann M., *The Normative Order of the Internet: A Theory of Rule and Regulation Online* (Oxford University Press 2020).

Kim N. S. and Telman D. A., 'Internet Giants as Quasi-Governmental Actors and the Limits of Contractual Consent' (2015) 80 Missouri Law Review 723.

Kindt E. J., *Privacy and Data Protection Issues of Biometric Applications. A Comparative Legal Analysis* (Springer 2013).

Kirkpatrick M., 'Facebook's Zuckerberg Says the Age of Privacy is Over' The New York Times (10 January 2010) www.nytimes.com/external/readwriteweb/2010/01/10/10readwriteweb-facebooks-zuckerberg-says-the-age-of-privac-82963.html?source=post_page.

Kitchin R. and Lauriault T.P., 'Small Data, Data Infrastructures and Big Data' (2014) 80(4) GeoJournal 463.

Klabbers J., Peters A. and Ulfsein G., *The Constitutionalisation of International Law* (Oxford University Press 2009).

Klang M. and Murray A. (eds.), *Human Rights in the Digital Age* (Cavendish 2005).

Klonick K., 'The Facebook Oversight Board: Creating an Independent Institution to Adjudicate Online Free Expression' (2020) 129(8) The Yale Law Journal 2232.

Klonick K., 'The New Governors: The People, Rules, and Processes Governing Online Speech' (2018) 131 Harvard Law Review 1598.

Knight W., 'China Plans to Use Artificial Intelligence to Gain Global Economic Dominance by 2030' MIT Technology Review (21 July 2017) www.technologyreview.com/2017/07/21/150379/china-plans-to-use-artificial-intelligence-to-gain-global-economic-dominance-by-2030/.

Knox J. H., 'Horizontal Human Rights Law' (2008) 102(1) American Journal of International Law 1.

Kohl U., *Jurisdiction and the Internet: Regulatory Competence over Online Activity* (Cambridge University Press 2007).

Kokott J. and Sobotta C., 'The Distinction between Privacy and Data Protection in the Jurisprudence of the CJEU and the ECtHR' (2013) 3 International Data Privacy Law 222.

Koltay A., *New Media and Freedom of Expression. Rethinking the Constitutional Foundations of the Public Sphere* (Hart 2019).

Koops B. J., 'The Trouble with European Data Protection Law' (2014) 4(4) International Data Privacy Law 250.

Kosseff J., 'Defending Section 230: The Value of Intermediary Immunity' (2010) 15 Journal of Technology Law & Policy 123.

Kosseff J., *The Twenty-Six Words That Created the Internet* (Cornell University Press 2019).

Kostka G., 'China's Social Credit Systems and Public Opinion: Explaining High Levels of Approval' (2019) 21(7) New Media & Society 1565.

Kreimer S. F., 'Censorship by Proxy: The First Amendment, Internet Intermediaries, and the Problem of the Weakest Link' (2006) 155 University of Pennsylvania Law Review 11.

Kreiss D. and Mcgregor S. C., 'The "Arbiters of What Our Voters See": Facebook and Google's Struggle with Policy, Process, and Enforcement around Political Advertising' (2019) 36(4) Political Communication 499.

Krisch N., *Beyond Constitutionalism. The Pluralist Structure of Postnational Law* (Oxford University Press 2010).

Kuczerawy A., 'Safeguards for Freedom of Expression in the Era of Online Gatekeeping' (2018) 3 Auteurs & Media 292.

Kuczerawy A., 'The Power of Positive Thinking. Intermediary Liability and the Effective Enjoyment of the Right to Freedom of Expression' (2017) 3 Journal of Intellectual Property, Information Technology and Electronic Commerce Law 182.

Kuczerawy A. and Ausloos J., 'From Notice-and-Takedown to Notice-and-Delist: Implementing Google Spain' (2016) 14 Columbia Technology Law Journal 219.

Kumm M., 'Constituent Power, Cosmopolitan Constitutionalism, and Post-Positivist Law' (2016) 14(3) International Journal of Constitutional Law 2016.

Kumm M. and Ferreres Comella V., 'What Is So Special about Constitutional Rights in Private Litigation? A Comparative Analysis of the Function of State Action Requirements and Indirect Horizontal Effect' in Andras Sajó and Renata Uitz (eds.), *The Constitution in Private Relations: Expanding Constitutionalism* (Eleven 2005).

Kumm M. and Walen A. D., 'Human Dignity and Proportionality: Deontic Pluralism in Balancing' Grant Huscroft and others (eds.), *Proportionality and the Rule of Law: Rights, Justification, Reasoning* (Cambridge University Press 2014).

Kuner C., 'Extraterritoriality and Regulation of International Data Transfers in EU Data Protection Law' (2015) 5(4) International Data Privacy Law 235.

Kuner C., 'The Internet and the Global Reach of EU Law' in Marise Cremona and Joanne Scott (eds.), *EU Law Beyond EU Borders: The Extraterritorial Reach of EU Law* (Oxford University Press 2019).

Kuner C. and others, 'Machine Learning with Personal Data: Is Data Protection Law Smart Enough to Meet the Challenge?' (2017) 7(1) International Data Privacy Law 1.

Kuner C. and others, 'Risk Management in Data Protection' (2015) 5(2) International Data Privacy Law 95.

Kwet M., 'Digital Colonialism: US Empire and the New Imperialism in the Global South' (2019) 60(4) Race & Class 3.

Laidlaw E. B., 'A Framework for Identifying Internet Information Gatekeepers' (2012) 24(3) International Review of Computer Law and Technology 263.

Laney D., '3D Data Management: Controlling Data Volume, Velocity and Variety' (2001) Application Delivery Strategies.
Langvardt K., 'Regulating Online Content Moderation' (2018) 106 The Georgetown Law Journal 1353.
Lawson G., 'The Rise and Rise of the Administrative State' (1994) 107 Harvard Law Review 1231.
Leczykiewicz D., 'Horizontal Application of the Charter of Fundamental Rights' (2013) 38(3) European Law Review 479.
Lenaerts K., 'Exploring the Limits of the EU Charter of Fundamental Rights' (2013) 8(3) European Constitutional Law Review 375.
Lessig L., 'An Information Society: Free or Feudal' (2004) World Summit on the Information Society (WSIS) www.itu.int/wsis/docs/pc2/visionaries/lessig.pdf.
Lessig L., *Code: And Other Laws of Cyberspace. Version 2.0* (Basic Books 2006).
Lessig L., 'Reading the Constitution in Cyberspace' (1996) 45(3) Emory Law Journal 869.
Lessig L., 'The New Chicago School' (1998) 27(2) The Journal of Legal Studies 661.
Lessig L. and Resnick P., 'Zoning Speech on the Internet: A Legal and Technical Model' (1998) 98 Michigan Law Review 395.
Lessin J., 'Facebook Shouldn't Fact Check. New York Times', The New York Times (29 November 2016) www.nytimes.com/2016/11/29/opinion/facebook-shouldnt-fact-check.html.
Liang F. and others, 'Constructing a Data-Driven Society: China's Social Credit System as a State Surveillance Infrastructure' (2018) 10(4) Policy & Internet 415.
Lidsky L. B., 'Public Forum 2.0' (2011) Boston University Law Review 1975.
Linskey O., 'Grappling with "Data Power": Normative Nudges from Data Protection and Privacy' (2019) 20(1) Theoretical Inquiries in Law 189.
Lobel O., 'The Law of the Platforms' (2016) 101 Minnesota Law Review 87.
Lohr S., *Data-Ism: The Revolution Transforming Decision Making, Consumer Behavior, and Almost Everything Else* (Blackstone 2015).
Loi M. and Dehaye P. O., 'If Data is the New Oil, when is the Extraction of Value from data Unjust?' (2018) 7(2) Philosophy & Public Issues 137.
Lucchi N., 'Freedom of Expression and the Right to Internet Access' in Monroe E. Price, Stefaan G. Verhulst, Libby Morgan (eds.), *Routledge Handbook of Media Law* (Routledge 2013).
Luhman N., *Social System* (Stanford University Press 2016).
Lynskey O., 'Regulating Platform Power' (2017) LSE Legal Studies Working Paper 1 http://eprints.lse.ac.uk/73404/1/WPS2017-01_Lynskey.pdf.
Lynskey O., 'Regulation by Platforms: The Impact on Fundamental Rights' in Luca Belli and Nicolo Zingales (eds.), *Platform Regulations How Platforms Are Regulated and How They Regulate Us* (FGV Direito Rio 2017).
Lynskey O., *The Foundations of EU Data Protection Law* (Oxford University Press 2015).
Lyon D., *Surveillance After Snowden* (Polity Press 2015).
Lyon D., *The Culture of Surveillance: Watching as a Way of Life* (Polity Press 2018).

Lyons K., 'India reportedly orders social media platforms to remove references to "Indian variant" of COVID-19' The Verge (23 May 2021) www.theverge.com/2021/5/23/22449898/india-social-media-platforms-remove-indian-variant-covid-19-coronavirus.

Maceinate M., 'The "Riskification" of European Data Protection Law through a two-fold Shift' European Journal of Risk Regulation (2017) 8(3) European Journal of Risk Regulation 506.

MacKinnon R., *Consent of the Networked: The Worldwide Struggle for Internet Freedom* (Basic Books 2013).

Macnish K., 'Unblinking Eyes: The Ethics of Automating Surveillance' (2012) 14 Ethics and Information Technology 151.

Mahapatra S., Fertmann M. and Kettemann M. C., 'Twitter's Modi Operandi: Lessons from India on Social Media's Challenges in Reconciling Terms of Service, National Law and Human Rights Law' Verfassungsblog (24 February 2021) https://verfassungsblog.de/twitters-modi-operandi/.

Malgieri G., 'Automated Decision-Making in the EU Member States: The Right to Explanation and Other "Suitable Safeguards" in the National Legislations' (2019) 35(5) Computer Law & Security Review 105327.

Malgieri G. and Comandè G., 'Why a Right to Legibility of Automated Decision-Making Exists in the General Data Protection Regulation' (2017) 7 International Data Privacy Law 234.

Mann M., 'The Limits of (Digital) Constitutionalism: Exploring the Privacy-Security (Im)Balance in Australia' (2018) 80 International Communication Gazette 369.

Mann M. and Matzner T., 'Challenging Algorithmic Profiling: The Limits of Data Protection and Anti-Discrimination in Responding to Emergent Discrimination' (2019) 6(2) Big Data & Society https://journals.sagepub.com/doi/pdf/10.1177/2053951719895805.

Mansell R. and Javary M., 'Emerging Internet Oligopolies: A Political Economy Analysis' in Arthur S. Miller, Warren J. Samuels (eds.), *An Institutionalist Approach to Public Utilities Regulation* (Michigan State University Press 2002).

Mantelero A., 'From Group Privacy to Collective Privacy: Towards a New Dimension of Privacy and Data Protection in the Big Data Era' in Linnet Taylor and others (eds.), *Group Privacy* (Springer 2017).

Mantelero A., 'The Future of Consumer Data Protection in the EU Re-Thinking the "Notice and Consent" Paradigm in the New Era of Predictive Analytics' (2014) 30(6) Computer Law & Security Review 643.

Manyika J. and others, 'Big Data: The Next Frontier for Innovation, Competition, and Productivity', McKinsey Global Institute (2011) www.mckinsey.com/business-functions/mckinsey-digital/our-insights/big-data-the-next-frontier-for-innovation.

Maple C., 'Security and Privacy in Internet of Things' (2017) 2 Journal of Cyber Policy 155.

Marks S., *The Riddle of All Constitutions: International Law, Democracy, and the Critique of Ideology* (Oxford University Press 2004).

Marsden C., *Internet Co-Regulation: European Law, Regulatory Governance and Legitimacy in Cyberspace* (Cambridge University Press 2011).

Mayer-Schönberger V. and Cukier K., *Big Data: A Revolution That Will Transform How We Live, Work, and Think* (Houghton Mifflin Harcourt 2013).

McCrudden C., 'Human Dignity and Judicial Interpretation of Human Rights' (2008) 19(4) European Journal of International Law 655.

Mcdonald A. M. and Cranor L. F., 'The Cost of Reading Privacy Policies' (2008) 4(3) I/S: A Journal of Law and Policy for the Information Society 543.

Mcgregor S. C., 'Personalization, Social Media, and Voting: Effects of Candidate Self-Personalization on Vote Intention' (2017) 20(3) News Media & Society 1139.

McIlwain C. H., *Constitutionalism: Ancient and Modern* (Amagi 2007).

McLuhan M., *Understanding Media. The Extensions of Man* (MIT Press 1994).

McPherson M., Smith-Lovin L. and Cook J. M., 'Birds of a Feather: Homophily in Social Networks' (2001) 27 Annual Review of Sociology 415.

McStay A. and Urquhart L., 'This Time with Feeling? Assessing EU Data Governance Implications for Out of Home Emotional AI' (2019) 24(10) First Monday https://firstmonday.org/ojs/index.php/fm/article/download/9457/8146.

Meiklejohn A., *Free Speech and Its Relation to Self-Government* (Lawbook Exchange 2011).

Meiklejohn A., 'The First Amendment Is an Absolute' (1961) The Supreme Court Review 245.

Meldman J. A., 'Centralized Information Systems and the Legal Right to Privacy' (1969) 52 Marquette Law Review 335.

Mendez R., 'Google Case in Italy' (2011) 1(2) International Data Privacy Law 137.

Mendoza I. and Bygrave L. A., 'The Right Not to Be Subject to Automated Decisions Based on Profiling' in Tatiani Synodinou and other (eds.), *EU Internet Law: Regulation and Enforcement* (Springer 2017).

Mill J. S., *On Liberty* (1859).

Miller A. R., 'Personal Privacy in the Computer Age: The Challenge of a New Technology in an Information-Oriented Society' (1969) 67 Michigan Law Review 1089.

Milton J., *Aeropagitica* (1644).

Mittelstadt B., 'From Individual to Group Privacy in Big Data Analytics' (2017) 30 (4) Philosophy and Technology 475.

Mittelstadt B. and Floridi L., 'The Ethics of Big Data: Current and Foreseeable Issues in Biomedical Contexts' (2016) 22 Science and Engineering Ethics 303.

Mittelstadt B. and others, 'The Ethics of Algorithms: Mapping the Debate' (2016) 3 Big Data & Society https://journals.sagepub.com/doi/pdf/10.1177/2053951716679679.

Mittelstadt B. D. and others, 'The Ethics of Algorithms: Mapping the Debate' (2016) 3(2) Big Data & Society https://journals.sagepub.com/doi/pdf/10.1177/2053951716679679.

Moazed A. and Johnson N. L., *Modern Monopolies: What It Takes to Dominate the 21st Century Economy* (St Martin's Press 2016).

Moeller J. and Helberger N., 'Beyond the Filter Bubble: Concepts, Myths, Evidence and Issues for Future Debates. A Report Drafted for the Dutch Media Regulator' (2018) https://dare.uva.nl/search?identifier=478edb9e-8296-4a84-9631-c7360d593610.

Moerel L., 'The Long Arm of EU Data Protection Law: Does the Data Protection Directive Apply to Processing of Personal Data of EU Citizens by Websites Worldwide?' (2011) 1(1) International Data Privacy Law 28.

Möller J. and others, 'Do Not Blame it on the Algorithm: An Empirical Assessment of Multiple Recommender Systems and Their Impact on Content Diversity' (2018) 21(7) Information, Communication & Society 959.

Moore M. and Tambini D. (eds.), *Digital Dominance: The Power of Google, Amazon, Facebook, and Apple* (Oxford University Press 2018).

Morozov E., *The Net Delusion: The Dark Side of Internet Freedom* (Public Affairs 2011).

Morozov E., *To Save Everything, Click Here: The Folly of Technological Solutionism* (Public Affairs 2013).

Mortelmans K., 'The Common Market, the Internal Market and the Single Market, What's in a Market?' (1998) 35(1) Common Market Law Review 101.

Mourby M. and others, 'Are "Pseudonymised" Data Always Personal Data? Implications of the GDPR for Administrative Data Research in the UK' (2018) 34 Computer Law & Security Review 222.

Mueller M., 'Hyper-Transparency and Social Control: Social Media as Magnets for Regulation'(2016) 39(9) Telecommunications Policy 804.

Mueller M. L., 'Against Sovereignty in Cyberspace' (2020) 22(4) International Studies Review 779.

Murray A., 'Internet Regulation' in David Levi-Faur (ed.), *Handbook on the Politics of Regulation* (Edward Elgar 2011).

Murray A., *Information Technology Law: The Law and Society* (Oxford University Press 2013).

Murray A., 'Nodes and Gravity in Virtual Space' (2011) 5(2) Legisprudence 195.

Murray A., *The Regulation of Cyberspace* (Routledge 2007).

Musiani F., 'Network Architecture as Internet Governance' (2013) 2(4) Internet Policy Review https://policyreview.info/node/208/pdf.

Napoli P. M., *Social Media and the Public Interest: Media Regulation in the Disinformation Age* (Columbia University Press 2019).

Narayanan A. and Shmatikov V., 'Myths and Fallacies of Personally Identifiable Information' (2010) 53 Communications of the ACM 24.

Negroponte N., *Being Digital* (Alfred A Knopf 1995).

Nemitz P., 'Constitutional Democracy and Technology in the age of Artificial Intelligence' (2018) Royal Society Philosophical Transactions A 376.

Netanel N. W., 'Cyberspace Self-Governance: A Skeptical View from the Liberal Democratic Theory' (2000) 88 California Law Review 401.

Newell S. and Marabelli M., 'Strategic Opportunities (and Challenges) of Algorithmic Decision-making: A Call for Action on The Long-Term Societal

Effects of 'Datification' (2015) 24 The Journal of Strategic Information Systems 3.

Neyland D., 'Bearing Accountable Witness to the Ethical Algorithmic System' (2016) 41 Science, Technology & Human Values 50.

Nicas J., 'YouTube Tops 1 Billion Hours of Video a Day, on Pace to Eclipse TV' Wall Street Journal (27 February 2017) www.wsj.com/articles/youtube-tops-1-billion-hours-of-video-a-day-on-pace-to-eclipse-tv-1488220851.

Nissenbaum H., 'A Contextual Approach to Privacy Online' (2011) 140(4) Daedalus 32.

Nissenbaum H., 'From Preemption to Circumvention: If Technology Regulates, Why Do We Need Regulation (and Vice Versa)?' (2011) 26 Berkley Technology Law Journal 1367.

Nissenbaum H., 'Protecting Privacy in an Information Age: The Problem of Privacy in Public' (1998) 17 Law and Philosophy 559.

Noble S. U., *Algorithms of Oppression: How Search Engines Reinforce Racism* (NYU Press 2018).

Novet J., 'Pentagon Asks Amazon, Google, Microsoft and Oracle for Bids on New Cloud Contracts' CNBC (19 November 2021) www.cnbc.com/2021/11/19/pentagon-asks-amazon-google-microsoft-oracle-for-cloud-bids.html.

Novick S., *Honorable Justice* (Laurel 1990).

Nunziato D. C., 'The Death of The Public Forum in Cyberspace' (2005) 20 Berkeley Technology Law Journal 1115.

Ohm P., 'Broken Promises of Privacy: Responding to the Surprising Failure of Anonymization' (2010) 57 UCL Law Review 1701.

O'Neil C., *Weapons of Math Destruction: How Big Data Increases Inequality and Threatens Democracy* (Crown Pub 2016).

Orwell G., *1984* (Penguin Books 2008).

Oswald M., 'Algorithm-Assisted Decision-making in the Public Sector: Framing the Issues Using Administrative Law Rules Governing Discretionary Power' (2018) 376 Philosophical Transaction Royal Society A.

Padovani C. and Santaniello M., 'Digital Constitutionalism: Fundamental Rights and Power Limitation in the Internet Eco-System' (2018) 80 International Communication Gazzette 295.

Pagallo U., 'On the Principle of Privacy by Design and its Limits: Technology, Ethics and the Rule of Law' in Serge Gutwirth and others (eds.), *European Data Protection: In Good Health?* (Springer 2012).

Palfrey J. G., 'Four Phases of Internet Regulation' (2010) 77(3) Social Research 981.

Pariser E., *The Filter Bubble: What the Internet Is Hiding from You* (Viking 2011).

Parker G. G., Van Alstyne M. W. and Choudary S. P., *Platform Revolution – How Networked Markets are Transforming the Economy – And How To Make them Work for You* (WW Norton & Company Inc 2017).

Pasquale F., 'From Territorial to Functional Sovereignty: The Case of Amazon' Law and Political Economy (6 December 2017) https://lpeblog.org/2017/12/06/from-territorial-to-functional-sovereignty-the-case-of-amazon.

Pasquale F., 'Inalienable Due Process in an Age of AI: Limiting the Contractual Creep toward Automated Adjudication' in Hans-W. Micklitz and others (eds.), *Constitutional Challenges in the Algorithmic Society* (Cambridge University Press 2021).

Pasquale F, 'Internet Nondiscrimination Principles: Commercial Ethics for Carriers and Search Engines' (2008) University of Chicago Legal Forum 263.

Pasquale F., *New Laws of Robotics. Defending Human Expertise in the Age of AI* (Belknap Press 2020).

Pasquale F., 'Platform Neutrality: Enhancing Freedom of Expression in Spheres of Private Power' (2016) 17 Theoretical Inquiries in Law 487.

Pasquale F., 'Reforming the Law of Reputation' (2015) 47 Loyola University of Chicago Law Journal 515.

Pasquale F., *The Black Box Society: The Secret Algorithms That Control Money and Information* (Harvard University Press 2015).

Pasquale F. A., 'Privacy, Autonomy, and Internet Platforms' in Marc Rotenberg, Julia Horwitz and Jeramie Scott (eds.), *Privacy in the Modern Age, the Search for Solutions* (The New Press 2015).

Paul K. and Milmo D., 'Facebook Putting Profit Before Public Good, Says Whistleblower Frances Haugen' The Guardian (4 October 2021) www.theguardian.com/technology/2021/oct/03/former-facebook-employee-frances-haugen-identifies-herself-as-whistleblower.

Paul K. and Vengattil M., 'Twitter Plans to Build "Decentralized Standard" for Social Networks' Reuters (11 December 2019) www.reuters.com/article/us-twitter-content/twitter-plans-to-build-decentralized-standard-for-social-networks-idUSKBN1YF2EN.

Peguera M., 'The Shaky Ground of the Right to Be Delisted' (2016) 18 Vanderbilt Journal of Entertainment & Technology Law 507.

Peppet S. R., 'Regulating the Internet of Things: First Steps Toward Managing Discrimination, Privacy, Security, and Consent' (2014) 93 Texas Law Review 85.

Pernice I., 'Global Constitutionalism and the Internet. Taking People Seriously' HIIG Discussion Paper Series Discussion Paper (10 March 2015) https://papers.ssrn.com/sol3/papers.cfm?abstract_id=2576697.

Pernice I., 'Multilevel Constitutionalism and the Crisis of Democracy in Europe' (2015) 11(3) European Constitutional Law Review 541.

Pernice I., 'The Treaty of Lisbon: Multilevel Constitutionalism in Action' (2009) 15(3) Columbia Journal of European Law 349.

Perritt, Jr. H. H., 'Cyberspace Self-Government: Town Hall Democracy or Rediscovered Royalism?' (1997) 12 Berkeley Technology Law Journal 413.

Perritt, Jr. H. H., 'The Internet as a Threat to Sovereignty? Thoughts on the Internet's Role in Strengthening National and Global Governance' (1998) 5 Indiana Journal of Global Legal Studies 423.

Peters J., 'The "Sovereigns of Cyberspace" and State Action: The First Amendment's Application (or Lack Thereof) to Third-Party Platforms' (2018) 32 Berkeley Technology Law Journal 988.

Petit N., *Big Tech and the Digital Economy. The Moligopoly Scenario* (Oxford University Press 2020).
Petkova B., 'Privacy as Europe's First Amendment' (2019) 25(2) European Law Journal 140.
Pistor K., 'Statehood in the Digital Age' (2020) 27(3) Constellations 3.
Pitruzella G. and Pollicino O., *Disinformation and Hate Speech: A European Constitutional Perspective* (Bocconi University Press 2020).
Plantin J.-C. and others, 'Infrastructure Studies Meet Platform Studies in the Age of Google and Facebook' (2018) 20(1) New Media & Society 293.
Pohle J., 'Digital Sovereignty' (2020) 9(4) Internet Policy Review https://policyreview.info/pdf/policyreview-2020-4-1532.pdf.
Pollicino O., 'Contact Tracing and COVID-19: Commission and Member States Agree on Specifications' EU Law Live (16 June 2020) https://eulawlive.com/contact-tracing-and-covid-19-commission-and-member-states-agree-on-specifications/.
Pollicino O., 'Fighting COVID-19 and Protecting Privacy under EU Law. A Proposal Looking at the Roots of European Constitutionalism' EU Law Live (16 May 2020) https://eulawlive.com/weekend-edition/weekend-edition-no17/.
Pollicino O., 'Judicial Protection of Fundamental Rights in the Transition from the World of Atoms to the Word of Bits: The Case of Freedom of Speech' (2019) 25 European Law Journal 155.
Pollicino O., *Judicial Protection of Fundamental Rights on the Internet: A Road Towards Digital Constitutionalism?* (Hart 2021).
Pollicino O., 'Right to Internet Access: Quid Iuris?' in Andreas von Arnauld, Kerstin von der Decken and Mart Susi (eds.), *The Cambridge Handbook on New Human Rights. Recognition, Novelty, Rhetoric* (Cambridge University Press 2019).
Pollicino O. and Apa E., *Modeling the Liability of Internet Service Providers: Google vs. Vivi Down. A Constitutional Perspective* (Egea 2013).
Pollicino O. and Bassini M., 'Bridge Is Down, Data Truck Can't Get Through … A Critical View of the Schrems Judgment in the Context of European Constitutionalism' (2017) 16 Global Community Yearbook of International Law and Jurisprudence 245.
Pollicino O. and Bassini M., 'Free Speech, Defamation and the Limits to Freedom of Expression in the EU: A Comparative Analysis' in Andrej Savin and Jan Trzaskowski (eds.), *Research Handbook on EU Internet Law* (Edward Elgar 2014).
Pollicino O. and Bassini M., 'Reconciling Right to Be Forgotten and Freedom of Information in the Digital Age: Past and Future of Personal Data Protection in the EU' (2014) 2 Diritto pubblico comparato ed europeo 641.
Pollicino O. and Bassini M., 'The Law of the Internet between Globalisation and Localization' in Miguel Maduro, Kaarlo Tuori and Suvi Sankari (eds.), *Transnational Law. Rethinking European Law and Legal Thinking* (Cambridge University Press 2016).
Pollicino O. and De Gregorio G., 'A Constitutional-Driven Change of Heart: ISP Liability and Artificial Intelligence in the Digital Single Market' (2019) 18 The Global Community Yearbook of International Law and Jurisprudence 237.

Pollicino O. and Romeo G. (eds.), *The Internet and Constitutional Law: The Protection of Fundamental Rights and Constitutional Adjudication in Europe* (Routledge 2016).

Popper B., 'A Quarter of the World's Population now Uses Facebook Every Month' The Verge (3 May 2017) www.theverge.com/2017/5/3/15535216/facebook-q1-first-quarter-2017-earnings.

Poullet Y., 'Data Protection Between Property and Liberties. A Civil Law Approach' in Henrik W. K. Kaspersen and Anja Oskamp (eds.), *Amongst Friends in Computers and Law. A Collection of Essays in Remembrance of Guy Vandenberghe* (Kluwer Law International 1990).

Poullet Y., 'Data Protection Legislation: What is at Stake for our Society and Democracy' (2009) 25 Computer Law & Security Review 211.

Price M. E. and Verhulst S. G., *Self-Regulation and the Internet* (Kluwer 2004).

Puetz T., 'Facebook: The New Town Square' (2014) 44 Southwestern Law Review 385.

Purtova N., *Property Rights in Personal Data: A European Perspective* (Kluwer Law International 2011).

Purtova N., 'The Law of Everything. Broad Concept of Personal Data and Future of EU Data Protection Law' (2018) 10(1) Law, Innovation and Technology 40.

Puschmann C. and Burgess J., 'Big Data, Big Questions. Metaphors of Big Data' (2014) 8 International Journal of Communication 1690.

Quelle C., 'Enhancing Compliance under the General Data Protection Regulation: The Risky Upshot of the Accountability- and Risk-based Approach' (2018) 9(3) European Journal of Risk Regulation 502.

Quintais J. P. and others, 'Safeguarding User Freedoms in Implementing Article 17 of the Copyright in the Digital Single Market Directive: Recommendations from European Academics' (2019) 10(3) Journal of Intellectual Property, Information Technology and E-Commerce Law 277.

Radin M. J., *Boilerplate the Fine Print, Vanishing Rights, and the Rule of Law* (Princeton University Press 2013).

Rahman K. S., 'The New Utilities: Private Power, Social Infrastructure, and the Revival of the Public Utility Concept' (2018) 39 Cardozo Law Review 1621.

Ranchordas S. and Goanta C., 'The New City Regulators: Platform and Public Values in Smart and Sharing Cities' (2020) 36 Computer Law and Security Review 105375.

Redeker D. and others, 'Towards Digital Constitutionalism? Mapping Attempts to Craft an Internet Bill of Rights' (2018) 80 International Communication Gazette 302.

Regan P. M., *Legislating Privacy, Technology, Social Values and Public Policy* 321 (University of North Carolina Press 1995).

Reidenberg J. R., 'Governing Networks and Rule-Making Cyberspace' (1996) 45 Emory Law Journal 911.

Reidenberg J. R., 'Lex Informatica: The Formulation of Information Policy Rules through Technology' (1997–8) 76 Texas Law Review 553.

Reidenberg J. R., 'States and Internet enforcement' (2004) 1 University of Ottawa Law & Techonology Journal 213.

Rheingold H., 'Habermas Blows Off Question about the Internet and the Public Sphere', SmartMobs (5 November 2007) www.smartmobs.com/2007/11/05/habermas-blows-off-question-about-the-internet-and-the-public-sphere/.

Richards N. M., *Intellectual Privacy: Rethinking Civil Liberties in the Digital Age* (Oxford University Press 2015).

Richards N. M., 'The Dangers of Surveillance' (2013) 126 Harvard Law Review 1935.

Richards N. M., 'The Information Privacy Law Project' (2006) 94 Georgetown Law Journal 1087.

Richards N. M. and King J. H., 'Three Paradoxes of Big Data' (2013) 66 Stanford Law Review Online 41.

Roberts S. T., *Behind the Screen: Content Moderation in the Shadows of Social Media* (Yale University Press 2019).

Roberts S. T., 'Content Moderation' in Laurie A. Schintler and Connie L. McNeely (eds.), *Encyclopedia of Big Data* (Springer 2017).

Roberts S. T., 'Digital Detritus: "Error" and the Logic of Opacity in Social Media Content Moderation (2018), 23(3) First Monday https://firstmonday.org/ojs/index.php/fm/rt/printerFriendly/8283/6649.

Robertson V. H. S. E., 'Excessive Data Collection: Privacy Considerations and Abuse of Dominance in the Era of Big Data' (2020) 57(1) Common Market Law Review 161.

Robin-Olivier S., 'The 'Digital Single Market' and Neoliberalism: Reflections on Net Neutrality' in Margot E. Salomon and Bruno De Witte (eds.), *Legal Trajectories of Neoliberalism: Critical Inquiries on Law in Europe* (RSCAS R 2019).

Rocher L., Hendrickx J. M. and de Montjoye Y. A., 'Estimating the Success of Re-identifications in Incomplete Datasets Using Generative Models' (2019) 10 Nature Communications 3069.

Rodotà S., *Vivere la democrazia* (Laterza 2019).

Romei A. and Ruggieri S., 'A Multidisciplinary Survey on Discrimination Analysis' (2014) 29 The Knowledge Engineering Review.

Rosen J., 'The Deciders: The Future of Privacy and Free Speech in the Age of Facebook and Google' (2012) 80 Fordham Law Review 1525.

Rosenfeld M. and Sajo A., 'Spreading Liberal Constitutionalism: An Inquiry into the Fate of Free Speech Rights in New Democracies' in Sujit Choudhry (ed.), *The Migration of Constitutional Ideas* (Cambridge University Press 2007).

Rouvroy A., 'Technology, Virtuality and Utopia: Governmentality in an Age of Autonomic Computing' in Mireille Hildebrandt and Antoniette Rouvroy, *Law, Human Agency and Autonomic Computing: The Philosophy of Law Meets the Philosophy of Technology* (Routledge 2011).

Rouvroy A. and Poullet Y., 'The Right to Informational Self-Determination and the Value of Self-Development: Reassessing the Importance of Privacy for Democracy' in Serge Gutwirth and others (eds.), *Reinventing Data Protection?* (Springer 2009).

Rozenshtein A. Z., 'Surveillance Intermediaries' (2018) 70 Stanford Law Review 99.

Rubinstein I. and Good N., 'Privacy by Design: A Counterfactual Analysis of Google and Facebook Privacy Incidents' (2013) 28 Berkeley Technology Law Journal 1333.

Rubinstein I. S., 'Big Data: The End of Privacy or a New Beginning?' (2013) 3(2) International Data Privacy Law 74.

Rubinstein I. S., 'Regulating Privacy by Design' (2012) 26 Berkeley Technology Law Journal 1409.

Ruggles R., de Pemberton Jr J. and Miller A. R., 'Computers, Data Banks, and Individual Privacy' (1968) 53 Minnesota Law Review 211.

Rutherglen G, 'State Action, Private Action, and the Thirteenth Amendment' (2008) 24(6) Virginia Law Review 1367.

Sabeel Rahman K., 'Monopoly Men' Boston Review (11 October 2017) http://bostonreview.net/science-nature/k-sabeel-rahman-monopoly-men.

Sabeel Rahman K., 'The New Utilities: Private Power, Social Infrastructure, and the Revival of the Public Utility Concept' (2018) 39 Cardozo Law Review 1621.

Sadowski J., 'When Data Is Capital: Datafication, Accumulation, and Extraction' (2019) 6 Big Data & Society 1.

Sajó A. and Uitz R., *The Constitution of Freedom: An Introduction to Legal Constitutionalism* (Oxford University Press 2017).

Sánchez Graells A., *Public Procurement and the EU Competition Rules* (Hart 2015).

Sander B., 'Democratic Disruption in the Age of Social Media: Between Marketized and Structural Conceptions of Human Rights Law' (2021) 32(1) European Journal of International Law 159.

Sander B., 'Freedom of Expression in the Age of Online Platforms: The Promise and Pitfalls of a Human Rights Based Approach to Content Moderation' (2020) 43(4) Fordham Journal of International Law 939.

Santaniello M. and others, 'The Language of Digital Constitutionalism and the Role of National Parliaments' (2018) 80 International Communication Gazette 320.

Sartor G., '"Providers" Liabilities in the New EU Data Protection Regulation: A Threat to Internet Freedoms?' (2013) 3(1) International Data Privacy Law 3.

Sartor G., 'Providers Liability. From the eCommerce Directive to the Future' (2017) In-depth analysis for the IMCO Committee www.europarl.europa.eu/RegData/etudes/IDAN/2017/614179/IPOL_IDA(2017)614179_EN.pdf.

Sartor G. and Viola de Azevedo Cunha M., 'The Italian Google-Case: Privacy, Freedom of Speech and Responsibility of Providers for User-Generated Contents' (2010) 18(4) International Journal of Law & Information Technologies 15.

Sartori G., 'Constitutionalism: A Preliminary Discussion' (1962) 56(4) The American Political Science Review 853.

Sassen S., *Losing Control? Sovereignty in the Age of Globalization* (Columbia University Press 1996).

Sassen S., 'On the Internet and Sovereignty' (1998) 5 Indiana Journal of Global Legal Studies 545.

Scassa T., 'Pandemic Innovation: The Private Sector and the Development of Contact-Tracing and Exposure Notification Apps' (2021) 6(2) Business and Human Rights Journal 352.

Schaurer F., 'The Exceptional First Amendment' in Michael Ignatieff (ed.), *American Exceptionalism and Human Rights* (Princeton University Press 2005).

Schermer B. W., 'The Limits of Privacy in Automated Profiling and Data Mining' (2011) 27(1) Computer Law & Security Review 45.

Schermer B. W., Custers B. and van der Hof S., 'The Crisis of Consent: How Stronger Legal Protection May Lead to Weaker Consent in Data Protection' (2014) 16 Ethics and Information Technology 171.

Schiller D., *Digital Capitalism. Networking the Global Market System* (MIT Press 1999).

Schudson M., 'Was There Ever a Public Sphere? If So, When? Reflections on the American Case' in John Calhoun (ed.), *Habermas and the Public Sphere* (MIT Press 1992).

Schutze R., '"Delegated" Legislation in the (New) European Union: A Constitutional Analysis' (2011) 74 (5) Modern Law Review 661.

Schwab K., *The Fourth Industrial Revolution* (Crown 2016).

Schwartz P. and Solove D., 'The PII Problem: Privacy and a New Concept of Personally Identifiable Information' (2011) 86 NYU Law Review 1814.

Schwartz P., 'Global Data Privacy: The EU Way' (2019) 94 NYU Law Review 771.

Schwartz P. M. and Peifer K. N., 'Transatlantic Data Privacy' (2017) 106 Georgetown Law Journal 115.

Scott J., 'Extraterritoriality and Territorial Extension in EU Law' (2018) 62 American Journal of Comparative Law 87.

Selbst A. D. and Powles J., 'Meaningful Information and the Right to Explanation' (2017) 7 International Data Privacy Law 233.

Shadmy T., 'The New Social Contract: Facebook's Community and Our Rights' (2019) 37 Boston University International Law Journal 307.

Shapiro A., 'The Disappearance of Cyberspace and the Rise of Code' (1998) 8 Seton Hall Constitutional Law Journal 703.

Shapiro A. L., *The Control Revolution: How the Internet is Putting Individuals in Charge and Changing the World we Know* (Public Affairs 1999).

Simon H. A., 'Designing Organizations for an Information-Rich World' in Martin Greenberger (ed.), *Computers, Communications, and the Public Interest* (Johns Hopkins Press 1971).

Simoncini A. and Longo E., 'Fundamental Rights and the Rule of Law in the Algorithmic Society' in Hans-W. Micklitz and others (eds.), *Constitutional Challenges in the Algorithmic Society* (Cambridge University Press 2021).

Simoncini M., *Administrative Regulation Beyond the Non-Delegation Doctrine: A Study on EU Agencies* (Hart 2018).

Slawson D., 'Standard Forms of Contract and Democratic Control of Lawmaking Power' (1967) 84 Harvard Law Review 529.

Solove D., *Nothing to Hide: The False Tradeoff Between Privacy and Security* (Yale University Press 2013).

Solove D. J., 'A Brief History of Information Privacy Law' (2006) Proskauer on Privacy.

Sommer J. H., 'Against Cyberlaw' (2000) 15 Berkeley Technology Law Journal 1145.

Spano R., 'Intermediary Liability for Online User Comments under the European Convention on Human Rights' (2017) 17(4) Human Rights Law Review 665.

Spoerri T., 'On Upload-Filters and other Competitive Advantages for Big Tech Companies under Article 17 of the Directive on Copyright in the Digital Single Market' (2019) 10(2) Journal of Intellectual Property, Information Technology and E-Commerce Law 173.

Squires C. R., Rethinking the Black Public Sphere: An Alternative Vocabulary for Multiple Public Spheres' (2002) 12(4) Communication Theory 446.

Srnicek N., *Platform Capitalism* (Polity Press 2016).

Stalla-Bourdillon S. and Knight A., 'Anonymous Data v. Personal Data - A False Debate: An EU Perspective on Anonymisation, Pseudonymisation and Personal Data' (2017) 34 Wisconsin International Law Journal 284.

Stark B. and others, 'Are Algorithms a Threat to Democracy? The Rise of Intermediaries: A Challenge for Public Discourse' Algorithm Watch (26 May 2020) https://algorithmwatch.org/wp-content/uploads/2020/05/Governing-Platforms-communications-study-Stark-May-2020-AlgorithmWatch.pdf.

Stasi M. L., 'Ensuring Pluralism in Social Media Markets: Some Suggestions' (2020) EUI Working Paper RSCAS 2020/05 https://cadmus.eui.eu/bitstream/handle/1814/65902/RSCAS_2020_05.pdf?sequence=1&isAllowed=y.

Stein L., 'Policy and Participation on Social Media: The Cases of YouTube, Facebook, and Wikipedia' (2013) 6(3) Communication, Culture & Critique 353.

Stewart L., 'Big Data Discrimination: Maintaining Protection of Individual Privacy Without Disincentivizing Businesses' Use of Biometric Data to Enhance Security' (2019) 60 Boston College Law Review 347.

Stone Sweet A. and Mathews J., *Proportionality Balancing and Constitutional Governance. A Comparative and Global Approach* (Oxford University Press 2019).

Stroud N. J., 'Polarization and Partisan Selective Exposure' (2010) 60(3) Journal of Communication 556.

Sunstein C. R., *Infotopia: How Many Minds Produce Knowledge* 9 (Oxford University Press 2006).

Sunstein C. R., *Republic.com* (Princeton University Press 2002).

Sunstein C. R., *Republic.com 2.0* (Princeton University Press 2007).

Suzor N., 'Digital Constitutionalism: Using the Rule of Law to Evaluate the Legitimacy of Governance by Platforms' (2018) 4(3) Social Media + Society, https://journals.sagepub.com/doi/pdf/10.1177/2056305118787812.

Suzor N., *Lawless. The Secret Rules That Govern Our Digital Lives* (Cambridge University Press 2019).

Svantesson D. J. B., 'A "Layered Approach" to the Extraterritoriality of Data Privacy Laws' (2013) 3(4) International Data Privacy Law 278.

Svantesson D. J. B., *Solving the Internet Jurisdiction Puzzle* (Oxford University Press 2017).

Taddeo M., 'Modelling Trust in Artificial Agents, a First Step Toward the Analysis of E-Trust' (2010) 20 Minds and Machines 243.

Taddeo M. and Floridi L. (eds.), *The Responsibilities of Online Service Providers* (Springer 2017).

Taylor R. B., 'Consumer-Driven Changes to Online Form Contracts' (2011–12) 67 NYU Annual Survey of American Law 371.

Tene O. and Polonetsky J., 'Big Data for All: Privacy and User Control in the Age of Analytics' (2013) 11 Northwestern Journal of Technology and Intellectual Property 239.

Teubner G., *Constitutional Fragments: Societal Constitutionalism and Globalization* (Oxford University Press 2012).

Teubner G., *Law as an Autopoietic System* (Blackwell 1993).

Teubner G., 'Societal Constitutionalism: Alternatives to State-Centered Constitutional Theory?' in Christian Joerges, Inger-Johanne Sand and Gunther Teubner (eds.), *Transnational Governance and Constitutionalism* (Hart 2004).

Teubner G., 'The Anonymous Matrix: Human Rights Violations by "Private" Transnational Actors' (2006) 69(3) Modern Law Review 327.

Teubner G. 'The Project of Constitutional Sociology: Irritating Nation State Constitutionalism' (2013) 4 Transnational Legal Theory 44.

Tewksbury D. and Rittenberg J., 'Online News Creation and Consumption: Implications for Modern Democracies' in Andrew Chadwick and Philipp N. Howard (eds.), *The Handbook of Internet Politics* (Routledge 2008).

Thurman N. and Schifferes S., 'The Future of Personalization at News Websites: Lessons from a Longitudinal Study' (2012) 13(5–6) Journalism Studies 775.

Trotter Hardy I., 'The Proper Legal Regime for "Cyberspace"' (1994) 55 University of Pittsburgh Law Review 993.

Tsai C. W. and others, 'Big Data Analytics: A Survey' (2015) 2 Journal of Big Data 21.

Tsamados A. and others, 'The Ethics of Algorithms: Key Problems and Solutions' (2021) AI & Society https://link.springer.com/article/10.1007/s00146-021-01154-8#citeas.

Tufekci Z., 'Algorithmic Harms Beyond Facebook And Google: Emergent Challenges of Computational Agency' (2015) 13 Colorado Technology Law Journal 213.

Tully S., 'A Human Right to Access the Internet? Problems and Prospects' (2014) 14(2) Human Rights Law Review 175.

Tully J., 'The Imperialism of Modern Constitutional Democracy' in Martin Loughlin and Neil Walker (eds.), *The Paradox of Constitutionalism: Constituent Power and Constitutional Form* (Oxford University Press 2008).

Tuori K., *European Constitutionalism* (Cambridge University Press 2015).

Turilli M. and Floridi L., 'The Ethics of Information Transparency' (2009) 11(2) Ethics and Information Technology 105.

Turkle S., *Life on the Screen, Identity in the Age of Internet* (Simon & Schuster 1997).
Tushnet M., 'The Issue of State Action/Horizontal Effect in Comparative Constitutional Law' (2003) 1(1) International Journal of Constitutional Law 79.
Tushnet M., 'Shelley v. Kraemer and Theories of Equality' (1988) 33 New York Law School Law Review 383.
Tushnet M., 'The Inevitable Globalization of Constitutional Law' (2009) 49 Virginia Journal of International Law 985.
Tushnet M., 'The Issue of State Action/Horizontal Effect in Comparative Constitutional Law' (2003) 1(1) International Journal of Constitutional Law 79.
Tushnet R., 'Power Without Responsibility: Intermediaries and the First Amendment' (2008) 76 George Washington Law Review 986.
Tutt A., 'The New Speech' (2014) 41 Hastings Constitutional Law Quarterly 235.
Urban J. M. and others, *Notice and Takedown in Everyday Practice* (American Assembly 2016).
Vaihyanathan S., *Anti-Social Media* (Oxford University Press 2018).
Van Alsenoy B., 'Allocating Responsibility Among Controllers, Processors, And "Everything In Between": The Definition of Actors and Roles in Directive 95/46' (2012) 28 Computer Law & Security Review 30.
Van Alsenoy B., 'Liability under EU Data Protection Law from Directive 95/46 to the General Data Protection Regulation' (2016) 9(2) Journal of Intellectual Property, Information Technology and Electronic Commerce Law 271.
van der Sloot B., 'Do Privacy and Data Protection Rules Apply to Legal Persons and Should They? A Proposal for a Two-tiered System' (2015) 31 Computer Law and Security Review 26.
van der Sloot B., 'Welcome to the Jungle: The Liability of Internet Intermediaries for Privacy Violations in Europe' (2015) 3 Journal of Intellectual Property, Information Technology and Electronic Commerce Law 211.
van Dijk J. and Poell T., 'Understanding Social Media Logic' (2013) 1(1) Media and Communication 2.
van Dijck J, Poell T. and de Waal M., *The Platform Society: Public Values in a Connective World* (Oxford University Press 2018).
Van Eecke P., 'Online Service Providers and Liability: A Plea for a Balanced Approach' (2011) 48 Common Market Law Review 1455.
van Hoboken J., 'The Proposed EU Terrorism Content Regulation: Analysis and Recommendations with Respect to Freedom of Expression Implications' Transatlantic Working Group on Content Moderation Online and Freedom of Expression (2019) www.ivir.nl/publicaties/download/TERREG_FoE-ANALYSIS.pdf.
Van Loo R., 'The Corporation as Courthouse' (2016) 33 Yale Journal on Regulation 547.
Veale M., Binns R. and Ausloos J., 'When Data Protection by Design and Data Subject Rights Clash' (2018) 8 International Data Privacy Law 105.
Veliz C., *Privacy Is Power: Why and How You Should Take Back Control of Your Data* (Bantam Press 2020).

Vermeule A., Common Good Constitutionalism (Wiley & Sons, forthcoming).
Vestager M., 'Algorithms and Democracy' Algorithmic Watch (30 October 2020) https://ec.europa.eu/commission/commissioners/2019-2024/vestager/announcements/algorithms-and-democracy-algorithmwatch-online-policy-dialogue-30-october-2020_en.
Viellechner L., 'Responsive Legal Pluralism: The Emergence of Transnational Conflicts Law' (2015) 6(2) Transnational Legal Theory 312.
Viola de Azevedo Cunha M. and others, 'Peer-to-Peer Privacy Violations and ISP Liability: Data Protection in the User-Generated Web' (2012) 2(2) International Data Privacy Law 50.
Volokh E., 'In Defense of the Market Place of Ideas / Search for Truth as a Theory of Free Speech Protection' (2011) 97(3) Virginia Law Review 591.
von Daniels D., *The Concept of Law from a Transnational Perspective* (Ashgate 2010).
Wachter S. and Mittelstadt B. D., 'A Right to Reasonable Inferences: Re-Thinking Data Protection Law in the Age of Big Data and AI' (2019) Columbia Business Law Review 494.
Wachter S. and Mittelstadt B. and Russell C., 'Why Fairness cannot be Automated: Bridging the Gap between EU Non-discrimination Law and AI' (2021) 41 Computer Law & Security Review 105567
Wachter S. and others, 'Why a Right to Explanation of Automated Decision-Making Does Not Exist in the General Data Protection Regulation' (2017) 7 International Data Privacy Law 76.
Wagner B., *Global Free Expression: Governing the Boundaries of Internet Content* (Springer 2016).
Wagner B., 'Understanding Internet Shutdowns: A Case Study from Pakistan' (2018) 12 International Journal of Communication 3917.
Wagner B. and others (eds.), *Research Handbook on Human Rights and Digital Technology: Global Politics, Law and International Relations* (Edward Elgar 2019).
Wakabayashi D. and others, 'Big Tech Could Emerge from Coronavirus Crisis Stronger Than Ever' The New York Times (23 March 2020) www.nytimes.com/2020/03/23/technology/coronavirus-facebook-amazon-youtube.html.
Waldron J., 'Constitutionalism: A Skeptical View' (2012) NYU, Public Law Research Paper No. 10-87 https://papers.ssrn.com/sol3/papers.cfm?abstract_id=1722771&rec=1&srcabs=1760963&alg=1&pos=1.
Walker N., *Intimations of Global Law* (Cambridge University Press 2015).
Walkila S., *Horizontal Effect of Fundamental Rights in EU Law* (European Law Publishing 2016);
Ward J. S. and Barker A., 'Undefined By Data: A Survey of Big Data Definitions' ArXiv http://arxiv.org/abs/1309.5821.
Warf B., 'Geographies of Global Internet Censorship' (2011) 76 GeoJournal 1.
Warner M., *Publics and Counterpublics* (MIT University Press 2002).
Warren S. D. and Brandeis L. D., 'The Right to Privacy' (1890) 4 Harvard Law Review 193.

Wauters E., Lievens E. and Valcke P., 'Towards a Better Protection of Social Media Users: A Legal Perspective on the Terms of Use of Social Networking Sites' (2014) 22 International Journal of Law & Information Technology 254.

Weber R. H., 'Corporate Social Responsibility as a Gap-Filling Instrument' in Andrew P. Newell (ed.). *Corporate Social Responsibility: Challenges, Benefits and Impact on Business* (Nova 2014).

Weber R. H., 'Internet of Things – New Security and Privacy Challenges' (2010) 26(1) Computer Law & Security Review 23.

Webster J. G., 'User Information Regimes: How Social Media Shape Patterns of Consumption' (2010) 104 Northwestern University Law Review 593.

Weiler J. H. H., *The Constitution of Europe* (Cambridge University Press 1999).

Weiler J. H. H. and Wind M. (eds.), *European Constitutionalism beyond the State* (Cambridge University Press 2003).

Weinberg J., 'ICANN and the Problem of Legitimacy' (2000) 50 Duke Law Journal 187.

Weinrib L., 'Human Dignity as a Rights-Protecting Principle' (2004) 17 National Journal of Constitutional Law 330.

Wen Y., *The Huawei Model: The Rise of China's Technology Giant* (University of Illinois Press 2020).

Werro F., 'The Right to Inform v. the Right to be Forgotten: A Transatlantic Crash' in Aurelia Colombi Ciacchi and others (eds.), *Liability in the Third Millennium, Liber Amicorum Gert Bruggemeier* (Nomos 2009).

West S. M., 'Censored, Suspended, Shadowbanned: User Interpretations of Content Moderation on Social Media Platforms' (2018) 20(11) New Media & Society 4380.

Westin A. F., *Privacy and Freedom* (Athenum 1967).

Whitman J. Q., 'On Nazy "Honour" and the New European Dignity' in Christian Joerges and Navraj Singh Ghaleigh, *Darker Legacies of Law in Europe: The Shadow of National Socialism and Fascism Over Europe and Its Legal Traditions* (Hart 2003).

Whitman J. Q., 'The Two Western Cultures of Privacy: Dignity Versus Liberty' (2004) 113(6) Yale Law Journal 1151.

Wiener A. and others, 'Global Constitutionalism: Human Rights, Democracy and the Rule of Law' (2012) 1 Global Constitutionalism 1.

Wiener N., *The Human Use of Human Beings: Cybernetics and Society* (Da Capo Press 1988).

Wolfsfeld G. and others, 'Social Media and the Arab Spring: Politics Comes First' (2013) 18(2) The International Journal of Press/Politics 115.

Wu F. T., 'Collateral Censorship and the Limits of Intermediary Immunity' (2011) 87(1) Notre Dame Law Review 293.

Wu T., 'Cyberspace Sovereignty? The Internet and the International Systems' (1997) 10(3) Harvard Law Journal 647.

Wu T., *The Attention Merchants: The Epic Scramble to Get Inside our Heads* (Knopf 2016).

Wu T., *The Curse of Bigness: How Corporate Giants Came to Rule the World* (Atlantic Books 2020).

Xenidis R. and Senden L., 'EU Non-discrimination Law in the Era of Artificial Intelligence: Mapping the Challenges of Algorithmic Discrimination' in Ulf Bernitz and others (eds.), *General Principles of EU law and the EU Digital Order* (Kluwer Law International 2020).

Yakovleva S., and Irion K., 'Toward Compatibility of the EU Trade Policy with the General Data Protection Regulation' (2020) 114 AJIL Unbound 10.

York J. C., 'Policing Content in the Quasi-Public Sphere' Open Net Initiative' Bulletin (September 2010) https://opennet.net/policing-content-quasi-public-sphere.

York J. C., *Silicon Values: The Future of Free Speech Under Surveillance Capitalism* (Verso Books 2021).

York J. C. and Schmon C., 'The EU Online Terrorism Regulation: A Bad Deal' EFF (7 April 2021) www.eff.org/it/deeplinks/2021/04/eu-online-terrorism-regulation-bad-deal.

Zalnieriute M., 'Google LLC v. Commission Nationale de l'Informatique et des Libertés (CNIL)' (2020) 114(2) American Journal of International Law 261.

Zanfir-Fortuna G., 'Forgetting About Consent: Why The Focus Should Be on "Suitable Safeguards" in Data Protection Law' in Serge Gutwirth, Ronald Leenes and Paul De Hert (eds.), *Reloading Data Protection* (Springer 2014).

Zanzotto F. M., 'Viewpoint: Human-in-the-loop Artificial Intelligence' (2019) 64 Journal of Artificial Intelligence Research 243.

Zarsky T., 'Incompatible: The GDPR in the Age of Big Data' (2017) 47 Seton Hall Law Review 1014.

Zarsky T., 'Social Justice, Social Norms and the Governance of Social Media' (2015) 35 Pace Law Review 154.

Zarsky T., 'The Trouble with Algorithmic Decisions: An Analytic Road Map to Examine Efficiency and Fairness in Automated and Opaque Decision Making' (2016) 41 Science, Technology, & Human Values 118.

Zarsky T., 'Transparent Predictions' (2013) 4 University of Illinois Law Review 1507.

Zarsky T., 'Understanding Discrimination in the Scored Society' (2014) 89 Washington Law Review 1375.

Zeno-Zencovich V., *Freedom of Expression: A Critical and Comparative Analysis* (Routledge 2008).

Zerilli J. and others, 'Algorithmic Decision-making and the Control Problem' (2019) 29 Minds and Machines 555.

Ziccardi-Capaldo G., *The Pillars of Global Law* (Ashgate 2008).

Zimmer D., 'Digital Markets: New Rules for Competition Law' (2015) 6(9) Journal of European Competition Law & Practice 627.

Zittrain J., 'History of Online Gatekeeping' (2006) 19(2) Harvard Journal of Law & Technology 253.

Zittrain J., *The Future of the Internet and How to Stop It* (Yale University Press 2008).

Zittrain J. and Edelman B., 'Empirical Analysis of Internet Filtering in China' (2003) Harvard Law School Public Law Research Paper No. 62.

Zuboff S., 'Big Other: Surveillance Capitalism and the Prospects of an Information Civilization' (2015) 30(1) Journal of Information Technology 75.

Zuboff S., *The Age of Surveillance Capitalism: The Fight for a Human Future at the New Frontier of Power* (Public Affairs 2018).

Zuckerberg M., 'Bringing the World Closer Together', Facebook (22 June 2017) www.facebook.com/notes/mark-zuckerberg/bringing-the-world-closer-together/10154944663901634/.

Zuckerberg M., 'Building Global Community' Facebook (16 February 2017) www.facebook.com/notes/mark-zuckerberg/building-global-community/10154544292806634/.

Zuiderveen Borgesius F. J. and others, 'Online Political Microtargeting: Promises and Threats for Democracy' (2018) 14(1) Utrecht Law Review 82.

Zuiderveen Borgesius F. J. and others, 'Should We Worry about Filter Bubbles?' (2016) 5(1) Internet Policy Review https://policyreview.info/node/401/pdf.

Zumbansen P., 'The Law of Society: Governance Through Contract' (2007) 14(1) Indiana Journal of Global Legal Studies 191.

Index

Footnotes are indicated by n. after the page number.

For EU product safety concerns, contact us at Calle de José Abascal, 56–1°, 28003 Madrid, Spain or eugpsr@cambridge.org.

www.ingramcontent.com/pod-product-compliance
Lightning Source LLC
LaVergne TN
LVHW011702200926
848484LV00004B/1037
* 9 7 8 1 3 1 6 5 1 2 7 7 7 *